Twenty-First Century
PENN

WRITINGS ON THE
Faith and Practice
Of the PEOPLE called
QUAKERS
by *William Penn*

Translated into Modern English

by Paul Buckley

EARLHAM
SCHOOL *of* RELIGION
Richmond, Indiana

Twenty-First Century Penn

Library of Congress Cataloguing-In-Publication Data

Buckley, Paul, 1949-

Twenty First Century Penn: Writings on the Faith and Practice of the People called Quakers by William Penn / Paul Buckley

ISBN 1-879117-13-4

1. Religion   2. Quakerism

2003111077

Contents

Preface

This translation of five of the theological works of William Penn was inspired by my repeated and unsuccessful attempts to read them in their original formats. I began each attempt convinced that the contents were so important that my education in Quaker Studies would be incomplete without them. Each ended when I realized the amount of effort that would be required to really understand what Penn was saying. When the opportunity arose to devote two years to translating these works into modern English, I grabbed it.

Comments and encouragement from Jay Marshall and Stephen Angell of the Earlham School of Religion have helped to keep me focused over that period of time, and a number of books on Penn and his writings have been invaluable in my work. In particular, footnotes in Hugh Barbour's *William Penn on Religion and Ethics* have frequently pointed me toward information that I would not have easily found on my own. Barbara Mays has been invaluable in reviewing the manuscript and offering a host of helpful comments.

But most importantly, my wife, Peggy Spohr, has endured my long hours of contemplation on the ultimate meaning of three hundred year old words – keeping me appropriately clothed, fed, and rested. I could not have done it without her.

Introduction

The period surrounding the English Civil Wars was one of great religious ferment. Dozens of new religious movements sprang up in England, but only one, the Religious Society of Friends (Quakers), has survived. Among the foremost reasons for this remarkable endurance was the work and writings of William Penn.

Most people, if they know anything about him at all, can identify William Penn as the founder of Pennsylvania. Many also know that he was a Quaker, but most people (even Quakers) do not know his role within the Society of Friends in the second half of the seventeenth century or the enduring mark he had on the development of that religious body.

William Penn was raised at the center of the English political establishment. His father, Sir William Penn, had been a Rear Admiral in the Parliament's Navy, a General of the English fleet during the Commonwealth, and instrumental in the restoration of King Charles II to the throne of England. The younger William was prepared to step, as an adult, into the role of confidant, advisor, and friend of kings. He had attended Oxford University, studied theology at Saumur, the leading French Protestant University, and read the law at Lincoln's Inn in London. He was trained in the classics and was exceptionally well acquainted with ancient Greek and Latin writings, as well as those of the early Christian theologians.

When the twenty-three-year-old Penn came to the Religious Society of Friends in 1667, he was a capable seventeenth-century English gentleman. The political skills and connections that he brought with him were essential in achieving its legal acceptance and his scholarly training was instrumental in directing the evolution of the movement. Five of his more influential texts are translated in this book.

Early Quakerism

The beginning of the Quaker movement is usually dated to 1652. In that year, George Fox, a self-trained, itinerant minister, received a revelation of a great people to be gathered for God. Within a few years, Fox had enlisted dozens of other religious seekers to join in spreading the Quaker message. In the remaining years of that decade, the growth of what was to become the Religious Society of Friends was phenomenal.

Although these early Quakers were subject to intermittent harassment under the Commonwealth government of Oliver Cromwell, their fortunes changed radically when that government fell. Between the restoration of Charles II in 1661 and the Act of Toleration in 1689, Quakers experienced periods of cruel persecution. Thousands were jailed, fortunes were seized, and hundreds died. While stubbornly resisting its oppressors, the Society of Friends also responded by redefining itself and its relationships to the wider world. Over this period, a self-confident, aggressive, and confrontational movement was transformed into a quiet and nonviolent sect.

In their early years, Quakers were convinced that they were members of the one true church of Jesus Christ – that they represented the revival of Primitive Christianity. They mercilessly attacked what they saw as the substitution of outward ceremonies and rituals for the proper worship of God and abandoned such common activities as the celebration of holy days and water baptism. They reordered their daily lives to be faithful in all things. When in the presence of a social superior, they pointedly refused to offer 'hat honor', to bow and scrape, or to use the second person plural pronouns, 'you' or 'your' when addressing a single person. All honor and glory is reserved for God alone; any attempt to honor a mere human needed to be resisted, even if it meant arrest and imprisonment in the vilest dungeon. Yet thirty years later, this most intolerant of people had completely redefined themselves. The rude insults and peculiar practices of the 1650s remained, but they had been recast as mere Quaker 'distinctives.' The original insistence that all must follow the one Truth that they had discovered was abandoned in favor of a cry for toleration on the part of the wider society they had once rejected. At the heart of this transformation was William Penn.

As can be seen in this book, Penn's writing both reflected and led Friends in these changes. Like the religious society he had joined, his earliest pamphlets reveal a brash young man and impassioned new convert – a man out to share his new faith with the world. His early works focused on the differences between his new beliefs and those both of the established church and of other religious dissenters. He had found the Truth and was anxious to spread it. As he aged, the emphasis in his writing shifted and he became more concerned with demonstrating the orthodoxy of Quaker beliefs. He did not repudiate his earlier views, but rather chose to concentrate on different topics. For example, the first two pieces below, *A Sandy Foundation Shaken* and *Innocency with Her Open Face*, written when Penn was in his mid twenties, contain material related to an esoteric argument over the Trinity. While Penn and other early Friends believed in God as Father, Son, and Spirit, they rejected the wider church's Trinitarian doctrine. Friends saw this specific formulation of the triune God as a human innovation based on Greek philosophy rather than the scriptures. But, less than a decade later Penn apparently saw no reason to include commentary on trinitarianism in *The Christian Quaker*. While he continued to profess the Quaker view of God throughout his life, he had come to understand that emphasizing theological differences did not advance his primary goal – gaining toleration for the Religious Society of Friends.

Truth, Revelation, and Apostasy

Before beginning the texts below, it may be helpful to review a few of Penn's basic religious concepts. Perhaps the most important of these is that Penn believed in Truth with a capital 'T.' Not only did ultimate truth exist, but it was humanly knowable – although never in its entirety.

Penn saw the history of God's interactions with humanity as the story of continuing divine revelation. In each succeeding age, people could come to know more and more of God's Truth. The Bible records a series of dispensations or ways in which God interacts with humanity. But, the scriptures only record the revelations to Jews and Christians. God does not abandon any part of humanity – God's will has been revealed to all people in all ages through the work of the Light within each individual soul.

But the story is not so simple. Central to Penn's understanding of God's dealings with humanity was a theory of apostasy. Briefly stated, this theory held that in each age God would gather a people and reveal a measure of truth to them. In each case, they would remain faithful to that revelation for a period of time, but inevitably they would fall away from it. Apostasy would supplant true religion as people substituted their own ideas for those they had received from God.

Penn was not alone in this belief. Some concept of apostasy was necessary for Protestants to justify breaking away from the Roman Church. Unless the Church of Rome had fallen into apostasy, those who rejected it were not reformers, but heretics. To Penn, Quakers were the most recent of God's chosen peoples and were finishing the work of cleansing Christianity that the Reformation had begun, but failed to complete.

In Penn's view, apostasy is particularly inevitable whenever the church is directly linked to the state, allowing the use of civil power to compel people to deny their consciences and to submit to the dictates of an established church. Wedding the power of the state to the church, and the moral authority of the church to the goals of the state, corrupts those who exercise that power and in due course the institutions of the church. The classic example of this process was the transformation of early Christianity from a pacifist, outsider sect into a rich, powerful and corrupt institution after it had become the official religion of the Roman Empire. Penn saw this pattern repeated throughout history – even among Protestants. New sects that had been founded in opposition to a corrupt established church fell into apostasy themselves whenever they succeeded in achieving state power.

To the early Friends, apostasy was the work of the devil and only unrelenting spiritual warfare could overcome it. There was no possibility of compromise with Satan. But over time, the pressures of persecution drove them, under the political leadership of William Penn, to advocate religious toleration. In promoting this goal, Penn distinguished between 'essential' and 'non-essential' aspects of faith and practice, arguing that the outward differences that distinguished Quakers from other Christians were not essential or necessary and, therefore, should not be points of contention.

The Bible

It is important when reading Penn to understand the way in which the Bible was viewed in the seventeenth century. Society was steeped in the scriptures. Beginning late in the previous century, English-language Bibles had been printed in great numbers and had become readily available to common people. For many, it was the only book they had ever read, and the stories and language of the Bible were familiar to all. It was accepted as an accurate history of the Jews and of Primitive Christianity. But it would be a mistake to confuse the naïve literalism of the seventeenth century with contemporary scriptural literalism. Religious thinkers of that time did not have to contend with evolution, modern science, or biblical criticism – they were not rejecting another way of viewing the scriptures; for them, belief in the historical accuracy of biblical accounts was simply the natural thing to do.

Nevertheless, while early Friends recognized the Bible as authoritative, they did not accept it as the final authority. Scripture is a limited record of the word of God, while the Word, Spirit, or Light that inspired its writers is unlimited and new revelation remains possible. Just as the written scriptures were the product of divine inspiration in the past, the ministry of contemporary Quakers may be the product of new divine inspiration. This was not, however, license for individuals to unilaterally elevate their own ideas to the level of divine revelation. To early Friends, God is unchanging and the works of the Holy Spirit are consistent — what is truly a divine revelation today will not contradict what has been revealed by the Holy Spirit in the past. New revelations build on and complement older revelations.

Of course, any particular claim of divine inspiration may be in error. We are fallible human beings and may mistake the products of our own egos as ultimate truth. Moreover, we may be intentionally misled by the devil. To avoid such errors, a way is required that will distinguish the true word of God from all other things. For Friends, the collective judgment of the community provides a surer (although still not infallible) test.

The Translation

Penn wrote prolifically, publishing more than one hundred books and pamphlets on topics ranging from the law, politics, and international relations to business, education, and science and on to philosophy and theology. For one hundred and fifty years after his death, his works were definitive among Friends, sitting beside *The Journal of George Fox*, and Robert Barclay's *Apology*. While *The Journal* has remained in print and Dean Freiday's *Barclay's Apology in Modern English* has revived interest in that work, Penn's theological works have fallen from favor. In large measure, this is due to Penn's background and training. He was a gentleman and a courtier, and he wrote like one. His sentences are long and involved. His word choices are often unfamiliar to modern readers — even when a word looks familiar, its meaning may have changed in the intervening three hundred years.

In this volume, I have attempted to overcome these barriers by treating his original work as if it was written in a foreign language. What is presented below is simply a translation into modern English. To the best of my ability, I have retained Penn's concepts while putting them in words that a twenty-first century reader can easily understand. As with any translation, certain choices have been made. Most English words have retained their meanings over the last three hundred years, but in some cases, the primary meaning of a word is now very different. There are two ways to deal with such changes.

An example of the first method is in how the word 'prove' has been treated. If I were to say that I am going to prove a proposition, most people today would understand that I am aiming to demonstrate that the idea is true — implying, therefore, that I believe the proposition to be true. In the seventeenth century, the same phrase would be understood to mean that the truth of the proposition is to be tested and, therefore, that it may or may not be true. Consequently, depending on the context, 'test' has sometimes been substituted for 'prove' or 'proof' in the translation.

The second approach is illustrated by the more concrete example of the word 'apology' – which Penn uses especially in the second work included in this collection, *Innocency with Her Open Face*. The various meanings of this word allow different readers to understand the work in different ways. *Innocency* was written when Penn was imprisoned and facing charges of blasphemy – charges based on the contents of *A Sandy Foundation Shaken*. In ordinary use, an apology can be read as an expression of sorrow and regret. But, to an attorney in those times, it was the name used to describe a defense against a criminal charge and, to a theologian, it was a reasoned argument in favor of a particular theological view. No single modern English word will convey all of these meanings to a twenty-first-century reader, and substituting a phrase may destroy the intended ambiguity. In this translation, the original word has been retained and a footnote appended to provide the reader with additional information.

There are two terms that could particularly mislead a modern reader.

'Evangelical' has taken on new meanings since the 1800s. In twenty-first century America, it is used to describe Protestant Churches that emphasize a personal relationship with Jesus Christ, but when Penn used the term, he was referring to the gospel. To avoid confusion, the word 'gospel' has generally been substituted for 'evangelical.'

Likewise, since the early nineteenth century, 'universalism' has come to be understood as a belief that God will eventually save everyone. Penn, however, lived in a time in which many believed that salvation was available only to a chosen few. He rejected such claims. For early Friends, the universal infusion of the Light proclaimed in John 1:9 ("*That* was the true Light, which lighteth every man that cometh into the world") creates the possibility, but not the promise, of salvation for all – Christian, Jew, Muslim, or Pagan. To be faithful to this meaning and avoid confusion, where possible 'universal' has been replaced with other words.

Penn could assume widespread biblical literacy. Even those who had not read the Bible themselves were well acquainted with it. As a result, he could quote a passage, or even a few words, and assume that readers would identify the reference and know its context. Such an assumption can no longer be made. To give a modern reader a sense of this way of reading, the text has been heavily footnoted with relevant scriptural references.

Although Penn's text has been translated into modern English, it was felt that the flavor of his text would be better represented by presenting these in the language of the King James Version.

Standards for punctuation and capitalization have changed considerably in the last three hundred years. As part of the translation, the punctuation has been made to conform to modern standards, but some of Penn's original capitalization has been retained. As noted above, Penn distinguished between ordinary truth and ultimate truth. Ultimate truth is spelled with a capital 'T'. Words that are used as the name of God or that describe attributes of God (e.g., Wisdom, the Word, and the Light) are capitalized. In a few cases, capitals were used for emphasis and have been retained.

Some aspects of Penn's writing may be unattractive, even offensive, to modern readers. Seventeenth-century English society was defined by a rigid class structure that Penn and virtually all his contemporaries saw as natural – even as ordained by God. The roles of men and women; master, servant, and slave; nobility and commoner were well known, understood, and accepted. The superiority of Christianity to Judaism (much less any other religion) was taken for granted. In the translations below, efforts have been made to avoid unnecessarily exclusive or offensive language – such as the use of male pronouns for God – but this cannot be done entirely without reducing the value of these works by distorting the view they give us of Penn, his times, and his message.

These texts were written to challenge their original readers, both Quaker and non-Quaker. They present an evolving understanding of how God relates to humanity and how the Religious Society of Friends would relate to the world surrounding it. More than *The Journal of George Fox* or Robert Barclay's *Apology*, they set the direction for the development of that faith community for the next one hundred and fifty years and, consequently, the shape of that religious body today.

THE

Sandy Foundation

S H A K E N :

O R,

Those so generally believed
and applauded D O C T R I N E S,

Of

One God subsisting in three distinct and separate Persons,
The Impossibility of God's pardoning Sinners,
without a plenary Satisfaction, and
The Justification of impure persons, by an
imputative Righteousness,

Refuted

From the Authority of Scripture Testimonies and Right Reason.

By W. P. j.

A Builder on that Foundation which cannot be moved.

But to us there is but one God the Father of all things. 1 Corinthians *8:6*

*Who is a God like unto thee, that pardoneth Iniquity? He retaineth not his anger
for ever, because he delighteth in mercy.* Micah *7:18*

For I will not justifie the wicked, &c. Exodus *23:7*

London, Printed in the Year, *1668*.

To the Unprejudiced Reader

Out of weakness, some in ancient times replaced God's law with their own traditions, and it certainly seems that some are doing so again in our day. God Almighty, in the fullness of time, made and perfected the second covenant. This covenant was foretold by the prophets, instituted by Jesus Christ, and established among the primitive believers. When I seriously consider the spiritual nature and purpose of that covenant, it is clear to me that it not only utterly abolishes all forms of ceremony in worship, but writes that spiritual law on the heart[1] and infuses fear of the Lord into the inmost part of each person.[2] In this way, all are able in some degree to know God – not on the slender grounds of their own "Look here, or look there!" interpretations – but from direct experience of an infallible sign within themselves. The kingdom of God is within.[3] There, God alone must be the teacher.

But on the other hand, every sect firmly asserts that its way of knowing God's will is infallible, so I accept the need for an impartial examination of our ways.

Alas! All have lost the purity of both the scriptural record and of the example set by those primitive believers. They accept as infallible doctrine questionable ideas and uncertain decisions made by early Church Councils, whose intrigues, prejudices, and cruelties soon became as great as those of the heathens who had persecuted them. It is both astonishing and regrettable that the decisions of those incompetent and unqualified men should remain unquestioned up to the present time. Blind faith has always been the product of ignorance, idleness, and fear; and blind faith never questions whether these predetermined opinions, imposed on the church, are consistent with reason or with true religion.

---

[1] Heb. 8:10: "For this *is* the covenant that I will make with the house of Israel after those days, saith the Lord; I will put my laws into their mind, and write them in their hearts: and I will be to them a God, and they shall be to me a people." (Also Heb. 10:16 and Jer. 31:33)

[2] Jer. 32:40: "And I will make an everlasting covenant with them, that I will not turn away from them, to do them good; but I will put my fear in their hearts, that they shall not depart from me."

[3] Luke 17:21: "Neither shall they say, Lo here! or, lo there! for, behold, the kingdom of God is within you."

3

But what is most regrettable of all, is that Protestants, who have disproved and dismissed human traditions and human prescriptions in doctrines that are not essential, have in word and deed embraced the authority of tradition for things that are not merely important, but essential. This is obvious to anyone who observes their Anathemas[4] – damning others for refusing to accept doctrines that are solely the products of human imagination.

This is the position maintained by those of us who are with contempt called Quakers, against the world. It is undoubtedly the reason for our mistreatment at its hands. God Almighty has raised us up for no other purpose than to declare that which our eyes have seen, our ears have heard, and our hands have touched of the Eternal Word[5] – in opposition to all human opinions, conjectures, and interpretations about God and religion. Sound judgment has been lost, and this has caused all of mankind's religious divisions and moral corruption. We have been called forth so that all people might be brought to faith in and obedience to that universal grace that brings salvation.[6] Only this can restore sound judgment and bring redemption from sin.

I will describe one incident that clearly demonstrates how we have been and are mistreated and is, in fact, the reason I have written this essay.

Recently, two people from the congregation of Thomas Vincent (who calls himself a presbyter) in Spitalfields visited one of our meetings to hear what we preach and to determine the truth of it for themselves. They wanted to know if we really deserved the scorn our enemies have heaped on us. By Divine Goodness, the Light of God came over them and turned them away from human ideas, outward forms of worship, willfulness, and foolishness. They gave up their former sect and become Children of the Day.[7] Although the Light they received was small, it was sufficient to reveal to them that they had been inhabitants of the night. This is the Light of God that can never be ignored, but shows us our guilt.

---

[4] Anathema: A formal declaration of heresy, excommunication, and damnation.

[5] Matt. 13:16: "But blessed *are* your eyes, for they see: and your ears, for they hear."

[6] Titus 2:11: "For the grace of God that bringeth salvation hath appeared to all men."

[7] 1 Thess. 5:5: "Ye are all the children of light, and the children of the day: we are not of the night, nor of darkness."

Leaving their old congregation so incensed this Presbyterian preacher that he flew beyond the bounds of Christian moderation, and even those of simple civility. In his rage (and harming his own argument), he said it would have been better if they had gone to a brothel than to hear the erroneous and damnable doctrines preached at a Quaker meeting. Pointing to a window, he said, "If there were a cup of poison in that window, I would rather drink it than suck in their damnable doctrines." He turned on one of them and bellowed, "If you ever go again, I will give up on you, and God will give up on you! You will be caught in their lies, and be damned for it!"

His storms of foul and abusive accusations failed to wash away their new-found grains of faith. Nor were the appeals of others in the congregation any more successful. Knowing that they needed the approval of the head of their household,[8] he went to the husband of one (and father of the other) and asked him to violate the liberty of their consciences by blocking all visits to them from Quakers and prohibiting their attendance at our meetings.

For truth's sake, we could not let this pass in silence, and therefore we challenged him to a public meeting in which we could answer his charges against us and our principles. After some negotiations, he picked a day and time, two o'clock, for the meeting. To gather a sympathetic audience and (I am told) to keep our Friends from getting in first, he told his congregation to come at 1 o'clock. To ensure that he would not be tired by the debate, he also invited three others, Thomas Danson, Thomas Doolittle, and William Maddocks, to assist him. Each of them in turn (and out-of-turn) spoke. George Whitehead mostly answered the four of them. If any other persons spoke, it was only from following their own example.

The topic of the debate will be presented in the introduction to the essay below. Their manner of debate was so coarse, that I do not know how to better describe it than as a bare-knuckle brawl: undignified and crude, marked by laughing, hissing, shoving, and punching. We were slandered and called presumptuous fellows, impudent villains, blasphemers, etc. As is often the case when empty-headed people have little of value to say and want to prejudice the audience against their opponents, he frequently asked

---

[8] In seventeenth century England, it was expected that all members of a household, including servants, would attend the same church as the head of the household. To attend another church, a man's wife or child would normally need his permission.

if we weren't Jesuits – seeming to forget (or at least unwilling to let the audience know) that no one has been or is more insistent that God consists of three distinct persons than the Jesuits. If I had wanted, I could have turned the charge back on them and exposed their ignorance. In short, they would neither stick to the Scriptures themselves, nor allow others to do so. When George Whitehead tried to apply the Scriptures to their arguments, and thereby expose their foolish dependence on tradition to the audience, they claimed that this was deceptive and not answering their arguments. Then abruptly, Thomas Vincent fell to his knees, as if in prayer, and with many strange moans and whines, he falsely accusing us of being blasphemers. When he was finished, he tried to prevent us from answering this charge by ordering the audience to leave. Trying to set an example, he and his three friends scurried away. We wanted to stay and prove our innocence, but they tried to pull us down after them. They even blew out the candles. Several well-respected persons stayed, while we vindicated ourselves and refuted their accusations.

Even then, the congregation remained seated, so Thomas Vincent, looking very pale, came back down the stairs (carrying a candle) and again demanded that they leave. At this time he also agreed to our request for another meeting. He seems since to regret making that promise and, we are told, has no intention of keeping it, claiming that he is much too busy to do so. Instead, he has proposed to meet with George Whitehead and me in private. This can hardly be called 'another meeting.' He made his accusations before hundreds but suggests that we refute those charges before no one. It should be obvious to any unbiased person that our vindication should be as public as was our damning.

It was for this reason that we felt compelled to visit his meeting on Lecture Day.[9] We waited in silence throughout his worship service and, when it was over, modestly asked that we might be allowed to clear ourselves of his unjust accusations in front of the congregation. We offered to come back another time to continue the debate if he felt unprepared. But he, who had earlier been so willing to defame our reputations, slunk away like a coward, refusing even to defend his own principles. Nor was anyone

---

[9] By English law, Sunday sermons at this time were required to be based on the lectionary in the Book of Common Prayer. In order to address other scriptural passages, non-conforming congregations held a mid-week meeting which featured an alternate sermon. To avoid prosecution, these were referred to as lectures.

from the congregation willing to step forward, take his place at the pulpit, and justify his treatment of us or to defend their doctrines.

Reader, what is your opinion of such savage treatment? Would Socrates, Cato, or Seneca, whom they call heathens, have treated us so badly? I don't think so. It's good that truly humble and conscientious people are not subject to the severe lashings and spiteful treatment that seem to be inseparable from the use of the Scotch Directory[10] – whose cold and cutting gales nip and blast the fairest blossoms of greater reformation.

But so much for the past.

What remains is to inform the reader, as briefly as possible, that I will discuss and present a complete refutation of the following cardinal points and chief doctrines so firmly believed and so continually imposed on the church as articles of Christian faith:

1. The Trinity of separate persons, in the unity of essence.

2. God's inability to forgive without full satisfaction being paid by another.

3. The justification of impure persons by imputing[11] righteousness.

Let me tell you, Reader, that these principles are contrary to the Scriptures and to reason. They imperil your souls, but most importantly, they impugn God's honor by attacking God's unity, mercy, and purity.

Therefore, I implore you to read this short essay as dispassionately as possible. It was written in love to you. If you wish to know, love, and revere God Almighty beyond all human teachings, you will not achieve that end by blindly embracing tradition as if it were truth. With the nobility of a true Berean,[12] search and inquire. Let Truth, not a claim of antiquity (for some

---

[10] This refers to the Westminster Standards, produced by a gathering of Reformed Theologians that met at Westminster Abbey from 1643-49. These have served as significant doctrinal and governing documents in many Calvinist churches since that time.

[11] Impute: To attribute or bestow a characteristic of one thing or person on another. Penn is arguing against the claim that God would see people as righteous – even though they were not – by the imputation of Christ's righteousness to them.

[12] The reference is to Paul's visit to Beroea in Asia Minor (Acts 17:10-15). In particular to Acts 17:10-11 ("And the brethren immediately sent away Paul and

of these things are not ancient), and solid reason, not a too-hasty desire to believe, be the basis of your judgment. Then, your decisions will be marked by commitment and certainty.

A Short Summary and Disproof of the Charges Made against Us at Thomas Vincent's Meeting

When public debate is dull, it is either due to the debaters' ineffectiveness and lack of knowledge, or to the ignorance and prejudice of the audience. All of these attributes were well demonstrated by Thomas Vincent, his three associates, and his congregation.

The widespread accusation, that Quakers held damnable doctrines, was the subject of this debate. That being the case, George Whitehead was prepared to open the discussion with a plain statement of our principles and to defend them based on the authority of Scripture and by reason. Rather than allow this to take place, Thomas Vincent employed a tactic often used in lectures to the uneducated. Pretending he had accidentally slandered us in ignorance of our principles, he began to ask a series of questions supposedly to gain a better understanding.

The first question was whether we acknowledged that there was one Godhead, consisting of three distinct and separate persons as defined by the councils of the church. This we denied as it is found nowhere in Scripture. Hearing that, Thomas Vincent made the following argument, starting with the words of the beloved disciple:

> For there are three that bear record in heaven, the Father, the Word, and the Holy Ghost: and these three are one. (1 John 5:7)

> These are either three manifestations, three operations, three substances, or three somethings else besides subsistences.

> But they are not three manifestations, three operations, three substances, or three of anything else except subsistences.

> Therefore, they must be three subsistences.

Silas by night unto Berea: who coming *thither* went into the synagogue of the Jews. These were more noble than those in Thessalonica, in that they received the word with all readiness of mind, and searched the Scriptures daily, whether those things were so").

George Whitehead utterly rejected the premise of this argument – it is not found in the Scriptures nor is it a logical inference from John's text. He asked them to define their terms, saying that God did not choose to hide truth in the metaphysical language of heathens, but to reveal it plainly. They could offer no better definition of subsistence than person, and no better definition of person than the mode of a substance. George Whitehead and I then cited several scriptural passages that prove God's complete unity and asked how God was to be understood if God's existence was separate from God's substance. They stated that it was a matter more for wonder and reverence than for discussion.

Even a cursory examination of this argument shows him to be a poor scholar, just as the content shows him to be a poor Christian. As much as possible, I will overlook these personal shortcomings. Likewise, I will not comment on his first proposition, but concentrate on why we flatly reject the second proposition. Briefly stated, no single thing – or substance – can have three subsistencies – that is three ways of existing – and preserve its unity. Even with the most favorable definition of these terms, each subsistence must have its own substance. Therefore, three distinct subsistences, or manners of being, must have three distinct substances, or beings. Consequently, by the terms of their argument, there must be three Gods.

If the infinite Godhead exists in three separate manners or forms, then isn't each of them a perfect and complete subsistence without the other two? By definition then, each must be only a part of the whole and therefore finite and, therefore, something finite is in God. If that is not the case, then each must be infinite – that is, there must be three distinct infinite subsistences. We know that nothing is infinite but God, so doesn't this imply three Gods? By definition, any substance and its subsistence are inseparable. Therefore, contrary to their claims, the unity of substance in the Godhead is incompatible with a Trinity composed of separate and distinct subsistences.

When Thomas Danson quoted Hebrews,[13] he was asked, 'Of whom was Christ the express image?' He said, 'Of God's subsistence or manner of

---

[13] Heb. 1:1-3: "God, who at sundry times and in divers manners spake in time past unto the fathers by the prophets, Hath in these last days spoken unto us by *his* Son, whom he hath appointed heir of all things, by whom also he made the worlds; Who being the brightness of *his* glory, and the express image of his

being.' In reply, I observed that two things naturally follow from this: first, that it makes God a Father only by subsistence and second, Christ a Son without a substance. Besides which, the current English version of Hebrews is inaccurate since the Greek does not say *Charakter prosopo*, the exact likeness of his face, but *Charakter tes hypostasios*, the exact likeness of his being.

Danson's error, and an explanation of the truth, can be seen by carefully examining Col. 1:15, "He is the image of the invisible God."

George Whitehead tried to explain this foreign doctrine in terms that the audience would understand, comparing their three persons with three apostles. How, he asked, can Paul, Peter, and John be three persons and one apostle? This is an apt comparison and one that exposes the ridiculous nature of their doctrine. Maddocks, whose zeal exceeded his knowledge, began to bluster that he had important information that would resolve the question. Instead of doing so, (perhaps to save his companions from more embarrassment, or perhaps just to show off), he tried to end the discussion by offering a crude syllogism that cast inappropriate aspersions on George Whitehead's character:

> Anyone who scornfully and disgracefully compares our doctrine of the blessed Trinity of Father, Son, and Spirit – one in essence, but three in persons – to three finite men, Paul, Peter, and John, is a blasphemer.

George Whitehead has done so.

Therefore, George Whitehead is a blasphemer.

This is certainly a strange way to frame an argument. First, he assumes what he cannot prove to be true, and then, based on that assumption, asserts the truth of the very thing that is still in question. In this case, he takes for granted that there are three distinct and separate persons in one essence. Let him first prove the truth of his assumed Trinity and then charge us with blasphemy. But, I must not forget how he contradicted himself. Maddocks called each of the three "He," and if he can find a "He" without a substance, or prove that a subsistence is anything other than the form of a "He," he might avoid appearing ignorant.

---

person, and upholding all things by the word of his power, when he had by himself purged our sins, sat down on the right hand of the Majesty on high."

These weak hypotheses provide them with no basis for the charges they made against George Whitehead.

Remember that if what George Whitehead said is blasphemy, it is not based his own ideas, but on theirs. He has simply taken their own principles, drawn out the necessary implications of them, and re-stated what they themselves have already said. To find blasphemy or a blasphemer, they might simply look in a mirror.

The Trinity of Distinct and Separate Persons in the Unity of Essence

Refuted from Scripture

And he said, Lord God, there is no god like you,[14] *to whom will you compare me? Who shall be my equal? Says the Holy ONE.*[15] *– I am the Lord, and there is no other, there is no God besides me.*[16] *This is what the Lord, your Redeemer, the Holy ONE of Israel, says,*[17] *I will also praise you, O my God; I will sing to you, O Holy ONE of Israel;*[18] *Jehovah is ONE, and his name ONE.*[19]

These, with a cloud of other verses that might be cited, clearly demonstrate that in the days of the first covenant and the prophets, only ONE was the Holy God and none but God was that Holy ONE.

---

[14] 1 Kings 8:23: "And he said, LORD God of Israel, *there is* no God like thee, in heaven above, or on earth beneath, who keepest covenant and mercy with thy servants that walk before thee with all their heart."

[15] Isa. 40:25: "To whom then will ye liken me, or shall I be equal? saith the Holy One."

[16] Isa. 45:5-6: "I *am* the LORD, and *there is* none else, *there is* no God beside me: I girded thee, though thou hast not known me: That they may know from the rising of the sun, and from the west, that *there is* none beside me. I *am* the LORD, and *there is* none else."

[17] Isa. 48:17: "Thus saith the LORD, thy Redeemer, the Holy One of Israel; I *am* the LORD thy God which teacheth thee to profit, which leadeth thee by the way *that* thou shouldest go."

[18] Ps. 71:22: "I will also praise thee with the psaltery, *even* thy truth, O my God: unto thee will I sing with the harp, O thou Holy One of Israel."

[19] Zech. 14:9: "And the LORD shall be king over all the earth: in that day shall there be one LORD, and his name one."

Again: *And Jesus said to him, why do you call me good? There is only* ONE *who is good, and that is God.*[20] *And this is eternal life, that they may know you (Father) the only true God.*[21] *Since there is only* ONE *God who will justify.*[22] *There are many gods, but for us there is only* ONE *God, the Father, from whom all things come.*[23] ONE *God and Father, who is over all things.*[24] *For there is* ONE *God.*[25] *To the Only God be glory now and forever.*[26]

From all of these texts, I make one simple assertion: that the Scriptures, both the Old Testament and the New, testify that ONE is God and God is ONE. On this basis, I will make my argument.

If, as the Scriptures unanimously declare, God is the Holy ONE, then God is not a Holy Three nor does God exist as three separate and distinct Holy ONEs. The Scriptures above undeniably prove that ONE is God and God alone is that Holy ONE. God cannot be divided or subsist in THREE, or in THREE distinct and separate Holy ONEs.

Nor should these texts be distorted to support the distinction – frequently, but irrelevantly made – that God is ONE in substance, but THREE in persons or subsistencies. The Scriptures did not declare an incomplete God nor ask us to believe incompletely. God does not require us to worship an incomplete or abstract being, but to worship God, the

---

[20] Matt. 19:17: "And he said unto him, Why callest thou me good? *there is* none good but one, *that is*, God: but if thou wilt enter into life, keep the commandments."

[21] John 17:3: "And this is life eternal, that they might know thee the only true God, and Jesus Christ, whom thou hast sent."

[22] Rom. 3:30: "Seeing *it is* one God, which shall justify the circumcision by faith, and uncircumcision through faith."

[23] 1 Cor. 8:5-6: "For though there be that are called gods, whether in heaven or in earth, (as there be gods many, and lords many,) But to us *there is but* one God, the Father, of whom *are* all things, and we in him; and one Lord Jesus Christ, by whom *are* all things, and we by him."

[24] Ephesians 4:6: "One God and Father of all, who *is* above all, and through all, and in you all."

[25] 1 Tim. 2:5: "For *there is* one God, and one mediator between God and men, the man Christ Jesus."

[26] Jude 1:25: "To the only wise God our Saviour, *be* glory and majesty, dominion and power, both now and ever. Amen."

Holy ONE. Otherwise, God would be seen as, and we would be asked to pay homage to, something less than God. That truly is blasphemy.

These Trinitarians must either believe this scriptural testimony, that God is entirely and completely the Holy ONE (not abstractly or with some distinctions made), or they must deny the truth of Scripture. Likewise, if they acknowledge these Holy Testimonies, they must necessarily conclude that their kind of Trinity is a fiction.

Refuted by Right Reason [27]

1. If there are three distinct and separate persons, then there must be three distinct and separate substances, since each person is inseparable from its own substance. In our ordinary understanding of things, there is no person that is not a substance – an understanding the Scriptures agree with fully. Since, as the Trinitarians agree, the Father is God, the Son is God, and the Spirit is God; then, by their logic, either the Father, Son, and Spirit are three distinct nothings or they must be three distinct somethings, that is, three distinct Gods.

2. It is likewise obvious that these divine persons must be either finite or infinite. If they are finite, then it implies that something finite is inseparable from the Infinite Substance – that is, that something finite is in God. On the other hand, if these persons are infinite, then there are three distinct infinities, three that are all-powerful, three that are eternal, and thus, three Gods.

3. If each person is God, and God consists of three persons, then logically, in each of these persons there are three persons or Gods – each of the three is three itself, and they increase to nine. This logic can be applied again and again until there are an infinite number of Gods.

4. If the Trinitarians deny that these three persons, or subsistences, are infinite (to avoid the necessity of three Gods), then each must be finite; but this is just as absurd. The proposal that one essence is made up of three existences, is replaced with the preposterous notion of an infinite being that exists in three finite ways. But, a finite existence cannot correspond to an infinite essence. Even so, to try and understand their

---

[27] At the time that Penn was writing, 'reason' was understood to be a faculty of the mind that transcended logical understanding and allowed an individual to come to an awareness of the essences of things. Moreover, the mind was viewed as a property of the soul, not of the brain or body.

principle, let us suppose that there are three persons, each of which is finite by itself, but together, they are infinite. If we assume this, the distinctions between the supposed persons are lost. The resulting infinite substance is not completely defined by any one or two, but only by all three simultaneously. Even to make this argument, one must overlook the necessary assumption that the Father, Son, and Spirit are less than infinite.

5.   Furthermore, if these three persons are really one in the Godhead, then they are not truly separate and distinct. On the contrary, each must be able to take the place of the others. Consider this: if the one God is the Father and Christ is the one God, then Christ is the Father. At the same time, if the one God is the Son and the Spirit is that one God, then the Spirit is the Son, and so forth. Nor is it possible to stop there. If the divine nature is inseparable from the three persons – but intimately connected to each – and each person contains the whole of the divine nature, then the Son is in the Father, and the Spirit is in the Son, unless the Godhead is as separate from each of the persons as they are reported to be from each other. Or, perhaps it is assumed that each of the persons has been allocated a unique portion of the divine nature that is not shared with the other two persons. Such a proposal is not only absurd; it is shameful.

Much more might be said to demonstrate the complete self-contradiction of Trinitarian doctrine, as it is commonly understood, but I must be brief.

Information and Caution

Before I move on to a new topic, I must tell you about the origin of the idea of a Trinity. You can be sure that it is not found in the Scriptures or justified by reason (although those who concoct new theological ideas always try to show that their notions are consistent with the Holy Record). It was, my Friend, devised by a bishop of Alexandria,[28] who was in the midst of a hot dispute with Arius,[29] more than three hundred years after the

---

[28] Athanasius (c. 293-373), an early Christian theologian and Patriarch of Alexandria, played a leading role in the opposition to and eventual repudiation of the Arian heresy. In the course of this protracted fight, he was repeatedly banished.

[29] Arius (c. 250-336) was an early Christian priest who championed the belief that God alone is immutable and self-existing. According to Arius, Jesus, although

gospels were first proclaimed. This bishop developed the idea of the Trinity by the too-clever application of his imagination to a set of extraordinarily selective theological distinctions. The dispute they were engaged in overflowed into contentiousness, animosity, and persecution. In the end, both the bishop and Arius were consumed by it.

Thus, it is an idea conceived in ignorance and brought forth and maintained by cruelty. Ultimately, the Trinitarians prevailed by persecution. They imposed their beliefs by force and have maintained them ever since within the Church of Rome. It is called Athanasian, after Athanasius (a stubborn man who alienated even his patron, the Emperor Constantine[30]) for the lead role he is supposed to have played in writing the creed in which this doctrine is asserted. Yet, I suspect that creed is more likely the product of Roman Catholic scholastics[31] – I could say more on this, but I need to be brief.

Beware, Reader. Do not accept too quickly the decisions of prejudiced church councils as gospel doctrines. They go far beyond what is clearly in the Scriptures or what was believed by the primitive saints. They exceed anything that I have read in the works of the first, second or third centuries. These notions are wholly foreign to the works of Irenaeus, Justin Martyr, Tertullian, Origen, Theophilius, or any of the other early Christian writers. These doctrines, though generally accepted, are the children of human minds (and not even the most ingenious of those). They are products of the past – let them remain in the past. For yourselves, turn your minds to that Light and Grace which brings salvation and by your obedience, those mists that tradition has cast before your eyes will be dispersed. Then you will receive secure knowledge of that God, whom to know is life eternal, who is indivisible, the ONE pure, complete, and eternal being. You will know the God who in the fullness of time sent forth his Son[32] as the true Light that

---

the son of God, is a created being with a real beginning in time. Arianism was condemned and Arius declared a heretic by the Council of Nicea in 325.

[30] Constantine (c. 280-337) was the first Roman emperor to profess Christianity and was instrumental in the condemnation of Arianism.

[31] Penn seems to be asserting that the Nicene Creed was written by Catholic academics sometime between the ninth and fourteenth centuries.

[32] Gal. 4:4: "But when the fulness of the time was come, God sent forth his Son, made of a woman, made under the law."

enlightens everyone;[33] that whoever followed him (the Light) might be turned from the fables of darkness[34] and the empty foolishness of human ideas to this Holy Light.[35] Only in this Light are sound judgment and eternal life obtainable; this was promised so many hundreds of years ago, by Christ in person. All have received sufficient Light to enable them to follow Christ's example.

The Common Doctrine of Satisfaction, as Dependent on the Second Person of the Trinity

The Doctrine: Because humanity has broken the Righteous Law of God and therefore deserves the penalty of eternal wrath, it is utterly impossible for God to forgive them without receiving complete and perfect satisfaction.[36] There was no other way for God to obtain this satisfaction, or to save humanity, than by inflicting infinite wrath and vengeance on Jesus Christ, the Second Person of the Trinity. Christ has taken on the whole of our guilt for all sins, past, present, and to come, and has paid our debt (whether for all or only for some) to the offended infinite justice of his Father.

---

[33] John 1:9: "*That* was the true Light, which lighteth every man that cometh into the world."

[34] Titus 1:14: "Not giving heed to Jewish fables, and commandments of men, that turn from the truth."

[35] Acts 26:18: "To open their eyes, *and* to turn *them* from darkness to light, and *from* the power of Satan unto God, that they may receive forgiveness of sins, and inheritance among them which are sanctified by faith that is in me."

[36] The words 'satisfy' and 'satisfaction' are used throughout this section in their theological sense, that is, to indicate the repayment of the spiritual debt to God that humanity incurs each time anyone sins.

Refuted from Scripture

1. "And the Lord passed in front of Moses proclaiming, The Lord, the Lord God merciful and gracious, steadfast in his love for thousands, forgiving iniquity, transgression and sin."[37] From this text, I conclude that since God has proclaimed himself to be a gracious, merciful, and forgiving God, it is not inconsistent with God's nature to pardon humanity – receiving no compensation other than God's own love. A God for whom it is impossible to pardon – who requires repayment to the last penny – is a God who cannot truthfully be called merciful and gracious.

2. "For if you turn back to the Lord, the Lord your God is gracious and merciful, and will not turn his face away from you."[38] How natural it is to see here that God's forgiveness of sin is grounded on repentance. It is not impossible for God to pardon without full satisfaction. This verse tells us of the possibility – no, the certainty – of just the opposite: God's grace and mercy is the ultimate cause and reason for this loving invitation to return.

3. "They were stiff-necked, and would not follow your Commandments, but you are a God ready to pardon, gracious and merciful."[39] Can any honest-hearted reader believe that a God this merciful, at the same time, demands payment to the last full measure of the law? Is that God

---

[37] Exod. 34:6-7: "And the LORD passed by before him, and proclaimed, The LORD, The LORD God, merciful and gracious, longsuffering, and abundant in goodness and truth, Keeping mercy for thousands, forgiving iniquity and transgression and sin, and that will by no means clear *the guilty*; visiting the iniquity of the fathers upon the children, and upon the children's children, unto the third and to the fourth *generation*."

[38] 2 Chron. 30:9: "For if ye turn again unto the LORD, your brethren and your children *shall find* compassion before them that lead them captive, so that they shall come again into this land: for the LORD your God *is* gracious and merciful, and will not turn away *his* face from you, if ye return unto him."

[39] Neh. 9:16-17: "But they and our fathers dealt proudly, and hardened their necks, and hearkened not to thy commandments, And refused to obey, neither were mindful of thy wonders that thou didst among them; but hardened their necks, and in their rebellion appointed a captain to return to their bondage: but thou *art* a God ready to pardon, gracious and merciful, slow to anger, and of great kindness, and forsookest them not."

unable to forgive a debt unless it is paid by another? I can not believe that.

4. "Let the wicked give up their ways, and the unrighteous their thoughts; let them return to the Lord and he will have mercy on them; and to our God, who will abundantly pardon."[40] Let the unprejudiced judge for themselves whether this Scripture-doctrine says that God's nature prohibits forgiving sin and, therefore, that Christ must pay full satisfaction or God certainly will take his vengeance. A strange opinion, indeed!

5. "Behold the days are coming, says the Lord, when I will make a new covenant with the house of Israel; I will put my law within them; I will forgive their iniquity, and remember their sin no more."[41] Here God's pure grace is asserted, not an alleged necessity for satisfaction to gain God's pardon. Paul acknowledges the coming of this new covenant in the eighth chapter of his letter to the Hebrews.[42] The doctrine of

---

[40] Isa. 55:7: "Let the wicked forsake his way, and the unrighteous man his thoughts: and let him return unto the LORD, and he will have mercy upon him; and to our God, for he will abundantly pardon."

[41] Jer. 31:31-34: "Behold, the days come, saith the LORD, that I will make a new covenant with the house of Israel, and with the house of Judah: Not according to the covenant that I made with their fathers in the day *that* I took them by the hand to bring them out of the land of Egypt; which my covenant they brake, although I was an husband unto them, saith the LORD: But this *shall be* the covenant that I will make with the house of Israel; After those days, saith the LORD, I will put my law in their inward parts, and write it in their hearts; and will be their God, and they shall be my people. And they shall teach no more every man his neighbour, and every man his brother, saying, Know the LORD: for they shall all know me, from the least of them unto the greatest of them, saith the LORD: for I will forgive their iniquity, and I will remember their sin no more."

[42] The Letter to the Hebrews is no longer generally ascribed to the apostle, Paul. The text referred to is Heb. 8:10-12 ("For this *is* the covenant that I will make with the house of Israel after those days, saith the Lord; I will put my laws into their mind, and write them in their hearts: and I will be to them a God, and they shall be to me a people: And they shall not teach every man his neighbour, and every man his brother, saying, Know the Lord: for all shall know me, from the least to the greatest. For I will be merciful to their unrighteousness, and their sins and their iniquities will I remember no more").

satisfaction contradicts the essence and promise of the second covenant.[43] In short, it denies God's mercy and omnipotence.

6. "Who is a God like you, who pardons sins and forgives the transgression of the remnant of your inheritance? A God does not stay angry forever, but delights in showing mercy."[44] Is there any passage clearer than this? It declares not only the possibility, but God's desire to pardon sin and *not stay angry forever*. Micah challenges all other gods to compare their limited powers with those of his God. He proclaims God's supremacy and the unlimited nature of God's power, *who pardons sins and does not stay angry forever*. Perhaps instead the 'satisfactionists' should ask, "Who is a God like ours, that cannot pardon sins nor forgive transgression, but stays angry until someone pays full satisfaction?" My answer is, "You will find that God many times among the harsh and severe rulers of the earthly nation; but my God is exalted above them all, seated on the Throne of Mercy, *who pardons sins and does not stay angry forever.*

7. "And forgive us our debts, as we have also forgiven our debtors."[45] Nothing could be more obvious than that when a debt is forgiven, it has not been repaid. If it is our duty to forgive without satisfaction, and if it is true that God will forgive us as we have forgiven others, then satisfaction is totally excluded. Christ further elaborates on that part of his prayer in verse 14: "For if you forgive others when they sin against you, your heavenly Father will also forgive you." Jesus proclaims the justice of receiving God's forgiveness in the same way that we forgive others and encourages us to follow God's merciful example by forgiving others in the same way that we have been forgiven. Christ returns to this message in chapter 18, where the Kingdom of Heaven (which is founded on righteousness) is represented by a King, who when faced with a delinquent debtor, had compassion, and forgave the debt; but that debtor went and threw a fellow servant into prison for

---

[43] In this context, the second covenant is the set of mutual promises made between God and humanity that were instituted by Jesus. This is contrasted with the first covenant, or Covenant of the Law, which was made between God and the children of Israel.

[44] Mic. 7:18: "Who *is* a God like unto thee, that pardoneth iniquity, and passeth by the transgression of the remnant of his heritage? he retaineth not his anger for ever, because he delighteth *in* mercy."

[45] Matt. 6:12: "And forgive us our debts, as we forgive our debtors."

failing to repay his own debt. In anger, the king handed the wicked servant over to the torturers until he had repaid in full.[46] Would that servant have been at fault without the merciful example of the King? How can anyone dare assert that forgiveness is impossible for God? This is despicable and, I am forced to say, blasphemous. Forgiveness is not only possible, it is God's command.

8. "For God so loved the world that he gave his only Son, so that everyone who believed in him will not perish but have eternal life."[47] In this text, it is plainly stated that God's love is not the result of Christ's act of satisfaction. Rather, Christ is the gift and product of God's love.

9. "All the prophets testify that everyone who believes in him receives forgiveness of sins through his name."[48] Here we are told that forgiveness comes from believing Christ's preaching, and obeying his precepts. Not by an alleged satisfaction.

10. "If God is for us, who is against us? God, who did not hold back his own Son, but gave him up for us all."[49] This quite evidently declares it to be God's act of love. If God must be paid, he is paying himself, because God gave him up for us all.

11. "All things are from God, who has reconciled us to himself through Jesus Christ, and given us the ministry of reconciliation; that is, in Christ God reconciled the world to himself, and did not count their sins against them."[50] How undeniably apparent it is that God does not stand off in anger and indignation, contracting with his Son for satisfaction, and unable in any other way to be reconciled with us. God became the Reconciler through Christ, and afterwards through the

---

[46] Matt. 18:23-35.

[47] John 3:16: "For God so loved the world, that he gave his only begotten Son, that whosoever believeth in him should not perish, but have everlasting life."

[48] Acts 10:43: "To him give all the prophets witness, that through his name whosoever believeth in him shall receive remission of sin."

[49] Rom. 8:31-32: "What shall we then say to these things? If God *be* for us, who *can be* against us? He that spared not his own Son, but delivered him up for us all, how shall he not with him also freely give us all things?"

[50] 2 Cor. 5:18-19: "And all things *are* of God, who hath reconciled us to himself by Jesus Christ, and hath given to us the ministry of reconciliation; To wit, that God was in Christ, reconciling the world unto himself, not imputing their trespasses unto them; and hath committed unto us the word of reconciliation."

Apostles, God's messengers, to whom the ministry of reconciliation was entrusted.

12. "In him we have redemption through his blood, the forgiveness of sins, in accordance with the riches of his grace."[51] Now, what relation does satisfaction have to the forgiveness of sins? How could anyone, even the least educated among us, confuse grace with justice?

13. "But the God of all grace has called us to eternal glory through Christ Jesus."[52] Peter does not say that God's justice was satisfied by Christ's sacrifice, and therefore God has forgiven us for our past, present, and future sins and called us to his eternal glory. Rather, we are called because of God's grace.

14. "This is how God showed his love for us: He sent his only Son into the world that we might live through him."[53] This plainly names Christ, in his doctrine, life, miracles, death, and sufferings, as the gift and expression of God's eternal love – all for our salvation.

   a. The old covenant of external and shadowy[54] ordinances that could not clear their consciences was abolished.[55]

   b. Christ offered free and universal life and salvation to all who believed and followed him (the Light) in all his righteousness. The particular purpose of his coming into the world was to destroy the works of the Devil, and we come to know this only when we walk humbly with God, following the guidance of that measure of Light and Grace with which we have each been enlightened.

---

[51] Ephesians 1:7: "In whom we have redemption through his blood, the forgiveness of sins, according to the riches of his grace."

[52] 1 Pet. 5:10: "But the God of all grace, who hath called us unto his eternal glory by Christ Jesus, after that ye have suffered a while, make you perfect, stablish, strengthen, settle *you*."

[53] 1 John 4:9: "In this was manifested the love of God toward us, because that God sent his only begotten Son into the world, that we might live through him."

[54] 'Shadowy' is used here to describe the nature of the old covenant. It is contrasted with the new covenant which is rooted in spiritual substance – to Friends, epitomized by the testimony of the inward Light.

[55] Heb. 9:9: "Which *was* a figure for the time then present, in which were offered both gifts and sacrifices, that could not make him that did the service perfect, as pertaining to the conscience."

c.   Signs, miracles, and the example of his own most-innocent life were used to present his doctrines.

d.   The truth of all he had said (with great love and in complete submission to his Father) was sealed and confirmed when he offered up his body to be crucified by wicked hands.[56] He has now ascended above all the heavens and has become a most complete captain[57] and perfect example.[58]

Therefore, I must openly declare that the Scriptures of Truth are not merely silent with respect to this so-called Doctrine of Satisfaction, but they repudiate it. This doctrine denies the dignity of God and is contrary to the foundation, the essence, and the purpose of the second covenant. Of this, there can be no question.

Absurdities that are Unavoidably Revealed when this Doctrine is Compared with the True Sense of the Scripture

1.   God wishes to forgive, but it is impossible for God to do so unless the debt of sin is fully paid.

2.   We finite and impotent creatures are more capable of showing mercy and forgiveness than the Infinite and Omnipotent Creator.

3.   "God so loved the world, he gave his only Son to save it;"[59] and yet, at the same time, God remained angry with us and condemned us until Christ's death had satisfied his offended justice.

There are many more such absurd and obvious inferences that might be drawn.

---

[56] Acts 2:23: "Him, being delivered by the determinate counsel and foreknowledge of God, ye have taken, and by wicked hands have crucified and slain."

[57] Penn is probably alluding to Heb. 2:10 ("For it became him, for whom *are* all things, and by whom *are* all things, in bringing many sons unto glory, to make the captain of their salvation perfect through sufferings.") where 'captain' might be read as 'guide.'

[58] 1 Pet. 2:21: "For even hereunto were ye called: because Christ also suffered for us, leaving us an example, that ye should follow his steps."

[59] John 3:16: "For God so loved the world, that he gave his only begotten Son, that whosoever believeth in him should not perish, but have everlasting life."

Refuted from Right Reason

Suppose we assume that the Scriptures' silence leaves open the possibility that Christ's death was intended to satisfy his Father's injured justice. In this case, the contradictions are obvious and an insult to our intelligence. Anyone whose thinking is not limited by mindless tradition, and who has not surrendered their judgment to the unspoken assumptions of self-important people, will easily understand this point.

We must ask ourselves: If we make God into a creditor (that is, one who is owed a debt), and Christ paid that debt, then (to use their own terms) did Christ pay that debt as God, as a man, or as both?

Not as God

Christ cannot have paid the debt as God because:

1. It divides the unity of the Godhead by having God engaged in several pairs of contradictory acts at the same time: God is offended and not offended; demanding punishment and pleading for mercy; requiring satisfaction and giving it.

2. If Christ pays the debt as God, then the Father and the Spirit (being God) must also be paying the debt.

3. Since they claim that God requires satisfaction, and Christ is God, then Christ must require satisfaction. Who will satisfy Christ's infinite justice?

4. But if Christ has satisfied God the Father, then Christ (being also God) has satisfied himself (which cannot be).

5. And, since God the Father needed satisfaction, and it is impossible for the Father to satisfy himself, then neither can the Son or the Spirit (because they are the same God). Logically, then, the debt remains unpaid.

Thus far, the 'satisfactionists' are still at a loss.

Not as Man

Christ cannot have paid the debt as a man because:

6. God's justice is infinite and an offense to it is also necessarily infinite. It correspondingly will require an infinite satisfaction, which Jesus Christ, as a mere, finite man, could never offer – no finite cause can produce an infinite effect. We might just as well claim that finite humanity could bring about the existence of God, since nothing less than divinity itself can be truly infinite.

Not as God and Man

7. It should be obvious that if each of two propositions is false, then the combination of the two must also be false. We have refuted the claims that Christ paid the debt as God and as man. Putting the two claims together cannot make them true.

But, let us suppose for the moment that one of these three ways of repaying the debt of sin is possible. Even then, we must consider the notion that God cannot pardon sinners without such a satisfaction. This idea results in consequences that are both ridiculous and unworthy of God.

Irreligious and Irrational Consequences

1. It is unlawful and impossible for God Almighty to be gracious and merciful or to pardon transgressors. What statement could be more unworthy of God?

2. God was irresistibly forced to use this way to save humanity from sin. Does this not deny God's uncontrollable nature?

3. God is not permitted to pardon, but is permitted to inflict punishment on the innocent and to require satisfaction when none is due.

4. The true purpose and great example given us by Christ's life and death is denied. If so, then God does not deserve praise for his greatest act of love for us and goodness to us.

5. It portrays the Son as more compassionate and kind than the Father. But if both are the same God, then either the Father must be as loving as the Son, or the Son as angry as the Father.

6. It claims that the Son purchased our salvation by giving himself to God as satisfaction for our sins. Thus, God is robbed of the gift of the Son

for our redemption (which the Scriptures call unmerited love for the world).

7.   Christ cannot satisfy a debt he does not owe. In offering payment to the Father, the debt is not erased, but merely transferred. Whatever satisfaction humanity owed to the Father, it now owes to the Son.

8.   Because it denies the possibility of humanity ever repaying its debt, we cannot be seen as obligated to God – a debt that cannot be repaid is not an obligation. The value of Christ's acts is Christ's alone; any benefit, Christ's alone. This denies Scripture's testimony of God's good will toward us. – What a shameful picture this paints of the infinite Goodness! Is this your repayment, injurious satisfactionists?

9.   Since God's justice is satisfied for all sins – past, present, and to come – aren't God and Christ denied both the power to require our Godliness and the right to punish our disobedience? What has been paid once – the penalty for future sins – cannot be claimed again. If repayment is again demanded for anyone's debts, either the demand is unlawful or Christ's repayment was insufficient. Do not forget that we are told that all must appear before the judgment seat of Christ, so that each may be punished or rewarded for what has been done during life.[60] Truly, all must give an account of themselves to God.

These, and many more vulgar absurdities and blasphemies, are the true fruits of this grotesque and presumptuous Doctrine of Satisfaction.

---

[60] This combines two texts:

2 Cor. 5:10: "For we must all appear before the judgment seat of Christ; that every one may receive the things *done* in *his* body, according to that he hath done, whether *it be* good or bad."

Rom. 14:10&12: "But why dost thou judge thy brother? or why dost thou set at nought thy brother? for we shall all stand before the judgment seat of Christ. ... So then every one of us shall give account of himself to God."

A Caution

Let me advise, no, *warn* you, Reader, this is not a principle to dabble in, no matter who recommends it. It not only strips God of his sovereign power (both to pardon and to punish), but just as plainly invites us to licentiousness – or at least to take liberties that are inconsistent with the ancient Gospel message as preached by the primitive saints. And all done just to maintain the notion of a satisfaction paid once and for all.

I, on the other hand, call on you to repent and cease troubling God's Holy Spirit, which has been placed within you. Allow yourself to be taught by that Holy Spirit – turn your back on all ungodliness and follow it into all righteousness. If you do not, at the Tribunal of the Great Judge, your pleas will be denied and you will be judged by those things you have done while in the flesh. "Do not deceive yourself, because God will not be deceived; you will reap what you sow."[61]

This brings us to the consideration of the third topic, that is, Justification by Imputed Righteousness.

The Justification of Impure Persons by Imputed Righteousness

*T*he Doctrine: There is no way for a sinner to be justified in the sight of God, except by the imputation of Christ's righteousness. Sanctification, or Godliness, does not precede, but follows justification.

Refuted from Scripture

1. "Have nothing to do with anything false and do not put an innocent or honest person to death, for I will not justify the wicked."[62] Clearly, we are required to live righteous lives. This is the only way to gain God's acceptance, because God will never justify the wicked. If this is so, then imputed righteousness must regenerate and redeem the soul from sin. Otherwise, we are as justified with it as we were without it. From the authority and power of this Scripture text, I can say with absolute certainty that as long as any person is truly guilty of anything false, he or she cannot be in a state of justification. Likewise, since God will

---

[61] Gal. 6:7: "Be not deceived; God is not mocked: for whatsoever a man soweth, that shall he also reap."

[62] Exod. 23:7: "Keep thee far from a false matter; and the innocent and righteous slay thou not: for I will not justify the wicked."

never justify the wicked, then logically it must equally be true that God will never condemn the just – only these are the justified of God.

2. "Both those who justify the wicked and those who condemn the innocent are an abomination to the Lord."[63] If it is such a great abomination for a human being to justify the wicked or to condemn the guilty, how much greater would it be for God to do so? But isn't that exactly what this Doctrine of Imputed Righteousness implies, that God is so uninvolved with the people justified that their guilt will not condemn them, nor would innocence save them? But isn't the abomination greatest of all when God condemns an innocent in order to save the wicked? This is the implication of their doctrine: that a Righteous and Merciful God condemned and punished his innocent Son in order to be satisfied for our sins and thereby to justify us by the imputation of Christ's perfect righteousness – although we remain unsanctified. Why would any Christian assert such a detestable notion?

3. "Children shall not suffer for the sins of their parents; the righteousness of the righteous shall be their own, and the wickedness of the wicked shall be their own. If the righteous turn away from righteousness, they will die; and if the wicked turn away from all their sins, and keep all my commandments, and do what is right and just, they will save their souls; but the house of Israel says, 'The way of the Lord is not fair.' Are my ways unfair?"[64] If God's ways were fair before, they are still fair now, because God's ways are unchangeable. Therefore, I must make this argument: a person's condemnation or justification is not due to the imputation of any other's righteousness, but only to their

---

[63] Prov. 17:15: "He that justifieth the wicked, and he that condemneth the just, even they both *are* abomination to the LORD."

[64] Eze. 18:20, 26-29: "The soul that sinneth, it shall die. The son shall not bear the iniquity of the father, neither shall the father bear the iniquity of the son: the righteousness of the righteous shall be upon him, and the wickedness of the wicked shall be upon him. ...When a righteous *man* turneth away from his righteousness, and committeth iniquity, and dieth in them; for his iniquity that he hath done shall he die. Again, when the wicked *man* turneth away from his wickedness that he hath committed, and doeth that which is lawful and right, he shall save his soul alive. Because he considereth, and turneth away from all his transgressions that he hath committed, he shall surely live, he shall not die. Yet saith the house of Israel, The way of the Lord is not equal. O house of Israel, are not my ways equal? are not your ways unequal?"

own acts in keeping God's righteous laws and commandments – otherwise, God would not be fair and just. How wickedly unfair and unjust are those who would ignore this scriptural testimony? Based only on their own unenlightened guesswork and convoluted interpretations of obscure passages, they have created a doctrine completely and obviously inconsistent with God's perfect and just nature. They would require God to condemn the righteous to death and spare the guilty for eternal life, on account of the imputation of another's righteousness – this is a most unfair way indeed!

4.   "Not everyone who says to me, 'Lord, Lord,' will enter the Kingdom of Heaven, but only those who do the will of my Father... Everyone then who hears these words of mine and acts on them will be like a wise man who built his house on rock..."[65] How very fruitful the Scriptures of Truth are in testifying against this absurd and dangerous doctrine. The words above seem to specify a two-fold righteousness: the first part based on sacrifice and the second, on obedience. One makes for a 'talking' Christian; the other, a 'doing' Christian. In short, I argue that if no one can enter into the Kingdom of Heaven unless they do the Father's will, then likewise no one is justified unless they do the Father's will – because no one can enter the Kingdom who is not justified. Therefore, since there is no admittance without living in harmony with that righteous will and doing what the holy and perfect sayings require, what value will imputed righteousness have to a poor soul, still polluted by sin, when it is awakened by the impatient calls of Death to appear before the Judgment Seat? There, it will be impossible to justify the wicked and only those who have done the will of God will escape condemnation.

5.   "If you keep my commandments, you will abide in my love, just as I have kept my Father's commandments and abide in the Father's love."[66] If no one is truly justified who does not abide in Christ's love,

---

[65] Matt. 7:21, 24-25: "Not every one that saith unto me, Lord, Lord, shall enter into the kingdom of heaven; but he that doeth the will of my Father which is in heaven... Therefore whosoever heareth these sayings of mine, and doeth them, I will liken him unto a wise man, which built his house upon a rock: And the rain descended, and the floods came, and the winds blew, and beat upon that house; and it fell not: for it was founded upon a rock."

[66] John 15:10: "If ye keep my commandments, ye shall abide in my love; even as I have kept my Father's commandments, and abide in his love."

and no one abides in his love who does not keep Christ's commandments, then necessarily, no one is justified except those who keep his commandments. This is the plainest possible refutation of an imputed righteousness: Christ is telling his listeners that he lives within his Father's love because of his obedience. Christ does not say that others could be justified on account of his obedience being imputed to them (while they themselves remain outside his love). No, he says that unless they keep his commandments – obeying for themselves – there will be no acceptance; they will be rejected completely. In this, Christ offers himself as our example.

6. "You are my friends if you do what I command you."[67] Here, we have the precise words and the same message: Unless we are Christ's friends, we cannot be justified; and unless we keep his commandments, it is impossible to be his friend. It necessarily follows from this that unless we keep his commandments, we cannot be justified. If, in short, the way to be Christ's friend is to keep his commandments, then the way to be justified is likewise to keep the commandments. No one can achieve that friendship and remain unjustified, nor can anyone be truly justified while remaining an enemy – and certainly those who do not keep his commandments are his enemies.

7. "For it is not the hearers of the law who are righteous in God's sight, but the doers the law who will be declared righteous."[68] From this, unanswerably I observe that unless we become doers of that law – which Christ came not to destroy, but to fulfill as an example to us[69] – we can never be justified before God. Obedience is so absolutely necessary, that without it, we cannot be accepted. Don't believe that Christ has fulfilled the law for you and relieved you of that obligation! Christ was our model. "For unless you follow me," Christ said, "you cannot be my Disciples."[70] To believe otherwise is not only

---

[67] John 15:14: "Ye are my friends, if ye do whatsoever I command you."

[68] Rom. 2:13: "For not the hearers of the law *are* just before God, but the doers of the law shall be justified."

[69] Matt. 5:17: "Think not that I am come to destroy the law, or the prophets: I am not come to destroy, but to fulfil."

[70] This is a combination of two verses from Luke:

Luke 9:23: "And he said to *them* all, If any *man* will come after me, let him deny himself, and take up his cross daily, and follow me"

unreasonable, but precisely contrary to the Scriptures. If Christ had repaid our debt for us, and did not at the same time enable us to follow his example, the Scripture would not speak of 'doers,' but only one 'doer' of the law who was justified before God. In short, no one can be justified without obeying God's Righteous Law. Hearing about the law will not save you. The imputation of another's righteousness, while you remain a lawbreaker yourself, will not save you. "You do well if you fulfill the royal law; so speak and act as those who are going to be judged by the law."[71]

8. "If you follow your sinful nature, you will die; but if, through the Spirit, you subdue the desires of your body, you will live."[72] No one can be spiritually dead and justified before God. Those who follow their sinful nature will be condemned. Only those who are spiritually alive can be justified. If the living are justified and not the dead, and none can be alive to God except those who have, by the Spirit, conquered their bodily desires, then no one can be justified except those who have, by the Spirit, overcome the desires of their bodies. In other words, justification does not come before, but after, the renunciation of desire and the sanctification of the soul by the power of the Spirit.

9. "For all who are led by the Spirit of God are children of God."[73] Only the most stubborn or capricious would deny that righteousness grows as we become obedient to the leadings of the Spirit. If we cannot be children of God unless we are led by the Spirit of God, then we cannot be justified unless we are led by the Spirit of God, because to be justified is to be a child of God. The way to righteousness and adoption by God is through obedience to the Spirit's leadings, demonstrated by the innocent ways in which we live our lives.

Luke 14:27: "And whosoever doth not bear his cross, and come after me, cannot be my disciple."

[71] James 2:8&12: "If ye fulfil the royal law according to the Scripture, Thou shalt love thy neighbour as thyself, ye do well... So speak ye, and so do, as they that shall be judged by the law of liberty."

[72] Rom. 8:13: "For if ye live after the flesh, ye shall die: but if ye through the Spirit do mortify the deeds of the body, ye shall live."

[73] Rom. 8:14: "For as many as are led by the Spirit of God, they are the sons of God."

10. "Let each person examine his or her own work and take pride in that alone – not in the work of others...Do not deceive yourselves: whatever you sow, that is what you will reap."[74] Acceptance by God will be gained (or lost) from your own work – you may sow in the flesh or in the Spirit. Taking pride in the works of another, or expecting to be accepted for those works, is utterly rejected. We will each reap according to what we have each sown; we must each bear our own burdens.

11. "Was not our ancestor Abraham justified by works when he offered his son Isaac on the altar? You see then that a person is justified by works and not by faith alone."[75] Read the second chapter of the Epistle of James. You will undoubtedly recognize "Satisfactionists" and "Imputarians" among those to whom he was writing. They would have been pleased to have discovered a justification by faith alone or support of the imputation of another's righteousness in his writings; but James, an Apostle of the Most High God, knew what true faith and justification were by direct experience. By Abraham's self-denying example, James showed that without faith in the perfecting power of God's grace – overthrowing our most cherished desires, freeing us from the clutches of every Delilah,[76] and leaving us willing to sacrifice Isaac[77] – faith is a lie; it is a body without a soul. Righteousness in one person cannot justify the unrighteousness in another. Anyone who claims to be justified by faith, but who has not been led into all the Ways of Truth and Works of Righteousness, will find in the end that their Faith is a Fiction.

12. "Little children, let no one deceive you. Those who act righteously are righteous, just as God is righteous, but those who commit sin are

---

74 Gal. 6:4-5&7: "But let every man prove his own work, and then shall he have rejoicing in himself alone, and not in another. For every man shall bear his own burden... Be not deceived; God is not mocked: for whatsoever a man soweth, that shall he also reap."

75 James 2:21&24: "Was not Abraham our father justified by works, when he had offered Isaac his son upon the altar? ... Ye see then how that by works a man is justified, and not by faith only."

76 The reference is to Judges 16, in which Delilah tricked Samson into revealing the source of his strength, cut off his hair, and delivered him to the Philistines.

77 The reference is to the story in Genesis 22 in which Abraham is asked to sacrifice his son, Isaac.

children of the Devil."[78] No one can be in a state of justification by claiming the benefits of another's righteous acts. Each must be free from acts of sin. If those who commit sin are children of the Devil, then how can anyone be completely justified before God who is not completely free of sin? If anyone who is still a captive to desire can be justified, then the Devil's Seed can be justified – but this is impossible. Those who act righteously are righteous, just as God is righteous, but in no other way are they like God, nor are they otherwise defensible. If they deviate from those works of faith directed by a pure conscience, they are no longer righteous or justified, but condemned as transgressors, disobedient to the Righteous Commandment. To achieve a true state of justification, we must in all things follow the guidance of the Holy Spirit and the instruction of that unction[79] to which the Apostle pointed the ancient churches.[80] Only in this way can we be led out of all ungodliness and into Truth and Holiness. Only in this way can we find acceptance with the Lord, who will never justify the wicked.[81]

Refuted by Right Reason

1. This doctrine requires God to see the wicked as righteous by the imputation of another's righteousness, but that is impossible. God cannot be reconciled with anything that is opposed to or destructive of his nature.

2. In its original state of innocence, humanity was justified before God. We were not condemned until we fell from that pure state, and we can never become justified again while we continue to sin. To be justified, our redemption must be as complete as our fall.

3. Sin came into the world by a real act, not by imputation – God does not condemn us for what we did not do, but for what we have done.

---

[78] 1 John 3:7-8: "Little children, let no man deceive you: he that doeth righteousness is righteous, even as he is righteous. He that committeth sin is of the devil; for the devil sinneth from the beginning. For this purpose the Son of God was manifested, that he might destroy the works of the devil."

[79] Unction: The spiritual influence of the Holy Spirit acting on a person.

[80] 1 John 2:20: "But ye have an unction from the Holy One, and ye know all things."

[81] Exod. 23:7: "Keep thee far from a false matter; and the innocent and righteous slay thou not: for I will not justify the wicked."

Likewise, to again be acceptable to God, our righteousness must be as personal as our sin. Otherwise, two things can be logically concluded: First, we can be sinners but not condemned for our sin. And second, the power of the first Adam to bring death was greater than the power of the second Adam to bring life.[82]

4. If actual sin brought death and condemnation, how can anything less than actual obedience and righteousness restore life and justification? Death and life, condemnation and righteousness – these are irreconcilably opposed. No one can be actually dead and yet still alive by imputation, but this much-admired and much-advocated doctrine proposes just that: that one can be actually sinful and yet, by imputation, righteous – which is to say that we will in reality be judged and condemned, but, by imputation, justified and glorified; we will be damned, yet saved by imputation. This is truly a gross absurdity! Doesn't it make more sense that the obedience required for our justification be as real and complete as was our disobedience in earning condemnation? Ask yourselves, how are the words 'sanctification,' 'righteousness,' 'resurrection,' 'justification,' etc. best understood? As real or imputed things?

5. Those who assert an imputed righteousness seek to imitate the Scripture in their doctrine, but they miss the mark. The words, *impute, imputed, imputes, imputing*, are used in Scripture to describe people as they really and truly are. If someone is imputed to be guilty, it is because he or she is guilty. People are imputed to be forgiven, because they are forgiven; righteous, because they are righteous. For instance: "If anyone of the house of Israel slaughters an ox, and does not bring it to the door of the tabernacle as an offering to the Lord, blood will be imputed to him."[83] That is to say, that person is guilty of bloodshed. Likewise,

---

[82] 1 Cor. 15:22&45: "For as in Adam all die, even so in Christ shall all be made alive... And so it is written, The first man Adam was made a living soul; the last Adam *was made* a quickening spirit."

[83] Lev. 17:3-4: "What man soever *there be* of the house of Israel, that killeth an ox, or lamb, or goat, in the camp, or that killeth *it* out of the camp, And bringeth it not unto the door of the tabernacle of the congregation, to offer an offering unto the LORD before the tabernacle of the LORD; blood shall be imputed unto that man; he hath shed blood; and that man shall be cut off from among his people."

"Shimei said to the king, 'May my lord not impute iniquity to me, for your servant knows that I have sinned.'"[84]

6. "Sin is not imputed when there is no law."[85] Again, it is obvious that there can be no charge or imputation of guilt to anyone who is not really guilty. Next, consider how 'impute' is used with respect to remission of sin: "Blessed are those to whom the Lord imputes no iniquity" or, as stated in the previous verse, "Blessed are those whose transgression is forgiven."[86] This non-imputation does not declare sin unreal; the sin is as real as God's forgiveness. Otherwise, there would be nothing to forgive – nor would there be a real pardon offered, but only the suggestion of one. According to the logic of this doctrine, God's forgiveness is imaginary.

Again, consider: "God in Christ was reconciling the world to himself, not imputing their sins to them."[87] As before, 'not imputing' describes real forgiveness of actual sins. That being the case, 'imputing' is actually charging a person with real guilt. Lastly, the word is used in relation to 'righteousness:' "Was not our ancestor Abraham justified by works when he offered his son Isaac? And faith was made perfect by works and the Scripture that says, 'Abraham believed God, and righteousness was imputed to him,' was fulfilled."[88] The blind Imputarians of our day deny that

---

[84] 2 Sam. 19:18-20: "And there went over a ferry boat to carry over the king's household, and to do what he thought good. And Shimei the son of Gera fell down before the king, as he was come over Jordan; And said unto the king, Let not my lord impute iniquity unto me, neither do thou remember that which thy servant did perversely the day that my lord the king went out of Jerusalem, that the king should take it to his heart. For thy servant doth know that I have sinned: therefore, behold, I am come the first this day of all the house of Joseph to go down to meet my lord the king."

[85] Rom. 5:13: "For until the law sin was in the world: but sin is not imputed when there is no law."

[86] Ps. 32:1-2: "Blessed *is he whose* transgression *is* forgiven, *whose* sin *is* covered. Blessed *is* the man unto whom the LORD imputeth not iniquity, and in whose spirit *there is* no guile."

[87] 2 Cor. 5:19: "To wit, that God was in Christ, reconciling the world unto himself, not imputing their trespasses unto them; and hath committed unto us the word of reconciliation."

[88] James 2:21-23: "Was not Abraham our father justified by works, when he had offered Isaac his son upon the altar? Seest thou how faith wrought with his works, and by works was faith made perfect? And the Scripture was fulfilled

Abraham's very personal offering was a justifying act of righteousness; they claim that God was simply pretending that it was – but God does not pretend. There is no imputation of another's righteousness to Abraham; on the contrary, his personal and real obedience is the reason for this well-deserved imputation of righteousness.

From all these passages, we can conclude that no one in the Scriptures is justified by the imputation of another's righteousness – God does not declare someone to be righteous who is not righteous within. To believe that God grants us something that is not our honest possession is ridiculous and dangerous: Ridiculous, since it is like calling a penniless person a millionaire, because someone else is rich. Dangerous, because it convinces many people that they are saved while they remain captive to desires that will bring them ultimate condemnation. Many who claim to be religious say that God does not see them as they are, but as they are in Christ – as if they could truly be in Christ and not be new creatures.[89] No one is a new creature who has not stripped off their old garments, but remains wrapped in the corruption of the old man.[90]

Irreligious and Irrational Consequences

1. This doctrine makes God guilty of what the Scriptures name an abomination, that is, that God justifies the wicked.[91]

2. It requires God to see people as they are not, or to show partiality among them, which is unworthy of God's most equal nature.[92]

3. If sinners are justified, then they would be at peace with God, who said, "There is no peace with the wicked."[93]

---

which saith, Abraham believed God, and it was imputed unto him for righteousness: and he was called the Friend of God."

[89] 2 Cor. 5:17: "Therefore if any man *be* in Christ, *he is* a new creature: old things are passed away; behold, all things are become new."

[90] Col. 3:9-10: "Lie not one to another, seeing that ye have put off the old man with his deeds; And have put on the new *man*, which is renewed in knowledge after the image of him that created him."

[91] Prov. 17:15: "He that justifieth the wicked, and he that condemneth the just, even they both *are* abomination to the LORD."

[92] Rom. 2:11: "For there is no respect of persons with God."

[93] Isa. 57:21: "*There is* no peace, saith my God, to the wicked."

4. Not only does it imply reconciliation with them in this world, but throughout eternity, "for those he justified, he also glorified."[94] In other words, sinners are justified and glorified, while remaining sinners.

5. Sinners are freed from the consequences of their sin, but not from enslavement to sin. In this way, something that is sinful becomes justified, and something that is corrupt enters God's kingdom.

6. It declares us to be justified and condemned, dead and alive, redeemed and unredeemed – all at the same time. We are one thing by imputed righteousness and the other by our personal unrighteousness.

7. It deludes us into believing we can indulge our worldly desires and still be justified. This undermines the purpose of Christ's appearance among us: to destroy the works of the Devil[95] and take away the sins of the world.[96] Instead the Satisfactionists and Imputarians of our day would have us believe that Christ came to do just the opposite: to give satisfaction for their sins and, by Christ's imputed righteousness, to make them appear holy while allowing them to remain unholy in themselves. But, Christ came to take away sin and destroy the Devil's works (which were not in him, but in us). It is, therefore, undeniably true that those from whom sin has not been taken and in whom the works of the Devil are undestroyed have no understanding (despite all their pretensions) of the purpose or the products of Christ's mission.

---

[94] Rom. 8:30: "Moreover whom he did predestinate, them he also called: and whom he called, them he also justified: and whom he justified, them he also glorified."

[95] 1 John 3:8: "He that committeth sin is of the devil; for the devil sinneth from the beginning. For this purpose the Son of God was manifested, that he might destroy the works of the devil."

[96] Heb. 10:11-12: "And every priest standeth daily ministering and offering oftentimes the same sacrifices, which can never take away sins: But this man, after he had offered one sacrifice for sins for ever, sat down on the right hand of God."

Conclusion by way of a Caution

*T*hus Reader, I have led you through a consideration of three generally accepted doctrines. Although my disproofs have been brief, I hope that you have understood them. Now, I call the Righteous God of Heaven as a witness, to testify on my behalf, that in this document I have tried only to defend God's unity, mercy, and purity against the rash and ignorant assaults of tradition, both from the pulpit and in print. What I hear of these daily, leads me almost to believe that there is a conspiracy to tear down Truth and betray gospel doctrines in favor of idle traditions. But God will rebuke the winds[97] and the enemies of God's anointed will face destruction. Make no mistake, we have never disowned Father, Word, and Spirit, which are ONE[98] – we deny only human innovations:

1. Their *Trinity* cannot be found in the Scriptures.

2. This notion first appears three hundred years after the founding of the primitive church.

3. Conflict over it caused so much blood to be shed, that in 355 A.D. the Council of Sirmium decreed that, henceforth, the controversy should never again be brought up since God's Scriptures did not mention it. Why then should it now be mentioned? Why are those who oppose this obscure opinion threatened with excommunication?

4. This notion has undoubtedly been the cause of idolatry. As an example, look no further than the Popish images of Father, Son, and Holy Ghost.

5. It scandalizes Turks, Jews, and Infidels and is an obstacle to their acceptance of the Christian faith.

Nor is either of the other two so-called doctrines any more defensible. Can anyone find even one scriptural text that in any way approximates the Doctrine of Satisfaction (much less one that contains that name)? It cannot be done, even considering the degree to which this doctrine has been stretched. We do not deny – indeed, we profess – that Jesus Christ, in his

---

[97] Matt. 8:26: "And he saith unto them, Why are ye fearful, O ye of little faith? Then he arose, and rebuked the winds and the sea; and there was a great calm."

[98] 1 John 5:7: "For there are three that bear record in heaven, the Father, the Word, and the Holy Ghost: and these three are one."

life, doctrine, and death, fulfilled his Father's will and offered himself up as an atoning sacrifice. But that sacrifice was not offered to pay God, or help him to save humanity (as if God were unable to do so in any other way). It was not to provide justification by an imputed righteousness – an imaginary justification – and therefore we reject it. Here is what we confess and we know to be justifying before God: There is no abiding in Christ's love without keeping his commandments.[99] In love, therefore, I must tell you plainly, no matter what religious sect you are in now, do not deceive yourselves. Do not let yourselves be seduced by human ideas masquerading as divine mysteries. Know that God has given each of us sufficient grace to see what is good, so that we may obey and do it. If you follow that guidance, you will be led out of all unrighteousness, and in your obedience you will receive power to become a child of God.[100] It is only in that state of happy obedience that God can be known by us and in which we can know that we are justified before God. In that way, we can know, through our own experience, life eternal through Jesus Christ.[101]

Postscript: A Critique of the Contradictions in Thomas Vincent's Sermon on the Fifth Chapter of the First Epistle of John, Delivered this Evening in Spittle-Yard

"Everyone born of God overcomes the world."[102]   *"There is a two-fold victory, the first is complete, the second incomplete."*

The explanation offered contradicts not only the text it seeks explain, but simple common sense. The Scripture does not say that those who are born of God cannot perfectly overcome the world, but rather just the opposite. What does he mean by an incomplete victory? One in which the enemy is not slaughtered, but overwhelmed and taken captive? But if the enemy is so defeated and disarmed that it can no longer threaten its conqueror, then the victory is ultimately complete – the dispute between

---

[99] John 15:10: "If ye keep my commandments, ye shall abide in my love; even as I have kept my Father's commandments, and abide in his love."

[100] Rom. 8:14: "For as many as are led by the Spirit of God, they are the sons of God."

[101] Rom. 6:23: "For the wages of sin *is* death; but the gift of God *is* eternal life through Jesus Christ our Lord."

[102] 1 John 5:4: "For whatsoever is born of God overcometh the world: and this is the victory that overcometh the world, *even* our faith."

them has been completely resolved. Anything incomplete is unfinished –
but it is on the way to being finished. Victory is the completion of what was
incomplete.

"Those who are born again in Christ overcome sin. They have stripped off their old self and have come to be completely new."

"Worldly desires can never be totally rooted out of God's people in this world."

How can they be born again as children of God and have a place in the
body of Christ if sin must have a place in them? How can they strip off the
old self and put on the new if the desires of this world are still rooted
within them?

"God's children are the greatest conquerors. Alexander and Caesar were conquerors, but God's children have overcome their desires."

"God's children cannot achieve complete victory over the desires of the world; sometimes their desires take them captive."

What a strange divinity! God's people will be conquerors, and yet, they
are captives; they will overcome the world, and yet, be overcome by it.

"Sin may rule as a tyrant over believers."

"But sin will not reign; it is in captivity, it is in chains."

Is there anyone more unlawful or uncontrollable than a tyrant? And yet,
this tyrant will not reign, but be held captive in chains. Is there any
common sense in this? Only a madman could believe both of these things
at once.

"You must kill or be killed; either you will overcome the world or it will overcome you. If you fight, you will win."

"We overcome only incompletely. We can smash their forces and take them captive in chains; but not all are slain, and sometimes they take us captive."

"Kill or be killed" leaves no alternatives, no escape. Yet we are told that
Sin and God's children will each take the other captive and that those who
fight will win, but only incompletely and therefore they remain in danger of
being held captive in turn. This is a very strange doctrine.

Moreover, Thomas Vincent goes on to tell us, "Whoever is born of
God conquers worldly desires,[103] and anyone that conquers worldly desires,

---

[103] 1 John 5:4: "For whatsoever is born of God overcometh the world: and this is the victory that overcometh the world, *even* our faith."

conquers all the Devils of Hell. God's children face a conquered enemy."
Yet in all this, he asks us to understand that he means this only in an
incomplete sense. He challenges us to fight for that incomplete victory. He
holds out the fruits of conquest, that is, "All who conquer will be allowed
to eat the fruit of the Tree of Life[104] and the hidden manna. I will give them
a white stone, a new name, power over the nations, [105] and clothing of the
purest white;[106] I will make them pillars in the Temple of my God; they will
remain in God's presence forever,[107] and I will allow them to sit with me on
my Throne."[108] I admit that these are amazing privileges! But are they
promised to *incomplete* conquerors? I don't think so.

Reader, from this, you can probably guess the rest of my argument; and
since I began with Thomas Vincent and his comrades, let me end with
them. Despite all their proud boasting and malicious slanders, they have
avoided every opportunity – offered in letters, verbal messages, and
personal visits – to speak with us directly. If they had any real belief in their
principles, cared for their reputations, or kept their promises, they would
have accepted one of our invitations for a face-to-face, public discussion.

Instead, I have had to resort to this publication to answer them. Now, I
am told – that as a result of malicious misinterpretations of my answers on
the part of some busybodies –it is being said that "A certain Quaker has
taken up a dispute with Ralph Farmer, in which he has grossly
misrepresented the Christian religion; in particular, by denying that Christ

---

[104] Rev. 2:7: "He that hath an ear, let him hear what the Spirit saith unto the
churches; To him that overcometh will I give to eat of the tree of life, which is
in the midst of the paradise of God."

[105] Rev. 2:17: "He that hath an ear, let him hear what the Spirit saith unto the
churches; To him that overcometh will I give to eat of the hidden manna, and
will give him a white stone, and in the stone a new name written, which no man
knoweth saving he that receiveth *it.*"

[106] Rev. 3:5: "He that overcometh, the same shall be clothed in white raiment; and I
will not blot out his name out of the book of life, but I will confess his name
before my Father, and before his angels."

[107] Rev. 3:12: "Him that overcometh will I make a pillar in the temple of my God,
and he shall go no more out: and I will write upon him the name of my God,
and the name of the city of my God, *which is* new Jerusalem, which cometh
down out of heaven from my God: and *I will write upon him* my new name."

[108] Rev. 3:21: "To him that overcometh will I grant to sit with me in my throne,
even as I also overcame, and am set down with my Father in his throne."

came bodily into the world." Although there are other, equally offensive accusations, I will not dignify them with an answer.

Reader, I ask that you alone consider this uncharitable accusation and be my judge. First of all, since I do not know Ralph Farmer, I could not have directed my arguments against him – I am not looking for a quarrel with anyone, except those who seek to distort God's Truth. I must admit, however, that his opinions may be contradicted by this plain and simple work.

Lastly, concerning the accusation that I deny Christ, this is not a new slander, but nevertheless a false one. On behalf of that despised people who are commonly called Quakers, I declare that the Grace about which we preach has never led us to proclaim any other God than the Father of all things,[109] who fills heaven and earth.[110] Nor has that Grace led us to acknowledge any Lord but the Lord Jesus Christ who appeared so many hundred years ago, who was born of a virgin,[111] and is like us in every way, except sin.[112] Nor do we deny any doctrine that Jesus practiced or preached. Therefore, let every mouth be stopped up and never opened again that speaks any evil against God's Innocent People. We will, in principle, life, and death, bear unanimous testimony of the One, True God, the true Christ, and the Doctrines of Heaven. This truth is publicly declared by

William Penn, Junior

---

[109] 1 Cor. 8:6: "But to us *there is but* one God, the Father, of whom *are* all things, and we in him; and one Lord Jesus Christ, by whom *are* all things, and we by him."

[110] Jer. 23:24: "Can any hide himself in secret places that I shall not see him? saith the LORD. Do not I fill heaven and earth? saith the LORD."

[111] Matt. 1:23: "Behold, a virgin shall be with child, and shall bring forth a son, and they shall call his name Emmanuel, which being interpreted is, God with us."

[112] Heb. 4:15: "For we have not an high priest which cannot be touched with the feeling of our infirmities; but was in all points tempted like as *we are, yet without sin.*"

INNOCENCY

WITH

Her Open Face

PRESENTED

By way of Apology for the Book entitled
The Sandy Foundation Shaken,

To all Serious and Inquiring Persons,
PARTICULARLY
The *Inhabitants* of the City of

LONDON:

By W. P. *j.*

*He that uttereth a Slander is a Fool; and a False Balance is an
Abomination to the Lord,* Proverbs *10:8* and *11:1*

Printed in the Year, *1669.*

RELIGION: It is the calamity of our times that although there can be nothing of greater concern, nor anything more essential to a person's immortal happiness, nevertheless there is nothing people are less attentive to or less serious in practicing. People seem to believe that it consists merely of a vague adherence to and rote confession of some humanly invented traditions and precepts, while ignoring the more orthodox definition of the Apostle James. "Religion that is pure and undefiled before God is to care for orphans and to keep oneself unstained by the world."[113] They believe instead that they are performing a great service when they deprive others of reputation, liberty, and property – if not of life itself[114] – for failing to share their stubbornly held beliefs. Even though those they are oppressing possess more virtue, but cannot agree to each and every aspect of those beliefs.

It is common knowledge that I am a victim of such persecution. No proverb was ever better proved than by the lying lips[115] that have so outrageously attacked me. I have been slandered, reviled, and defamed from the pulpit, in the press, and by common gossip. I have been called a blasphemer, a seducer,[116] and a Socinian.[117] I have been accused of denying the divinity of Christ the Savior. All this is due to a pamphlet[118] I recently published as part of a dispute with some Presbyterians. The purpose of this short apology[119] is to demonstrate the injustice of these accusations. Had I

---

[113] James 1:27: "Pure religion and undefiled before God and the Father is this, To visit the fatherless and widows in their affliction, *and* to keep himself unspotted from the world."

[114] In the seventeenth century, the punishment for a blasphemy conviction was execution. Penn was accused of blasphemy, but not formally charged with it.

[115] Prov. 10:18: "He that hideth hatred *with* lying lips, and he that uttereth a slander, *is* a fool."

[116] Penn is not being accused of sexual impropriety, but of spiritual seduction – i.e., leading people away from true belief. This use of the term is biblical; for example, see Mark 13:22 ("For false Christs and false prophets shall rise, and shall shew signs and wonders, to seduce, if it were possible, even the elect").

[117] Socinians were followers of Laelius and Faustus Socinus, sixteenth century Italian theologians who denied the divinity of Christ.

[118] The pamphlet referred to is *A Sandy Foundation Shaken*.

[119] The choice of the word 'apology' to describe this essay is important. In the seventeenth century, 'apology' had several meanings that are no longer in common use. In a legal forum, it was used to describe a formal defense against

not been anticipating a hearing on the charges against me, this would have been published earlier. If I succeed in demonstrating the injustice of my adversaries' accusations, I hope it will put an end to this situation. To that end, I ask the reader to give my innocence a fair hearing in its own defense. Just as Innocence can only reveal the truth of what has been done, so she will easily disprove her enemies, showing their accusations to be fictitious. I ask only this: that you not judge me before you read this nor that you believe any more than what you can see for yourself.

I.   I am credibly informed that the principal reason for my imprisonment, and for the suggestion of blasphemy that has been the subject of so much recent gossip, is the charge that I have denied the Divinity of Christ and his Eternal Godhead. This charge has been urged on those in authority and maliciously spread among the common people. Please, be impartial and considerate in reviewing my defense, which is presented to you in the fear of Almighty God and written in simple, scriptural words. I hope it will prove my innocence beyond any doubt.

The Proverbs which most people agree refer to Christ the Savior are:

"By me kings reign, and rulers decree what is just."[120]

"I (Wisdom[121]) walk the Paths of Judgment."[122]

"I was established from eternity."[123]

Some of Paul's words also allude to this:

---

an accusation. Theologically, an apology was a statement of faith. By titling this work an apology, Penn could be read as admitting that he had made a mistake and that he was expressing sorrow for it by those who were looking for an admission of guilt. He seems, however, to intend the term to be understood in the legal sense – as a defense against unfair and untrue charges. In some places in the text, the theological meaning might also be conveyed. It seems likely that this ambiguity is intentional.

[120] Prov. 8:15: "By me kings reign, and princes decree justice."

[121] Prov. 8:12: "I wisdom dwell with prudence, and find out knowledge of witty inventions."

[122] Prov. 8:20: "I lead in the way of righteousness, in the midst of the paths of judgment."

[123] Prov. 8:23: "I was set up from everlasting, from the beginning, or ever the earth was."

"To those who are called (we preach) Christ the power of God and the wisdom of God."[124]

And from this, I conclude Christ the Savior to be God. Otherwise, God would not be God, because if Christ is God's Power and Wisdom, and is distinct from God, then God would be without his own Power and Wisdom. Surely, it is impossible for God's Power and Wisdom to be distinct and separate from God. Therefore, Christ, who is God's Power and Wisdom, is not distinct from God, but is entirely that very same God.

Next, consider the testimony of the Prophets David and Isaiah:

"The Lord is my Light and my Salvation."[125]

"I will make you a Light to the Gentiles."[126]

"For the Lord will be your Everlasting Light."[127]

To this, John the Evangelist adds,

"That was the true Light which enlightens everyone who comes into the world."[128]

"God is Light, and in God there is no darkness at all."[129]

On the basis of these verses, I affirm the unity of God and Christ. Though they are nominally distinguished, both are essentially the same Divine Light. If Christ is that Light and that Light is God, then Christ is

---

[124] 1 Cor. 1:23-24: "But we preach Christ crucified, unto the Jews a stumblingblock, and unto the Greeks foolishness; But unto them which are called, both Jews and Greeks, Christ the power of God, and the wisdom of God."

[125] Ps. 27:1: "The LORD *is* my light and my salvation; whom shall I fear? the LORD *is* the strength of my life; of whom shall I be afraid?"

[126] Isa. 49:6: "I will also give thee for a light to the Gentiles, that thou mayest be my salvation unto the end of the earth."

[127] Isa. 60:20: "Thy sun shall no more go down; neither shall thy moon withdraw itself: for the LORD shall be thine everlasting light, and the days of thy mourning shall be ended."

[128] John 1:9: "*That* was the true Light, which lighteth every man that cometh into the world."

[129] 1 John 1:5: "This then is the message which we have heard of him, and declare unto you, that God is light, and in him is no darkness at all."

God. Likewise, if God is that Light and that Light is Christ, then God is Christ. Look also at the Book of Revelation:

> "And the city has no need for the sun, for the glory of God lights it, and the Lamb (Christ) is its Light."[130]

In this text, the oneness of these Lights is made plain, because God is not God without God's own glory, and it is God's glory that lights the city, (which it could not do if it were not Light). And the Lamb, or Christ, is declared to be that very same Light. Can there be any conclusion but that Christ the Light and God the Light are the ONE pure and eternal Light?

Now, let us consider the word 'Savior':

> "I, only I, am the Lord, and besides me, there is no other Savior."[131]

> "You shall know no God but Me, for there is no Savior besides Me."[132]

> "And Mary said, my spirit rejoices in God my Savior."[133]

> "And the Samaritans said to the woman who met Jesus at the well, now we know that this is truly the Christ, the Savior of the world."[134]

> "According to his grace revealed through the appearing of our Savior Christ Jesus."[135]

---

[130] Rev. 21:23: "And the city had no need of the sun, neither of the moon, to shine in it: for the glory of God did lighten it, and the Lamb *is* the light thereof."

[131] Isa. 43:11: "I, *even* I, *am* the LORD; and beside me *there is* no saviour."

[132] Hos. 13:4: "Yet I *am* the LORD thy God from the land of Egypt, and thou shalt know no god but me: for *there is* no saviour beside me."

[133] Luke 1:46-47: "And Mary said, My soul doth magnify the Lord, And my spirit hath rejoiced in God my Saviour."

[134] John 4:42: "And said unto the woman, Now we believe, not because of thy saying: for we have heard *him* ourselves, and know that this is indeed the Christ, the Saviour of the world."

[135] 2 Tim. 1:9-10: "Who hath saved us, and called *us* with an holy calling, not according to our works, but according to his own purpose and grace, which was given us in Christ Jesus before the world began, But is now made manifest by the appearing of our Saviour Jesus Christ, who hath abolished death, and hath brought life and immortality to light through the gospel."

"Simon Peter said to those who have received a faith as precious as ours through the righteousness of our God and our Savior Jesus Christ."[136]

"To achieve this end we accept disgrace, because we trust in the living God, the Savior of all people."[137]

"To the only God, our Savior, be glory, etc."[138]

From all of these, I conclude that Christ is God. If no one can save, or correctly be called the Savior, but God; and Christ is said to save, and is correctly called the Savior, then it must be the case that Christ the Savior is God.

Lastly:

"In the beginning, was the (logos) Word, (which the Greeks sometimes understood to mean Wisdom and divine Reason) and the Word was with God, and the Word was God."[139]

"Through him all things were made; without him nothing was made that has been made."[140]

"For by him all things in heaven and on earth were created."[141]

"He is before all things; in him all things hold together."[142]

"And he sustains all things by his powerful word, etc."[143]

---

[136] 2 Pet. 1:1: "Simon Peter, a servant and an apostle of Jesus Christ, to them that have obtained like precious faith with us through the righteousness of God and our Saviour Jesus Christ."

[137] 1 Tim. 4:10: "For therefore we both labour and suffer reproach, because we trust in the living God, who is the Saviour of all men, specially of those that believe."

[138] Jude 1:25: "To the only wise God our Saviour, *be* glory and majesty, dominion and power, both now and ever. Amen."

[139] John 1:1: "In the beginning was the Word, and the Word was with God, and the Word was God."

[140] John 1:3: "All things were made by him; and without him was not any thing made that was made."

[141] Heb. 1:10: "And, Thou, Lord, in the beginning hast laid the foundation of the earth; and the heavens are the works of thine hands."

[142] Col. 1: 17: "And he is before all things, and by him all things consist."

By all this, I am convinced of Christ the Savior's Divinity. If he made all things and by him all things are held together and are sustained; and he was before all things, and therefore not himself made or maintained by another; then he is God. This logos or Word made flesh,[144] or Christ the Light, Power and Wisdom of God, and Savior of humanity, has made all things and holds together and sustains all things, having been before they existed (as is obvious from the scripture passages cited). Therefore he was not made, nor is he sustained by any power other than his own, and is truly God.

In short, this conclusive proof that Christ the Savior is God should certainly convince all serious Readers of my innocence and of my adversaries' malice. He who is the Everlasting Wisdom, the Divine Power, the true Light, the only Savior, the creating Word of all things (visible and invisible[145]), who sustains all things by his own Power, is without question God. All these qualifications and divine properties are ascribed to the Lord Jesus Christ by the testimony of Scripture. Therefore without the least doubt, I call him, and believe him to be, Almighty God. If you wish to have an even more complete description, please refer to page 28 of my reply to J. Clapham[146] in which my beliefs on Christ's Divinity and Eternity are fully detailed.

I appeal to you, impartial Readers – be my judge. Decide whether or not my reputation as a Christian has been slanderously misrepresented by those who have published their books against me (*while I remain a closely guarded prisoner*). Judge for yourself the empty arguments they produce while fighting their own shadows. They have asserted that things I have never thought, much less written, are the heart of my argument. Then, starting with that false assumption, they furiously attacked – thinking that I will feel

---

[143] Heb. 1:3: "Who being the brightness of *his* glory, and the express image of his person, and upholding all things by the word of his power, when he had by himself purged our sins, sat down on the right hand of the Majesty on high."

[144] John 1:14: "And the Word was made flesh, and dwelt among us, (and we beheld his glory, the glory as of the only begotten of the Father,) full of grace and truth."

[145] 1 Cor. 1:16: "For by him were all things created, that are in heaven, and that are in earth, visible and invisible, whether *they be* thrones, or dominions, or principalities, or powers: all things were created by him, and for him."

[146] William Penn, *Guide Mistaken*, 1668.

the sting of every punch they throw. So far, I am unaffected by their petty fits of rage.

As for my being a Socinian, I must confess that I have read about a man named Socinus, a member of (what is called) a noble family in Siena, Italy. As a young man, in about 1574, he voluntarily gave up the glories, pleasures, and honors he enjoyed in the Court of the great Duke of Tuscany at Florence (a place noted for its worldly delicacies) and became a perpetual Exile for Conscience. He was renowned in the Polish and Transylvanian churches for his abilities, wisdom, authority, and honesty.

However, I have never become a follower of this man nor have I endorsed his beliefs. I must therefore reject this attempt to defame me. If there is any similarity between what I write or have written and his works, it is for Truth's sake — he was blessed with a clearer understanding of various things than were many of his contemporaries. This no more makes me a Socinian than a child of the Anglican Church. Even though I agree with many of that church's principles against the Roman Church, I am and will remain a Quaker.

II.   As for the Doctrine of Satisfaction, the argument I am about to make has been anticipated by a person[147] who is well respected by English Protestants. The idea to which I most objected in my previous writings was that Divine forgiveness is impossible unless Christ pays the debt to God's justice by suffering Infinite Vengeance and Eternal Death for all sins, past, present, and in the future. In this recent discourse about Christ's sufferings, *Against Crellius*, he quite plainly states both the possibility of God pardoning sins (as debts) without a rigid requirement of satisfaction and the impossibility of Christ suffering in this way for the world. He notes that those he is answering have given the enemies of the church an opportunity to believe that they have triumphed over Faith.

But, for those whose arguments are based more on zeal than judgment, the only possible victory is over their own mistakes. In fact, on page 160,

---

[147] Edward Stillingfleet (1635-1699) was a young Church of England clergyman when he was asked by the Bishop of London to examine Penn. Stillingfleet had recently addressed the issue of satisfaction in *Six Sermons ... with a Discourse concerning the True Reason for the Sufferings of Christ wherein Crellius' Answer to Crotius is considered (R. White for Henry Mortlock, 1669)*. Stillingfleet had been chaplain to Charles II in 1667, and was later dean of St. Paul's Cathedral in London (1678) and bishop of Worcester (1689-99).

this work states very well one of the primary goals I had for writing my earlier discourse.[148] If they believe that Christ came into the world to reform it, "The Wrath of God is now revealed from Heaven against all unrighteousness.[149] God's Love, now shown to the World, will deliver them from the hands of their enemies so that they might serve God in righteousness and holiness all the days of their lives.[150] They should not assume that salvation is bestowed on them merely by their overwhelming reliance and vehement conviction that Christ has done all and suffered all for them." This is a reasonable restatement of the hypothesis or proposition for which I have also argued. Despite the various misconceptions some have held about me (and no matter how vehemently I reject my opponents unscriptural notions of Satisfaction), you can be sure of this: I know of no other name by which remission of sins, atonement, and salvation can be obtained, but Jesus Christ the Savior, the Power and Wisdom of God.

III.   As for Justification by Imputed Righteousness, I still say that whoever believes in Christ shall have remission and justification, but this is a faith that cannot live without works any more than a body could live without a spirit. In other words, true faith embraces gospel obedience. On this point, Dr. Stillingfleet again supports my position (though it needs no outside support) by a plain declaration of the necessity for obedience: Those who conclude that the Gospels require nothing more than belief should be careful that their hearts are sounder than their heads – and by delineating the flaws and dangers of that notion. My intention (and God Almighty supports it) was nothing less, and nothing more, than to pull that beloved and sin-pleasing principle out of the hands, heads, and hearts of people. I sought to turn them away from the idea that they could be justified by the personal righteousness of any other (regardless of their own obedience) and that they could continue to sin without fear until their deaths. My purpose was to turn them to the serious pursuit of holiness by accepting the guidance of God's Holy Spirit. Without this, no one will ever

---

[148] *The Sandy Foundation Shaken.*

[149] Rom. 1: 18: "For the wrath of God is revealed from heaven against all ungodliness and unrighteousness of men, who hold the truth in unrighteousness."

[150] Luke 1:74-75: "That he would grant unto us, that we being delivered out of the hand of our enemies might serve him without fear, In holiness and righteousness before him, all the days of our life."

see the Lord.[151] I will conclude my apology[152] for religious matters, with a short confession[153] so that all can see, in the most important matters of Eternal Life, the simplicity and scriptural integrity of my statement of faith.

I sincerely acknowledge, and honestly believe (by virtue of the sure knowledge and experience I have received as a gift of the Holy Unction[154] and Divine Grace from on high) in one holy, just, merciful, almighty and eternal God, who is the Father of all things, who many times and in various ways appeared to the Patriarchs and Prophets of old.[155] And I believe in ONE Lord Jesus Christ, the Everlasting Wisdom, Divine Power, True Light, Only Savior and Preserver of All, the same one holy, just, merciful, almighty and eternal God, who in the fullness of time[156] took flesh, and lived in the world.[157] At that time he preached (and after his death, his Disciples preached) the everlasting gospel of repentance and the promise of the remission of sins,[158] and of eternal life to all that heard and obeyed. It is he who said, the one that is with you (in the flesh) shall be in you (by the Spirit) and though he left them (in the flesh), he did not leave them

[151] Heb. 12:14: "Follow peace with all *men*, and holiness, without which no man shall see the Lord."

[152] In this sentence, Penn continues the redefinition this piece of writing. 'Apology' is here used it in its religious sense, as a statement of beliefs. Implicitly, it defines this pamphlet as a defense of the opinions in *A Sandy Foundation Shaken* rather than as an admission of error.

[153] Again, Penn seems to be taking advantage of dual meanings, in this case of the word 'confession.' In common use, it is an admission of guilt. Penn uses it here in its religious sense, as a declaration of one's beliefs.

[154] 1 John 2:20: "But ye have an unction from the Holy One, and ye know all things."

[155] Heb. 1:1: "God, who at sundry times and in divers manners spake in time past unto the fathers by the prophets."

[156] Gal. 4:4: "But when the fullness of the time was come, God sent forth his Son, made of a woman, made under the law."

[157] John 1:14: "And the Word was made flesh, and dwelt among us, (and we beheld his glory, the glory as of the only begotten of the Father,) full of grace and truth."

[158] Luke 24:47: "And that repentance and remission of sins should be preached in his name among all nations, beginning at Jerusalem."

comfortless,[159] for he promised to come to them again (in the Spirit)[160] for a little while, and although they would not see him (in the flesh), after a little while they would see him (in the Spirit).[161] The Lord (Jesus Christ) is that Spirit[162] and is revealed to all for their spiritual benefit.[163] And I believe in the Holy Spirit, who is the same Almighty and Eternal God and who, in those times, swept away the shadows and became the infallible Guide to all that would walk in the Light. In that way, they were adopted as heirs and co-heirs of God's glory.[164]

I am a living witness that the holy, just, merciful, almighty and eternal God is now the same as then (after the long night of Idolatry, Superstition, and human notions that has spread over the world).[165] God is and has been gloriously revealed to show us our sins, to save us from all iniquity, and to lead us to the Holy Land of pure and endless peace that is to live within us. I also firmly believe that remission of sins and eternal life can never be obtained without repenting, giving up our past sins, and walking in obedience to this heavenly voice. Only that voice can guide you to and secure you in the Truth. Only those who fear God's name and keep his

---

[159] John 14:17-18: "*Even* the Spirit of truth; whom the world cannot receive, because it seeth him not, neither knoweth him: but ye know him; for he dwelleth with you, and shall be in you. I will not leave you comfortless: I will come to you."

[160] John 14:28: "Ye have heard how I said unto you, I go away, and come *again* unto you. If ye loved me, ye would rejoice, because I said, I go unto the Father: for my Father is greater than I."

[161] John 16:16: "A little while, and ye shall not see me: and again, a little while, and ye shall see me, because I go to the Father."

[162] 2 Cor. 3:17: "Now the Lord is that Spirit: and where the Spirit of the Lord *is*, there *is* liberty."

[163] 1 Cor. 12:7: "But the manifestation of the Spirit is given to every man to profit withal."

[164] Rom. 8:14&17: "For as many as are led by the Spirit of God, they are the sons of God... And if children, then heirs; heirs of God, and joint-heirs with Christ; if so be that we suffer with *him*, that we may be also glorified together."

[165] Penn is referring to the apostasy of the Christian Church that began at the time of the apostles. His claim is that Quakerism represents the revival of true Christianity.

commandments shall have the right to the tree of life.[166] For the sake of his name, I have been made willing to give up all the vain fashions, enticing pleasures, alluring honors and glittering glories of this temporary world[167] and have willingly accepted being called a fool by this sneering generation. I have become a man of sorrows,[168] and a perpetual reproach[169] to my friends and family.[170] It is with the greatest cheerfulness[171] that I formally re-affirm that this is my faithful confession (and I expect, as a result, nothing less than the loss of everything this world holds dear). My eyes are fixed on a more enduring substance and a more lasting inheritance than this world can offer. When my time is no more, I am unshakably convinced that (if I remain faithful) I will inherit the mansions of eternal life[172] and be received into God's everlasting home of rest and glory.

---

[166] Rev. 22:14: "Blessed *are* they that do his commandments, that they may have right to the tree of life, and may enter in through the gates into the city."

[167] Penn has noted Matt. 10:37-39 ["He that loveth father or mother more than me is not worthy of me: and he that loveth son or daughter more than me is not worthy of me. And he that taketh not his cross, and followeth after me, is not worthy of me. He that findeth his life shall lose it: and he that loseth his life for my sake shall find it."] in the margin. This may be a personal reference. In becoming a Quaker, Penn risked losing the wealth and position that he was due to inherit from his father.

[168] Isa. 53:3: "He is despised and rejected of men; a man of sorrows, and acquainted with grief: and we hid as it were *our* faces from him; he was despised, and we esteemed him not."

[169] Ps. 78:66: "And he smote his enemies in the hinder parts: he put them to a *perpetual reproach*."

[170] Penn seems to be drawing a parallel between the treatment of Christ before his crucifixion and his own confinement in the Tower of London. He has noted the following in the margin:

Luke 18:32. ["For he shall be delivered unto the Gentiles, and shall be mocked, and spitefully entreated, and spitted on."]

Luke 23:36. ["And the soldiers also mocked him, coming to him, and offering him vinegar."]

[171] Penn has noted 1 Pet. 4:14 ["If ye be reproached for the name of Christ, happy *are ye*; for the spirit of glory and of God resteth upon you: on their part he is evil spoken of, but on your part he is glorified."] in the margin.

[172] John 14:2: "In my Father's house are many mansions: if *it were* not *so*, I would have told you. I go to prepare a place for you."

IV.   Lastly, it is not unreasonable to observe that (despite how some people – religious dissenters, no less – have tried to portray me) I have not violated any truly Fundamental Law relating to external property or good behavior – only the law as it relates to religious beliefs. Friends are determined to maintain good works[173] and keep our consciences clear of any offense.[174] Following the humble example of our Lord Jesus Christ, we are both actively and passively obedient in all things.

All may also be aware of how eager I was to debate these matters before a gathering of serious and thoughtful individuals – rather than the ignorant mob we faced in Spitalfields. Despite promises to the contrary, our opponents have refused to do so, and I have been forced to put my defense into writing. My intention was simply to answer their slanders against the Truth, but Oh! how my few pages have been tossed, tumbled, and torn at their hands. They accuse me of monstrous plotting and go so far as to charge me with the subversion of the Christian Religion (when nothing could be further from the truth). You can see for yourselves how excessive and unjust my adversaries have been in their vilifications, slanders, and defamations.[175] They call me a seducer, a heretic, a blasphemer, a deceiver, a Socinian, a Pelagian,[176] and a Simon Magus.[177] They accuse me of impiously robbing Christ of his divinity and warn me to beware of the vengeance of the Last Judgment. These things are not merely whispered in private – they are thundered from pulpits and spewed out in books as if some Bull[178] had recently been received from Rome. And all this has been justified as acts of zeal and love for Jesus Christ; but Christ's gentle and humble example was

---

[173] Titus 3:8: "*This is* a faithful saying, and these things I will that thou affirm constantly, that they which have believed in God might be careful to maintain good works. These things are good and profitable unto men."

[174] Acts 24:16: "And herein do I exercise myself, to have always a conscience void of offence toward God, and *toward* men."

[175] Penn has noted "See Tho. Vincent's late railing piece against the Quakers, also Thomas Danson's and Dr. Owen's" in the margin.

[176] Pelagius (354?-418?) was an English monk who rejected the Augustinian belief in predestination, arguing that humans are endowed with free will and can choose between good and evil. He was excommunicated as a heretic in 418.

[177] Simon Magus is mentioned in the book of Acts where he attempts to buy spiritual gifts (Acts 8:18, "...when Simon saw that through laying on of the apostles' hands the Holy Ghost was given, he offered them money").

[178] Bull: A papal edict.

to endure any injury or insult without complaint and without repaying it in kind – this is the mark of a true Christian. How can my adversaries call themselves righteous or faithful Christians when they conspire to destroy me on false religious grounds? Have they not also been the victims of religious persecution?[179] Are they not the descendents of those who were persecuted by the Church of Rome?

Please answer one question. When the great reformer Luther, whom you so revere, was summoned to appear at the Diet of Worms, what did he demand of the Emperor? Simply this, that his doctrines should be judged by the Scriptures alone and that if those doctrines were pronounced erroneous that his sentence should be based on the words of Gamaliel to the Jewish Council, "If it is not the work of God, it will not stand."[180] If you will not condemn the man who first subjected the so-called Christian World (that had slept so soundly throughout the long dark night of apostasy) to his own private judgment, how can you so furiously attack others for following his example? But above all else, remember that you for the last eight years have refused to conform to the Church of England and have written passionately in favor of Liberty of Conscience – a liberty you yourselves have only recently enjoyed.[181] What compelling argument do you offer to justify your unwillingness to grant to others what you have so passionately begged for yourselves? Does this not expose your true feelings and demonstrate that only a lack of power protects others from your injustice?

All Protestants need to consider this question: Do you believe that your persecution is Christian while persecution by Papists is Antichristian? You condemned Roman persecution as a sign of the weakness in their religion – yet in your own, you consider it a compelling argument. Contrary to what you believe, your oppression is the easiest way to enhance the reputation of

---

[179] This is addressed to those of Penn's opponents who are Dissenters, that is members of congregations that had separated themselves from the national church, and who had suffered persecution under the Restoration government.

[180] Acts 5:38-39: "And now I say unto you, Refrain from these men, and let them alone: for if this counsel or this work be of men, it will come to nought: But if it be of God, ye cannot overthrow it; lest haply ye be found even to fight against God."

[181] The Clarendon Codes were four acts passed while the Earl of Clarendon was Lord Chancellor. These greatly restricted the rights of Dissenters and were repealed in 1665.

those you persecute and to hasten the spread of those beliefs you wish to suppress. You were incredulous when others claimed infallibility, but seem to believe that it is impossible to err yourselves. Have Whitaker, Reynolds, Laud, Owen, Baxter, Stillingfleet, Poole, etc. wrestled the weapons of oppression from the Church of Rome so that you can use them on harmless fellow citizens? Let the example and teachings of Christ, who came not to destroy, but to save,[182] guide you. Consider carefully his impartial law: Do to others as you would have them do to you.[183]

Remember that I have not rejected God, subverted Faith, released any from obedience, nor denied belief in an eternal reward. I have not harmed any of you or in any way deviated from the holy principles, insisted on by Philosophers and Lawyers as the basis of good laws and a good life. If you will only let them, your own consciences will argue my case for me. It is enough to say that we (who have been called Quakers) have, after every change in government and official religion, been the most degraded, abused, disdained, despised, and persecuted of all people. It is as if God had indeed made us a spectacle to the world, to angels, and to men.[184] You act as if we have given up our common rights and our membership in human society.

Do not accept the products of hatred or ignorance as a true description of our lives or of our doctrines. Judge us by what you know yourselves – not by second-hand reports. We know too well the effects of such uninformed and thoughtless zealotry. If you will make your own impartial examination of the facts, we know we can depend on your sense of justice as much as we depend on our own innocence.

Some of our adversaries are so perversely devoted to their own ideas that they rarely give any consideration to whether any religion other than their own might be true or false, or what might happen if they were to tolerate the practice of another religion. Instead, with a fury matched in intensity only by their ignorance, they cry, Crucify! Crucify! Remember that

---

[182] Luke 9:56: "For the Son of man is not come to destroy men's lives, but to save *them*. And they went to another village."

[183] Luke 6:31: "And as ye would that men should do to you, do ye also to them likewise."

[184] 1 Cor. 4:9: "For I think that God hath set forth us the apostles last, as it were appointed to death: for we are made a spectacle unto the world, and to angels, and to men."

the Pharisees claimed to serve God and to honor the words of God's Prophets while they persecuted God's Son and righteous servants – persecution is always cruel, blind, and obstinate.

Let the words of our humble example, Jesus Christ, guide us. Call not for fire any longer, let the weeds grow with the wheat,[185] give up the use of that sword that was to be sheathed so many hundred years ago.[186] You may believe that we are the enemies of true faith, but be careful that you are not acting like Saul on his errand to Damascus[187] – helping those in power to oppress God and his chosen people. Use fair and impartial discussion to judge between religious differences, not Imperial Decrees. In that way, at least a civil unity, if not a religious unity, can be maintained. But if you choose harshness, it will destroy that unity. Our case will never change. Our happiness will never be diminished – no human edict can possibly deprive us of that glorious presence that makes even the most dismal prison into a palace of delights or deprive us of God's heavenly fellowship that fills our solitary souls to overflowing with divine consolation. I have been taught by that Holy, Meek, and Harmless Spirit to freely forgive and fervently pray for all of my adversaries. Fare well.

William Penn, junior

---

[185] Matt. 13:30: "Let both grow together until the harvest: and in the time of harvest I will say to the reapers, Gather ye together first the tares, and bind them in bundles to burn them: but gather the wheat into my barn."

[186] Matt. 26:52: "Then said Jesus unto him, Put up again thy sword into his place: for all they that take the sword shall perish with the sword."

[187] The reference is to the apostle, Paul, who was on his way to persecute the Christians in Damascus when he was struck from his horse and converted (see Acts 9).

A Questionary Postscript

*W*here in Scripture does it say that Christ suffered an Eternal Death and Infinite Vengeance? Did Christ not rise on the third day?[188] Wouldn't infinite vengeance and eternal death be endless? Didn't God say he was well pleased with his son before his death?[189] Wasn't Christ's offering acceptable? Didn't the Apostle Paul say that the saints were accepted in Christ[190] who was God's beloved? This was after Christ died and rose. God was said to be well-pleased with his Son, both before he suffered, in his suffering, and after he suffered, though God was displeased with those that caused him to suffer.

---

[188] Luke 24:46: "And said unto them, Thus it is written, and thus it behoved Christ to suffer, and to rise from the dead the third day."

[189] Mark 1:11: "And there came a voice from heaven, *saying*, Thou art my beloved Son, in whom I am well pleased."

[190] 1 Cor. 1:2: "Unto the church of God which is at Corinth, to them that are sanctified in Christ Jesus, called *to be* saints, with all that in every place call upon the name of Jesus Christ our Lord, both theirs and ours."

THE

Christian-Quaker

AND HIS
DIVINE TESTIMONY

VINDICATED

BY

Scripture, Reason and Authorities;

AGAINST

The *Injurious Attempts*, that have been lately made by several *Adversaries*, with Manifest Design to render HIM Odiously Inconsistent with CHRISTIANITY and Civil Society.

By *William Penn.*

Veritas fatigari potest, vinci non potest, *Etherius & Beatus*, libr. 1

Thus saith thy LORD, and thy God that pleadeth the Cause of his People; Behold I have taken out of thy Hand the Cup of Trembling, even the Dregs of the Cup of my Fury, thou shalt no more drink it again: But I will put it into the Hand of them that Afflict thee. Isaiah 51:22-23

Printed in the year 1674.

TO THE NOBLE *BEREANS* [191] OF THIS AGE

*A*mong the commands of our dear Lord Jesus Christ, the Blessed Author of the Christian Religion, when he first sent his Disciples forth to proclaim the happy approach of the Kingdom of Heaven,[192] was this one: when you enter any city or town, ask who in it is righteous.[193] He foresaw the many ways in which unworthy people would misuse his message – how the stubborn Pharisees and the clever Scribes would try to subvert the Right Way of the Lord, and turn the common people away from that Excellent Testimony.

And as the impious abused our Blessed Savior and his faithful followers, so the Pharisees and Scribes of our own day have more maliciously resented, more bitterly envied, and more furiously attacked the people called Quakers than any other people. In this desperate situation, we seek a few worthy Readers – people who dare to form their own opinions rather than blindly accepting those of others, who will recognize self-interest and ignorance and who, in these dark times, will serve as sincere, diligent, and impartial judges.

Of all the peoples mentioned in the Scriptures, none is more honorable in the eyes of the Holy Spirit than the Bereans who searched after Truth impartially and, when they found it, embraced it readily. They stood in contrast to the Jews of Thessalonica, who feared the spread of the Gospel among your ancestors and attempted to stir up the people against those who earnestly preached it.[194] For this they were called Noble. It is to the Noble Bereans of our own day that we, the slandered supporters of the Cause of Truth, dedicate this Defense of our Religious Principles.

---

191 Acts 17:10-11: "And the brethren immediately sent away Paul and Silas by night unto Berea: who coming *thither* went into the synagogue of the Jews. These were more noble than those in Thessalonica, in that they received the word with all readiness of mind, and searched the Scriptures daily, whether those things were so."

192 Matt. 10:5&7: "These twelve Jesus sent forth, and commanded them, saying… as ye go, preach, saying, The kingdom of heaven is at hand."

193 Matt. 10:11: "And into whatsoever city or town ye shall enter, enquire who in it is worthy; and there abide till ye go thence."

194 Acts 17:13: "But when the Jews of Thessalonica had knowledge that the word of God was preached of Paul at Berea, they came thither also, and stirred up the people."

Our modern Thessalonians will go to any extreme to incite hatred of the Quakers. Not only do they condemn what they see as the worst in us (charges we will not address yet); but cleverly try to insinuate that even our best is criminal.

They describe our seriousness as a fraud and our incessant preaching and godly lives as decoys, designed to lure others to join us. When they question us, if we say nothing, it is called sullenness or an inability to answer. If we say anything, it is presumptuousness or mere lies. They tell us that we do not really believe what we claim to believe, but what they want us to believe. This they state as offensively as possible so that they can then taunt us for them. Nor can our writings mean what we say they mean, but what they tell us they mean. Distorted in this way, they can be used as proof of our guilt. As David said, "All day long they twist my words and plot to harm me."[195] It is to David's God, and to you, the Bereans of our time, that we submit our slandered case. Follow the example of those earlier Bereans. If you do, we trust that we will receive a fair hearing and an honest judgment.

May the God and Father of our Lord Jesus Christ multiply your desires for the Truth, give you clear discernment of the Truth, enable you to readily receive the Truth, and grant you the steadfastness to hold onto the Truth. We are

> Your greatly maligned, but truly Christian Friends,
>
> William Penn and George Whitehead.
>
> Rickmersworth, the 16th of 10th Month, 1674.[196]

---

[195] Ps. 56:5: "Every day they wrest my words: all their thoughts *are* against me for evil."

[196] December 16, 1674, according to the modern calendar.

PREFACE

*A*n insatiable thirst for religious or civil domination has filled nearly every age with strife, but rarely has anyone fought for Pure Religion.

To write about the disorders in the first six hundred years after Christ (let alone the even greater disorders of the years following) is simply to write an Ecclesiastical History. Religion quickly became a disguise for political domination and claims of truth, an excuse for revenge.[197]

What has happened since, our modern stories tell us. Certainly, most sects that have been established, regardless of how right they were to break their ties with older institutions, have quickly degenerated first into shameless self-promotion, and then to attempts at domination of others' consciences. In pursuing these aims, they have used the same tools of persecution that they found so cruel when in the hands of others.

I know very well that there is something in all people that draws them toward religion and that thing is not to be found in tradition nor in mere formal rituals. But in order to appear devout and pious, people engage in needless activities and mix their own conceptions in with divine commands. As a result, what is called religion becomes more a human creation than the work of Truth. People become so attached to these inventions that, like the ancient tyrants, they impose them on the consciences of others to secure their domination in this world.

If you doubt the truth of this claim, look only to the days of your own great grandparents. It is not even two hundred years since bold and honorable steps were taken to free Christianity from the apostate Church of Rome. These proved to be successful and many kingdoms were freed from Roman tyranny. God certainly blessed the work of those conscientious people who gave their fortunes, time, and lives to that truly holy, but longsuffering, war.[198]

---

[197] At this point, Penn listed a number of sources for ecclesiastical history and commentary in the margin.

[198] In the margin, Penn refers the Reader to a book on the debate between Martin Luther and Johann von Eck, as well as the works of Ulrich Zwingli, John Calvin, and Theodore Beza.

Tragedy came when these heroes were taken by death. Their successors failed to act in the same simplicity or out of the same convictions. Instead, they began to think they could honor their martyred ancestors by gaining worldly power for what they called religion and took up outward swords to do so. Mixing in their own additions, they declared the resulting new and adulterated religion to be the most true, certain, and infallible. Wielding the power of the state, they offered dissenters a choice of conformity or death – the same detestable actions that Rome had used against those earlier martyrs.[199]

While their predecessors had labored to overcome power by suffering, their work was to promote religion by the use of power. Forming alliances, sending out dignified ambassadors, holding great conventions, raising armies, waging war with one state or seeking peace with another filled the minds of most. Foremost was a desire to defend the dignity and pompous grandeur of their religion, though by so doing they demonstrated how much they had lost a true sense of the religion they claimed to be advancing.

There were some who denounced this state of affairs. In the English Church, they condemned the superstitions and rituals that had unfortunately been retained when it broke with Rome. These, they said, were mere human inventions and anti-Christian. They believed that the people were being corrupted and laid the blame on the pride, greed, lusts, and ignorance of the clergy. These Protestants stripped away most of the formalities and seemed to promote a stricter way of life than what was generally observed. These people were called Puritans.[200]

But both civil and religious leaders were tied to their customs and laws were enacted, and executed in blood, to prevent further purification of religion as much as to guard against renewed debasement. Surely, this was more a protection of their own power, interests, and friends than of religion. Without doubt, the Puritans' arguments were never answered by their opponents. The people, both the gentry and the common people, and

---

[199] In the margin, Penn has noted Peter Heylyn's *Ecclesia Restauranta.*

[200] In the margin, Penn has noted William Camden's *Annales: The True and Royal History of Elizabeth Queen of England* and John Rushworth's *Historical Collection of Private Passages of State.*

especially those who were most religious, took up these complaints. And when the Long Parliament was chosen, Puritans had a clear majority.[201]

The Church of England, showing disdain for its so-called reformation and determined to maintain all of its civil and religious splendor, wealth, and privileges, resisted – calling them disturbers of both civic and religious peace. The lessons of persecution that the heathens had taught the Papists, and the Papists in turn had taught the Protestants, were now taught to the Puritans – to be firm and determined in the defense of their separation. The church's rebuke was met by denial; heated words escalated to armed confrontation and finally to war. Feud, hatred, ruin, and the most lamentable slaughter – on a scale not seen for ages – were the rotten fruits of that contest for religion.[202] With victory, the Puritans degenerated, seeking to impose a harsh Presbyterianism on the country. Those who had earlier called the Church of England anti-Christian for trying to coerce them into conformity now took their turn at intolerance. The definitions of scriptural faith, proper forms of worship, and church discipline that their synods adopted were imposed and enforced by the harshest penalties known up to that time. The Liberty of Conscience they had so recently gained for themselves was denied to others. So prejudiced and blind is self-interest.

But our story does not end here. Seeming to forget the faithfulness and humility with which they confronted the degeneracy of the English clergy (as those had earlier confronted Rome), the Puritans were quickly reminded by those who were called Independents and Baptists.[203] These people, who had a clearer understanding of religious matters and were more devoted to true reformation, charged the Puritans with neglect and tried to push things a step further. They loudly denounced the moral looseness found in Puritan

---

[201] After years of ruling alone, King Charles I called Parliament into session in 1640 to raise money for a war with Scotland. Parliament demanded more accountability from the king in return for the new taxes. When the king resisted, parliament raised its own army. This lead to the English Civil War and, in 1649, the execution of Charles and the establishment of the Commonwealth. Called the Long Parliament, it finally dissolved itself in 1660 just prior to the restoration of Charles II.

[202] In the margin, Penn has noted *Hist. Wars of Engl.* This may refer to The Earl of Clarendon's *History of the Rebellion and Civil Wars in England.*

[203] Independents and Baptists had rejected the attempted organization of parishes into Presbyterian synods by the Commonwealth government.

parishes and the practice of administering the sacraments to all – whether true Christians or not. They decried the control of the national church over individual parishes and the requirement that ministers have university training.[204] Finally, they passionately denounced any attempt to impose articles of faith or forms of worship and the use of any physical penalties against those who dissented for the sake of conscience.

You would think that these people, having seen the effects of a spirit of superstition and revenge – how their predecessors had been split by it – would have learned the lesson. So many earlier attempts at reformation (driven at first by an inward sense of the corrupt and unchristian state of things) had ended up producing conceit, pride, superstition, and the despicable coercion of conscience. Knowing this, they should have lived lives of complete subjugation to the Holy Spirit of Truth. Such a life would have rejected worldly desires, covetousness, and revenge and would have preserved them in the ways of meekness, patience, long-suffering, and holiness,[205] without which no one will see God.[206] But, alas! Just as reformation from pope and prelate was soon pushed aside by self-promotion and contention between sects, the makers of this reformation also quickly took up the old, outward weapons to advance themselves and suppress others.

The Papists taught the Protestants; the Protestants taught the Presbyterians; and the Presbyterians taught the Puritans. But unlike their predecessors, the Puritans were not strong enough to hold power alone. There were too many Presbyterians and their definitions were too narrow – not in our church, not in the faith; not dipped in our water, not Christian. Without an alliance, their grip on the government, and all the advantages that gave them, would be lost. So (against their will), they invited some Presbyterians – the moderates and especially those in the so-called parochial churches – to a partial share in the administration of the civil government. Though this was done with regret and even jealousy, an acceptable arrangement was found.

---

[204] Many Baptist congregations were led by common people with no formal schooling.

[205] 1 Tim. 6:11: "But thou, O man of God, flee these things; and follow after righteousness, godliness, faith, love, patience, meekness."

[206] Matt. 5:8: "Blessed *are* the pure in heart: for they shall see God."

There is a story of a poor priest who (because several of the apostles were fishermen) would have a fisherman's net spread on his table to remind him of his humble predecessors. When this man was elected Pope, the net was again brought out, but seeing it, he cried out, "Take it away! Take it away! The fish is caught!" In the same way, the Puritans had caught a great two-headed fish – one head wearing the crown of civil power and the other the miter of ecclesiastic power – and like the Laodiceans they were content, rich, and wanting nothing more.[207] They were willing to forget their humble origins, their Father's house,[208] their convictions, their righteousness, and their humility. Oh! What falseness, cruelty, covetousness, and folly they fell into! They broke faith with their membership, and the most solemn covenants with God, seeking security through blood and establishing their church by persecution. Like the Ottoman Emperors, they never felt more secure on their thrones than by the murder of their compatriots.[209] Above all others, they denounced tyranny and persecution, but were the source of both. It is as if they were unable to use power without abusing it.

Succeeding times may have surpassed them in wickedness, but no others, in any time I know, have equaled them in treacherous hypocrisy. To be fair, there were those among them who expressed their revulsion, but this only seemed to drive the rest to greater apostasy. In the end, the treacherous treated these few disaffected worse than any others. For a more complete description, I refer the Reader to the first and second narratives, printed in 1659.[210]

---

[207] Rev. 3:14-17: "And unto the angel of the church of the Laodiceans write; These things saith the Amen, the faithful and true witness, the beginning of the creation of God; I know thy works, that thou art neither cold nor hot: I would thou wert cold or hot. So then because thou art lukewarm, and neither cold nor hot, I will spue thee out of my mouth. Because thou sayest, I am rich, and increased with goods, and have need of nothing; and knowest not that thou art wretched, and miserable, and poor, and blind, and naked."

[208] Ps. 45:10: "Hearken, O daughter, and consider, and incline thine ear; forget also thine own people, and thy father's house."

[209] Hugh Barbour suggests that this reference to Turkey may be based on Sir Paul Rycaut's *The Present State of the Ottoman Empire*.

[210] Barbour suggests that the 'first and second narratives' may refer to Sir George Wharton's *Gesta Brittanorum, or a Succinct Chronology* and *A Second Narrative of the late Parliament*.

Certainly, it was then time for God to intervene and make his enemies known. Disguised as the most glorious show of reformation that had been seen in fourteen hundred years, they had crucified the holy life of religion – suffocating spirituality with new rituals, empty forms, and the mere tinkling cymbals[211] of sin-pleasing doctrines. Their original loving-tenderness was worn off by time and status and no one was more superstitious or persecuted more zealously than those who had once so clearly condemned it – out of charity, I will not name names. In short, pride, self-seeking, and the pursuit of glory, wealth, and worldly possessions undermined the honor and honesty that had been stirring in their hearts. They built a chest to hold their beliefs – glorious on the outside and empty on the inside! They claim, like the Jews, to be children of Abraham and heirs of God's promise,[212] but they are servants to sin.[213] They claim to be Christians by imputation, but lack any qualification to that title. They say they are saved in Christ, but in themselves, they are lost in sin. They assert that they pray by the Spirit, but take as their duty, unholy things. Behold Babylon![214]

It was at this time, serious Reader, when Religion was so often talked about and so little practiced, the Eternal Wise God, whose ways are unsearchable,[215] appeared and let himself be known to those the world rejects and ignores – shepherds and others of the lowest class. Their outward abilities seemed as inadequate to convince others as their outward appearance was to attract them.

These were plain, simple people who desired nothing more than to know the true and unchangeable way of God. All the religion that had been taught or that they had found in books, together with their own simplicity and zeal, was unable to protect them from the enemies of their souls. Often

---

[211] 1 Cor. 13:1: "Though I speak with the tongues of men and of angels, and have not charity, I am become *as* sounding brass, or a tinkling cymbal."

[212] Gal. 3:29: "And if ye *be* Christ's, then are ye Abraham's seed, and heirs according to the promise."

[213] Rom. 6:17: "But God be thanked, that ye were the servants of sin, but ye have obeyed from the heart that form of doctrine which was delivered you."

[214] Rev. 18:2: "And he cried mightily with a strong voice, saying, Babylon the great is fallen, is fallen, and is become the habitation of devils, and the hold of every foul spirit, and a cage of every unclean and hateful bird."

[215] Rom. 11:33: "O the depth of the riches both of the wisdom and knowledge of God! how unsearchable *are* his judgments, and his ways past finding out."

they felt deep despair, but they were willing to take up any cross[216] that might help them to the knowledge of Truth; they thirsted after this more than any other food.[217]

In order that no one would boast in his presence,[218] Almighty God poured out his spirit on the poor and the despised. By his terrible power, God shook the old foundations[219] – spreading fear and terror – because of the glory of the majesty[220] revealed. Judgment was established over sin,[221] righteousness was set up as a guide,[222] and an honest scale was erected. All the world's claims for religion were scattered by it, like chaff in the wind.[223] All the pretty pictures of religion that tradition, education, and imagination had drawn in people's minds were consumed on this Day of Judgment.[224] This, the poor and despised were compelled to preach, and both those who claim to believe and those who do not were astonished by their words.

These witnesses rejected outward religion that (no matter how sophisticated) served only to alienate the whole world from God. Because

---

[216] Mark 8:34: "And when he had called the people *unto him* with his disciples also, he said unto them, Whosoever will come after me, let him deny himself, and take up his cross, and follow me."

[217] Matt. 5:6: "Blessed *are* they which do hunger and thirst after righteousness: for they shall be filled."

[218] 1 Cor. 1:29: "That no flesh should glory in his presence."

[219] Ps. 18:7: "Then the earth shook and trembled; the foundations also of the hills moved and were shaken, because he was wroth."

[220] Isa. 2:19: "And they shall go into the holes of the rocks, and into the caves of the earth, for fear of the LORD, and for the glory of his majesty, when he ariseth to shake terribly the earth."

[221] Isa. 59:9: "Therefore is judgment far from us, neither doth justice overtake us: we wait for light, but behold obscurity; for brightness, but we walk in darkness."

[222] Isa. 28:17: "Judgment also will I lay to the line, and righteousness to the plummet: and the hail shall sweep away the refuge of lies, and the waters shall overflow the hiding place."

[223] Ps. 1:4: "The ungodly are not so: but are like the chaff which the wind driveth away."

[224] Isa. 5:24: "Therefore as the fire devoureth the stubble, and the flame consumeth the chaff, *so* their root shall be as rottenness, and their blossom shall go up as dust: because they have cast away the law of the LORD of hosts, and despised the word of the Holy One of Israel."

of the iniquity and unrighteousness that covered the earth as the waters cover the sea,[225] they knew that the time of the kindling of Almighty God's wrath[226] had come. Their preaching cut to the heart of matters, not arguing about outward organization, church government, or mere articles of faith. They spoke of the inward principle of righteousness that restores the soul to heaven's order and of that faith that overcomes the world.[227] In the name of God[228] and by the arm of the Lord,[229] they went into the towns, cities, and countries, proclaiming that the day of God's controversy with humanity[230] had arrived. By the action of God's Holy Light, Power, or Spirit in their hearts and consciences, they condemned all the notions about Christ that mankind had invented. They called on the lofty cedars to bow and the sturdy oaks to bend before the Heavenly Appearance of the Lord.[231] All knowledge of God not obtained by an inward judgment – by God's Light within and by the experience of the operation of God's saving hand within – was declared accursed of God. The sea of wickedness within human hearts will be consumed by the refiner's fire,[232] and its fiery heat will

---

[225] Isa. 11:9: "They shall not hurt nor destroy in all my holy mountain: for the earth shall be full of the knowledge of the LORD, as the waters cover the sea."

[226] Deut. 11:16-17: "Take heed to yourselves, that your heart be not deceived, and ye turn aside, and serve other gods, and worship them; And *then* the LORD'S wrath be kindled against you."

[227] 1 John 5:4: "For whatsoever is born of God overcometh the world: and this is the victory that overcometh the world, *even* our faith."

[228] Isa. 50:10: "Who *is* among you that feareth the LORD, that obeyeth the voice of his servant, that walketh *in* darkness, and hath no light? let him trust in the name of the LORD, and stay upon his God."

[229] Isa. 53:1: "Who hath believed our report? and to whom is the arm of the LORD revealed?"

[230] Isa. 61:2: "To proclaim the acceptable year of the LORD, and the day of vengeance of our God; to comfort all that mourn."

[231] Isa. 2:12-13: "For the day of the LORD of hosts *shall be* upon every *one that is* proud and lofty, and upon every *one that is* lifted up; and he shall be brought low: And upon all the cedars of Lebanon, *that are* high and lifted up, and upon all the oaks of Bashan."

[232] Mal. 3:1-2: "Behold, I will send my messenger, and he shall prepare the way before me: and the Lord, whom ye seek, shall suddenly come to his temple, even the messenger of the covenant, whom ye delight in: behold, he shall come, saith the LORD of hosts. But who may abide the day of his coming? and who

cause the heavens of human knowledge to roll up as a scroll,[233] making way
for a new heaven and a new earth.[234] There, a real (not imputed), essential,
and eternal righteousness will dwell and will be known directly – formed by
the Word of God in the human heart.[235]

With the sound of their harsh and terrible trumpets, these people
alarmed the nation[236] that had taken so long a nap in pleasant, easy, and
fleshly religion and gave birth to extraordinary and unfamiliar fears among
the people.

Some were enraged and cried out, "What can we do to be saved?"
while hiding like wolves and foxes to stop the blessed work of the Lord by
cunning and cruelty. The Priests (who were as corrupt as any of them,
teaching for pay and divining for money, bargaining for so much per year to
'preach the gospel,' as they call it), were like foxes whose den has been
discovered and who no longer had a place to hide. They knew that no one
could remain at peace with God[237] who continued to sin.

They feared that this steadfast testimony would turn the people to the
Light in their consciences.[238] Then the people would come to see that all
knowledge about the things of God that has not been received through
holy submission to God's Heavenly Appearance within themselves was
going beyond the teachings of the True Teacher and sufferings of the Cross

---

shall stand when he appeareth? for he *is* like a refiner's fire, and like fullers'
soap."

[233] Isa. 34: 4: "And all the host of heaven shall be dissolved, and the heavens shall
be rolled together as a scroll: and all their host shall fall down, as the leaf falleth
off from the vine, and as a falling *fig* from the fig tree."

[234] Isa. 65:17: "For, behold, I create new heavens and a new earth: and the former
shall not be remembered, nor come into mind."

[235] Rom. 10:8: "But what saith it? The word is nigh thee, *even* in thy mouth, and in
thy heart: that is, the word of faith, which we preach."

[236] Joel 2:1: "Blow ye the trumpet in Zion, and sound an alarm in my holy
mountain: let all the inhabitants of the land tremble: for the day of the LORD
cometh, for *it is* nigh at hand."

[237] Rom. 5:1: "Therefore being justified by faith, we have peace with God through
our Lord Jesus Christ."

[238] Acts 26:18: "To open their eyes, *and* to turn *them* from darkness to light, and *from*
the power of Satan unto God, that they may receive forgiveness of sins, and
inheritance among them which are sanctified by faith that is in me."

of Christ – as the apostle said, whatever may be known of God is manifest within.[239] Like Saul,[240] they ran to the civil authorities, crying out great tirades of lies and slanders and trying to arouse a wolf-like nature in them. The priests called on the magistrates to put a stop to the progress of this blessed outpouring of the Eternal Light of Righteousness by the exercise of merciless power. A few of these could not be fooled, but most – seeing that their worldly honors and (even more importantly) their easy religion was under attack, root and branch – went to the assistance of the priests. With the force of arms, they furiously attacked the poor preachers. Some were imprisoned, others whipped, several bruised, not a few murdered, and many robbed.

Showing their true character, some priests could not even wait for the magistrates to give them a pretence of legality. They inflamed their congregations to assault both men and women, young and old alike.

The cries of the innocents were heard by the then supreme authority[241] but no relief could be obtained. One book after another came out, appealing to the authorities to use their power to wipe out what they called seducers. They commanded the common people to have no contact with them, but to avoid them like the plague – as if they were witches and sorcerers. It would take too long to tell even half of their schemes. Even their mercies were cruelties! Even so, we wrote many things that demonstrated our innocence. Some, who sought the redemption of Israel and the right way of God, believed. Here and there was a Simeon,[242] a Centurion,[243] a Priest,[244] a Lawyer,[245] a physician,[246] a tax collector,[247] and a

---

[239] Rom. 1:19: "Because that which may be known of God is manifest in them; for God hath shewed *it* unto them."

[240] This is a reference to Paul's activities as a persecutor of Christians before his conversion and name change.

[241] The 'then supreme authority' was Oliver Cromwell. At the time Penn was writing, the monarchy had been restored and a direct reference to Cromwell may have been politically unwise.

[242] Luke 2:25: "And, behold, there was a man in Jerusalem, whose name *was* Simeon; and the same man *was* just and devout, waiting for the consolation of Israel: and the Holy Ghost was upon him."

[243] Matt. 8:5-6: "And when Jesus was entered into Capernaum, there came unto him a centurion, beseeching him, And saying, Lord, my servant lieth at home sick of the palsy, grievously tormented."

[244] Perhaps a reference to Zacharias, the father of John the Baptist.

fisherman.[248] Above all, there was an abundance of laborers, for the poor eagerly accepted the gospel. But Alas! Neither the truth of our preaching, nor the enormity of our suffering, satisfied that growing spirit of cruelty. Nor did the dreadful conditions of our imprisonments change the minds of the priests or the rulers in the smallest way. There were occasional small acts of kindness, but these were soon overwhelmed by a new, more terrible storm of violence. There was no legal justification for this vicious treatment, so at the urging of the priests, the lawmakers created one. First, they enacted a law forbidding travel on the Sabbath Day, so that they could punish us as criminals for assembling to worship the living God. Next, they decreed that anyone who was found so many miles from home and not having a good explanation for it would be whipped as a vagabond. By these laws they brutally oppressed our Friends, including many of high standing, treating us worse than any vagabond. The first of these laws they justified as protecting God's Day of Rest; the second, as providing prudent care for the good of the Commonwealth.[249]

Nor was this all. Acting as if they wished to surpass the suffering of cruel popery and degenerate prelacy, they embraced the Oath of Queen Mary[250] – an oath enacted against Protestants who denounced the idolatry and superstitions of Roman Catholic worship – as a means of venting their

---

[245] Luke 10:27: "And he (the lawyer) answering said, Thou shalt love the Lord thy God with all thy heart, and with all thy soul, and with all thy strength, and with all thy mind; and thy neighbour as thyself."

[246] Col. 4:14: "Luke, the beloved physician, and Demas, greet you."

[247] Matt. 9:9: "And as Jesus passed forth from thence, he saw a man, named Matt., sitting at the receipt of custom: and he saith unto him, Follow me. And he arose, and followed him."

[248] Matt. 4:18-19: "And Jesus, walking by the sea of Galilee, saw two brethren, Simon called Peter, and Andrew his brother, casting a net into the sea: for they were fishers. And he saith unto them, Follow me, and I will make you fishers of men."

[249] The laws referred to are parts of the Clarendon Code – in particular to the Conventicle Act which outlawed Dissenter (and Quaker) worship services and to the Corporation Act which forbade those who did not take the sacraments at a parish church from holding public office.

[250] Queen Mary (1516-1558, ruled 1553-1558), known as Bloody Mary, tried to re-impose Roman Catholicism on England during her reign. Among other measures, she required all to take an oath of allegiance to the Roman church. A similar oath was required following the Restoration.

cruelty and revenge upon us. When we would bear our faithful testimony against their formal and hypocritical declarations, they would demand that we swear we were not Catholics. In this way, they sought to take advantage of our faithfulness in never swearing,[251] labeling us Papists and Jesuits. Their plain design was to make us odious in the sight of others and to hide their own cruelty. These pretended reformed Protestants have outdone themselves when they try to secure their religion by the enforcement of laws passed originally by brutal Papists to suppress the truly reformed Protestants of an earlier day. They practice themselves what they previously condemned in the Papists. Knowing that we do not swear at all, they treacherously seek to entrap us with a counterfeit and wickedly contrived oath, and then punish us for not swearing against the Papists. This is the cloak they use to conceal their malice, but it has grown short, ragged, and out of fashion. The bruises, bloodshed, awful beatings, and wearying imprisonments which we have endured are now seen as the detestable things they are by nearly all. Their descendents will hold their acts in utter abhorrence.

Oh! What a bloodthirsty spirit ruled that day! These great pretending Presbyterians, Independents, and Anabaptists! Fighting, punching, kicking, robbing, imprisoning, and murdering an innocent people, whose only goal was to tear down the false-fronted doctrines of the times and to turn people to a true Holy Principle within themselves. When people are obedient to that principle, they know that sin has been conquered and find peace with God – desiring this above all human traditions or the most sublime power of human ministry.

But, as many of us saw in the Eternal Light, this stubborn rejection of Heavenly Truth by both priests and rulers could lead only to their downfall (and though we often warned them of this in our writings and in person, they scorned our honest advice, turning it back on us, and saying it was we who would soon vanish). So within a few years, God brought about the wonderful revolution[252] and those who had been our chief persecutors – those who had wickedly stolen lands and power for themselves in the name of the country – now fell under the new rulers' greatest displeasure. Their

---

[251] James 5:12: "But above all things, my brethren, swear not, neither by heaven, neither by the earth, neither by any other oath: but let your yea be yea; and *your* nay, nay; lest ye fall into condemnation."

[252] The restoration of the monarchy in 1660.

acts can be called nothing other than usurpation – wickedly designed to fulfill their own desires, not those of the nation.

Behold the justice of the Almighty! Those who had refused us our liberty, after making loud and solemn oaths to God and man for the preservation of civil and religious liberties, lost their own. Those who had robbed us were robbed in turn by others. Those who had crushed us under their boot heels now found themselves our equals. At that time, we both worked to secure freedom for our consciences. Whether we won or not, some hoped that this change of affairs would work a change in their hearts and they would never again cut or wound a people who had in no way wronged them. Some hoped that they would take time to reflect on their past abuses of power and unjust cruelty toward us and others and that this would lead to sincere sorrow rather than continued hostility. But so far, these hopes have been in vain – their hatred has outlived their power to inflict it on us. It is true that in times of persecution they have asked about us out of their hiding places (finding that long practice in persecuting had not prepared them to receive it). From the top of the city walls, or other convenient vantage points, they have diligently observed the state of things. By observations and by inquiry they have carefully tracked our successes (since our disappearance would expose them directly) – as one of them remarked, we were the front line of defense and absorbed the brunt of the attack. Even so, their malice has been relentless. When King Charles first arrived, they thought they would help themselves by letting him know that they had not supported the Quakers and by broadcasting to the world that we were not part of them. This in fact helped us, distinguishing us from those noisy, disorderly, bloodthirsty, covenant-breaking, and government-destroying Anabaptists. No sooner were the storms of persecution past than, like forgetful sailors, they fell back to their old works of bitter envy. No matter what happens – whether it is that some have left their church or that the Quakers are successful in their labors – they can scarcely conceal their resentment of us and the blessed Truth.

When I have seen it, grief has truly overwhelmed my soul, and pity for their sakes has filled my heart. All these trials, which if they rightly understood them and took them to heart, would have been a source of great advantage to them, were instead lost like water spilled on the ground.

We have had many instances of this since they lost the throne of power; particularly in the years 1668 and 1669 when there was a temporary reprieve from violent persecution on account of conscience. What preaching was heard in nearly every one of their meetings against the dangerous errors of the Quakers (as they were pleased to call us)! And how they slandered us in print at every opportunity. We could scarcely walk the streets without hearing a sales pitch for the *Antidote Against Quakerism*, the *Synopsis of Quakerism*, or *The Damnable Heresy of the Quakers*[253] and other, equally poisonous expressions designed to increase their sales to the curious or the prejudiced.

While they lobbied for the king for freedom to worship for their own parties, and publicly commended him for his clemency, they diligently sought my imprisonment. They did not hesitate to describe me as both the most wretched and most monstrous of men on account of a book that they (in a sense) had extorted from me.[254] To show the extent of their wickedness, at that time, when my body was imprisoned and my life in mortal danger, they continued to maintain that my confinement was justified.

But let that pass and, instead, let us examine the consequences of succeeding troubles. The laws mentioned earlier were surpassed by the passage of one that was even more sharp and cruel.[255] We had hoped that this new act would cure these so-called believers forever of their long love of persecution. Their brave claims to legality quickly vanished in the face of a few threats. While God, by his Almighty and Invisible Power, held us up through all the hardships of bruises, bloodshed, broken limbs, disheartening imprisonments, and the seizure of our property (enough to melt the hearts of infidels), when persecution reappeared, they would come, Nicodemus-like,[256] to give us their night-encouragement. Some thanked God that we were there to absorb the force of persecution and serve as a buffer for them. Yet once again, when we were released from prison, their kindnesses cooled. Instead of congratulations, we were met with a fraud from Lincoln and a lie from Dover. The former was produced by R. James[257] and the

---

[253] These are titles of anti-Quaker tracts published in 1668-69.

[254] Penn wrote *A Sandy Foundation Shaken* when opponents refused to publicly debate him. Using the contents of that pamphlet as evidence, Penn's opponents had him imprisoned in 1669 for blasphemy in the Tower of London. At the time, blasphemy was a capital offense.

[255] The Conventicle Act was revised in 1670.

[256] Nicodemus was a 'ruler of the Jews' who came to talk with Jesus only under cover of darkness (John 3:1-21).

[257] According to Barbour, this is Ralph James, *A True and Impartial Narrative of the Eminent Mind of God* (1672).

latter by T. Hobbs,[258] both Anabaptists, as they are commonly called (to their own shame) and both works a disgrace to their claims of faith.

Following these first rotten fruits, Reader, the Dissenters in general pressed their attack, whether by preaching, public debate, writing, or other more secret communications, both in the cities and in the country, but especially in London. There, the enormity of our sufferings from the civil powers seems to have been outdone by the malicious practices of the Dissenters. They are so relentless in their assaults on us that they would rather cause troubles for themselves than to let us be in peace. They do not care who they abuse, if the end result is to make the Quakers seem more loathsome. Consider among others a libel, called *The Spirit of the Quakers Tried*, a letter signed by J. G. and *A Dialogue* by T. H. (two members of the same sect mentioned above).[259]

The authorities have since granted these people toleration. Behold the use, in their gratitude, that they make of it! Their policy has been to loose a torrent of virulent abuse against us. Daily, they pour out their ungodly hatred, as if by their persecution they could cancel the king's tolerance for us. They seem to need to take revenge on us for our liberty —as if this can be a time of peace only for themselves. But, what makes it worse, I have heard that some envious spirits among them wished for another storm of persecution to shipwreck the Quakers. What a bizarre situation! They envy our successes so much that they would risk their own continued existence. Perhaps they are content to return to their old habits, hiding their meetings like so many mice in garrets, cheese-lofts, coal bins, and similar places – in worship, they have become more elusive than a Catholic priest hiding his profession.

Truly, this is lamentable situation that they would separate religion from charity and faith from those good works of patience, mercy and universal love. They act as if quarrelling about religion was itself religious and as if name calling and jeering demonstrated passion and intelligence.

In summary and conclusion, this has been the burden of every reformation – that its founders have fallen away from their initial understanding (which was to practice religion with a clean conscience,

---

[258] According to Barbour, this is Richard Hobbs and Thomas Partridge, *A True and Impartial Relation* (1667).

[259] According to Barbour, J. G. may be John Garkin. T. H may be Thomas Hicks. The letter is not identified.

without pride, walking with God,[260] rather than talking about God) to self-promotion and persecution of all who dissent from their sect. Briefly, the cause of this deterioration is this: they wander away from the heavenly Light within themselves, inventing new forms of faith and practice even before they have succeeded in washing away the contrivances of those who came before them. They become so taken with their innovations that they desire to spread them widely. When others resist having new forms imposed on them, cruelty follows. Every nation has drunk from this cup – whether their faith is sophisticated or vulgar.

It is no wonder then that God first appeared to, empowered, and sent forth plain people to declare plain Truth – to turn all from the darkness that covered their hearts (despite their earnest professions of faith) to the Light that shined uncomprehended within,[261] which when obeyed was sufficient to salvation.[262] These plain people were first slandered and then persecuted – but persecution did not always come from the civil powers, often others took this on themselves. Even now, they are diligently pursued by their old adversaries, the Separatists, who cry out "Heresy! Error! Blasphemy!" – seeking to portray them as a burden on the earth. Note the many printed books, particularly, *The Spirit of the Quakers Tried, The Letter, The Dialogue betwixt a Christian and a Quaker, Quakerism no Christianity,* and *The Controversy Ended.* In answer to them all, from beginning to end, I dare present the world with our clear and full defense so far as concerns: **Christ, the true Light, enlightening all that ever came, and do or shall come into the world, with a saving Light, and what is the general rule of faith.**

Consider our case, presented below with any other objections I thought might carry any weight against us. I will lay out our fundamental principles. If these are proved they will knock the common notions (Satisfaction for sins past, present, and to come; Justification without Righteousness; the fearful doctrine of Predestination; and the Pleas against Perfection) tumbling to the ground.

---

[260] Mic. 6:8: "He hath shewed thee, O man, what *is* good; and what doth the LORD require of thee, but to do justly, and to love mercy, and to walk humbly with thy God?"

[261] John 1:5: "And the light shineth in darkness; and the darkness comprehended it not."

[262] Heb. 5:9: "And being made perfect, he became the author of eternal salvation unto all them that obey him."

I earnestly beseech you, Reader, in the love and awe of God, not to believe every wandering book or story that is out against us. Hear us before you pass judgment. Let your conscience tell you if we are not the true apostolic Christians, promoting the rights and privileges of the pure spiritual apostolic religion. What we believe and publicly declare is what we ourselves have witnessed – we do not steal nor rob our neighbors. God has shown this to us, beyond all imitation. This religion God has made our own through his operations within us. There is no standing against these convictions and without them, there can be no solid knowledge. It is the lack of this knowledge that makes the world miserable and renders us unknown.

This is the history from which this discourse grows. God, the Righteous Judge of all is my witness. This comes in perfect love to all and with ill will to no one, so that the absolute Truth of all things may be brought to light. It is written to provide a better understanding of the controversy now underway between the much-despised Quakers and their adversaries. Let everyone be clear, I am not writing to promote controversy, but simply for conscience sake. I do not seek empty victories, but hope that true conversion may result from my labors for the Lord my God who is over and above every name, worthy of eternal praises and dominion. I will close this preface with these earnest desires in uprightness of soul to God – that Truth, Righteousness, and Peace may prevail, that Error may be more plainly seen, and that all Envy and Prejudice may be utterly defeated.

Introduction

Part I

A book titled *A Dialogue Between a Christian and a Quaker* has recently come into my hands. This and several others recently published against us is the reason for this response.

I was very anxious to see in what way that book would try to distinguish between Quakers and Christians. In my own religious search, I have wanted nothing more than to understand and unite with that group of believers I had reason to believe was the most truly Christian.

Although I tried to be impartial, I found the book's arguments to be weak, and that it was more favorable to the idea that Quakers are Christians than the title would indicate. I was also surprised to find my name among several that were frequently cited – and each time, the author had undeservedly abused it. If there are errors in my thinking, they should not be attributed to the Quakers as a whole, but if I am not in error, then I feel able and obliged to answer on my own behalf. This will not be hard to do, given the scarcity of reason and the abundance of ranting in that book. The author seems more interested in scolding me than in proving me wrong or showing the world that he is better at abuse than argument.

This personal affront, I confess, was what first moved me to reply. Not that the Truth wasn't foremost in my mind, but because I knew that the person against which his attack was most directed was both willing and able to reply, I thought that I might be excused.

But when I considered how much burden fell on that person, I found myself drawn to take on this work – though my experience in debating some other adversaries had left me a bit battle-scarred and tired of contentiousness. I had hoped not to be drawn into further controversy.

But, just as the people of ancient Syracuse suffered through several very bad tyrants only to find each succeeded by one that was worse, so it has truly happed to us. We no sooner rout one adversary than another, twice as jealous, prejudiced, and spiteful, appears. They seem to debate only to score points, rather than to find the truth. Oh, the dreadful ways that these people take advantage of our love and efforts on their behalf! I have also heard that, failing to make a good case for themselves, they resolve instead simply to have the last word in any dispute, and these words are scurrilous lies and deceitful abuse. They believe that among the common people, this approach can have great advantage and tip the scales in their favor.

Truly, judging by the character of the author – using his book as our guide – I would be amazed that any honest, upright Christian could avoid thinking very poorly of him. Even the slightest, most impartial glance at his book demonstrates that he writes about religion without any sense of either religion or good manners.

But let us not dwell on that – let his book speak for (or against) itself. I shall only comment that although I have noted above his manner of writing, and my response is in reply to that book and several other recent publications that have attacked the Truth, this work is not the product of personal offence nor is it directed at anyone directly, immediately, or personally. The content of this discourse, both with respect to the Light and to our Beliefs, I have stated affirmatively and defended by plain Scripture, sound reason, and the universal wisdom of former ages. Whenever I quote – either directly from our adversaries' books (especially from T. Hicks'), arguments, or objections or from my own memory of them – I will try to be faithful to the original source and not put words that they never thought in my antagonists' mouths. It is not my desire to set up a straw man of my own design, knock it down, and then claim brag of a great victory (as T. Hicks has done). In short, exactly what I have against this book in general – and for the Truth and for myself in particular – I will cite below in the text. I will try to be brief in my responses.

First, he has taken a very unfair way in opposing our principles, if we can still call them ours. Instead of collecting what we have actually written, and choosing from among those writings the strongest arguments in our defense (which honesty and justice demand), he fabricates a dialogue between a Christian and a Quaker, both speaking words of his own invention. His characterization of a Quaker is dishonest and his 'Christian' hardly better. He puts his own beliefs in the mouth of the Christian rather than the beliefs of a true Christian in his own, and the poor, despised Quaker is contrived to say whatever would be most ridiculous, weak, or most irrelevant to the discussion. This form of argument is disgraceful and unchristian: by it, the wisest person can be painted a fool and Truth itself overcome by the weakest possible foe. This technique was employed more ingeniously, though equally injuriously, to bring the greatest heathen of his time to utter disgrace in the eyes of those who had formerly (and properly) admired him. I speak of the caricatures of Socrates by Anytus and Aristophanes. Living a blameless life of unparalleled virtue, Socrates led the Greeks by his strict teachings and example to reject those comedians and their immoral followers. They found it impossible to oppose him until a frivolous spirit was revived in the people by their ludicrous parodies of Socrates in a play.

I think that this man's writing aspires to the same result, although its lack of refinement and wit shows to be of a much different class. Give me the worst possible position to defend, but the ability to write all of my opponent's answers, and I will not fear the outcome of any debate. But who would agree to debate me under those terms? Let me apply his own technique to T. Hicks' defense of adult baptism, and I can make him appear to be from the Church of England, pleading for the baptism of children. But would he allow others to do to him as he has done to others? If this is the essence of our adversary's strength – to color us as weak in order to appear to be strong – I think that we need to say no more, but leave it to every unprejudiced conscience to judge the true meaning. Certainly it is obvious that we have not been treated justly, nor have our principles been weighed fairly in the scales of righteousness; but such is the inevitable result of his manner of writing.

Part II

Next, in order to make us seem silly or irrelevant, he portrayed us as misrepresenting ourselves and our principles. This is so uncharitable, indeed so very wicked, that I think any serious and impartial Reader should be justly scandalized by the whole work. We are made not only to answer in his terms, but to lie in the course of our answer, and on top of that, to deny our principles and our conscience! In a single stroke, he exposes both his hatred for us and the lunacy of his cause.

Can anyone who knows us well believe that if we were asked, as his fictitious Christian does on page 66 of his *Dialogue*, "Do you believe the Scriptures to be true sayings of God?" we would answer, "So far as they agree with the Light in me." In a sense this is true, the true Light within is the same Light as that which shined in the hearts of the holy writers of the Scriptures, and therefore it must agree with itself in its various revelations in different ages. Consequently, the Light is a true judge of which sayings are of God and which are those of wicked people. Yet, by fraudulently twisting and placing those words in the mouth of his supposed Quaker, he has depicted us as saying what he cannot find any, much less all, Quakers to have said.

Again, in another place of his abusive catechism, he asks, "Then may I not conclude that the reason you so freely rant against and revile your opponents is simply to impress those you might convert?" The Quaker is made to answer, "There is some truth in what you say." Oh, what an impudent forgery! Could any true follower of Christ, especially an Anabaptist preacher – who might be considered a serious person – produce such a fabrication? I will leave it to the Readers to judge for themselves. I have to believe that many Anabaptists have too much sensitivity and conscience to support this fraud. In short, his technique is to draw on an uncharitable spirit in asking his questions and a lying spirit when answering. God is our witness in this matter.

But he proceeds:

Christian: "Will you attack whether or not your opponent gives you cause?"

Quaker: "Our goals are to make them the objects of ridicule and have our friends believe that they do nothing but contradict themselves."

Christian: "But doesn't this reveal you as dishonest and malicious?"

Quaker: "We don't care what you might think — as long as our friends don't agree."

Christian: "Doesn't William Penn, in his book against the author of *The Spirit of the Quakers Tried*, express great displeasure with the man for concealing his name and suggesting that if he knew it that they would probably do something to disgrace him?"

(I will not take up space with my own defense, but carefully read, courteous Reader, the answer that he would have the world believe to be ours.)

Quaker: "Whatever you or others may think of our writings, we will claim to have both answered and refuted every one of our adversaries' charges. Our friends will believe it, and that is enough for us."

Oh! Lies, madness, and folly! Certainly, Reader, by this time you must agree that I had more than enough reason to take exception to *A Dialogue*. I sincerely hope that even such a bitter adversary might, on serious reflection, re-consider and see us as the Christians we are. In the love, awe, and reverence of Almighty God, we appeal to the consciences of all those who might ever read us: In his dialogue and catechism, has this man treated us with meekness, righteousness, and truth? These are, or ought to be, the rule and guide for Christians in all their undertakings, but especially in the most important matters of religion. Indeed, we need no defense in this case beyond the obvious foolishness of his answers. The entire world will think that we had little need to seek the good will of our friends — which we had already — but will instead conclude that we care greatly what others say or believe about us. It seems that our opponent pays little attention to his own conscience or to the Light of Truth that should be its teacher — there is little evidence of it in his dialogue. But, no matter how much he attempts to elevate his own defective notions above the dictates of the heavenly Light in his conscience (as his unconscionable treatment of us demonstrates), it remains our desire to faithfully follow that Light ourselves and seek the successful workings of it in others. This — not clever writing that equates our own notions with Christian faith, much less lies and absurdities — is our only answer and the best answer to our adversaries.

Part III

Not only has he made us say whatever he pleased – absurdly and untruly – but he portrays us as irreverent, taunting, and frivolous. What is worse he misuses the simple and serious expressions that honest, religious people may have sometimes uttered. These are used as answers to his questions, but in such a way as to mislead the serious Reader. Perhaps we need to repeat what is said on page 2, "You speak eloquently, making many fine distinctions, and seem to enjoy much worldly knowledge, but I tell you, 'Dust is the serpent's food.'[263]"

Some examples:

To a question about the sufficiency of the Light, he has the Quaker reply, "What you have said makes it clear that you are a poor, dark creature – truly, this is revealed by the Light."

Another time, the Quaker says, "You are a wicked creature – the deepest darkness is reserved you. You are a serpent with the eternal curse of God on you."

"You reveal your darkness and that you are still stuck in human imaginings."

"You look for words, but you must be silent."

"We are its witnesses. Poor creature, you chase after the letter of the law, but what do you experience within yourself?"

"I command you to be silent. I bear witness against you."

"Yes, truly. Alas for you, these are your own dark imaginings. Now you seek meaning in them – we deny their meaning. You reveal a wicked spirit. We deny all social and churchly distinctions. You tempt others with your notions."

These, impartial Reader, and other similar answers, he presents as if they were our strongest answers to his questions – several of which we have been given, and may yet be given, better, rational, and satisfactory answers. However, if such answers have been given to unfortunate questions from empty-headed and deceitful persons, these are no more ridiculous than was

---

[263] Isa. 65:25: "The wolf and the lamb shall feed together, and the lion shall eat straw like the bullock: and dust *shall be* the serpent's meat. They shall not hurt nor destroy in all my holy mountain, saith the LORD."

Christ's immoveable silence when questioned by Herod. Nor has T. Hicks acted honorably if, as he seems to believe, he has attacked our weakest responses.

But it is least excusable for someone who calls himself an Anabaptist – a sect subject to nearly as much contempt as the Quakers – to take such pains, not only to make serious people look ridiculous (even though the attempt will backfire), but to attempt with common taunts and street-language to mock their serious words. This is worthy of a comedian entertaining the rabble, not of a Christian speaking to other religious people. Certainly, Reader, we would have to be heathens (as he would have others believe) and desperate for any religion before we would accept this from such a source. How can we trust someone who seems to have so forgotten how his own sect is treated that he inflicts the same scorn and mockery on others?

He would do well to remember the infamous plays of such so-called comic wits as Sylvester,[264] Shakespeare, or Jonson[265] in which the exactness and godly lives of the Puritans and other dissenters are abusively misrepresented for the entertainment of vain and irreligious persons. If we find this reprehensible in a secular playwright, how can we excuse it in a Christian or, should we say, one who calls himself a Christian? Certainly not, and it will weigh heavily against him on the Day of the Lord's Judgment if he does not sincerely and publicly repent – providing an example to all who would lead a religious life not to tolerate such ungodly attacks. I think it reveals his complete foolishness that, instead of out-growing childish things, he makes use of undignified mockery and ridicule – especially, when speaking about religion. Has he grown so rash that he dares to handle holy things without fear and to carelessly take advantage of tender consciences? Is the Quakers' dissention from other Christians so offensive that an Anabaptist must show his little wit by mocking it? Certainly, dear Reader, both his bitterness and apparent frivolousness give us a substantial advantage over a man with such unwarranted claims to religiousness. However, our victory will be won by patience, innocence and

---

[264] Possibly Joshua Sylvester (1563-1618), an English translator. He was best known for translating Guillaume du Bartas' (1544-90) biblical epic, *Divine Weekes and Workes*, from the French. Based on the Book of Genesis, it was popular in England in the first half of the seventeenth century.

[265] Probably Ben Jonson (1572-1637), an English playwright, poet and critic. He wrote a number of satiric plays and masques for the court of King James I.

truth. Not that I believe that he thinks I lack the words to reply (indeed, he more than once implies that my having words to answer him is, in some way, criminal), and anyone who has read his works can see that he has supplied me with more than enough targets. But I do not take delight in spending time on invectives; if I did, I might produce a tragic comedy featuring a ranting Anabaptist in return for the ridiculous dialogue he tried unfairly to fasten on an unsuspecting Quaker. But my God forbids that I should take religion lightly, or to rant and abuse others for their religious belief. Using ridicule to try and change a person's religion is disgraceful; nor could I respect any sect that people joined out of shame. Conviction by the Light within is the most serious ground on which to receive faith. To disparage or mislead others can harden their hearts, but never open them to the workings of the Spirit – and this is the case with T. Hicks. I want him to know that our much-criticized Light within – which he claims has so little effect on his life – directs us away from 'an eye for an eye,' teaching us forbearance and forgiveness. These, we fear, are strangers to him. How else are we to interpret his zealous efforts to pluck out the eyes of those who have never harmed either of his eyes by their words or their writings? We may well join in the complaint of God's prophet, "I have become a laughingstock! All day long, everyone mocks me."[266] But let these worldly Christian-mockers beware! Though we endure their cruel mockings in this life, their bonds in the next life will be correspondingly stronger. The Lord of Hosts has promised destruction to those who persist in mockery.[267]

Having stated as briefly as possible all of my just complaints against the manner in which the dialogue was presented and the spirit of the author in general, I shall proceed to reply to the various distinct doctrines in it with a defense of Truth, the universality and sufficiency (that is that is it sufficient in itself to save) of the Light within, and a demonstration of the general rule of faith.

---

[266] Jer. 20:7: "O LORD, thou hast deceived me, and I was deceived: thou art stronger than I, and hast prevailed: I am in derision daily, every one mocketh me."

[267] Isa. 28:22: "Now therefore be ye not mockers, lest your bands be made strong: for I have heard from the Lord GOD of hosts a consumption, even determined upon the whole earth."

Chapter I

Three questions are proposed that state the matter that will be addressed.

T he Light of Christ within is the great principle of God in humanity – the root and spring of divine life and knowledge in the soul. By it, salvation is achieved and it is uniquely acknowledged by the people called Quakers as the foundation of their faith and testimony to the world. I will use three questions – addressing the principle, its power, and its adherents – to structure my discussion of it. As they naturally arise, I will do my best to meet any objections that my opponents have or reasonably could make to my argument. I offer these for my Readers' serious consideration and ask that they exercise patience and impartiality while making up their minds. It has been written as much for the Readers' spiritual benefit as for our defense. By it, I hope to give the Reader a clearer view of the path that the blessed have always followed to glory.

1. What is the SALVATION to which the Light leads?

2. What is this LIGHT and how does this Light lead to it? And

3. Who is HE or are THEY that obey this Light and, by obeying, gain salvation?

First, what is salvation? To be saved from sin as well as from wrath – not from wrath without sin.

By SALVATION we understand, as the Scripture teaches, being saved from Sin in this life and the wages of Sin, which is the wrath to come. We are taught to completely renounce and reject the usual understanding of it, that is, merely to be saved from punishment in the hereafter. In that false security – that fruitless expectation of salvation, while not really and actually saved by the invisible power of Christ from the power of sin and captivity to earthly desires – thousands die. T. Hicks is one of those that not only is enslaved himself, but earnestly claims that a meaningless faith and religion – one unable to deliver either himself or others from the power of sin – is the most Christian. In short, what we call salvation is Christ's putting an end to Sin, destroying the works of the devil, ending disobedience, binding the strong man and removing his goods from the hearts and consciences of men and women, and bringing his everlasting righteousness into the soul.

This cleanses, washes, regenerates, renews, and refreshes the soul – in the words of the Scriptures, it saves God's people from their SINS.[268]

These are the Times of Refreshment and this is the Day of Restitution.[269] Christ is King, to reign; Prophet, to give vision; and High Priest, to anoint with the holy oil that leads his people into all Truth.[270] His lips alone preserve knowledge. This is the unchangeable gospel-rule to believers – those who are freed from the power, nature, and defilement of sin. They are the only ones that are or shall ever be saved from Eternal Wrath and Vengeance – the heavy wages of sin. All this is what we understand by the word 'salvation.' This is the heart of the great and glorious prophecies and works of Christ.

Chapter II

Second, what is meant by the Light? It is a principle that reveals the condition of a person and leads to blessedness.

What is this LIGHT that leads to salvation and how does it lead to Salvation?

The word 'Light' is not used in a metaphorical sense, such as when Christ said to his disciples, "You are the Light of the world."[271] Nor as Paul did when he wrote, "Now, you are Light in the Lord."[272] Nor do I mean mere human spirit or reason. It is Christ, that glorious Sun of

---

[268] Matt. 1:21: "And she shall bring forth a son, and thou shalt call his name JESUS: for he shall save his people from their sins."

[269] Acts 3:19&21: "Repent ye therefore, and be converted, that your sins may be blotted out, when the times of refreshing shall come from the presence of the Lord ... Whom the heaven must receive until the times of restitution of all things, which God hath spoken by the mouth of all his holy prophets since the world began."

[270] 1 John 2:20: "But ye have an unction from the Holy One, and ye know all things."

[271] Matt. 5:14: "Ye are the light of the world. A city that is set on an hill cannot be hid."

[272] Eph. 5:8: "For ye were sometimes darkness, but now *are ye* light in the Lord: walk as children of light."

Righteousness[273] and Heavenly Luminary of the spiritual or invisible world. It is analogous to the great sun in the physical or visible world. When that natural light rises, it illuminates all things that have to do with that world. In the same way, when this Divine Light arises, it illuminates that other life for all who will accept what it reveals. This is the Light that enlightens everyone coming into the world[274] and that leads those who obey it to eternal salvation.[275] As the Scripture says, "In the Word of God was Life and that Life that was the Light of all, etc."[276]

But, to make this obvious to everyone, I shall demonstrate the nature and power of this principle by showing the holy effects of this Light – how it leads to salvation. Just as the tree is known by its fruit,[277] so the true Savior is known by his salvation. If I can show that the Light, when all its revelations and requirements are obeyed, is sufficient to lead us to salvation, then this debate with T. Hicks will end and all must acknowledge the power of the Light within.

I will demonstrate the saving properties of the Light, starting with the first step toward salvation, namely, seeing in oneself the reasons for damnation. I will prove by the Scriptures – the great record of saving truth and the blessed testimony that Christ left for his flock – that the Light within is necessary for this step.

---

[273] Mal. 4:2: "But unto you that fear my name shall the Sun of righteousness arise with healing in his wings; and ye shall go forth, and grow up as calves of the stall."

[274] John 1:9: "*That* was the true Light, which lighteth every man that cometh into the world."

[275] Heb. 5:9: "And being made perfect, he became the author of eternal salvation unto all them that obey him."

[276] John 1:4: "In him was life; and the life was the light of men."

[277] Luke 6:44: "For every tree is known by his own fruit. For of thorns men do not gather figs, nor of a bramble bush gather they grapes."

Chapter III

The Light within reveals all sin.

When people are enlightened by the Light, it is the natural consequence that it will make sin visible. All who do evil hate the Light and will not come to the Light for fear that their deeds will be exposed.[278] This implies that if they brought their deeds to the Light, the Light would have separated them out and made the character of each one obvious. This shows the Light to be the ultimate test, rule, and judge of conversion and of putting that conversion into practice. The Apostle Paul expressly bears witness to this in his epistle to the Ephesians, "Everything shameful is exposed by the Light and becomes visible."[279] The all-encompassing nature of the Apostle's claim shows that nothing shameful – whether thought, word, or deed – can be hidden from examination by the Light. There is nothing that is not known by the Light and exposed by the Light. It should be obvious to all that, if our adversary believes that all have sinned,[280] and all know that they have committed sin, then the Light must have come into all, in order to reveal that sin, and to point us to conversion. Without the Light to make it visible, how could we know that we have sinned? It is the same as if the Apostle had said, "Sin damns everyone, but it could not damn anyone if it were not shameful." And, sin would not be shameful except that the Light has made it visible to them and condemned it.

When our adversaries claim that the Light is not sufficient to discern all sin, it flatly contradicts Scripture and quite plainly calls the Apostle a liar. Paul says, "Everything shameful is exposed by the Light and becomes visible."[281] But Thomas Hicks says, "Everything shameful is not exposed by the Light and does not become visible." Stop here a moment, Serious Reader, and after some reflection, tell me who treats the Apostle and the

---

[278] John 3:20: "For every one that doeth evil hateth the light, neither cometh to the light, lest his deeds should be reproved."

[279] Eph. 5:13: "But all things that are reproved are made manifest by the light: for whatsoever doth make manifest is light."

[280] Rom. 3:23: "For all have sinned, and come short of the glory of God."

[281] Eph. 5:13: "But all things that are reproved are made manifest by the light: for whatsoever doth make manifest is light."

Holy Scriptures of Truth in a most unworthy manner? Is it T. Hicks or the Quakers?

Apostasy or sinfulness is not an argument against the Light.

An objection is raised by T. Hicks and some others: If the Light is in everyone, why is it that everyone is not convinced of their disobedience and guilt? Why don't they know their duty to God as well as the heathens of old did and as many infidels do today? Did the Light in Saul condemn him for persecuting the Church?

I answer that this objection in no way invalidates or lessens the power of the Light, although it greatly increases the guilt of those who rebelled against the Light. There were heathens who, to the degree they had the Light, set up their own laws and did the things that were contained in the Law of the Old Testament.[282] For this they were esteemed above those Jews who did not keep the Law. The Apostle Paul himself speaks to this in the second chapter of the epistle to the Romans. Nor are other histories silent on this point. On the contrary, they loudly trumpet the godly accomplishments which several famous Gentiles achieved by this Light. Credible historians have recorded their belief in One Eternal Being, God's communication of Divine Light to humanity, the necessity of holy living, and the reality of immortality. The praise of these writers has been greatly added to by those of later times – including by Christians. Some of these heathens are Pythagorus, Timaeus, Solon, Bias, Chilon, Anaxagorus, Socrates, Plato, Antisthenes, Xenocrates, Zeno, Antipater, Seneca, Epictetus, Plutarch, and Marcus Aurelius Antonius.

But what if Jews and Gentiles at some times did apostatize? In particular, Saul persecuted the Church of God, believing disobedience to be his duty and murder his service! Does this prove that the Light was insufficient? By no means! Rather, it shows that Saul, like many who went before him, was rebellious, stiff-necked, and resisted the Holy Spirit. These are the words of Scripture: he kicked against the goads.[283] From this it is plain that there were goads; and where were these guides to right action if not in his conscience? And were they anything other than the revelations of

---

282 Rom. 2:14: "For when the Gentiles, which have not the law, do by nature the things contained in the law, these, having not the law, are a law unto themselves."

283 Acts 9:5: "And he said, Who art thou, Lord? And the Lord said, I am Jesus whom thou persecutest: *it is* hard for thee to kick against the pricks."

the Light of Christ within him – the Light that makes evil visible and condemns the deeds it leads to? This Light was the Son of God that, as Paul wrote to the Galatians, "It pleased God to reveal in me,"[284] though Paul did not know him or his voice – his eyes had been blinded and his ears deafened by the god of this world, who had crept into the outward forms of religion then, as now. That false God had many cunning agents who denounced that pure, heavenly, and invisible life of truth and righteousness, which then, as now, lived in the hearts of many and who turned people to the idolatries of the Gentiles and to the outward practices and services of both Jews and worldly Christians.

On God's behalf, I affirm that it is most preposterously absurd for anyone to claim that human rebelliousness is due to an insufficiency of the Light. If people are wicked, isn't it despite their knowledge of the good? And, if so, where does the responsibility lie? Any claim that people are wicked despite their desire to be good – that they do not know any better – is a serious and malignant charge, indeed a blasphemous one, against a good and righteous God of heaven and earth. It supposes that God did not give humanity, either inwardly or outwardly, the ability to do what was required of them and, as a consequence of that failure, they are sentenced to eternal misery. I do not know how convincing this argument is to an impartial Reader, but I confess that I almost despair of ever understanding some of our adversaries. Their souls are confined within the narrow bounds of a most detestable and unmerciful kind of predestination. Like some of the ancients, they fear that they cannot be like God, so they will make a God who will be like them – a God as unfair as they themselves are.

How are we to understand this attack on the adequacy of the Light within? They seem to say, in short, that the gift of God is not perfect, or capable of salvation, because it does not compel obedience from all – the talent that God has given us is insufficient, because some hide it in a napkin.[285]

---

[284] Gal. 1:15-16: "But when it pleased God, who separated me from my mother's womb, and called *me* by his grace, To reveal his Son in me, that I might preach him among the heathen; immediately I conferred not with flesh and blood."

[285] This is an allusion to Luke 19:20 ("And another came, saying, Lord, behold, *here is* thy pound, which I have kept laid up in a napkin"). In this parable, three servants are given money while their master is away. Two invest the money and are rewarded. The third hides it away, returning it without interest when the master returns. For this, he is punished.

What do they think of this argument: When I sow seed on good ground, it grows, but then I sow it on barren ground, it does not. Shall I blame the seed or the ground?

The rituals of the Jews reveal no imperfection in the Light, but rather in the people.

Is there anyone who does not know how tradition and habit have replaced conviction and blinded the world? And that it is through worldly desires and pleasures that people become deadened to the invisible things of God? Today's so-called believers delight in external appearances and religious revelations. Alas! There would never have been so much need for these, if humanity not turned from the inward Light and Life of Righteousness. Mankind has become so scattered that it seemed good to God to grant us some external wonder in order to turn us back home again – to our first love, to that Light of Life, which was given by God as the way and guide to salvation.

But those things could not cleanse the conscience.[286] Therefore God, through his servants and prophets, continued to admonish and warn the people of old to end their evil ways, to give up evil and learn to do good, and to wash and cleanse themselves,[287] and that all their careful outward observances were no more pleasing than cutting a dog's throat.[288] In the Scriptures, the abolition of all outward religious forms and practices and the return of humanity to its original state of inward Light and Righteousness are called the times of refreshment and restoration of all things.[289]

---

[286] Heb. 9:9: "Which *was* a figure for the time then present, in which were offered both gifts and sacrifices, that could not make him that did the service perfect, as pertaining to the conscience."

[287] Isa. 1:16-17: "Wash you, make you clean; put away the evil of your doings from before mine eyes; cease to do evil; Learn to do well; seek judgment, relieve the oppressed, judge the fatherless, plead for the widow."

[288] Isa. 66:3: "He that killeth an ox *is as if* he slew a man; he that sacrificeth a lamb, *as if* he cut off a dog's neck; he that offereth an oblation, *as if he offered* swine's blood; he that burneth incense, *as if* he blessed an idol. Yea, they have chosen their own ways, and their soul delighteth in their abominations."

[289] Acts 3:19&21: "Repent ye therefore, and be converted, that your sins may be blotted out, when the times of refreshing shall come from the presence of the Lord ... Whom the heaven must receive until the times of restitution of all

In short, although by God's decree there have been many external observations and ordinances in the world, they were the images and shadows of the good things to come. These were granted either to prevent the Jews from adopting the Gentile's splendid outward forms of worship in order to maintain a special sovereignty over them, or to point them toward the more hidden and invisible glory. This remains true forever, that the Light was there and that the ancients saw their sins by it; that they could not be acceptable to God unless they walked in that Light[290] and were taught by it to put aside their evil ways. According to one notable passage, "The path of the righteous is like the light of dawn, which shines brighter and brighter until the full light of day."[291] Could this 'day' have been anything other than the day of salvation? Can there be any imperfection or darkness in this day? Surely not! What if their Light was dimmer? Could it still bring salvation? Surely, yes! But, just as when much is given, much is expected in return,[292] when little is given, little is required. If the Light was not so gloriously manifested before our Lord Jesus Christ came in the flesh, then less would be required at that time. Nevertheless, it does not follow that there were two Lights, or that the Light was not capable of saving those who lived in Holy Obedience to it before the visible appearance of Christ.

If the Light is insufficient because some people are wicked, the same could be said of the Scriptures.

I think all would agree that blindness is not an argument against the existence of the sun. By the same token, this Light cannot be called insufficient just because the people of one nation or another remained blind to it – clinging to worthless customs and evil practices. If such a doctrine were accepted, what would become of our adversaries' opinion that the Light found in the Scriptures is sufficient in itself to provide people with

---

things, which God hath spoken by the mouth of all his holy prophets since the world began."

[290] Isa. 2:5: "O house of Jacob, come ye, and let us walk in the light of the LORD."

[291] Prov. 4:18: "But the path of the just *is* as the shining light, that shineth more and more unto the perfect day."

[292] Luke 12:48: "But he that knew not, and did commit things worthy of stripes, shall be beaten with few *stripes*. For unto whomsoever much is given, of him shall be much required: and to whom men have committed much, of him they will ask the more."

knowledge of God?[293] By this same logic, if those who have the Scriptures fail to know, believe, and obey God as they ought to do, then the fault would lie with the Scriptures, not with them. Certainly this argument can be applied equally well to the Scriptures as to the Light within. Let Thomas Hicks and those who agree with him be careful not to hold too strongly to a position that would overturn the authority of the Scriptures as easily as that of the Light within.

Chapter IV

Another objection against the Light's ability to reveal what ought to be done – even if it can reveal what should be avoided.

There is a second objection: There is, they claim, an obvious insufficiency in the Light in that while it can reveal many things, it does not and cannot reveal other necessary things. Although it may show an individual all that is shameful, it cannot disclose everything which is essential for that person either to believe or to do.

The Light does not tell us all it knows, or that we might come to know in the future. This does not prove that the Light does not know all things.

I answer that this is merely an elaboration on the objection already considered. The problem is that people do not do what they should. The suggested conclusion is that they don't know all that they might need to know in order to be saved and therefore the Light is insufficient to guide them to salvation. The first part of this has been answered by what I have already said above. There is little difference between the objection that people do not do what they should and the objection that people do what they should not. The answer to one is the same as the answer to the other.

As for the charge that people do not know all they need to know, I deny it completely. Remember a thing is necessary only at its proper time. What is needed tomorrow may not be needed today. It is appropriate for children to learn to read, but it is necessary that they first learn to spell. Would it be just for a schoolmaster to be charged with incompetence if he did not tell little children everything he knows when they first came to him?

---

[293] 2 Tim. 3:15: "And that from a child thou hast known the holy Scriptures, which are able to make thee wise unto salvation through faith which is in Christ Jesus."

Should the first lesson contain everything? Students who are willing to learn and who listen to and follow the directions of a capable teacher will grow in knowledge. If they do not attend to the master, their failure to learn should be laid at their feet, not the teacher's. The teacher who presents material that is beyond the students' present abilities will overwhelm and discourage them. Likewise, if a tutor does not tell a pupil all he or she needs to learn in the first lesson, it does not imply a defect in the tutor or that the tutor is ignorant.

Consider this from the gospel of John: "If you do my will, you will learn more of my doctrine.[294] I have much more to say to you, more than you can now bear."[295] In short, to charge the Light of the Gospel[296] (a description of Paul's epistle with which T. Hicks would agree) with insufficiency, because it failed to reveal every ineffable thing Paul knew to every believer, would be false and antichristian. In his zeal to attack, Thomas Hicks has driven himself to this extreme. He charges the blessed Light of the Son of God, who enlightens everyone, with insufficiency because it fails to reveal to every individual, in every age, everything that he or she will ever know himself as well as everything that will be revealed to others in the future.

People know more than their acts reveal. Let them first obey what they already know – then more will be revealed to them.

The Light is not insufficient even though it does not tell all at one time that will be known by the end of the world. It shows me (as it does everyone) my daily duty. The Light is sufficient if, at each point in time, it shows us more than we then do and which we ought to do. Will T. Hicks say, and can he prove, that he has come to the final conclusion of the Light's teachings? Has he learned everything that it is possible for the Light of Christ to teach him, and yet found that there is still something more needed? If he has, he will have shown himself to be superior to all other

---

[294] This seems to be an amalgam of John 7:17 ("If any man will do his will, he shall know of the doctrine, whether it be of God, or *whether* I speak of myself") and John 15:14 ("Ye are my friends, if ye do whatsoever I command you").

[295] John 16:12: "I have yet many things to say unto you, but ye cannot bear them now."

[296] 2 Cor. 4:4: "In whom the god of this world hath blinded the minds of them which believe not, lest the light of the glorious gospel of Christ, who is the image of God, should shine unto them."

people and to God as well, who is the Fountain of all Light,[297] who searches the hearts, and examines the minds[298] of all humanity by the illumination of the revealing Light. This Light, when it is obeyed, leads to God who is the fullness of all Light and Life. To all who rebel against it, this Light carries the stench of death (the wages of sin).[299] But, to those who are obedient to it, it brings the sweet smell of life. These people will not walk in darkness, but will have the Light of Life.[300] Thomas Hicks argues against the possibility of being in a sinless state – and shows his sinful state by his writings. Let him cover his face in shame for his attempts to deny the Light's sufficiency. In his current state, he will never know the Life and Power of the Light.

To conclude, if all things shameful are made visible by the Light, then logically, it should also be capable of revealing all things that are worthy of approval with respect to our faith, salvation, and duty. If the Light tells us that it is evil not to believe in God, then it follows that to believe in God is consistent with the Light. If it reprimands T. Hicks for being rash and hot-tempered, it also teaches him that he ought to be patient. If the Light condemns theft, it necessarily commends honesty. If it scolds me for following my own will, it implies that I ought to do God's will. And, if it condemns sin, then it points toward holiness, without which no one will see God. In short, if it reveals some things as shameful, at the same time that it condemns them, it teaches those things that are contrary to them. The fruitless works of darkness[301] are judged by the Light so that the Holy Fruits of the Light may appear. "You were darkness, but now you are Light in the Lord."[302] "Discipline and instruction are the way to life."[303] Whoever comes

---

[297] Ps. 36:9: "For with thee *is* the fountain of life: in thy light shall we see light."

[298] Penn is drawing on an expression used in various Scripture texts, e.g., Ps. 26:2 ("Examine me, O LORD, and prove me; try my reins and my heart.").

[299] Rom. 6:23: "For the wages of sin *is* death; but the gift of God *is* eternal life through Jesus Christ our Lord."

[300] John 8:12: "Then spake Jesus again unto them, saying, I am the light of the world: he that followeth me shall not walk in darkness, but shall have the Light of Life."

[301] Eph. 5:11: "And have no fellowship with the unfruitful works of darkness, but rather reprove *them*."

[302] Penn has noted Eph. 5:8 ["For ye were sometimes darkness, but now *are ye* light in the Lord: walk as children of light"] in the margin.

out of the rejected darkness, walks in the accepted Light. To those who accept the Holy Rebuke, the Instruction of the Way of Life is revealed.

This brings me to the third property of the Light: It does not merely reveal and condemn sin, or disclose purity and point us toward it, but, if it is followed (or rather that principle that is the Light is followed), it has both the power and the ability to redeem us from sin and to lead us to the highest state of bliss. "I am the Light of the world (said Jesus himself), whoever follows me will never walk in darkness, but will have the Light of Life."[304] In this, it is obvious that the same Light that reveals the darkness will redeem us from it, and lead us into a state of Light and Life. That is to say, those who confidently believe in Christ, the Light in their consciences that condemns sin, have been illuminated. Those who obediently follow its Holy Requirements and yield to the Heavenly Message of that Blessed Appearance – giving up the temporary pleasures of sin, desire, and their own wills and taking up the daily cross[305] – shall find that Divine Principle. This principle illuminates our dark state, convincing us of our need to repent – it is rightly called Light. It is the true revelation with the power and the ability to save us from that which condemns and to bring us to the Glory we hope for. This Word of God, the true Light that enlightens all, is the Life, Power, Wisdom, and Righteousness of the Father – in whom is hidden all the Treasures of Wisdom.[306] All power both in heaven and on earth is his;[307] he is the heir of all things.[308] He also said, "While you have Light (because their day of visitation was almost over), believe in the Light that you may be children of it." (Or, as it would be better translated, "While you have a little Light in you, believe and walk in it.") Again, he says, "I

---

[303] Penn has noted Prov. 6:23 ["For the commandment *is* a lamp; and the law *is* light; and reproofs of instruction *are* the way of life"] in the margin.

[304] Penn has noted John 8:12 ["Then spake Jesus again unto them, saying, I am the light of the world: he that followeth me shall not walk in darkness, but shall have the Light of Life"] in the margin.

[305] Luke 9:23: "And he said to *them* all, If any *man* will come after me, let him deny himself, and take up his cross daily, and follow me."

[306] Col. 2:3: "In whom are hid all the treasures of wisdom and knowledge."

[307] Matt. 28:18: "And Jesus came and spake unto them, saying, All power is given unto me in heaven and in earth."

[308] Heb. 1:2: "Hath in these last days spoken unto us by *his* Son, whom he hath appointed heir of all things, by whom also he made the worlds."

have come as a Light to the world, so that no one who believes in me will remain in darkness."[309]

A sincere faith in and obedience to the Light of Christ – shining in the heart to give living and direct knowledge of the glory of God – is the way to be redeemed from darkness and be made a child of the Light. There is sufficient ability and power in the Light to re-claim the souls of those who faithfully follow it from the power of darkness. Just as the true knowledge of God is life eternal, whatever may be known of God is revealed within.[310] This revelation cannot be truly understood without the Light whose distinctive property is to bring enlightenment – revealing the mind and will of God to humanity. As the apostles said, "Whatever makes things visible is Light" and "In him was Life, and that Life was the Light of all."[311] It is not, however, the life of all people when considered spiritually and taken as a whole, but rather the unique privilege of those who believe and walk in it.

There is a difference between Light and Life – not in the principle itself, but in the way it is experienced. Those who truly believe in and obey really do enjoy a new nature, a new spirit, and a new life. But what is 'it?' The Word-God is that true Light that illuminates, or reveals, the secrets of the heart and conscience. In this sense, it may be said that just as Christ, in his life, was Light to humanity; so the Light, by his obedience, gave new Life to humanity. Jesus said, "Whoever follows me will never walk in darkness, but will have the Light of Life."[312] Life and Light do not differ in nature, but in the ways they work on humanity. Those who doubt this, do so at their peril. As the Light is received and believed, it creates life, motion, heat, and the divine qualities of the new birth. In this way, the Life of the

---

[309] Penn has noted John 12:36&46 ["While ye have light, believe in the light, that ye may be the children of light. These things spake Jesus, and departed, and did hide himself from them ... I am come a light into the world, that whosoever believeth on me should not abide in darkness"] in the margin.

[310] Penn has noted Rom. 1:19 ["Because that which may be known of God is manifest in them; for God hath shewed *it* unto them"] in the margin.

[311] Penn has noted the following in the margin:

Eph. 5:13. ["But all things that are reproved are made manifest by the light: for whatsoever doth make manifest is light."]

John 1:4. ["In him was life; and the life was the light of men."]

[312] Penn has noted John 8:12 ["Then spake Jesus again unto them, saying, I am the light of the world: he that followeth me shall not walk in darkness, but shall have the Light of Life"] in the margin.

Word – and the Light of the Word – generates a new life in the soul, so that it is not the old person who lives, but Christ – the Word-God, who is put on[313] and who becomes each person's Life and Light – who dwells within.[314]

Do not depend on what you dimly understand, from scant knowledge of the letter of the Scriptures. Do not trust arguments against that which you have not tried and have not obeyed, and therefore whose power and abilities you do not know. This principle brings salvation to all who turn to it and live in it.

The Scriptures are explicit in their defense of the sufficiency and necessity of the Light for salvation. Indeed, it seems to have been at the heart of Jesus' instructions to his disciples to preach the everlasting gospel: "Open the eyes of the people and turn them from darkness to Light, and from the power of Satan to God, so that they may receive forgiveness of sins and a place among those who are sanctified by faith in me."[315] Who does he mean by 'me?' It is the one who is the Light of the world and the power of God for salvation. Certainly the eyes that needed to be opened were not natural eyes, but spiritual eyes (and the Light and darkness are likewise spiritual Light and darkness) that had been blinded by the god of this world[316] who rules in the hearts of the children of disobedience.[317] It is no wonder that the Light was not understood by the darkness[318] and that

---

[313] Gal. 3:27: "For as many of you as have been baptized into Christ have put on Christ."

[314] Gal. 2:20: "I am crucified with Christ: nevertheless I live; yet not I, but Christ liveth in me: and the life which I now live in the flesh I live by the faith of the Son of God, who loved me, and gave himself for me."

[315] Acts 26:18: "To open their eyes, and to turn them from darkness to light, and from the power of Satan unto God, that they may receive forgiveness of sins, and inheritance among them which are sanctified by faith that is in me."

[316] 2 Cor. 4:3-4: "But if our gospel be hid, it is hid to them that are lost: In whom the god of this world hath blinded the minds of them which believe not, lest the light of the glorious gospel of Christ, who is the image of God, should shine unto them."

[317] Eph. 2:2: "Wherein in time past ye walked according to the course of this world, according to the prince of the power of the air, the spirit that now worketh in the children of disobedience."

[318] Penn has noted John 1:5 ["And the light shineth in darkness; and the darkness comprehended it not"] in the margin.

the blind could not see the Light; but this plainly shows that there was Light, even though it was not seen. The powerful ministry of the apostles was to open these blind or dark eyes into people's minds — which the god of this world had blinded[319] — and then to turn them from the darkness to the Light. The place where darkness abounded and that needed to be illuminated was within them, and so therefore was the Light. Consequently, the way to be carried from Satan's domain to God's — to gain forgiveness of sins and a place with those who are sanctified — is to be turned from the darkness in the heart to the marvelous Light that has long shined there without being understood. It is for this reason that the gospel is called both the Light[320] and the power of God.[321]

The same apostle, in his epistle to the Romans, is more explicit concerning the holy nature and effectiveness of the Light in bringing salvation. He urges them, "The night is far gone, the day is near, so let us then put aside the works of darkness and put on the armor of Light. Let us behave decently, as in the daytime, not in reveling and drunkenness, not in debauchery and licentiousness, not in quarreling and jealousy. Instead, put on the Lord Jesus Christ, and make no provision to gratify the desires of the flesh."[322] Based on this, I will make three points, which support not only our purposes in this matter, but defend Truth itself.

---

[319] John 12:40: "He hath blinded their eyes, and hardened their heart; that they should not see with *their* eyes, nor understand with *their* heart, and be converted, and I should heal them."

[320] 2 Corinthians 4:3-4, 6: "But if our gospel be hid, it is hid to them that are lost: In whom the god of this world hath blinded the minds of them which believe not, lest the light of the glorious gospel of Christ, who is the image of God, should shine unto them. ... For God, who commanded the light to shine out of darkness, hath shined in our hearts, to *give* the light of the knowledge of the glory of God in the face of Jesus Christ."

[321] Rom. 1:16: "For I am not ashamed of the gospel of Christ: for it is the power of God unto salvation to every one that believeth; to the Jew first, and also to the Greek."

[322] Rom. 13:12-14: "The night is far spent, the day is at hand: let us therefore cast off the works of darkness, and let us put on the armour of light. Let us walk honestly, as in the day; not in rioting and drunkenness, not in chambering and wantonness, not in strife and envying. But put ye on the Lord Jesus Christ, and make not provision for the flesh, to *fulfil* the lusts *thereof*."

1. There is an absolute opposition between Light and darkness. Darkness can only hide the Light from our understanding, while Light can reveal and melt away that darkness. Or, more succinctly, the Light exposes and condemns the works of darkness, for "what fellowship is there between Light and darkness?"[323] The difference between them is evidence of the capabilities of the Light.

2. In this Light, there is armor; and when that armor is put on, it provides a defense against darkness and can conquer darkness, making the soul safe from the evil of darkness. Otherwise, it would be very strange for the apostle to urge people to put it on.

3. Putting on the armor of the Light, or putting on the Lord Jesus Christ (the Light of the world), are synonymous, or one and the same thing, and achieve one and the same purpose (again in the apostle's words): to behave decently, not to engage in reveling and drunkenness, debauchery and licentiousness, or quarreling and jealousy. Put on the Lord Jesus Christ and make no provision to gratify the desires of the flesh.

I hope then that it will be admitted that Christ is that Light with which all are enlightened (more will be said about this later) and that the Light we urge all to obey is complete and sufficient – searching, expelling, and powerful, arming us against darkness and all its unfruitful works – and therefore saving.

The beloved disciple emphatically testifies to this in his first epistle, where he describes the apostolic mission: "This is the message we have heard from him and proclaim to you, that God is Light and in him there is no darkness at all. If we say that we have fellowship with God while we are walking in darkness, we lie and do not do what is true; but if we walk in the Light as he himself is in the Light, we have fellowship with one another, and the blood of Jesus his Son cleanses us from all sin."[324]

---

[323] Penn has noted 2 Cor. 6:14 ['Be ye not unequally yoked together with unbelievers: for what fellowship hath righteousness with unrighteousness? and what communion hath light with darkness?'] in the margin.

[324] 1 John 1:5-7: "This then is the message which we have heard of him, and declare unto you, that God is light, and in him is no darkness at all. If we say that we have fellowship with him, and walk in darkness, we lie, and do not the truth: But if we walk in the light, as he is in the light, we have fellowship one with another, and the blood of Jesus Christ his Son cleanseth us from all sin."

This is a summary, stating the whole great case for salvation:

1. What is God? Light.

2. Who can have no fellowship with God? Those who walk in darkness and sin.

3. Who has fellowship with God? Those who walk in the Light, because God is Light.

4. Why? Because those who walk in the Light feel the power of Christ's blood to cleanse them from all unrighteousness.

Notice that the Light, leading us out of darkness (i.e., out of unrighteousness), is the same as the blood of Jesus Christ cleansing us from all sin. Sin and darkness – to be cleansed from one or carried away from the other – are the same in the Scriptures. Otherwise, someone could be set free from the darkness and walk in the Light and not be cleansed from sin (which is that darkness). This is absurd and impossible. In short, they go together. Walking in the Light leads us directly to God and to fellowship with God – the saving Light and salvation for all nations. Consequently, the Light leads to salvation.

There is no essential difference between the Seed, the Light, the Word, the Spirit, the Life, the Truth, the Power, the Unction, the Bread, the Water, or the Flesh and Blood. These are merely different names for the various effects and different manifestations of the one Divine Principle.

Scripture often gives many names to one and the same thing. Christ is called the Word,[325] the Light, the Way, the Truth, the Life,[326] the Life-giving Spirit,[327] the Saving Power for all Nations,[328] the Savior,[329] Emmanuel, a Rock,[330] a Door,[331] a Vine,[332] a Shepherd,[333] etc. A state of sin is called darkness, death, disobedience, barrenness, rebellion, stiffneckedness, and eating sour grapes.[334] The wicked are called briars, thorns, thistles, weeds, dead trees, wolves, goats, etc. On the other hand, a state of conversion is sometimes described by such words as purged, refined, washed, cleansed, sanctified, justified, led by the Spirit, baptized by the Spirit into one body, circumcised without the use of human hands,[335] regenerated, redeemed,

---

[325] John 1:1: "In the beginning was the Word, and the Word was with God, and the Word was God."

[326] John 14:6: "Jesus saith unto him, I am the way, the truth, and the life: no man cometh unto the Father, but by me."

[327] 1 Cor. 15:45: "And so it is written, The first man Adam was made a living soul; the last Adam was made a quickening spirit."

[328] Ps. 67:2: "That thy way may be known upon earth, thy saving health among all nations."

[329] Luke 2:11: "For unto you is born this day in the city of David a Saviour, which is Christ the Lord."

[330] 1 Cor. 10:4: "And did all drink the same spiritual drink: for they drank of that spiritual Rock that followed them: and that Rock was Christ."

[331] John 10:7: "Then said Jesus unto them again, Verily, verily, I say unto you, I am the door of the sheep."

[332] John 15:1: "I am the true vine, and my Father is the husbandman."

[333] John 10:11: "I am the good shepherd: the good shepherd giveth his life for the sheep."

[334] Jer. 31:30: "But every one shall die for his own iniquity: every man that eateth the sour grape, his teeth shall be set on edge."

[335] Col. 2:11: "In whom also ye are circumcised with the circumcision made without hands, in putting off the body of the sins of the flesh by the circumcision of Christ."

saved, bought at a price,[336] etc. God's people are the children of God, children of the Light, children of the kingdom, heirs of glory, lambs, sheep, wheat, etc.

What brought them to that state is called Light, Spirit, Grace, Word, Fire, Sword, Hammer,[337] Power, Seed, Truth, Way, Life, Blood, Water, Bread, and Anointing to know all Truth.[338] Within each category, regardless of which phrase or name is used, all are one and the same. Sin, or a sinful state, is named differently to reflect the various works and revelations of its nature seen in the wicked. Similarly the varieties of virtues in good and holy people receive different titles, although all are the work of one divine principle that preserves and protects them. The primitive saints named the works of the one holy principle according to how they perceived it. To those in darkness, it was Light. To those who believed and obeyed, it was a leader. To those who had witnessed their sins conquered, their desires overcome, their hearts opened, and their souls washed, redeemed, and daily nourished by the Truth, it was a sword, a fire, a hammer, water, flesh, blood, bread, and the seed of life. In short, the same heavenly principle became Light, Wisdom, Power, counsel, redemption, sanctification, and eternal salvation to those who believed in it. The variety of expressions in Scripture must not be understood as listing distinct things – either in their nature or, sometimes, in their effects.

Indeed, despite the Light that some claim is found in the literal text of the Scriptures (exclusive of the Spirit), if all the wisest people in the world were to meet together, they would be unable to agree on one understanding of what the Scriptures say unless they experienced, and were faithful witnesses to, the work of the Holy Spirit within it. In a civil court, hearsay is inadmissible – only an eyewitness can testify. Just so, no one can give evidence about God or Christ who has not heard or seen or witnessed the Light, Spirit, Grace, and Word of God in their hearts. A person, who is not named in a will or a deed, has no claim to a property. I can confidently affirm that no one, who is not an heir of that blessed condition, can claim the glorious promises declared in the Scriptures. The time has come for

---

[336] 1 Cor. 6:20: "For ye are bought with a price: therefore glorify God in your body, and in your spirit, which are God's."

[337] Jer. 23:29: "Is not my word like as a fire? saith the LORD; and like a hammer that breaketh the rock in pieces?"

[338] 1 John 2:20: "But ye have an unction from the Holy One, and ye know all things."

people to look around and prepare themselves so that when they are suddenly awakened at midnight, they will still have oil for their lamps.[339] I must tell T. Hicks and his companions, in the words of the beloved disciple, "Anyone who claims to be in the Light but hates a brother or sister is still in darkness."[340] In my own words, those who show such jealous displeasure with a harmless, suffering people who have never offended or provoked them are in darkness. If they would only bring their thoughts, words, and deeds to this Light in their own consciences and let a true judgment be passed on them – if they would patiently accept heaven's reprimand for their disobedience to and vilification of that Light – then they could witness a turning from darkness to Light and begin to walk in it. In all generations, the Lord's ransomed have walked and will walk in that holy way, which leads to the enjoyment of eternal peace.

Such is the wondrousness of Christ, the true Light of the soul, the first and the last![341] When all outward ceremonies, writings, and worship – indeed the whole world – shall come to an end, the value and excellence of this Light will remain forever. As John the Divine says, "They will see his face, and his name will be on their foreheads. There will be no more night. They will not need light from a lamp or from the sun, for the Lord God will give them Light. And they will reign for ever and ever. Amen."[342]

---

[339] See the parable of the ten Bridesmaids, Matt. 25:1-13.

[340] 1 John 2:9: "He that saith he is in the light, and hateth his brother, is in darkness even until now."

[341] Rev. 1:8: "I am Alpha and Omega, the beginning and the ending, saith the Lord, which is, and which was, and which is to come, the Almighty."

[342] Rev. 22:4-5: "And they shall see his face; and his name shall be in their foreheads. And there shall be no night there; and they need no candle, neither light of the sun; for the Lord God giveth them light: and they shall reign for ever and ever."

Chapter V

Scripture proves that the Light saved from the time of Adam and Eve, through the holy patriarchs and prophets, and down to Christ's life.

I have now plainly shown from Scripture that the Light has brought salvation since the time of Christ. From its first appearance in humanity, it has revealed sin, condemned sin, and redeemed from sin all who obey it. The same principle that is called the Light is the Seed, Grace, Truth, Word, Spirit, Power, Anointing, Water, Way, Life, Flesh, and Blood. Therefore, T. Hicks and all who believe Scripture must acknowledge that it is not distinct from the one who saves. I call it the Light of Salvation or the Light that leads to salvation.[343]

---

[343] Penn has listed the following references in the margin:

Gal. 4:16. ["Am I therefore become your enemy, because I tell you the truth?"]

Titus 2 [probably verse 11: "For the grace of God that bringeth salvation hath appeared to all men."]

John 14:6. ["Jesus saith unto him, I am the way, the truth, and the life: no man cometh unto the Father, but by me."]

John 1:1-4, 9. ["In the beginning was the Word, and the Word was with God, and the Word was God. The same was in the beginning with God. All things were made by him; and without him was not any thing made that was made. In him was life; and the life was the light of men. ... *That* was the true Light, which lighteth every man that cometh into the world."]

1 Cor. 15:45&47. ["And so it is written, The first man Adam was made a living soul; the last Adam *was made* a quickening spirit. ... The first man *is* of the earth, earthy: the second man *is* the Lord from heaven."]

1 Cor. 1:24. ["But unto them which are called, both Jews and Greeks, Christ the power of God, and the wisdom of God."]

1 John 2:27. ["But the anointing which ye have received of him abideth in you, and ye need not that any man teach you: but as the same anointing teacheth you of all things, and is truth, and is no lie, and even as it hath taught you, ye shall abide in him."]

1 John 5:6-8. ["This is he that came by water and blood, *even* Jesus Christ; not by water only, but by water and blood. And it is the Spirit that beareth witness, because the Spirit is truth. For there are three that bear record in heaven, the Father, the Word, and the Holy Ghost: and these three are one.

There are still several objections to be answered. When that is done, we will immediately proceed to the question: Who, or what, is this Light?

An objection to the Light existing before Christ's coming into the world.

Some object: "Though you have proven from the Scriptures the universality of the saving Light since Christ's life, death, resurrection, and ascendance, you have not told us where this Light was before then. Did anyone have this saving Light before the birth of Jesus? Shouldn't there be if your doctrine of the Light is true?"

I will answer from Scripture, history, and reason.

     I.   The first Scripture I will quote is from Genesis: "God created people in his own image, in the image of God he created them."[344] From this, I conclude that if humanity was made in God's image, then because God is Light, Adam and Eve necessarily had a share of the Divine Light. As the image of God, they would have been in the image of this Light, so long as they walked in it, because no one walks in the Light without becoming a child of the Light. As the apostle Paul expresses it, writing about those who were turned from error to the Light, "Once you were darkness, but now you are Light in the Lord."[345] In other words, through obedience to the Light of the Lord Jesus, with which you were enlightened, you have become Light in the Lord and Lights to your generation. If anyone says that Adam and Eve did not have Light, then their original, innocent state is equated with darkness. Instead of God's image – who is, was, and always will be Light – they would have been completely ignorant of the one in whose image they were created.

And there are three that bear witness in earth, the Spirit, and the water, and the blood: and these three agree in one."]

    John 6:51-53. ["I am the living bread which came down from heaven: if any man eat of this bread, he shall live for ever: and the bread that I will give is my flesh, which I will give for the life of the world. The Jews therefore strove among themselves, saying, How can this man give us *his* flesh to eat? Then Jesus said unto them, Verily, verily, I say unto you, Except ye eat the flesh of the Son of man, and drink his blood, ye have no life in you."]

[344] Gen. 1:27: "So God created man in his *own* image, in the image of God created he him; male and female created he them."

[345] Eph. 5:8: "For ye were sometimes darkness, but now *are ye* light in the Lord: walk as children of light."

II.   Moses directed the children of Israel to the Light when he, on God's behalf, recommended and earnestly urged them to keep God's commandment and word in their hearts: "What I am commanding you today is not hidden or beyond your reach. It is not up in heaven, so that you have to ask, 'Who will go up to heaven to get it so that we may hear it and obey it?' No, the word is very near to you; it is in your mouth and in your heart so that you can do it.' See, today I set before you life and prosperity, death and destruction."[346] In this passage, we can see three things:

1. God's commandment and word are better than and greater than all written commandments and words.

2. This commandment and word is near – in each person's heart. No one can excuse disobedience by pleading ignorance or claiming unfamiliarity.

3. Setting life and prosperity, death and destruction before them was and could only be by and through the shinings of the Light within them. Otherwise, how could they have seen good and evil set before them? The Lord put these before them within their hearts. Note that this verse immediately follows the one in which Moses has proved that the Word is in their hearts. I hope that no one will complain (because I know who will confirm this) if I say that this commandment is the one which David spoke of when he said, "The commandment of the LORD is pure and enlightens the eyes."[347] Likewise, the holy Word is the same as that which David called a lamp to his feet and a light for his path,[348] which God hid in his heart,[349] and young people prepare

---

[346] Deut. 30:11-15: "For this commandment which I command thee this day, it *is* not hidden from thee, neither *is* it far off. It *is* not in heaven, that thou shouldest say, Who shall go up for us to heaven, and bring it unto us, that we may hear it, and do it? Neither *is* it beyond the sea, that thou shouldest say, Who shall go over the sea for us, and bring it unto us, that we may hear it, and do it? But the word *is* very nigh unto thee, in thy mouth, and in thy heart, that thou mayest do it. See, I have set before thee this day life and good, and death and evil."

[347] Ps. 19:8: "The statutes of the LORD *are* right, rejoicing the heart: the commandment of the LORD *is* pure, enlightening the eyes."

[348] Ps. 119:105: "Thy word is a lamp unto my feet, and a light unto my path."

[349] Ps. 119:11: "Thy word have I hid in mine heart, that I might not sin against thee."

God's way by living according to it.[350] It is the same Word that Paul called the Word of Faith.[351] Paul preached that the just live by it,[352] from this, we can be sure it was, and is, the Commandment, Word, and Light of salvation for those who believe and obey it.

III.   The next Scripture to consider is this: "You are my lamp, O Lord; you turn my darkness into Light."[353] Now if God was the Light and lamp at that time, certainly then they had a Light and one that led to salvation – unless we blasphemously deny God to be both Light or Savior. If it is claimed that David was merely speaking metaphorically, then I answer, Amen! His words were intended to demonstrate that they had something to show them the way in which God would have them walk – a revealing power that assisted them in walking righteously and safely to glory – and this is what we say, too.

IV.   Light condemned the wicked, just as it protected the good. "There are those who rebel against the Light, who do not know its ways or stay in its paths,"[354] said Job. Here, it is obvious that the wicked have Light, otherwise, it would have been completely impossible for them to rebel against it. It is also obvious that the Light they rebel against is the same Light that guides those who are righteous. This point is reinforced by another emphatic passage in the same book, "Can God's armies be counted? Is there anyone on whom his Light does not arise?"[355] Certainly, this universality strongly supports our belief in the Light.

If people would just allow it to come close to their consciences, I cannot help but believe that they would recognize its availability to all before the coming of Christ. I will not go into its effectiveness at that time

---

[350] Ps. 119:9: "Wherewithal shall a young man cleanse his way? by taking heed thereto according to thy word."

[351] Rom. 10:8: "But what saith it? The word is nigh thee, *even* in thy mouth, and in thy heart: that is, the word of faith, which we preach."

[352] Rom. 1:17: "For therein is the righteousness of God revealed from faith to faith: as it is written, The just shall live by faith."

[353] 2 Sam. 22:29: "For thou *art* my lamp, O LORD: and the LORD will lighten my darkness."

[354] Job 24:13: "They are of those that rebel against the light; they know not the ways thereof, nor abide in the paths thereof."

[355] Penn has noted Job 25:3 ["Is there any number of his armies? and upon whom doth not his light arise?"] in the margin.

(although one would think that Light always distinguishes a good way from a bad one) – more on that later. But, I will observe that Job, when he was deeply troubled in his spirit, cried out, "How I long for the way I was in months gone by, when God's lamp shone upon my head, and I walked through darkness by his Light!"[356] It is very apparent that Job attributes his salvation from the darkness (which stands for both sin and affliction) to the Light with which God had enlightened him. Certainly, it would have been utterly impossible for the various important things that are found in the book of Job to have been known and so vividly described had they not been seen by the Light and candle of the Lord. In the whole book, I cannot find a single verse that refers to other Scripture – it is original and undoubtedly was written very early.

V. David was no stranger to this doctrine. He very often honors the Light and its divine properties. I will mention only a few of the many I might offer.

"The Lord is my Light and my Salvation – whom shall I fear?"[357]

This significant passage of the Royal Prophet is a lively testimony to the true Light. In it, David confesses what the beloved disciple later called his gospel message, that is, "that God is Light."[358] Next, not only is God Light, but of immediate comfort. God is Light personally for David: "The Lord is my Light and my Salvation."[359] In other words, because the Lord is my Light, I know him to be my salvation or the one through whom my salvation is gained.

In short, God is my salvation because he is my Light – because I have obeyed and made him my Light, I know I am saved. Oh! If those who claim to be open-minded Christians would only consider what David's Light was and what was his salvation! David established this as his guide, saying, "God is the Lord, who has shown us Light. Your word is a lamp to my feet

---

[356] Penn has noted Job 29:3 ["When his candle shined upon my head, and when by his light I walked through darkness"] in the margin.

[357] Penn has noted Ps. 27:1 ["The LORD is my light and my salvation; whom shall I fear? the LORD is the strength of my life; of whom shall I be afraid?"] in the margin.

[358] 1 John 1:5: "This then is the message which we have heard of him, and declare unto you, that God is light, and in him is no darkness at all."

[359] Ps. 27:1: "The LORD is my light and my salvation; whom shall I fear? the LORD is the strength of my life; of whom shall I be afraid?"

and a Light for my path. I have not turned away from your laws, for you yourself have taught me."[360] This made him far wiser than his teachers in the secrets of life and the mystery of things. David had long seen beyond the types and figures foretelling the good things to come. He saw through the shadow to the substance – this was the source of his prophesies. He agreed with that famous passage, "The path of the righteous is like the light of dawn, which shines brighter and brighter until the full light of day."[361] This strongly implies that David, with the just of all ages, was blessed with the revelations and leadings of a Divine Light. Unless the path of righteousness is not the way to salvation, obedience to that Light makes people righteous. And, if that was true then, it is also true now, because David calls the Lord himself a Lamp, just as Moses had called the Lord the Word, which is "very near in your heart so you may obey it and do it."[362] This was the Word of reconciliation in every generation whose holy water cleansed the consciences of all who heard and obeyed it from sin.

So that you may see that this Light was not restricted to David or other good people, look at these two passages:

> "You use your mouth for evil and your tongue to deceive. You sit and speak against your brothers and sisters; you slander your own mother's child. You have done these things, and I have kept silent, so you thought I was like you. But I will condemn you and accuse you to your face."[363]

---

[360] Penn has noted the following in the margin:

Ps. 118:27. ["God is the LORD, which hath shewed us light: bind the sacrifice with cords, even unto the horns of the altar."]

Ps. 119:105. ["Thy word is a lamp unto my feet, and a light unto my path."]

Ps. 119:102. ["I have not departed from thy judgments: for thou hast taught me."]

[361] Penn has noted Prov. 4:18 ["But the path of the just is as the shining light, that shineth more and more unto the perfect day"] in the margin.

[362] Deut. 30:14: "But the word is very nigh unto thee, in thy mouth, and in thy heart, that thou mayest do it."

[363] Ps. 50:19-21: "Thou givest thy mouth to evil, and thy tongue frameth deceit. Thou sittest and speakest against thy brother; thou slanderest thine own mother's son. These things hast thou done, and I kept silence; thou thoughtest

"His lightning enlightened the world – the earth saw and trembled."[364]

On impartial consideration, it appears that in these two places God has enlightened the world and, by the Light that reveals the works and workers of darkness, God has rebuked the inhabitants of the earth, set their sins before them, and made the guilty tremble. This is notably confirmed in a passage from another prophet, "For lo! The one who forms the mountains and creates the wind; who makes darkness in the morning and walks in the highest places of the earth; and reveals his thoughts to humanity – the Lord God of Hosts is his name!"[365]

That the psalmist was well acquainted with this can be seen in these words, "Where can I go from your Spirit? Where can I flee from your presence?" These plainly show us that the Spirit of the Lord and the Lord's presence were everywhere and that the Light of them disclosed darkness to mankind. The question was not whether or not God, by his Spirit, was everywhere – all must grant that, if God is God – but, whether it was possible for David to hide anywhere where the eternal Spirit and presence of God (who is Light itself) were not present. Also, "O Lord, you have searched me and you know me. You understand my thoughts from far away. You are familiar with all my ways."[366] It is clear that God knew these things by the Light of his Spirit and David could not have known God, or knew that God knew him, except by that same Light.

In short, it must be evident to all unprejudiced Readers that, since it was impossible to be anywhere without it, David meant that he always had the Light of God's Holy Spirit present with him to admonish, inform, and comfort him. This proves that, although David lived over a thousand years

---

that I was altogether such an one as thyself: but I will reprove thee, and set them in order before thine eyes."

[364] Ps. 97:4: "His lightnings enlightened the world: the earth saw, and trembled."

[365] Penn has noted Amos 4:13 ["For, lo, he that formeth the mountains, and createth the wind, and declareth unto man what is his thought, that maketh the morning darkness, and treadeth upon the high places of the earth, The LORD, The God of hosts, is his name"] in the margin.

[366] Penn has noted Ps. 139:7 ["Whither shall I go from thy spirit? or whither shall I flee from thy presence?"] and verses 1-3 ["O LORD, thou hast searched me, and known me. Thou knowest my downsitting and mine uprising, thou understandest my thought afar off. Thou compassest my path and my lying down, and art acquainted with all my ways"] in the margin.

earlier, he knew very well the meaning of the doctrine that the apostle Paul preached to the Athenians, "God is not far from any one of us."[367] This can be truly witnessed, known, and experienced in the soul and, with humility received into the heart – not just as an accuser, but as a Comforter, Shepherd, Bishop, King, and Lord. This is the glory of the gospel dispensation in which God dwells within his people as a holy temple. This is the blessed Emanuel state, that is, God with us and God in us.[368]

I might also note the scriptural account of the great illumination of Daniel and the Gentiles' clear acknowledgment of it. Only some glimpse of the Divine Light could have allowed them to do so with such seriousness and conviction. It must have been the same Light, showing the same truths. But I will pass it over, along with several other passages from the Minor Prophets and conclude my proof from Scripture that the gift of the Light of God's Spirit preceded the birth of Christ with Stephen's testimony: "However, the Most High does not live in houses made by human hands. As the prophet says: 'Heaven is my throne, and the earth is my footstool. What kind of house can you build for me? says the Lord. Where will my resting place be? Has not my hand made all these things?' You stiff-necked people, with uncircumcised hearts and ears! You are just like your ancestors; you always resist the Holy Spirit!"[369] Plainly, those rebellious Jews had the Spirit of God trying to work within them, but they resisted it. If the rebellious had it, the obedient were not without it.

Lest it should be objected that it was only the Spirit in Stephen, or in the prophets of old, that was resisted – not within the rebellious themselves, remember Reader, what Nehemiah wrote, "You gave your good Spirit to instruct them. You did not withhold your manna from their

---

[367] Acts 17:27: "That they should seek the Lord, if haply they might feel after him, and find him, though he be not far from every one of us."

[368] 2 Cor. 6:16: "And what agreement hath the temple of God with idols? for ye are the temple of the living God; as God hath said, I will dwell in them, and walk in *them*; and I will be their God, and they shall be my people."

[369] Acts 7:48-51: "Howbeit the most High dwelleth not in temples made with hands; as saith the prophet, Heaven is my throne, and earth is my footstool: what house will ye build me? saith the Lord: or what is the place of my rest? Hath not my hand made all these things? Ye stiffnecked and uncircumcised in heart and ears, ye do always resist the Holy Ghost: as your fathers did, so do ye."

mouths."[370] Obviously, those who had manna to feed them also had the Spirit to instruct them, since all who received a portion of manna to eat, also had a portion of the Spirit to teach them. From this it is clear that the Light of God's Spirit, or the Spirit of God, was given to the rebellious as well as to the obedient – condemning sin as well as leading to all righteousness. Since we are to believe that God's Spirit, and the Light of it, is sufficient to bring salvation (since God's gifts are perfect and are given in order to perfectly achieve their purposes), we may, without causing any offense, conclude that God illuminated mankind with an adequate measure of Divine Light and Spirit throughout the long ages before the coming of Christ in the flesh.

Chapter VI

Another objection: Although Jews had it, it does not follow that the Gentiles were also illuminated.

Now I expect another objection – since I have virtually pushed our adversaries into it. That is, "Very well. We might grant that the Scriptures prove there was a saving Light or Spirit that was universally available to the Jews, but they were a distinct people, separated from the rest of the world, with a very special relationship with God. But what about the Gentiles? Were these gifts of God's Light or Spirit available to them? They constituted a much larger portion of the world's population."

Several Scriptures show the Gentiles were not ignored, but had a measure of the Light, some divine seed was sown in their hearts, some talents given to them, and that was sufficient to save them.

To that, I answer that I have already presented Scriptures which make it plain that the saving Light was available to all. But, because of the love deep in my soul for those who will read this treatise, I want to remove any doubt that I can possibly anticipate. Therefore, I will answer this objection first from Scripture, second from our best understanding of the doctrines and lives of heathens, and third from reason. God's love in the illumination of his Spirit was universal even before Christ's life on earth. All were

---

[370] Neh. 9:20: "Thou gavest also thy good spirit to instruct them, and withheldest not thy manna from their mouth, and gavest them water for their thirst."

enlightened with enough of the Light of God's Spirit to bring them to salvation; and everyone who received it, loved it, and obeyed it, knew this to be true. To begin with, I will return to the Scriptures; some I have already quoted, although not directly with respect to this topic.

I.   "My Spirit shall not strive with humanity forever."[371] Observe that no one nation is indicated more than any other, but rather all of humanity. From this, I conclude that humanity was not deprived of the Spirit, or Light, of the Almighty, although it might not be recognized as doing more than simply exposing and condemning sin. And, it follows that if people surrendered to the work of the Light within themselves, they would be redeemed from the spirit of evil that led to their fall from grace and resistance to God's will. This redemption, I call salvation from sin.

II.   "They are among those who rebel against the Light, who do not know its ways or follow its paths."[372] The Jews are not mentioned more than Gentiles in this passage, in this chapter, or in the whole book. Job is talking about the character of wicked people in general without reference to any particular nation. We may very well infer that he did not think of the Light as restricted to any particular people. If, as we are told, those who snatch an orphan from its mother's breast or seize an infant to secure a debt[373] are in rebellion against the Light and do not walk in its paths, then, because that vice was never limited to the Jews, it plainly follows that the Light against which they are rebelling was similarly not limited to the Jews but extended to the Gentiles as well. Otherwise, we would have to say that what was rebellion and wickedness for the Jews was not the same for the Gentiles. But sin was, and is, sin the whole world over, and Light was, and is, Light the whole world over – whether we acknowledge it or not.

III.   Let us read from the same book again. "Can God's armies be counted? Is there anyone on whom God's Light does not arise?"[374]

---

[371] Gen. 6:3: "And the LORD said, My spirit shall not always strive with man, for that he also is flesh: yet his days shall be an hundred and twenty years."

[372] Job 24:13: "They are of those that rebel against the light; they know not the ways thereof, nor abide in the paths thereof."

[373] Job 24:9: "They pluck the fatherless from the breast, and take a pledge of the poor."

[374] Job 25:3: "Is there any number of his armies? and upon whom doth not his light arise?"

This question carries with it very strong confirmation of the universality of God's Light. It asks who is there, from among all the sons and daughters of humanity, who can truly say, "I am not enlightened by God?" If no one can, then it follows that all are enlightened, Gentiles as well as Jews.

This is not our unique interpretation of this text, but is shared by many who are famous for explaining the Scriptures based on the original text. They unanimously interpret it to refer to the Light of the Divine Wisdom, the fountain of the Light – God himself. Rebelling against the Light is rebelling against God, the Light of Israel – an allusion to the psalmist, "The Lord is my Light and my Salvation."[375] Even to the Light mentioned by the apostle Paul, "You who were once darkness, are now Light in the Lord."[376] And that Light, which is said to have sprung up for those who sat in darkness,[377] is the Light of Truth, which all agree spreads the gospel and reveals Christ. The paths of Light are Light itself and lead to that Light that the wicked turn from and reject. This is the Light that arises on all and gives all a true view of themselves. Read the critics, Munsterius,[378] Vatablus,[379] Clarius, and Castellio,[380] on the seventeenth verse, but especially Drusius[381] and Codurcus who say that all people share in that Light and it is sufficient to reveal and drive away the Darkness of Error – it is the Light of Life. Indeed, Codurcus calls it a gospel principle and quotes John 1:9[382] to make his meaning clear.

---

[375] Ps. 27:1: "The LORD is my light and my salvation; whom shall I fear? the LORD is the strength of my life; of whom shall I be afraid?"

[376] Eph. 5:8: "For ye were sometimes darkness, but now are ye light in the Lord: walk as children of light."

[377] Matt. 4:16: "The people which sat in darkness saw great light; and to them which sat in the region and shadow of death light is sprung up."

[378] Possibly, Sebastian Münster (1489-1552), a Franciscan monk who became a Protestant.

[379] François Vatable (died 1547) was a French theologian and biblical exegete.

[380] Sebastian Castellion (1515-63) wrote a tract, *De Haereticis*, in 1553 calling for religious tolerance.

[381] Johannes van Dries (1550-1616) was a Protestant Orientalist and biblical exegete. Born in the Netherlands, he fled to England where he attended Cambridge.

[382] John 1:9: "That was the true Light, which lighteth every man that cometh into the world."

IV.   We are also taught much by two notable parables: the Parable of the Sower and the Parable of the Lord who gave Talents to his Servants. Those who believe the Scripture must recognize they represent God's dealings with mankind with respect to gifts, duties, and rewards. Look at the first parable:

> "That same day, Jesus went out of the house and sat by the lake. Such a large crowd gathered around him that he got into a boat and sat in it, while all the people stood on the shore. Then he told them many things in parables, saying: 'Pay attention! A farmer went out to sow his seed. As he was scattering the seed, some fell along the path, and the birds came and ate it up. Some fell on rocky places, where it did not have much soil. It grew quickly, because the soil was shallow. But when the sun came up, the plants were scorched and withered because they could not take root. Other seed fell among thorns, where it started to grow, but was choked. Still other seed fell on good soil, where it produced a crop – a hundred, sixty, or thirty times what was sown. Let anyone who has ears, hear'" (Matt. 13:1-9).

Everyone I know agrees that the farmer is Christ. The Scripture says, "The seed is the kingdom."[383] This must be the spiritual Word that is near, within the heart,[384] as it must be since Christ said the heavenly kingdom was within.[385] This is also known as the Light which is said to be sown for the righteous.[386] It is also the "grace that came by Christ"[387] and "has appeared, bringing salvation to all,"[388] and the Spirit that gives life.[389] Lastly, common

---

[383] Matt. 13:19: "When any one heareth the word of the kingdom, and understandeth it not, then cometh the wicked one, and catcheth away that which was sown in his heart. This is he which received seed by the way side."

[384] Rom. 10:8: "But what saith it? The word is nigh thee, even in thy mouth, and in thy heart: that is, the word of faith, which we preach."

[385] Luke 17:21: "Neither shall they say, Lo here! or, lo there! for, behold, the kingdom of God is within you."

[386] Ps. 97:11: "Light is sown for the righteous, and gladness for the upright in heart."

[387] John 1:17: "For the law was given by Moses, but grace and truth came by Jesus Christ."

[388] Titus 2:11: "For the grace of God that bringeth salvation hath appeared to all men."

[389] John 6:63: "It is the spirit that quickeneth; the flesh profiteth nothing: the words that I speak unto you, they are spirit, and they are life."

sense tells us tells us that the different types of ground in the parable encompass all of mankind – including the bad with the good – or else the seed would only have been sown on the good ground. But, the Scripture expressly distinguishes between the good and the bad ground and clearly states that seed falls on both. Therefore, God's gift is universal, but people, by their own wickedness, may have made their hearts stony or thorny or too shallow or in some other way defective and incapable of bringing forth fruit.

The other parable is also of very great significance and provides great support for our position.

"The kingdom of heaven is like a man preparing for a journey. He called in his servants and entrusted his property to them. To one he gave five talents, to another two talents, and to a third one talent – each according to his ability. Then he left. The one who had received five talents went off right away and traded with them, and made five more talents. In the same way, the one who had two talents earned two more talents. But the one who had received only one talent dug a hole in the ground and buried the money.

After a while, the master returned and asked for an accounting from them. First, the one who had received five talents came forward, bringing the five added talents. He said, 'Master, you gave me five talents; look, I have made five more talents.' His master said to him, 'Well done, good and faithful servant; you have acted responsibly in a few things, I will put you in charge of many things. Come and share your master's joy.' Then, the one with two talents also came, saying, 'Master, you gave me two talents; look, I have made two more talents.' 'Well done, good and faithful servant; you have acted responsibly in a few things, I will put you in charge of many things. Come and share your master's joy.'

Finally, the one who had received only one talent also approached, saying, 'Master, I knew that you are a harsh man, reaping where you do not sow, and harvesting where you do not plant, so I was afraid. I went and hid your talent in the ground. Here, you have back what is yours.' But his master replied, 'You wicked, lazy servant! You knew very well that I reap where I do not sow, and harvest where I do not plant! Why didn't you deposit my money in the bank? When I returned, I would have gotten my own money back with interest. Take the talent from him, and give it to the one with ten talents. To all who have, more will be given, and they will have plenty; but from those who have nothing, even what they have will be taken away. As for this worthless servant, throw him out into the darkness, where there will be weeping and gnashing of teeth.'

When the Son of Man comes in his glory, with all the angels, he will sit on the throne in glory. All the nations will be gathered before him, and he will separate the people as a shepherd separates sheep from goats. He will put the sheep at his right hand and the goats at his left" (Matt. 25:14-33).

Serious Reader, I have reproduced the parable in its entirety because of its great strength. It will lead to the conviction, I think, or at least the confusion of that narrow spirit that seeks to restrict the infinite goodness of God and render the Creator of the Universe a stingy benefactor. That spirit would restrict God's gifts to only a few and, in so doing, make him appear to favor some over others – like some human parents who (for no good reason) shower gifts and love on one, special child while neglecting their other children. To tell the truth, the over-fondness some have for their own ideas, together with their envious rejection of those who do not share their opinions, seems to have emptied them of all natural affection. In that condition, they dare to think that God is as unnatural as they are themselves. For myself, I have believed for some time that it arises from unwillingness on the part of some to accept that those who disagree with them can be saved. They hope to enforce compliance from others by the threat of eternal damnation and claim that they enjoy God's special favor. Who does not see (who has eyes, let them see), that God is the Lord in the parable? The Lord made mankind to be his servants and these three represent us all. So that all could be useful servants, each is given talents to improve on until he comes home – that is, until the Day of Recompense[390] – when all will be called to account. Those who improve their talents will be rewarded, while those who do not will be punished with eternal separation from God and all the holy angels.

I will conclude with these five observations:

1. Though it is God's sovereign prerogative to give whatever he chooses, the Lord has given every man and woman a talent from the celestial treasury.

---

[390] Isa. 34:8: "For it is the day of the LORD'S vengeance, and the year of recompences for the controversy of Zion."

2. This talent is in itself sufficient; but, like the best seed corn, if it is hidden in a napkin,[391] it cannot grow. But in that case, is not the talent's fault, but the fault of the one who hid it.

3. Those who do not improve their talent are also those who are most likely to charge God with reaping where he does not sow. We have met many, who claim to be Christians and agree that God will require a final accounting, but deny that he has given all sufficient talents to begin with.

4. Like the sheep and goats, each person's eternal blessing or punishment depends on whether they have improved or not improved the heavenly talent with which God has blessed them.

5. Lastly, the number of talents received is not the issue. It does not matter how many talents were given, but what has been done with them. The reward is greater for someone who starts with one talent and makes three out of it than for another person who starts with ten and ends up with fifteen. The first person has tripled what was given, while the second's gift has only been increased by one-half.

Blessed therefore are you all, and will you all be on the Day of Recompense, who pay no attention to the vanities, pleasures, cares, honors, and false religions of this world. Be diligent – attend to your own talent – and in the pure love, awe, and holy counsel of the Lord, improve it every day. Lay up treasure that is durable and everlasting in the high and heavenly place.[392]

V. This reasonable truth is further demonstrated in the important words of our Lord Jesus Christ, "All who do evil hate the Light, and will not come into the Light for fear that their deeds will be exposed."[393] To that, I add the words of the apostle, "Everything that is condemned is

---

[391] This is an allusion to Luke 19:20 ("And another came, saying, Lord, behold, *here is* thy pound, which I have kept laid up in a napkin"), which is in an alternate telling of the parable of the three servants.

[392] Matt. 6:20: "But lay up for yourselves treasures in heaven, where neither moth nor rust doth corrupt, and where thieves do not break through nor steal."

[393] John 3:20: "For every one that doeth evil hateth the light, neither cometh to the light, lest his deeds should be reproved."

exposed by the Light."[394] Certainly it is clear in the Scripture and to our reason that God has not let many millions of people across all the generations live in sin without a Light to show them the way or a law to guide them. To say otherwise is to call God unjust. It must be admitted that they had a Light and a law in their hearts and consciences[395] to convict them of sin. Those who obeyed it were helped and led to act righteously. They could not refuse to bring their deeds into the Light out of ignorance, but only intentionally – knowing that their deeds would be exposed and they would be condemned for doing them. This is proof both that they had a Light and that they knew they had it – even though they rebelled against it.

If I suppose that some of their evil deeds were not revealed to them, it would not mean that the Light was unable to do so. It is obvious that at least some of the things that the Gentiles did were condemned, and therefore that they had the Light. If they did not receive it fully, can the Light be blamed? That would be like blaming a guide because some travelers, who never even started to follow his directions, failed to reach their destination. Had the heathens been faithful to the Light that God had given them, and not blinded by the vain idolatries and superstitious traditions of their ancestors, they too could have learned and understood more fully the mind and will of their Creator. Indeed, as we will see below, some Gentiles did.

VI.   Listen to what the apostle Paul teaches in the first chapter of his Epistle to the Romans, "I am not ashamed of the gospel of Christ, because it is the power of God for the salvation of everyone who believes: for the Jews first and then for the Gentiles. In the gospel, the righteousness of God is revealed by faith from the beginning to the end, just as it is written: 'The righteous will live by faith.' The wrath of God against all the ungodliness and unrighteousness of those who wickedly suppress the truth is revealed from heaven. What can be known about God is revealed in them, because God has shown it to them. Since the creation of the world, God's invisible qualities – his eternal power and divine nature – have been seen clearly and understood by all creatures. Therefore, no one has an

---

[394] Eph. 5:13: "But all things that are reproved are made manifest by the light: for whatsoever doth make manifest is light."

[395] Rom. 2:15: "Which shew the work of the law written in their hearts, their conscience also bearing witness, and their thoughts the mean while accusing or else excusing one another."

excuse. Although all knew God, they did not glorify him as God or give thanks. They came to believe in what they thought up themselves, and their foolish hearts were darkened. And since they did not think it worthwhile to acknowledge God, he gave them over to a depraved mind – to do what ought not to be done" (Rom. 1:16-21, 28).

These notable lines from that great apostle provide an answer to all objections against either the universality or the sufficiency of the Light within. This should be apparent to the Reader:

1. The righteousness of God, from beginning to end, is revealed in the gospel of Christ.

2. Those who are just have always lived by this faith. What Paul quotes, when he says, "As it is written," can be dated to about seven hundred years before he wrote his epistle.[396]

3. Many, that is the Gentiles, had fallen from righteousness into ungodliness, against which the wrath of God was revealed from heaven.

4. Nevertheless, they once knew the Truth.

5. They had come to that knowledge of the Truth by the revelations of God (who is Light) within, since the apostle says, "What can be known about God is revealed in them, because God has shown it to them."

6. Their darkness was caused by their own rebellion against the revelation of Light and for not glorifying the God that had shown those things to them, although they saw those revelations and knew they were revealed by God. This shows that the Light that God had given them was sufficient to know and obey him. Since they choose not to acknowledge God, the fault was theirs, and not the Light's.

7. If their foolish hearts were darkened by their own disobedience, then it follows that the darkness came into their hearts as a consequence of sin. Prior to that sin, they had Light in their hearts, or a Light within, by which to know and to do their duty.

8. Lastly, God was angry only because of their actions. They wickedly suppressed the Truth and substituted their own notions for it. Only

---

[396] Hab. 2:4: "Behold, his soul which is lifted up is not upright in him: but the just shall live by his faith."

then were their hearts darkened. Certainly, if they had held fast to that enlightening principle that we call Truth and to the revelations of God within – preserving their faith in God as he was revealed to them, glorifying and acknowledging God – then mercy and peace, not wrath, would have been revealed from heaven. As the apostle says in the following chapter, "God will give eternal life to those who patiently and persistently seek for glory, honor, and immortality by doing good."[397]

In short, we can safely conclude that the righteousness revealed from beginning to end by the gospel of Christ (of which Paul was not ashamed) and by which, he testifies, the just ancients lived and were accepted by God, is the same in nature – although not in degree – as the Truth that the Gentiles had abandoned. That is why they are said to have lived in the world without faith, righteousness, or God. That is why God's wrath was revealed. Had they lived up to that Truth, glorifying God as God according to the revelations in their hearts and consciences, they would have been righteous and, like the just in all ages, they would have been acceptable to God – but without faith, no one can please God in any age. Without the holiness that flows from true faith, no one will ever see the Lord.[398]

---

[397] Rom. 2:7: "To them who by patient continuance in well doing seek for glory and honour and immortality, eternal life."

[398] Heb. 12:14: "Follow peace with all *men*, and holiness, without which no man shall see the Lord."

A challenge to provide an example of someone who was condemned by the Light for not believing that Jesus was the Christ is answered. Those who believed in the Light, and walked in it, received Christ when he came. The greatest hypocrites were those who opposed the Scriptures and crucified him. The Light from the Scriptures is seen to be universal and saving.

VII.   Lastly, I ask the unprejudiced Reader to consider two important passages and my reflections of them. These will conclude the proofs from Scripture that I will offer for the universality of the Light and Spirit of God prior to the birth of Jesus:

"Then Peter said, 'I now understand how true it is that God does not show favoritism, but accepts those from every nation who love and revere him and do what is right.'"[399]

"It is not those who hear the law who are righteous in God's sight – those who obey the law will be declared righteous. When Gentiles, who do not have the law, instinctively do the things that are required by the law, they are a law for themselves. Even though they do not have the law, they show that the requirements of the law are written on their hearts, and their consciences also bear witness. Their conflicting thoughts may accuse them or excuse them on the day my gospel declares that God, through Jesus Christ, will judge the secrets of all."[400]

These Scriptures strictly limit on any attempt to underestimate the blessed Light of God in humanity. The limits are revealed by examining these passages in detail:

---

[399] Acts 10:34-35: "Then Peter opened his mouth, and said, Of a truth I perceive that God is no respecter of persons: But in every nation he that feareth him, and worketh righteousness, is accepted with him."

[400] Rom. 2:13-16 "(For not the hearers of the law are just before God, but the doers of the law shall be justified. For when the Gentiles, which have not the law, do by nature the things contained in the law, these, having not the law, are a law unto themselves: Which shew the work of the law written in their hearts, their conscience also bearing witness, and their thoughts the mean while accusing or else excusing one another;) In the day when God shall judge the secrets of men by Jesus Christ according to my gospel."

1. God does not show favoritism. From this I conclude that all persons
    and all nations – Gentile as well as Jew – shared in and share in the
    Light.

2. There are those, uncircumcised by human hands,[401] who love and are
    awed by God, live righteously, and do what the law requires. They are
    not obligated to do so by an outward law – they do not have it – but by
    the inward workings of the law that is written on their hearts. This
    demonstrates that they had not only the Light as a judge, but also as a
    teacher and guide, leading them to love God and to live righteously.
    Elsewhere this is called the end of the matter and each person's whole
    duty.[402] No one who loves and reveres God and who lives righteously –
    who keeps the pure law of God in their hearts – can do so without the
    true Light. The Scriptures tell us that some Gentiles did. Hence, the
    objection that the heathens were ignorant of the true God (or that the
    Light within failed to condemn anyone who refused to accept that Jesus
    is our Savior) vanishes. All who sincerely lived up to the Light in their
    consciences instantly recognized that glorious appearance of the Light
    when it came in the flesh.

Those who would not come to Christ made much of the Scriptures –
tradition-bound, literal-minded, and legalistic people rejected and crucified
him. On the other hand, if Cornelius[403] and the Centurion[404] (and many
others) not conscientiously followed the Light within, Peter would not have
been received into the home of the first nor would Christ have been
followed by the second. The measure of the Divine Light that they had
obeyed, as the undoubted word of prophesy, led them naturally to the

---

[401] Eph. 2:11: "Wherefore remember, that ye being in time past Gentiles in the
flesh, who are called Uncircumcision by that which is called the Circumcision in
the flesh made by hands."

[402] Eccles. 12:13-14: "Let us hear the conclusion of the whole matter: Fear God,
and keep his commandments: for this is the whole duty of man. For God shall
bring every work into judgment, with every secret thing, whether it be good, or
whether it be evil."

[403] Cornelius is a Roman centurion who is shown in Acts 10:1-33 to be devout and
faithful.

[404] The unnamed centurion in Matt. 8:5-13 asks Jesus to heal his servant. In verse
10, Jesus says of him, "Verily I say unto you, I have not found so great faith,
no, not in Israel."

dawning of the day star.[405] This, although it was more glorious in appearance, was not a new or different Light, Life, or Spirit of God. There are not two Lights, two lives, two natures, or two Spirits in God. Despite the various ways God has been known and revealed at different times, God is *one* forever. God's Light is *one*, God's Truth is *one*, God's way is *one*, and God's rest is *one* forever.

Last of all, good people rejoice that, despite the hardheartedness of some in this world, the virtuous Gentiles will not be denied their reward in the next world. Despite all the heat, petulance, conceit, and worldly boasting of false Christians, we are assured that those who love and revere God – who live righteously and follow the law that is written in their hearts – will be accepted and justified by God on the day when, according to Paul's gospel, the secrets of all will be judged by Jesus Christ – if anyone preaches another gospel, let it be cursed.[406]

For the sake of brevity, I have purposely omitted many compelling and convincing selections – both from the Old and from the New Testament writings – in which the righteousness of the Gentiles has been more obvious than that of some of the Jews. This undoubtedly testifies to the sufficiency of the Light within, both to distinguish what is good from what is evil and to enable those who truly obey it to do the one and reject the other. These included Abimelech,[407] Cyrus,[408] Darius,[409] the ruler who came

---

[405] 2 Pet. 1:19: "We have also a more sure word of prophecy; whereunto ye do well that ye take heed, as unto a light that shineth in a dark place, until the day dawn, and the day star arise in your hearts."

[406] Gal. 1:9: "As we said before, so say I now again, If any *man* preach any other gospel unto you than that ye have received, let him be accursed."

[407] Penn has noted Gen. 20:4 &21:22 ["But Abimelech had not come near her: and he said, Lord, wilt thou slay also a righteous nation? ...And it came to pass at that time, that Abimelech and Phichol the chief captain of his host spake unto Abraham, saying, God *is* with thee in all that thou does"] in the margin.

[408] Penn has noted the following in the margin:

2 Chron. 36:23. ["Thus saith Cyrus king of Persia, All the kingdoms of the earth hath the LORD God of heaven given me; and he hath charged me to build him an house in Jerusalem, which *is* in Judah. Who *is there* among you of all his people? The LORD his God *be* with him, and let him go up."]

Ezra 1:2-5&6:3. ["Thus saith Cyrus king of Persia, The LORD God of heaven hath given me all the kingdoms of the earth; and he hath charged me to build him an house at Jerusalem, which *is* in Judah. Who *is there* among you of

to Christ,[410] and many others, which I will not list here. My primary purpose is to demonstrate the truth of my claims using their own writings.

---

all his people? his God be with him, and let him go up to Jerusalem, which *is* in Judah, and build the house of the LORD God of Israel, (he *is* the God,) which *is* in Jerusalem. And whosoever remaineth in any place where he sojourneth, let the men of his place help him with silver, and with gold, and with goods, and with beasts, beside the freewill offering for the house of God that *is* in Jerusalem. Then rose up the chief of the fathers of Judah and Benjamin, and the priests, and the Levites, with all *them* whose spirit God had raised, to go up to build the house of the LORD which *is* in Jerusalem. ... In the first year of Cyrus the king *the same* Cyrus the king made a decree *concerning* the house of God at Jerusalem, Let the house be builded, the place where they offered sacrifices, and let the foundations thereof be strongly laid; the height thereof threescore cubits, *and* the breadth thereof threescore cubits."]

[409] Penn has noted the following in the margin:

Ezra 6:12. ["And the God that hath caused his name to dwell there destroy all kings and people, that shall put to their hand to alter and to destroy this house of God which is at Jerusalem. I Darius have made a decree; let it be done with speed."]

Dan. 6:26-27. ["I make a decree, That in every dominion of my kingdom men tremble and fear before the God of Daniel: for he *is* the living God, and stedfast for ever, and his kingdom *that* which shall not be destroyed, and his dominion *shall be even* unto the end. He delivereth and rescueth, and he worketh signs and wonders in heaven and in earth, who hath delivered Daniel from the power of the lions."]

[410] Matt. 9:18: "While he spake these things unto them, behold, there came a certain ruler, and worshipped him, saying, My daughter is even now dead: but come and lay thy hand upon her, and she shall live."

Chapter VII

The Gentile understanding of divinity.

Having from the Scriptures proved briefly, though I hope fully and truly, that the Gentiles in general were lighted with a Divine Light, I shall now make it my business to provide evidence of that by a most undeniable source – their own writings. I will try to make the best and plainest possible defense that those works will allow, both of the Light within and of those who obey it.

First, from their own authorities, I am told that the Gentiles believe in One Holy, Infinite, and Eternal God.

Second, they came to this belief because of knowledge that God had implanted in their hearts. In our words, God enlightened all mankind with a Divine Light, which, if obeyed, will lead them to eternal happiness.

Third, they believed in and respected the sanctity of life.

Fourth, they recognized the immortality of the soul and that it would receive an eternal reward or punishment as a consequence of their obedience to or rebellion against the Eternal God and Creator.

These true, clear, and excellent principles are clearly laid out in their writings and, in my opinion, show the signs of divine inspiration. I hope that in this discourse I can call them inspired without offending anyone.

The Gentiles believed in one God.

Below, I will reproduce some of the writings that show that the Gentiles acknowledged and believed that there is One Supreme Being, who made all things, is eternal, infinite, almighty, omnipresent, holy, and good. In the footnotes, I will list some of the scriptural passages that support the same points. In this way, the Gentiles' assertions can be compared to a higher authority and their compatibility demonstrated. In doing so, I am following the example of the most ancient of the church fathers.

I.   Orpheus,[411] who lived more than twelve hundred years before Christ, expressed his belief in God like this, "His hand reaches to the end of the sea, his right hand is everywhere, and the earth is under his feet. He is

---

[411] Orpheus was a legendary ancient Greek hero endowed with superhuman musical skills.

the only One, self-created, and by him alone, all things are created. God is the first and the last."[412]

In this passage, Orpheus not only says that there is a God, but he attributes almighty power and omnipresence to God – showing that he meant no mere idol, but the God who made the heavens and the earth.

II.   Hesiod[413] wrote, "You are the King and Lord of all that do not die. No one can match your power."[414] This emphatically proves that he believed God to have been one and omnipotent.

III.   Thales,[415] a very ancient Greek philosopher tells us, "There is but one God, glorious forever and ever." He also openly confesses, "God is

---

[412] Penn has noted the following in the margin:

Isa. 23:11. ["He stretched out his hand over the sea, he shook the kingdoms: the LORD hath given a commandment against the merchant *city*, to destroy the strong holds thereof."]

Ps. 8:6. ["Thou madest him to have dominion over the works of thy hands; thou hast put all *things* under his feet."]

Josh. 2:11. ["And as soon as we had heard *these things*, our hearts did melt, neither did there remain any more courage in any man, because of you: for the LORD your God, he *is* God in heaven above, and in earth beneath."]

Rev. 22:13. ["I am Alpha and Omega, the beginning and the end, the first and the last."]

[413] Hesiod (c. 700 B.C.) was one of the earliest Greek poets. Two of his works have survived intact, *Theogony*, relating the myths of the gods, and *Works and Days*, describing peasant life.

[414] Penn has noted the following in the margin:

Matt. 22:32. ["I am the God of Abraham, and the God of Isaac, and the God of Jacob? God is not the God of the dead, but of the living."]

Ps. 10:16. ["The LORD *is* King for ever and ever: the heathen are perished out of his land."]

Ps. 95:3. ["For the LORD *is* a great God, and a great King above all gods."]

1 Tim. 1:17&6:15. ["Now unto the King eternal, immortal, invisible, the only wise God, *be* honour and glory for ever and ever. Amen. ... Which in his times he shall shew, *who is* the blessed and only Potentate, the King of kings, and Lord of lords."]

Ps. 45:6. ["Thy throne, O God, *is* for ever and ever: the sceptre of thy kingdom *is* a right sceptre."]

called *kardiognostis* – the one who knows hearts." When asked what God was, Thales replied, "That which has neither a beginning nor an end." When another person asked if anyone could do wrong and conceal it from God, he said, "How? When even an evil thought cannot be hidden." Quoting Thales, Cicero[416] says, "All should know that God sees all things."[417]

IV. Sibylla:[418] "There is one God who alone is infinite and without beginning."[419] "Who, with earthly eyes, can see the heavenly, true, and

---

[415] Thales (c. 624-c. 545 B.C.) was Greek philosopher who developed a cosmology based on the idea that water is the essence of all matter.

[416] Marcus Tullius Cicero (January 3, 106-December 7, 43 B.C.) was a Roman statesman, lawyer, scholar, and writer who sought to uphold republican principles in the civil wars that finally destroyed the Roman Republic.

[417] Penn has noted the following in the margin:

Exod. 15:11. ["Who *is* like unto thee, O LORD, among the gods? who *is* like thee, glorious in holiness, fearful *in* praises, doing wonders?"]

John 17:5. ["And now, O Father, glorify thou me with thine own self with the glory which I had with thee before the world was."]

Jer. 17:10. ["I the LORD search the heart, *I* try the reins, even to give every man according to his ways, *and* according to the fruit of his doings."]

Ps. 7:9. ["Oh let the wickedness of the wicked come to an end; but establish the just: for the righteous God trieth the hearts and reins."]

Amos 4:13. ["For, lo, he that formeth the mountains, and createth the wind, and declareth unto man what *is* his thought, that maketh the morning darkness, and treadeth upon the high places of the earth, The LORD, The God of hosts, *is* his name."]

Ps. 90:2. ["Before the mountains were brought forth, or ever thou hadst formed the earth and the world, even from everlasting to everlasting, thou *art* God."]

Heb. 7:3. ["Without father, without mother, without descent, having neither beginning of days, nor end of life; but made like unto the Son of God; abideth a priest continually."]

[418] Sibylla was a prophetess in Greek legend and literature. Tradition represented her as an ancient woman who prophesied in writing from an ecstatic frenzy.

[419] Penn has noted the following in the margin:

Ps. 86:10. ["For thou *art* great, and doest wondrous things: thou *art* God alone."]

immortal God whose seat is in the highest heavens?" This Sybil is dated as living more than two thousand years ago. The question just quoted implies her faith that God is a Spirit, just as Christ testifies.[420]

Christ enlightened all with a saving Light.

V.   Pythagoras,[421] a modest and private man, but diligent in his search after heavenly things, said, "It is humanity's duty to believe in God — that God exists, keeps them in mind, and cares for them. We need such care and ought never to oppose it. This care comes from the Divine in rightfully exercising dominion over all" and "God resembles Light and Truth." And, in another place, "God inhabits the lowest, highest, and the middle. There is no creature nor any place without God."[422]

Isa. 44:6. ["Thus saith the LORD the King of Israel, and his redeemer the LORD of hosts; I *am* the first, and I *am* the last; and beside me *there is* no God."]

1 Cor. 8:5-6. ["For though there be that are called gods, whether in heaven or in earth, (as there be gods many, and lords many,) But to us *there is but* one God, the Father, of whom *are* all things, and we in him; and one Lord Jesus Christ, by whom *are* all things, and we by him."]

[420] Penn has noted the following in the margin:

1 John 4:12. ["No man hath seen God at any time. If we love one another, God dwelleth in us, and his love is perfected in us."]

Acts 7:49. ["Heaven *is* my throne, and earth *is* my footstool: what house will ye build me? saith the Lord: or what *is* the place of my rest?"]

Ps. 11:4. ["The LORD *is* in his holy temple, the LORD'S throne *is* in heaven: his eyes behold, his eyelids try, the children of men."]

1 Kings 8:30. ["And hearken thou to the supplication of thy servant, and of thy people Israel, when they shall pray toward this place: and hear thou in heaven thy dwelling place: and when thou hearest, forgive."]

[421] Pythagoras (c. 575-c. 495 B.C.) was a Greek philosopher, mathematician, and founder of the Pythagorean brotherhood. He influenced the thought of Plato and Aristotle and contributed to the development of mathematics and Western philosophy.

[422] Penn has noted the following in the margin:

Heb. 11:6. ["But without faith it is impossible to please him: for he that cometh to God must believe that he is, and that he is a rewarder of them that diligently seek him."]

He also wrote, "God is one. He is not, as some believe, part of the world, but complete within himself – just as a circle is complete in itself – and watching over all generations. God is the life of all ages, the source of his own powers and works, the principle of all things – one heavenly luminary or Light and Father of all things – wisest and invisible, yet knowable."

This passionate account of the Divine Being corresponds amazingly with the words of Scripture, but was written by someone with no knowledge of it (I mean of the text of the Scriptures, since he obviously understands its message). As such, it deserves very serious consideration and acknowledgment by all, but especially by those who would try to restrict God's mercy to their own time or their own community.[423]

---

1 Chron. 29:11. ["Thine, O LORD, *is* the greatness, and the power, and the glory, and the victory, and the majesty: for all *that is* in the heaven and in the earth *is thine*; thine *is* the kingdom, O LORD, and thou art exalted as head above all."]

2 Chron. 16:9. ["For the eyes of the LORD run to and fro throughout the whole earth, to shew himself strong in the behalf of them whose heart is perfect toward him. Herein thou hast done foolishly: therefore from henceforth thou shalt have wars."]

Acts 17:24. ["God that made the world and all things therein, seeing that he is Lord of heaven and earth, dwelleth not in temples made with hands."]

Isa. 9:6. ["For unto us a child is born, unto us a son is given: and the government shall be upon his shoulder: and his name shall be called Wonderful, Counsellor, The mighty God, The everlasting Father, The Prince of Peace."]

Matt. 6:13. ["And lead us not into temptation, but deliver us from evil: For thine is the kingdom, and the power, and the glory, for ever. Amen."]

1 John 1:5. ["This then is the message which we have heard of him, and declare unto you, that God is light, and in him is no darkness at all."]

John 14:6. ["Jesus saith unto him, I am the way, the truth, and the life: no man cometh unto the Father, but by me."]

[423] Penn has noted the following in the margin:

Acts 17:27. ["That they should seek the Lord, if haply they might feel after him, and find him, though he be not far from every one of us."]

Jer. 23:23. ["*Am* I a God at hand, saith the LORD, and not a God afar off?"]

Eph. 4:6. ["One God and Father of all, who *is* above all, and through all, and in you all."]

All ought to live piously.

VI.   Heraclites,[424] a sensible and humble philosopher, speaks of the world's impieties and idolatries in much the same way. His deeply sorrowful, yet sharp and sound words reveal a profoundly sensitive mind. In a letter to his friend, Hermodorus, he seems, after a while, to be addressing Euticles and the rest of his enemies who condemned him as an enemy of their false gods. "I am condemned of impiety by the impious. What do you think? Am I impious for rejecting their gods? If the blind were to judge sight, they would say that blindness is sight. Oh, you ignorant people! Teach us first what God is, so that when you pronounce us impious, you might be believed. Where is God? Shut up in your temples? Oh, 'pious people'! You put God in the dark. You ignorant fools! Don't you know that God is not made with hands?"[425]

Job 25:3. ["Is there any number of his armies? and upon whom doth not his light arise?"]

1 Cor. 8:6. ["But to us *there is but* one God, the Father, of whom *are* all things, and we in him; and one Lord Jesus Christ, by whom *are* all things, and we by him."]

1 Tim. 1:17. ["Now unto the King eternal, immortal, invisible, the only wise God, *be* honour and glory for ever and ever. Amen."]

[424] Heraclites (c. 540-c. 480 B.C.) was a Greek philosopher who assumed the existence of the *logos*, that is, order or reason, as a unifying principle which guides all things. His views survive only in fragments quoted and attributed to him by later authors.

[425] Penn has noted the following in the margin:

1 Kings 8:27. ["But will God indeed dwell on the earth? behold, the heaven and heaven of heavens cannot contain thee; how much less this house that I have builded?"]

2 Chron. 6:18. ["But will God in very deed dwell with men on the earth? behold, heaven and the heaven of heavens cannot contain thee; how much less this house which I have built!"]

Acts 7:49. ["Heaven *is* my throne, and earth *is* my footstool: what house will ye build me? saith the Lord: or what *is* the place of my rest?"]

1 Tim. 6:16. ["Who only hath immortality, dwelling in the light which no man can approach unto; whom no man hath seen, nor can see: to whom *be* honour and power everlasting. Amen."]

Isa. 40:18. ["To whom then will ye liken God? or what likeness will ye compare unto him?"]

This is a clear and abundant testimony against their idols, mixed with religious mockery, and tempered by grief. Surely, Heraclites believed in God and that God was Light, too – a Light that would never fade. Elsewhere, he says that by God, "He had overcome the enemies of his soul."

VII.   Anaxagoras,[426] Socrates' mentor and an esteemed noble by birth, but even more esteemed for his knowledge and virtue, taught that, "God is an infinite, self-sufficient mind – the ultimate cause of all things. By that Divine Mind, everything being was made in its proper form. When all things were in confusion and mixed together, it came and put them in order."[427]

This undoubtedly is true and Anaxagoras must have had no small share in the Light to have given such a clear account of God and the creation. Indeed, he is remembered and celebrated by the Greeks for so greatly improving their understanding of God and immortality.

John 4:24. ["God *is* a Spirit: and they that worship him must worship *him* in spirit and in truth."]

[426] Anaxagoras (c. 500-c. 428 B.C.) was a Greek philosopher. He was the first to devise a molecular model of matter and to regard the physical universe as subject to the rule of reason.

[427] In the margin, Penn advises the Reader to read the first chapter of Genesis in which God creates the heavens and the earth with special attention to Gen. 1:2 ["And the earth was without form, and void; and darkness *was* upon the face of the deep. And the Spirit of God moved upon the face of the waters"]. He also noted the following:

1 Cor. 8:6. ["But to us *there is but* one God, the Father, of whom *are* all things, and we in him; and one Lord Jesus Christ, by whom *are* all things, and we by him."]

Job 38:4. ["Where wast thou when I laid the foundations of the earth? declare, if thou hast understanding."]

Acts 4:24. ["And when they heard that, they lifted up their voice to God with one accord, and said, Lord, thou *art* God, which hast made heaven, and earth, and the sea, and all that in them is."]

The soul is immortal. There is an eternal reward or punishment.

VIII.   Socrates,[428] that good heathen (if I can say that without offending so-called Christians), not only professes that there is one God, but I believe, gives good reasons for doing so. "The Mind, that is frequently called God, arranges and causes all things." Elsewhere he says, "God is *one*, perfect in himself, giving life and well-being to every creature."

He gives the following reasons: "God, not chance, made the world and all its creatures. This is obvious from the careful placement of each species so that it can feed itself, defend itself, and continue its species. This is particularly obvious in humanity – granted an excellent body and upright posture, the ability to speak, and especially a soul to give us insight and forethought. In caring for the whole species, each individual is nurtured. God has implanted knowledge within each person and, depending on their behavior, rewards those who please him and punishes those who do not. This has been recognized by the wisest and most civilized people in every city and in every age.[429] God sees all things and knows all things – even in

---

[428] Socrates (c. 470-c. 399 B.C.) was a Greek philosopher who, with Plato and Aristotle, is credited with laying the philosophical basis of for western culture. Cicero said of him that he "brought philosophy down from heaven to earth." He was Plato's mentor.

[429] At this point, Penn has placed a lengthy note in the margin, followed by a series of Scripture citations:

These notable arguments for the proof of a Divine Super-intelligent Being, Creator, and Providence may well agree with those earnest expressions of Job, the Psalmist, and several prophets, evangelists, and apostles concerning God's creating and sustaining the world – that God laid the foundations, watches over the lilies and sparrows, brings forth fruit in its season, and lights it by day and night. Also, that the disciples should give no thought to what they will eat or drink or wear, that there is a Spirit in each person, the inspiration of the Almighty, which gives us understanding, and, finally, that no one can hide in a place so secret that the Lord cannot see him. [Jer. 23:24: "Can any hide himself in secret places that I shall not see him? saith the LORD. Do not I fill heaven and earth? saith the LORD."]

Ps. 139:9. ["*If* I take the wings of the morning, *and* dwell in the uttermost parts of the sea."]

Prov. 8:15. ["By me kings reign, and princes decree justice."]

the most distant places – everything that is said or done or secretly desired. That God cares for all creatures is obvious from the benefits given to them: light, water, fire, and the fruits of the earth. That God particularly provides for humanity can be seen in the nurturing of all the plants and animals for our service – even those that vastly exceed us in strength. Humanity was given many senses with which to understand the all the things placed in the world for our use and pleasure. We enjoy the gifts of reason, memory, and speech, and through these God has developed law and the ability to govern states. God, although invisible, has a being – just as God's ministers, thunder and wind, are invisible but have substance. In the same way, the human soul (which partakes of that divine nature) is able to direct the workings of a body that cannot see it. Finally, God sees all, hears all, is everywhere, and orders all.

Here we have stated Socrates' faith in God and his reasons for it, drawn from the outward creation and from an inward divine sense, which came from the divine promptings or divine nature within him. In this faith, he lived and, as will be described below, he died.

Josh. 2:11. ["And as soon as we had heard *these things*, our hearts did melt, neither did there remain any more courage in any man, because of you: for the LORD your God, he *is* God in heaven above, and in earth beneath."]

Wis. 11:20&12:15. ["Yea, and without these might they have fallen down with one blast, being persecuted of vengeance, and scattered abroad through the breath of thy power: but thou hast ordered all things in measure and number and weight ... Forsomuch then as thou art righteous thyself, thou orderest all things righteously: thinking it not agreeable with thy power to condemn him that hath not deserved to be punished."]

Eph. 4:6. ["One God and Father of all, who *is* above all, and through all, and in you all."]

Gen. 1:1-3. ["In the beginning God created the heaven and the earth. And the earth was without form, and void; and darkness *was* upon the face of the deep. And the Spirit of God moved upon the face of the waters. And God said, Let there be light: and there was light."]

Acts 17:28. ["For in him we live, and move, and have our being; as certain also of your own poets have said, For we are also his offspring."]

Ps. 34:9-11. ["O fear the LORD, ye his saints: for *there is* no want to them that fear him. The young lions do lack, and suffer hunger: but they that seek the LORD shall not want any good *thing*. Come, ye children, hearken unto me: I will teach you the fear of the LORD."]

IX.   Timaeus of Locri,[430] in his work *Of Nature*, argues that God is "One principle by which all was created. It cannot be created itself, because then it could not be the creating principle, but whatever had created it would be that principle."[431]

Clement of Alexandria,[432] in refuting charges from Gentiles and proving the truth of the Scriptures, quoted this among a number of their own writings. In commentary on this passage, he wrote, "Hear, Oh Israel, the Lord your God, is one, and only him will you serve."[433]

Timaeus confirms that he believes "God is a Spirit and the source of all Light." How sound and true this statement is can be seen in the Scriptures I have noted.[434]

---

[430] Timaeus of Locri (420-380 B.C.) was a Pythagorean philosopher born in Locri, Italy. He is credited with the work *On the Soul of the Universe*, although some historians believe this may be an abridgement of Plato's dialogue, *Timaeus*.

[431] Penn has noted John 1:1-4 ["In the beginning was the Word, and the Word was with God, and the Word was God. The same was in the beginning with God. All things were made by him; and without him was not any thing made that was made. In him was life; and the life was the light of men."] in the margin.

[432] Clement of Alexandria (c. 150-c. 215), an early Christian theologian, sought to integrate Greek classical culture with Christian faith. The most important of his surviving works is a trilogy consisting of the *Protreptikos*, the *Paidagogos*, and the *Stromateis*.

[433] This combines Deut. 6:4 ("Hear, O Israel: The LORD our God *is* one LORD.") and Matt. 4:10 ("Then saith Jesus unto him, Get thee hence, Satan: for it is written, Thou shalt worship the Lord thy God, and him only shalt thou serve").

Penn has also noted the following in the margin:

2 Kings 19:19. ["Now therefore, O LORD our God, I beseech thee, save thou us out of his hand, that all the kingdoms of the earth may know that thou *art* the LORD God, *even* thou only."]

Mark 12:32. ["And the scribe said unto him, Well, Master, thou hast said the truth: for there is one God; and there is none other but he."]

1 Tim. 2:5. ["For *there is* one God, and one mediator between God and men, the man Christ Jesus."]

[434] Penn has noted the following in the margin:

John 4:24. ["God *is* a Spirit: and they that worship him must worship *him* in spirit and in truth."]

Gen. 1:3. ["And God said, Let there be light: and there was light."]

X.   Antisthenes,[435] who was part of Socrates school, seems to consider the question, "To whom will you compare me asks the Lord?"[436] and to answer it, "He is like no other, because no one has seen his picture or portrait."[437] From this, we can see that he did not believe God to be an image nor anything that could be known by an image or see by human eyes. This is a step beyond the Roman Catholics, who believe that they can teach about God using images.

XI.   Plato,[438] the learned and eminent Gentile philosopher, a student of Socrates, was given the honorary title "the Divine" by the Greeks because of his contemplation of the divine and pious life. He sums up his faith in God in these words, "God is First, Eternal, Inexpressible, Completely Autonomous – that is, needing no one and nothing – and Ever-Perfect. God is utterly complete at all times and perfect every way: in Divinity, in Essence, in Truth, in Harmony, and in Goodness. These names and attributes are not listed in order to distinguish one from another, but rather so that by knowing them all together can we can come to understand each one. God is said to be good for bestowing benefits – each person receiving whatever he or she needs – and is, therefore, the font of all that is

---

James 1:17. ["Every good gift and every perfect gift is from above, and cometh down from the Father of lights, with whom is no variableness, neither shadow of turning."]

[435] Antisthenes (c. 445-c. 365 B.C.) was an Athenian philosopher and a student of Socrates. Diogenes of Sinope credits him as the founder of the Cynic school of philosophy.

[436] Isa. 46:5: "To whom will ye liken me, and make *me* equal, and compare me, that we may be like?"

[437] Penn has noted the following in the margin:

Exod. 9:14. ["For I will at this time send all my plagues upon thine heart, and upon thy servants, and upon thy people; that thou mayest know that there *is* none like me in all the earth."]

Exod. 8:10. ["And he said, To morrow. And he said, *Be it* according to thy word: that thou mayest know that *there is* none like unto the LORD our God."]

Ps. 89:6. ["For who in the heaven can be compared unto the LORD? *who* among the sons of the mighty can be likened unto the LORD?"]

[438] Plato (428-347 B.C.) was an Athenian philosopher who built on the work of his mentor, Socrates. A rationalist, he was devoted to the proposition that reason must be followed wherever it leads. He founded the Academy, one of the great philosophical schools of antiquity.

good. Beautiful, because God is, in essence, both more and better than and equal to all beauty. Truth, because God is the source of all Truth – just as the sun is the source of all light."

"Moreover, God is not composed of parts that could be separated; God cannot be moved from place to place or changed in any way. If God could be altered, it must be by himself or by something else. But, if something else could change God, that thing must be more powerful than God. If God were to change himself, it must either to become better or worse – either of which is absurd."[439]

From these passages, it is plain that that God is a Spirit. And it is obvious how faithful, how reasonable, and how firm Plato's belief was in One Eternal Being and Father of All.

XII.   Lyricus Melanippides[440] offers this prayer, "Hear me Father, wonder of all humanity, who governs the living soul forever." This plainly

---

[439] Penn has noted the following in the margin:

Rev. 22:13. ["I am Alpha and Omega, the beginning and the end, the first and the last."]

Isa. 40:28. ["Hast thou not known? hast thou not heard, *that* the everlasting God, the LORD, the Creator of the ends of the earth, fainteth not, neither is weary? *there is* no searching of his understanding."]

Ps. 18:30. ["*As for* God, his way *is* perfect: the word of the LORD is tried: he *is* a buckler to all those that trust in him."]

Deut. 23:4 [Probably Deut. 32:4: "*He is* the Rock, his work *is* perfect: for all his ways *are* judgment: a God of truth and without iniquity, just and right *is* he."]

Isa. 45:5. ["I *am* the LORD, and *there is* none else, *there is* no God beside me: I girded thee, though thou hast not known me."]

Mal. 3:6. ["For I *am* the LORD, I change not; therefore ye sons of Jacob are not consumed."]

[440] Melanippides of Melos (fifth century B.C.) was the most famous lyre-player of the Classical period. It was said that he increased the number of lyre strings from eleven to twelve. Innovations in the composition of dithyrambs (hymns in praise of Dionysus) are also attributed to him. He spent the last years of his life at the court of the Macedonian king Perdikkas II. Fragments of three of his works, *Marsyas*, *Danaides*, and *Persephone*, have survived.

demonstrates belief in One Eternal God and in God's wondrous qualities.[441]

XIII.   Parmenides,[442] according to Plato in *Sophista*, wrote, "God is not created or subject to death, but like a chain with sturdy links and joined end-to-end so that it has no beginning." Who could this chain be, but the eternal God by whom all things are made? "The first and the last."[443]

XIV.   Zeno,[444] a grave and wise philosopher, established the Stoic way, but not the way of virtue. Although the teachings of both the Cynics and the Stoics tended to lead to a good life, both of these philosophies can be seen as coming from the work of Socrates, the most excellent man of his time. They can be distinguished on the basis of some over-scrupulousness, to which the mild, serious, and unaffected piety of Socrates gave no encouragement – though history tells us that none of them followed a more self-denying path than he walked in. As their doctrines will show, Zeno and his disciples vigorously maintained that there was One Infinite and Eternal God.

---

[441] Penn has noted the following in the margin:

Exod. 15:11. ["Who *is* like unto thee, O LORD, among the gods? who *is* like thee, glorious in holiness, fearful *in* praises, doing wonders?"]

Ps. 136:4-6. ["To him who alone doeth great wonders: for his mercy *endureth* for ever. To him that by wisdom made the heavens: for his mercy *endureth* for ever. To him that stretched out the earth above the waters: for his mercy *endureth* for ever."]

[442] Parmenides (c. 515-c. 450 B.C.) was a Greek philosopher who believed that true being and knowledge, which are discovered by the intellect, must be distinguished from appearance and opinion, which are based on the senses. He held that there is an eternal One, who is timeless, motionless, and changeless.

[443] Isa. 41:4: "Who hath wrought and done *it*, calling the generations from the beginning? I the LORD, the first, and with the last; I *am* he."

Penn has also noted the following in the margin:

Ps. 93:2. ["Thy throne *is* established of old: thou *art* from everlasting."]

Isa. 26:4. ["Trust ye in the LORD for ever: for in the Lord Jehovah *is* everlasting strength."]

[444] Zeno of Elea (c. 495 B.C.-c. 430 B.C.) was a Greek philosopher and logician. Aristotle called him the inventor of dialectic. He is especially known for his paradoxes which contributed to the development of logical and mathematical rigor and which were insoluble until the development of precise concepts of continuity and infinity.

Zeno tells us, "God is an immortal Being – rational, perfect, and intelligent; void of all evil; watching over the whole world and all things in the world. God is not of human form, but is the maker of all and Father of all" and "God and the Power of God governs all things and is governed by nothing and by no one. If anything was better in any way, then God could not be God."[445]

This was Zeno's faith in God and I cannot believe that even our worst opponent has so completely abandoned reason as to call it false or idolatrous. Proof that he taught it, as well as thought it, is provided by his followers.

XV.   Chrysippus,[446] a Stoic, also declares that he believes that, "the world was made by God" – from which, we can see that he believed that

---

[445] Penn has noted the following in the margin:

1 Tim. 1:17. ["Now unto the King eternal, immortal, invisible, the only wise God, *be* honour and glory for ever and ever. Amen."]

Prov. 22:2. ["The rich and poor meet together: the LORD *is* the maker of them all."]

Isa. 1:18. ["Come now, and let us reason together, saith the LORD: though your sins be as scarlet, they shall be as white as snow; though they be red like crimson, they shall be as wool."]

Lev. 11:44. ["For I *am* the LORD your God: ye shall therefore sanctify yourselves, and ye shall be holy; for I *am* holy: neither shall ye defile yourselves with any manner of creeping thing that creepeth upon the earth."]

Eph. 4:6. ["One God and Father of all, who *is* above all, and through all, and in you all."]

1 Cor. 8:6. ["But to us *there is but* one God, the Father, of whom *are* all things, and we in him; and one Lord Jesus Christ, by whom *are* all things, and we by him."]

Exod. 15:11. ["Who *is* like unto thee, O LORD, among the gods? who *is* like thee, glorious in holiness, fearful *in* praises, doing wonders?"]

Job 37:23. ["*Touching* the Almighty, we cannot find him out: *he is* excellent in power, and in judgment, and in plenty of justice: he will not afflict."]

Ps. 103:19. ["The LORD hath prepared his throne in the heavens; and his kingdom ruleth over all."]

[446] Chrysippus (c. 280-c. 206 B.C.) was a Greek philosopher from Soli. He systematized Stoic philosophy, and with Zeno co-founded the Athenian Stoa Academy. He is credited with about 750 writings and was among the first to organize propositional logic as an intellectual discipline.

there was one. "If there is anything that can create beings that humans, with all their understanding, cannot," he wrote, "that thing is necessarily stronger, greater, and wiser. But no person can make the heavens, and therefore, whatever made them surpasses humanity in art, wisdom, discernment, and power. What can that be, but God?"[447]

XVI.   Antipater,[448] a famous, serious, and shrewd Stoic, in his Discourse of God and the World, makes the following declaration, "We understand that what we call God is an intelligent and wise Spirit, a Living Nature or Divine Substance, blessed and incorruptible, doing good for mankind, present throughout the whole world, and called by many different names due to the diversity of appearances, variety of works, and multiplicity of effects with which the Divine Power is experienced."[449] Such a gospel definition may very well lead us to believe that he was a person who knew

---

[447] Penn has noted the following in the margin:

Acts 4:24. ["And when they heard that, they lifted up their voice to God with one accord, and said, Lord, thou *art* God, which hast made heaven, and earth, and the sea, and all that in them is."]

Ps. 90:2. ["Before the mountains were brought forth, or ever thou hadst formed the earth and the world, even from everlasting to everlasting, thou *art* God."]

Isa. 40:15. ["Behold, the nations *are* as a drop of a bucket, and are counted as the small dust of the balance: behold, he taketh up the isles as a very little thing."]

[448] Antipater of Tarsus (second century B.C.) was a Stoic philosopher.

[449] Penn has noted the following in the margin:

John 4:24. ["God *is* a Spirit: and they that worship him must worship *him* in spirit and in truth."]

Col. 2:3. ["In whom are hid all the treasures of wisdom and knowledge."]

Rom. 1:23. ["And changed the glory of the uncorruptible God into an image made like to corruptible man, and to birds, and fourfooted beasts, and creeping things."]

Ps. 145:9. ["The LORD *is* good to all: and his tender mercies *are* over all his works."]

Acts 17:27. ["That they should seek the Lord, if haply they might feel after him, and find him, though he be not far from every one of us."]

God, but not, we hope, one of those who "although they knew God, did not glorify him as God."[450]

Looking at all that we have quoted here, it can truly be called an account of divinity – no less because these are all written by Gentiles, since God is also present among them and can be admired by them. Their assertions, and the reasons they offer for them, are so forceful, so true, and so plainly evident – how could anyone continue to believe that there was not a share of the Eternal Fullness of all Divine Light shining in the hearts of these heathens, giving them some knowledge of the glory of the only true and invisible God? After all their declarations for and claims of Christianity, such a disbelief would reasonably lead others to call them utter Pharisees, overcast by the darkest clouds of envy and uncharitableness. For myself, I am of the opinion that many thousands of so-called Christians (and I do not mean the common people), do not so clearly believe in God nor are they able to give better reasons for what they believe, than do these Gentiles.

So much for those Gentile writings that concern God, creation, and divine providence.

---

[450] Rom. 1:21: "Because that, when they knew God, they glorified *him* not as God, neither were thankful; but became vain in their imaginations, and their foolish heart was darkened."

Chapter VIII

The Gentile belief that knowledge of God has been implanted in the minds of all.

It is now appropriate to tell what the Gentiles believe with respect to how and where God is revealed to humanity. In short, I will be addressing my second assertion, i.e., that knowledge of God is implanted in the minds of all. In other words, God has revealed himself to mankind by enlightening the soul with a Divine Light that, when it is obeyed, leads to blessedness. From the following very simple, yet vital expressions of belief, you can see for yourself whether or not this was their doctrine and the source of their knowledge of God.

I.   Pythagoras (and his disciples) say, "The mind sees only the Eternal God, the Ruler and Father of all things. What greater pleasure is there than to behold the serene face of God? No one knows what is agreeable to God, unless he or she hears God directly." They urged each other "not to separate themselves from God within themselves, but to care for and preserve their unity with God and with one another." Timaeus, one of the most careful members of that school, said, "The greatest thing to which the soul can attend is its guide or good genius[451] (that is to say, to its share of the Divine Light or Spirit). If the soul rebels against it, it will become her daemon or tormentor" and "But having overcome these things," said Pythagoras about evil, "you will know the union of immortal God and mortal humanity. The work of mortals is life; the work of God is eternal life and immortality."[452]

---

[451] In classical pagan belief, a 'genius' was a god or spirit assigned to each person at birth, to watch over and guide them, and at death to lead them out of the world. It is similar in some ways to a guardian angel.

[452] Penn has noted the following in the margin:

Matt. 5:8. ["Blessed *are* the pure in heart: for they shall see God."]

1 Tim. 6:16. ["Who only hath immortality, dwelling in the light which no man can approach unto; whom no man hath seen, nor can see: to whom *be* honour and power everlasting. Amen."]

Ps. 27:4. ["One *thing* have I desired of the LORD, that will I seek after; that I may dwell in the house of the LORD all the days of my life, to behold the beauty of the LORD, and to enquire in his temple."]

These Pythagorean writings are certainly enough to prove my claim. What spiritual intimacy or union is greater than to directly hear and see God, dwelling in the temple of his people?[453] Oh! The foolishness and uncharitableness of those so-called Christians! They exclude both such people and such knowledge of the kingdom of God because it was not delivered in the exact words of Scripture – although it conveys nearly the same message regarding divine vision, union with God, and eternal life! I wish they did not confuse imagination with knowledge, and speculation with understanding.

II.   Hieron,[454] an ancient philosopher, acknowledged the universal Light shining in the conscience and witnessing against evil, which, if obeyed, led all to immortality. He called this, "a domestic God, or God within the hearts and souls of all" and "The Eternal Mind is God, revealed within each individual. God is that which allows mortals to know about God directly."[455]

---

1 Cor. 2:10-11. ["But God hath revealed *them* unto us by his Spirit: for the Spirit searcheth all things, yea, the deep things of God. For what man knoweth the things of a man, save the spirit of man which is in him? even so the things of God knoweth no man, but the Spirit of God."]

2 Cor. 6:16. ["And what agreement hath the temple of God with idols? for ye are the temple of the living God; as God hath said, I will dwell in them, and walk in *them*; and I will be their God, and they shall be my people."]

1 Cor. 1:13. ["Is Christ divided? was Paul crucified for you? or were ye baptized in the name of Paul?"]

Rev. 21:3&7. ["And I heard a great voice out of heaven saying, Behold, the tabernacle of God *is* with men, and he will dwell with them, and they shall be his people, and God himself shall be with them, *and be* their God. ... He that overcometh shall inherit all things; and I will be his God, and he shall be my son."]

[453] 1 Cor. 3:16: "Know ye not that ye are the temple of God, and *that* the Spirit of God dwelleth in you?"

[454] This may be Hero (or Heron) of Alexandria, a first century A.D. mathematician and engineer.

[455] Penn has noted the following in the margin:

John 1:1. ["In the beginning was the Word, and the Word was with God, and the Word was God."]

Rom. 10:8. ["But what saith it? The word is nigh thee, *even* in thy mouth, and in thy heart: that is, the word of faith, which we preach."]

Certainly these Gentiles thought highly of that Light that revealed the darkness, making it their rule and guide – their domestic God. They did not see God as distant from them, but believed in God the Word who addressed them from within their own consciences.

III. Bias[456] was a prince of Priene. When that city was besieged by the Persians, some of the citizens gathered up their valuables and fled. Asked why he wasn't carrying his most prized possessions, Bias replied, "I have my riches with me." Valerius Maximus[457] explains, "He carried these in his heart, unseen by their eyes, but prized by the soul. They were enclosed within the bounds of his mind and not subject to destruction by mortal hands. This is what always remains with those who stay and is never deserted or abandoned by those who flee." Certainly, they held that this divine principle was the greatest treasure, the truest companion, and the best comforter – the soul's only refuge in the face of extreme danger, granting it piety, patience, and the contentment that lets it wade though the deepest disasters.

IV. Sophocles[458] also attests to the divine illumination. "May God grant that I always happily observe in my words and deeds the venerable sanctity of these noble laws which were made in heaven (meaning the laws

---

Isa. 57:15. ["For thus saith the high and lofty One that inhabiteth eternity, whose name *is* Holy; I dwell in the high and holy *place*, with him also *that is* of a contrite and humble spirit, to revive the spirit of the humble, and to revive the heart of the contrite ones."]

2 Cor. 6:16. ["And what agreement hath the temple of God with idols? for ye are the temple of the living God; as God hath said, I will dwell in them, and walk in *them*; and I will be their God, and they shall be my people."]

Rom. 1:19. ["Because that which may be known of God is manifest in them; for God hath shewed *it* unto them."]

456 Priene, an ancient Greek city in Ionia, was the birthplace of Bias (c. 600-c. 540 B.C.), listed by Diogenes as one of the seven sages of antiquity. Famous pronouncements of his include, "Not to be able to participate in misfortune is the greatest catastrophe." "Begin slowly but continue with vigor." "Action makes the man."

457 Valerius Maximus was a first century A.D. Roman historian and moralist who wrote a book of historical anecdotes.

458 Sophocles (496-406 B.C.) was, with Aeschylus and Euripides, one of classical Athens' three great tragic playwrights. The best known of his 123 dramas is *Oedipus Rex*.

written in the conscience). God, not mortals, is their author. They will never be forgotten or repealed, because they are the work of a great God who never grows old."[459] "This is a divine, sacred good – God keeping watch in the conscience." Surely, these are in themselves angelic sayings, showing a clear faith in God and in the inward revelations of God to mankind. Remember, too, that Sophocles said, "Truly there is only One God, who made the heavens and the earth."

V.   It has frequently been said of Socrates that, "he had the guide to his life within him. His father, Sophroniscus, was told that this would be worth more to him than five hundred master teachers. He called it his good angel or Spirit that inwardly suggested what was good and virtuous, inclining and disposing him to live a strict and pious life. It gave him divine knowledge, and very often impelled him to preach to the people in the streets – sometimes to severely criticize them, sometimes to inform them, and other times to gently persuade them to give up intemperance and vanity. In particular, he urged them to give up seeing plays and to take up self-denial, repentance, and reform if they hoped for immortality."[460]

VI.   Plato likewise casts his vote in favor of our claims and on behalf of the Gentiles. "The Light and Spirit of God are like wings for the

---

[459] Penn has noted the following in the margin:

Rom. 2:27-28. ["And shall not uncircumcision which is by nature, if it fulfil the law, judge thee, who by the letter and circumcision dost transgress the law? For he is not a Jew, which is one outwardly; neither *is that* circumcision, which is outward in the flesh."]

Isa. 40:8. ["The grass withereth, the flower fadeth: but the word of our God shall stand for ever."]

[460] Penn has noted the following in the margin:

Job 32:8. ["But *there is* a spirit in man: and the inspiration of the Almighty giveth them understanding."]

2 Tim. 2:22&25. ["Flee also youthful lusts: but follow righteousness, faith, charity, peace, with them that call on the Lord out of a pure heart. ... In meekness instructing those that oppose themselves; if God peradventure will give them repentance to the acknowledging of the truth."]

Rom. 8:14. ["For as many as are led by the Spirit of God, they are the sons of God."]

soul, raising it up into distinct union with God above that world in which our sluggish mortal minds become mired."[461]

Plotin,[462] a famous Platonist, adds, "God is the ultimate root or life of the soul" and "Humanity has a divine principle within, which makes a person true and good." [463] The Platonists in general held that there were three principles within each person. The first they called mind, intellect, spirit, or Divine Light; the second was the soul; and the third, the soul's image. "This," they said, "is the soul's vital energy on the body and its feminine power."

---

[461] Penn has noted the following in the margin:

Aratus [a Greek poet and Stoic, c. 315-c. 245 B.C.] was one of those quoted by Paul in Acts 17:28 [taken from the opening invocation to Zeus in Aratus's *Phaenomena*]. Paul described this as truth and uses it against his Athenian opponents to prove the existence of a true God and to introduce his gospel. If this shows his opponents' apostasy, it also implies that heathens rightly knew God – otherwise the apostle would certainly not have cited it as confirmation of his own doctrines.

John 1:5. ["And the light shineth in darkness; and the darkness comprehended it not."]

Ps. 36:9. ["For with thee *is* the fountain of life: in thy light shall we see light."]

Acts 17:27-28. ["That they should seek the Lord, if haply they might feel after him, and find him, though he be not far from every one of us: For in him we live, and move, and have our being; as certain also of your own poets have said, For we are also his offspring."]

[462] Plotinus (205-270), a Greek philosopher, was born in Egypt and lived in Rome. He was the founder of the Neoplatonic school of philosophy.

[463] Penn has noted the following in the margin:

John 16:13. ["Howbeit when he, the Spirit of truth, is come, he will guide you into all truth: for he shall not speak of himself; but whatsoever he shall hear, *that* shall he speak: and he will shew you things to come."]

Titus 2:11-12. ["For the grace of God that bringeth salvation hath appeared to all men, Teaching us that, denying ungodliness and worldly lusts, we should live soberly, righteously, and godly, in this present world."]

Mic. 6:8. ["He hath shewed thee, O man, what *is* good; and what doth the LORD require of thee, but to do justly, and to love mercy, and to walk humbly with thy God?"]

VII.   Cleanthes[464] the Stoic states "that mankind is not rightly governed by the dictates of its own nature – which barely renders people human – but by that Divine, Infinite, and Eternal Nature, which is God universally diffused or sown within the whole of humanity as a true and infallible guide and rule." He also states, "To live according to this knowledge and direction is truly to live virtuously – not doing anything that is forbidden. Human virtue and happiness depends on the close correspondence of the mortal mind with the divine will of the one who governs the universe" and "The knowledge of God is implanted in the minds of all."[465]

VIII.   Menander,[466] in demonstrating that God is good, says, "At birth, everyone is given a good spirit – a holy instructor for governing their life. Any spirit that harms a good person is evil. ... A good God is in all – perfect in goodness and good in all." On another occasion, he says, "God, who is always near, sees this; for God is not a God far away." [467]

IX.   Philo[468] (who was not a Gentile, but a Jew), a very refined and serious philosopher, gives his judgment positively and in support of our argument: "How could a human soul know God," he asks, "if God did not

---

[464] Cleanthes (331 B.C.-232 B.C.) became head of the Stoic school after the death of Zeno. Among his pupils was his successor, Chrysippus. Although Cleanthes produced little that is original, he brought a religious fervour to the teachings of Zeno, stressing the belief that the universe is a living entity and that God is the enlivening spirit of the universe. He wrote about fifty works, of which only fragments survive, the most important being his hymn to Zeus.

[465] Penn has noted Rom. 2:15 ["Which shew the work of the law written in their hearts, their conscience also bearing witness, and *their* thoughts the mean while accusing or else excusing one another"] in the margin.

[466] Menander (c. 342-c. 292 B.C.) was an Athenian comic playwright, famed for his realistic portrayal of situations and characters.

[467] Penn has noted the following in the margin:

1 Cor. 12:7. ["But the manifestation of the Spirit is given to every man to profit withal."]

Ps. 145:9. ["The LORD *is* good to all: and his tender mercies *are* over all his works."]

[468] Philo Judaeus (c. 20 B.C.-c. 45 A.D.), also known as Philo of Alexandria, was a Greek-speaking Jewish philosopher. His writings provide the clearest view of the development of Judaism in the Diaspora. He attempted to synthesize revealed faith and philosophic reason.

inspire it and, by divine power, take hold of it?" Again, he says, "The Divine Reason that we have received from God is an infallible law, not a mortal rule created by this or that mortal person. These are not lifeless instructions, written on pieces of paper, or chiseled on pillars, but immortal precepts, engraved by the Eternal Nature on the minds of all."[469] This is undeniable testimony that the law written in the heart is a more perfect teaching than any written on paper or carved in stone.

X.   Nor does Plutarch[470] fail to support this claim on behalf of the Gentiles. Writing about the principle of God in the conscience, he writes, "It is a law not written in books or on tablets, but dwelling in the mind – an ever-living rule, that never leaves the soul without an inward guide." Elsewhere, "To deny mankind's ancient faith – the natural belief planted in all thinking souls – is to overthrow the strong and everlasting foundation of virtue."[471] This is undoubtedly a very strong and sensible argument for an inward divine principle.

---

[469] Penn has noted the following in the margin:

　　1 Cor. 2:11. ["For what man knoweth the things of a man, save the spirit of man which is in him? even so the things of God knoweth no man, but the Spirit of God."]

　　Heb. 8:10-11. ["For this *is* the covenant that I will make with the house of Israel after those days, saith the Lord; I will put my laws into their mind, and write them in their hearts: and I will be to them a God, and they shall be to me a people: And they shall not teach every man his neighbour, and every man his brother, saying, Know the Lord: for all shall know me, from the least to the greatest."]

[470] Plutarch (c. 46-c. 120), a Greek biographer, historian, essayist, and moralist, has been described as one of the most influential writers who ever lived. Among his approximately 227 works, the most important are *Lives*, on Greek and Roman soldiers, legislators, orators, and statesmen, and the *Moralia* (or *Ethica*) a series of more than sixty essays on ethical, religious, physical, political, and literary topics.

[471] Penn has noted Rom. 1:19, 28, 26 ["Because that which may be known of God is manifest in them; for God hath shewed *it* unto them. ...And even as they did not like to retain God in *their* knowledge, God gave them over to a reprobate mind, to do those things which are not convenient ... For this cause God gave them up unto vile affections: for even their women did change the natural use into that which is against nature"] in the margin.

XI.   Epictetus,[472] was admired for his great virtue and way of living. His memory is greatly respected and preserved by many who call themselves Christians. Listen to what he says about this matter: "When you have shut your gates and made it all dark within – that is to say, when you have withdrawn alone into your own home – do not say that you are alone. You are not alone, God is within." His meaning is made clear in the following words. "What need is there for an outward light to reveal what has been done or to guide people to take good actions? All have God, the Divine Principle or Genius, as their Light."[473]

XII.   But, above all the Gentiles that have been mentioned – at least in terms of plain and positive words (because I prefer the exemplary life of the self-denying martyr, Socrates) – let us give greatest attention to the lectures of Seneca[474] on this subject. Truly, these are things of great importance. "The majority is the worst argument." He says, "To gain everlasting happiness, ask what is the best thing to be done, not what happens most often. Do not rely on the most common (and worst) interpreters of truth. I have a clearer and more certain Light by which I can distinguish truth from falsehood. The Eternal Mind directs us to those things that are most needed for the ultimate happiness of the soul." Undoubtedly, Seneca meant the Light within. Again, he says, "It is foolish for you to wish for what you cannot obtain. God is near you and in you. The Holy Spirit sits or lives within us, observing our good and evil acts. As we deal with God, God will deal with us." And, yet further, "We have this great gift. Virtue (meaning the Principle of Virtue or God) has sent her Light into the minds of all. Even those who do not follow her can see her."[475] Observe, Reader, how he attests to the universality of the Light and

---

[472] Epictetus (c. 50-c. 135) was a Greek Stoic philosopher who believed that people should concern themselves only with what they can control and accept what they cannot change.

[473] Penn has noted Ps. 139:1-2, 7 ["O LORD, thou hast searched me, and known *me*. Thou knowest my downsitting and mine uprising, thou understandest my thought afar off. ... Whither shall I go from thy spirit? or whither shall I flee from thy presence?"] in the margin.

[474] Lucius Annaeus Seneca, known as Seneca the Younger (c. 4 B.C.-65 A.D.) was a Roman philosopher, statesman, orator, and tragedian. He was the tutor of the emperor Nero and played a major role in governing the Roman Empire during the first eight years of Nero's reign.

[475] Penn has noted the following in the margin:

where he lays the blame for rebellion against it – not on the Light, as our enemies do, but on those who refuse to follow it. In rebelling, they voluntarily reject its heavenly revelations. Again, Seneca says, "Do you wonder that people go to God? God comes to them – no, nearer still – God comes into them. God dwells in the heart of every good person." Listen yet again, "Nothing is hidden from God. God is within our souls and comes into the midst of our thoughts." And last, "God has endowed everyone with something – if they do not forsake it, they will arise like God."[476]

How much more significant, sober and impartial Reader, are these inward doctrines of the virtuous Gentiles than the heated clamoring and uncharitable cries that empty Christians make against them? It seems they are afraid of nothing more than inherent holiness, even if it is the product

---

2 Pet. 1:19. ["We have also a more sure word of prophecy; whereunto ye do well that ye take heed, as unto a light that shineth in a dark place, until the day dawn, and the day star arise in your hearts."]

Mic. 6:8. ["He hath shewed thee, O man, what *is* good; and what doth the LORD require of thee, but to do justly, and to love mercy, and to walk humbly with thy God?"]

Acts 17:28. ["For in him we live, and move, and have our being; as certain also of your own poets have said, For we are also his offspring."]

Gal. 6:7. ["Be not deceived; God is not mocked: for whatsoever a man soweth, that shall he also reap."]

John 1:9. ["*That* was the true Light, which lighteth every man that cometh into the world."]

[476] Penn has noted the following in the margin:

Rev. 21:3. ["And I heard a great voice out of heaven saying, Behold, the tabernacle of God *is* with men, and he will dwell with them, and they shall be his people, and God himself shall be with them, *and be* their God."]

Amos 4:13. ["For, lo, he that formeth the mountains, and createth the wind, and declareth unto man what *is* his thought, that maketh the morning darkness, and treadeth upon the high places of the earth, The LORD, The God of hosts, *is* his name."]

John 12:36. ["While ye have light, believe in the light, that ye may be the children of light. These things spake Jesus, and departed, and did hide himself from them."]

1 John 1:5. ["This then is the message which we have heard of him, and declare unto you, that God is light, and in him is no darkness at all."]

of Christ's work. They claim that it undervalues Christ's blood when we experience the true (I mean the *inward*) benefit of it. They call us terrible heretics for agreeing with this greatest truth – that Christ's universal Light in the hearts of all is sufficient to lead them to salvation. They challenge us to prove it by Scripture or show it in any credible history. They claim that the heathens' ignorance and idolatry are stronger than the truth of the Light's revelations and the effectiveness of the Light's power. Against that, the Gentiles themselves provide our defense and, in so doing, demonstrate its power and universality.

Chapter IX

The earliest Christian writers knew and wrote that this was the doctrine and faith of the Gentiles.

*A*s I have shown, the Gentiles believed in One God and had a very clear understanding of the Light, or Divine Principle, that is implanted within each person and from which all heavenly knowledge is gained. They identified this Divine Light or Spirit or Principle as their most certain guide and an infallible rule of faith and practice. Further, I have shown that the Scriptures provide abundant confirmation of their doctrines. So that those angry people I have mentioned will not consider this to be disrespectful of the holy writ, or think I am the only person that ever had a favorable view of these Gentile doctrines, I will provide examples from the writings of some of the earliest and most widely approved fathers of the Christian Church. By briefly examining what they wrote, in their own words, we may more clearly see how they viewed these Gentiles. Indeed, we will see that they did not find them guilty of either faulty judgment or inaccuracy. If it is possible to do so, this may clear away their objections to the universality and sufficiency of this blessed Light.

I.   Justin Martyr,[477] whom I choose to begin with, earned his surname for his faithfulness when faced with martyrdom. He became an honest Christian after being trained as a philosopher. As a result, he is in an excellent position to tell us the difference between them. He shows no signs of repudiating the principle of God being within us as inconsistent with the purity of the Christian religion. He earnestly opposes any use of coercive

---

[477] Justin Martyr (c. 100-c. 165) was the first Christian apologist of non-Jewish heritage whose writings have survived. In these, he attempted to reconcile Christian revelation and Greek philosophy.

force on matters of conscience and condemns the heathens' ostentatious worship in their temples. As his *Apology* informs us, "God has built a natural temple in the consciences of all people, as the place in which we should worship. It is there that people ought to look for God's appearance and there they should adore and worship God."

II.   Clement of Alexandria, an earnest opponent of the apostate Gentiles, plainly agrees with this. More to the point, in a few examples offered below, he recommends that we look to the Light or Word within. "The voice of truth tells us that Light will shine out of darkness. It, therefore, shines within the hidden part of each person, that is, in the heart. Its rays of knowledge break forth, shining on and making visible each one's hidden, inward parts. Christ's most intimate friends and co-heirs are the disciples of Light."

Elsewhere, he adds, "Humanity cannot be void of divine knowledge. Each, coming into the world, naturally breathes in divine inspiration and therefore has a purer essence or nature than any other animal."

He frequently confirmed the truth of the doctrine of the Divine Light within as the companion of all our good works by using the works of ancient philosophers and other Gentiles (in responding to the Gentiles of his own time, he draws on no less than two hundred and fifty authors). One passage demonstrates this exceptionally well, "I earnestly encourage you, because I want you to be saved – as would Christ who offers you Life in one Word. You may ask, 'What is that word?' It is the Word of Truth, the incorruptible Word that regenerates mankind and leads all back to Truth. It is the spur that goads us toward salvation, banishes destruction, chases away death, and has built a temple in mankind, placing God within each person."

I do not know of any of the ancients who better understood the doctrines of the Gentiles than Clement of Alexandria. To prove the truth of the Christian religion to them, he frequently quoted the most respected Gentile writings. He accurately drew on the books of their most-admired ancestors to demonstrate the virtuousness and perfect goodness of Christianity and to show that their opposition to it was unreasonable. In this, he was imitating Christ, who proved himself the Messiah according to the Scriptures and, in so doing, exposing the hypocrisy of those who only pretended to believe in them.

III.   No one was sharper in attacking the depraved Gentiles of those times than Tertullian.[478] His careful and ingenious *Apology for the Christians* is a severe charge against their enemies. But in it, he says that it is neither heresy nor heathenism to believe and declare "that a life lived according to the holy guidings of the Universal Light in the conscience is a kind of natural Christianity – that is to say, to be a Christian by nature."

In his *Apology*, he uses his sharpest barbs of wit, reason, and truth to stab at the cause of degenerate philosophy and at those who do not deserve the title of philosopher. But he lays the greatest blame on their falling away from the noble principles that were so admirably held by their predecessors. Like the Pharisees among the Jews, they vainly believed that being their descendents and assuming their titles was sufficient to convert their pretenses into real science.

IV.   Origen[479] was twice a Christian – first by education and next, by choice. He was a strong defender of the faith, as his notable books against Celsus[480] and others abundantly prove. He calls the Divine Light with which God has illuminated all people a universal gift, calling it, "an immutable law, which, with the knowledge of good and evil, is written on the heart and grafted into the soul of all."

V.   Lactantius[481] was a student of Arnobius[482] (who wrote sharp criticisms of the apostate Gentiles). This good and perceptive man wrote, "The Light of God's law that has been made known to us is like the stars to

---

[478] Quintus Septimus Florens Tertullianus (c. 155-c. 245), an important early Christian theologian, polemicist, and moralist, was first major Christian writer to write in Latin rather than Greek. His work tends to be legalistic – a tendency that is carried on in Latin Christian writings.

[479] Oregenes Adamantius (185-254) was the most important theologian and biblical scholar of the early Greek church. His greatest work is the *Hexapla*, which is a synopsis of six versions of the Old Testament.

[480] Celsus the Platonist (second century A.D.) wrote *The True Word* or *The True Discourse*, an attack on Christian religion. Origen responded to this work.

[481] Lucius Caecilius Firmianus Lactantius (240-c. 320) was a Christian apologist and one of the most reprinted of the Latin Church Fathers. His *Divinae Institutiones* is a philosophical refutation of early-fourth-century anti-Christian tracts. It was the first systematic Latin account of the Christian attitude toward life.

[482] Arnobius the Elder, whose writings date to the early fourth century, was a Christian convert who defended Christianity by demonstrating to the pagans their own inconsistencies.

the sailor at night, clearly pointing out the path of wisdom. That law is pure and spotless reason – not inconsistent with nor unknowable by nature – which is spread over the whole world. It is unchangeable and eternal. By its commands and prohibitions, it faithfully shows all their duty and directs them away from wrongdoing. Elsewhere, he writes, "The way to ascend up to the House of Truth is to see within ourselves that there is one most high God who made and governs all things. Christ is God's builder and ambassador to mankind. As they receive him into their hearts, he builds a divine and immortal temple in them."

VI.   Let us carefully read what the greatly admired Athanasius[483] says to those Gentiles who frequently (and often vulgarly) posed the question, "How can you know that yours is the right way?" – A question Quakers are asked today.

"The way to gain knowledge of God is within us. Moses proved this, saying, 'The word of God is in your hearts.'[484] And Christ said, 'The faith and kingdom of God is within you.'[485] "If the kingdom of God is within us," Athanasius says, "then that is how we are able to understand the word or voice of God."

This solid, ancient, and great truth could only greatly increase the guilt of those who denied it, because it was simply the doctrine of their own renowned philosophers, although more clearly and scripturally expressed. It was on that basis that Christians believed and practiced their religion – not from tradition, however revered – but on inward assurance and revelation. No outward words guided them, only that great interpreter of the will and way of God – the eternal Word of God in their hearts. The souls of those who know that this Word or divine principle is reigning in their hearts have been sanctified. In them, the kingdom of God has come, and God's will is done.

---

[483] Athanasius (c. 296-373), a Christian theologian, was bishop of Alexandria, in Egypt. He was the most prominent opponent of Arianism, the heresy that Jesus, while the Son of God, was a creature composed of a similar, but not an identical, substance as God the Father.

[484] Deut. 30:14: "But the word *is* very nigh unto thee, in thy mouth, and in thy heart, that thou mayest do it."

[485] Luke 17:21: "Neither shall they say, Lo here! or, lo there! for, behold, the kingdom of God is within you."

VII.   Chrysostom[486] also honors this Holy Light. He not only declares that the Light in the first chapter of John's gospel is Christ, the Word-God who enlightens all who come into the world, but also proclaims that it can save all who believe in it and follow it. "Let no one who is not saved blame the Light, but their own rebellion." This, he solemnly calls, "A teacher or instructor, dwelling within our nature, so that all have a teacher to instruct, inspire, help, and assist them in the way that leads to eternal life."

I will conclude these Christian testimonies with a passage from Augustine.

VIII.   Augustine of Hippo[487] writes this notable example in his sermon on John: "God is by right the king of minds or souls[488] because, when taken in, God governs by divine power and spirit in the heart. Therefore, God's kingdom is not in the outward world, but within."

He clearly distinguishes between different qualities of reason: "There is a superior and an inferior reason. The inferior is that of a mere rational creature – the understanding that distinguishes humans from other creatures. The superior reason is a Light, a power within each person that dictates, reveals, and shows the way to divine, eternal, and entirely good things. For example, it will say of a thing, 'This is sin. Do not do it.' And if asked 'Why?' replies, 'Because it offends God.'"

I have quoted from primitive Christians who lived from about one hundred to four hundred years after Christ to illustrate the aspects of the Gentiles' understanding of divinity that are perhaps the most difficult to accept. It might seem to be a waste of time to quote so many early

---

[486] John Chrysostom (347-407) was a Father of the Eastern Church and Patriarch of Constantinople. His uncompromising reforms brought him into conflict with Byzantine authorities and led to his exile. The zeal and clarity of his preaching, which appealed especially to the common people, earned him the surname meaning "golden-mouthed."

[487] Augustine of Hippo (354-430), Christian philosopher and theologian, claimed that human knowledge would be impossible if God did not illumine the human mind and thereby allow it to see, grasp, or understand ideas. He is best known for *Confessions* and *City of God*. After the authors of the New Testament, he has probably been the most influential Christian writer.

[488] In the seventeenth century, the mind was considered to be a property of the soul, not of the brain.

Christians to prove the existence of God, the need for a holy life, or the immortality of the soul. Certainly, no one would doubt that they accepted such general truths. What is amazing (to some) is to hear language so similar to that of the unfairly condemned and abused Quakers – not only coming from the mouths of the best of the Gentiles, but also from the most highly respected primitive Christians. They speak of the Divine Light, Principle, Word, or Spirit within each person, whose inspiration provides infallible understanding. As people are guided by it, they are pulled up from the dirt and mire into which sin has plunged them. It frees them from the snares of earthly pleasures, enlightens their eyes, inspires their souls, and leads them gently by the hand into the way of eternal righteousness. Their reward from God will be immortal and eternal life.

Chapter X

The Gentiles lived virtuous lives and taught that this was indispensable for those who desired eternal life.

*I*t may now be time for me to address the other two parts of the Gentile understanding of God. I will try to be brief.

There are numerous instances of their pious doctrine and remarkable examples of their virtue. I will list only a few to convince, if I can, those who find it hard to believe that there is any good in them (and, I fear, that blame the Light for any examples of evil). I will show that their doctrines and practices, with respect to living uprightly, were and are very commendable and deserve to be approved by all good Christians.

I.   Pittacus of Mytilene[489] was known as one of the Seven Wise Men of ancient Greece. Among his maxims are:

"Do not do yourself what you call wicked in your neighbor. Do not criticize the unhappy; the hand of God is on them. Return what you have been given to hold in trust. Be patient with your neighbor. Love your neighbor. Do not scold a friend if you drift apart. Acquire honesty. Serve

---

[489] Pittacus of Mytilene (c. 650-c. 570), a statesman and sage, participated in the overthrow of the tyrant Melanchrus and was the commander for Sigium in a war with Athens. He was selected as dictator by the Mytileneans in about 590 B.C. and served in that post for ten years. Diogenes Laërtius quotes a number of sayings ascribed to him, five lines of lyric verse, and a spurious letter to Croesus.

others eagerly. Love discipline, temperance, prudence, truth, faith, experience, dexterity, friendliness, diligence, economy, and piety."[490]

II.   Chilon,[491] another of the Seven Wise Men, was so just in all his actions, that in his old age, he claimed that "he had never done anything contrary to anyone's conscience, although there was one instance about which he was doubtful. Having, according to the law, pronounced sentence on a friend, he advised that friend to appeal the judgment in order to preserve both his friendship and the integrity of the law." As Agellius[492] tells it, "When his life drew near to an end and he was ready to be taken by death, he spoke to the friends gathered around him, 'I have no need to repent for nearly any of the words or actions of my many years, as you may know. Truly, even at this moment, I am certain that I never done anything that troubles me in the least – except for one thing. I am not certain whether or not I was wrong. I was part of a three-judge panel in a capital case involving a friend. According to the law, my friend was guilty and must be condemned. It seemed either my friend would die or the law must be abused. Many things passed through my mind as I searched for a way out of this desperate situation. What I chose was the way that was easiest for me to bear. Silently, I condemned him, while persuading the other judges to absolve him. Thus, I was able to remain faithful to my duty both as a friend and as a judge. But, this action troubles me and I fear that it was deceitful. It seems dishonest in the same business, at the same time, and in a public

---

[490] Penn has noted the following in the margin:

Rom. 2:21. ["Thou therefore which teachest another, teachest thou not thyself? thou that preachest a man should not steal, dost thou steal?"]

Lev. 19:18. ["Thou shalt not avenge, nor bear any grudge against the children of thy people, but thou shalt love thy neighbour as thyself: I *am* the LORD."]

Phil. 4:8. ["Finally, brethren, whatsoever things are true, whatsoever things *are* honest, whatsoever things *are* just, whatsoever things *are* pure, whatsoever things *are* lovely, whatsoever things *are* of good report; if *there be* any virtue, and if *there be* any praise, think on these things."]

[491] Chilon (sixth century B.C.), the most famous of the ephor or magistrates of Sparta, was one of the Seven Wise Men of Greece.

[492] Aulus Gellius (second century A.D.) wrote *Noctes Atticae*, a collection of discussions of law, antiquities, and sundry other subjects in twenty books (of which nineteen and a fraction survive). The work is chiefly valuable as a storehouse of quotations from lost works.

affair, to persuade others to act contrary to what I believed was right.'"[493] Undoubtedly, this was a man of Light, insight, and conscience.

Of his maxims or sayings, only a few have been preserved by Diogenes Laertius:[494] "Foresight is the most human virtue."[495] When asked, "How do the learned differ from the ignorant?" He answered, "In being hopeful." When asked, "What is hard?" He replied, "To conceal secrets, to spend leisure time well, and to accept an injury." This is why Chilon said to his brother, "I can bear injuries; you cannot."

III.   Consider the general teachings of the Seven Wise Men of Greece (Thales, Solon,[496] Periander,[497] Cleobulus,[498] Chilon, Bias, and Pittacus) as they were collected by Sosiades more than two thousand years ago:

"Follow God, obey the law, worship God, respect your parents, suffer for justice, know yourself, consider mortal things, appreciate hospitality,

---

[493] Penn has noted Rom. 2:14 ["For when the Gentiles, which have not the law, do by nature the things contained in the law, these, having not the law, are a law unto themselves: Which shew the work of the law written in their hearts, their conscience also bearing witness, and *their* thoughts the mean while accusing or else excusing one another"] in the margin.

[494] Diogenes Laertius (second century) compiled a history of Greek philosophy. In it, he quotes hundreds of authorities, but, except for a few cases, his true sources have not been ascertained.

[495] Penn has noted the following in the margin:

Job 28:28. ["And unto man he said, Behold, the fear of the Lord, that *is* wisdom; and to depart from evil *is* understanding."]

Job 8:13. ["So *are* the paths of all that forget God; and the hypocrite's hope shall perish."]

1 Cor. 6:7. ["Now therefore there is utterly a fault among you, because ye go to law one with another. Why do ye not rather take wrong? why do ye not rather *suffer yourselves to* be defrauded?"]

[496] Solon (638-558 B.C.) was an Athenian statesman, poet, and one of the Seven Wise Men of Greece. He ended exclusive aristocratic control of the government, substituting a system of control by the wealthy, and introduced a new and more humane law code.

[497] Periander (died 588 B.C.) was the second tyrant of Corinth.

[498] Cleobulus of Lindus (c. 600 B.C.) was a poet, philosopher, and one of the Seven Wise Men of Greece.

discipline yourself, honor prudence, swear not, speak well of things that are good, criticize no one, praise virtue, do what is right, refrain from evil, teach your children, fear deceit, love wisdom, judge fairly, control your tongue, examine impartially, do what you will not regret, when you have sinned, be repentant, take care what you look at, strive for perfection, pursue what is worthwhile, be modest in childhood, temperate as a youth, just as an adult, and prudent in old age, so that you can die untroubled."

Reader, these weighty sayings are found in the Scriptures themselves – in the New Testament as well as the Old (so-called). Note especially that they say, "Swear not." Seven hundred years before Christ came into the world. These come from men who were called wise for their extraordinary virtue. Truly, they deserve to be called Christian and virtuous more than many who claim those titles today.

IV.   Pythagoras very truly tells us, "A Philosopher speaks in vain if no one is healed by it." Indeed, what use is any preaching or sacrament that does not cure? Why listen if it does not heal?

"Everything you decide to do should focus on and lead you to the recognition of God."

"Do not lie about your faults, but accept criticism to eliminate them."

"The first principle in any person's whole life is this: *follow God*. This is the sole basis of honest philosophy."[499]

"Purity is earned by doing penitence and refraining from murder and adultery and all pollution."[500]

"We ought to be silent and speak only when our words improve on the silence."

"Moderation is the strength of the soul; it is the light of the soul and free of passions."[501]

---

[499] Penn noted that the whole is summarized in Eccles. 12:13 ['Let us hear the conclusion of the whole matter: Fear God, and keep his commandments: for this *is* the whole *duty* of man.'] in the margin.

[500] Penn noted James 1:27 ['Pure religion and undefiled before God and the Father is this, To visit the fatherless and widows in their affliction, *and* to keep himself unspotted from the world'].

[501] In the margin, Penn noted, "In this sense I fear that we may say that some have no light in them." This echoes a number of scriptural passages, e.g., John 11:10

"It is better to die than to cloud the soul with intemperance or passions."

Pythagoras does not answer reproach with reproach.[502] Some who call themselves Christians reproach even when they are not reproached. The difference between a sincere heathen and these scolds is obvious – they are no Christians at all.

V.   Anaxagoras held, "The purpose of life is the contemplation of God and the freedom that results from such heavenly meditation." When he was accused of neglecting his country, he pointed to heaven and said, "You misjudge me. My greatest care is for my country."

Suidas[503] says, "Even though Pericles[504] pleaded on his behalf, the Athenians threw him into prison and banished him from the city for introducing new ideas about God."

Josephus[505] says, "He called the Athenians' belief that the sun was God nonsense and ignorance. For that, the votes of a few condemned him to death."

However, testimony to his good life and their belief that he would attain immortality was carved on his grave. As translated by Thomas Stanley,[506] it reads:

("But if a man walk in the night, he stumbleth, because there is no light in him.")

[502] Penn noted 1 Pet. 2:23 ["Who, when he was reviled, reviled not again; when he suffered, he threatened not; but committed *himself* to him that judgeth righteously"] in the margin.

[503] Suidas is the name attributed to the unknown author of a tenth century Greek lexicon or encyclopedia. More properly, this term refers to the lexicon itself which is one of the most valuable documents of Greek philology, grammar, and literary history, including material from the classical period down to the tenth century.

[504] Pericles (c. 495-429 B.C.) was an Athenian statesman largely responsible for the development of both democracy and empire, making Athens the political and cultural focus of Greece. His achievements included the construction of the Acropolis, which was begun in 447.

[505] Flavius Josephus (c. 37-c. 100), born Yoseph ben Matatyahu, was a Jewish general during the uprising of 66-70 A.D. After being captured by the Romans, he changed sides. Later, he wrote *Bellum Judaicum* and *Antiquitates Judaicae*.

"Here lies, who through the truest paths did pass

To the world celestial, ANAXAGORAS."

VI.   Socrates tells us,[507] "Right philosophy is the way to true happiness. This requires two things: to contemplate God and to free the soul from earthly sensations."[508]

"Doing good is the best course in life."[509]

"For the soul, virtue is beauty and vice deformity."

"Nobility is temperance in body and soul."

"The best way to worship is to do what God commands." (Hard for so-called Christians to hear, but a great truth.)

"Our prayers should be for blessings in general, because God knows best what is good for us. God looks for integrity, not philanthropy." (This condemns those who know only the outward rituals and worship of Christianity.)

"The path to wisdom is in discerning what is good and honest, while shunning that which is dishonest."

"Those who know what they ought to do and do not do it, are not wise or temperate, but fools and stupid."[510]

---

[506] Thomas Stanley (1625-April 12, 1678) was an English poet, translator, and the first English historian of philosophy.

[507] Penn has noted in the margin: "Reader, there is Scripture that mirrors each of these pithy maxims and pointed aphorisms – to list them all would be tedious and superfluous. In many cases, they are almost word-for-word the Scripture itself, as those who know the Scriptures plainly see."

[508] Penn has noted Ps. 111:10 ["The fear of the LORD *is* the beginning of wisdom: a good understanding have all they that do *his commandments*: his praise endureth for ever."] in the margin.

[509] Penn has noted Luke 9:23 ["And he said to *them* all, If any *man* will come after me, let him deny himself, and take up his cross daily, and follow me."] in the margin.

[510] Penn has noted Matt. 7:26-27 ["And every one that heareth these sayings of mine, and doeth them not, shall be likened unto a foolish man, which built his house upon the sand: And the rain descended, and the floods came, and the

Libanius[511] says, "Of all the things that people call their own, Socrates considered the soul to be the most important, and only when they have cleansed their souls of all sin can they be truly happy."[512]

He taught everywhere that "those who are just and those who are happy are the one and the same."

He said that he wondered at those who carve images out of stone. They take great care to make the stone resemble a human, but neglect themselves and come to resemble a stone. (Meaning, in the words of the prophet, that they had hearts of stone.[513])

When asked "Who lives without worry?" He answered, "Those without evil thoughts."[514]

Asked, "Who is richest?" He replied, "Whoever is content with the least. Contentment is natural riches."[515]

Challenged to define self-restraint, he responded, "Government of one's own bodily pleasures."

"Good people must let the world see that their behavior is dependable than their oath." (I again observe that this shows that Socrates knew and preferred integrity above a willingness to swear. But to proceed, let us hear the charges of his enemies and his defense.

---

winds blew, and beat upon that house; and it fell: and great was the fall of it."] in the margin.

[511] Libanius (314-393) was a Greek Sophist and rhetorician whose orations and letters are a major source of information on the political, social, and economic life of Antioch and of the eastern part of the Roman Empire in the fourth century.

[512] Penn has noted Matt. 5:8 ["Blessed *are* the pure in heart: for they shall see God."] in the margin.

[513] Zech. 7:12: "Yea, they made their hearts *as* an adamant stone, lest they should hear the law, and the words which the LORD of hosts hath sent in his spirit by the former prophets: therefore came a great wrath from the LORD of hosts."

[514] Penn has noted Gal. 5:22 ["But the fruit of the Spirit is love, joy, peace, longsuffering, gentleness, goodness, faith"] in the margin.

[515] Penn has noted 1 Tim. 6:6 ["But godliness with contentment is great gain."] in the margin.

VII.   Melitus,[516] the son of Melitus a Pythian, accused Socrates, son of Sophroniscus an Alopecian, saying, "Socrates has violated the law by refusing to believe in this city's gods – he has introduced a new God. Likewise, he violates the law by corrupting the youth. For this, the punishment is death." And to this day, the charge is the same. Good people are condemned for the words they speak – light is called darkness and darkness, light.

Anytus[517] was the true author of the charges, because Socrates had worked tirelessly to remove him and the rest of his comical associates (because they were comedians) from power. Soon after the charges were brought, he sent word privately, saying that if Socrates would not mention his occupation, all charges would be dropped. Socrates sent back "that he would never give up speaking the truth as long as he lived; that he would continue to speak of Anytus in the same way; and that the accusations that had been made were insufficient to force him to give up saying what he felt obligated to say."[518] You can see that he was resolute.

"It is likely that God, out of love for me, has determined that I will die at a good age and in the gentlest possible way. If I die by sentence of a court, I am allowed the benefit of the easiest kind of death and will, therefore, give my friends the least trouble." Further, "If, when I must account for my actions toward God and humanity, the judges see fit to condemn me, I would rather choose to die than to beg for a continued life that is worse than death. Dying unjustly will not trouble me – it will not reflect badly on me, but on those who condemned me. I am ready to follow the example of Palamedes,[519] who suffered a similar death. He is honored

---

[516] Melitus (or Meletus) is identified in Plato's *Apology of Socrates* as Socrates' principle prosecutor. He was a minor and obscure political figure.

[517] Anytus was the Athenian democrat behind the persecution of Socrates.

[518] Penn has noted in the margin: "Nothing they did could stop him from identifying the immoral comedians who sought his ruin."

[519] In Greek legend, Palamedes was the son of Nauplius, king of Euboea, and a hero of the Trojan War. Before the war he exposed Odysseus, who feigned madness to avoid military service. By placing the infant Telemachus in the path of Odysseus' plow in the field, he forced that king to admit his sanity. During the war, Odysseus falsely accused Palamedes of collaborating with the Trojans and had him executed as a traitor.

more than Odysseus[520] who arranged his death. The future will know that I never hurt or injured anyone. On the contrary, to my utmost ability, I have helped all that I have known, freely sharing whatever good I could."

"I think it is most unseemly for a philosopher to sell advice – this has always been contrary to my practice. Ever since, by God's command, I first took up the practice of philosophy,[521] I have never taken anything in return. I practice my craft in public, for anyone to hear; I do not lock the door when I teach or go around seeking crowds and extracting fees from my listeners." As, I might add, some in those days did and as some still do today.

Doesn't this make Socrates superior to the priests of our day? And by that I include some of the non-conformists among those who make a trade of it. The righteousness of this Gentile condemns the mercenary practices of those who pretend to be Christ's ministers – demonstrating a higher calling than the one that they have achieved.

VIII.   Antisthenes, the first of the Cynics and a student of Socrates, taught that virtue was the truest nobility, that piety alone was necessary for lasting happiness, and that true virtue came not from what was said, but what was done – not from higher education or many words, but from upright actions.[522] In short, he taught that the principle of virtue was sufficient to gain all necessary wisdom and that all other things are

---

[520] Odysseus (or Ulysses) was the conqueror of Troy. His nine year journey home to Greece was chronicled in Homer's *Odyssey*.

[521] Penn has noted in the margin: "Like many words, the meaning of 'philosopher' has changed since those days. At that time, it meant a love of the wisdom given by Pythagoras – wisdom that is the way of holy living – not engaging in silly and troublesome word-play about impractical things."

[522] Penn has noted the following in the margin:

1 Pet. 2:9. ["But ye *are* a chosen generation, a royal priesthood, an holy nation, a peculiar people; that ye should shew forth the praises of him who hath called you out of darkness into his marvellous light."]

Rev. 1:6. ["And hath made us kings and priests unto God and his Father; to him *be* glory and dominion for ever and ever. Amen."]

Luke 11:28. ["But he said, Yea rather, blessed *are* they that hear the word of God, and keep it."]

1 Cor. 1:20. ["Where *is* the wise? where *is* the scribe? where *is* the disputer of this world? hath not God made foolish the wisdom of this world?"]

secondary to it. Piety is the best armor[523] – no one can pierce it or seize it – and virtuous people are always friends. Antisthenes prefers the company of a just person to his own neighbor and says a woman's soul gains the same advantages from virtue as a man's. He considered pleasure the greatest source of mischief in this world. When he was asked, "What learning is best?" He answered, "Whatever unlearns evil. Those who wish to live forever must take care that the lives they live in this world are holy and just."[524]

IX.   From Diogenes,[525] his student and steadfast friend, comes a very true and noteworthy saying. In his account of Diogenes' doctrine, Laertius quotes him as saying of spiritual exercise, "Where human souls deeply and frequently engage in spiritual retreat from the world – waiting for divine strength in meditation on the eternal mind – holy revelations or illuminations will occur. These enlighten the soul and enable it to live and act virtuously."[526]

X.   The piety and wisdom of Xenocrates[527] were so highly respected that (four hundred years before the words, "swear not at all" were spoken by our Lord Jesus Christ), the Athenian judges refused to ask him

---

[523] Penn has noted Eph. 6:14 ["Stand therefore, having your loins girt about with truth, and having on the breastplate of righteousness"].

[524] Penn has noted the following in the margin:

Hab. 2:4. ["Behold, his soul *which* is lifted up is not upright in him: but the just shall live by his faith."]

Heb. 12:14. ["Follow peace with all *men*, and holiness, without which no man shall see the Lord."]

[525] Diogenes of Sinope (412-323 B.C.) is credited by some with originating the Cynic way of life, although he credits Antisthenes. Diogenes conveyed Cynic philosophy by personal example rather than any coherent system of thought.

[526] Penn has noted in the margin:

Isa. 40:31. ["But they that wait upon the LORD shall renew *their* strength; they shall mount up with wings as eagles; they shall run, and not be weary; *and* they shall walk, and not faint."]

Ps. 25:14. ["The secret of the LORD *is* with them that fear him; and he will shew them his covenant."]

[527] Xenocrates (fourth century B.C.) was a Greek philosopher and pupil of Plato. Except for fragments, his writings are lost, but according to Aristotle, his doctrines are similar to Plato's.

to take an oath when giving evidence, considering it an affront to his integrity. His unsworn word was accepted as more reliable than all the sworn testimony of others. Valerius Maximus says, "They dispensed with it for him, but required it of each other." – Proof that even among the heathens, the Light exposed oaths as a poor substitute for honesty; that they believed it nobler to maintain the kind integrity that needs no oaths. Fear of punishment for perjury provides only a poor imitation of the truth that comes from innate faithfulness. This also provides a more than sufficient answer to the question, "Without the Scriptures, how and by what Light could we have found the path to perfection?"

XI.   "The highest good, therefore," said Zeno, "is to live our lives according to the knowledge given us by the Eternal Being. When the soul enters into the path of virtue, it walks in the steps and under the guidance of right reason, and follows God."[528] This calls to mind several Stoic maxims attributed to Zeon by Laertius, Cicero, Quintilian,[529] and others, and recently collected by Thomas Stanley. In addition to those mentioned earlier, I add:

"The wise are free of passion. The wise are sincere. The wise are divine for they have God with them. But the wicked are atheists. The wicked oppose the good – God is good, so they oppose God. The wise are religious and humble. Only they can be priests. Only they can be prophets. They love and honor their parents. Only the wise are free. The wise are free of sin."

I must ask, aren't these the same things that the Scriptures teach? That "the fear of God is the beginning of wisdom" and those who turn away from wickedness have "a good understanding."[530]

---

[528] Penn has noted Rom. 2:14-15 ["For when the Gentiles, which have not the law, do by nature the things contained in the law, these, having not the law, are a law unto themselves: Which shew the work of the law written in their hearts, their conscience also bearing witness, and *their* thoughts the mean while accusing or else excusing one another"] in the margin.

[529] Marcus Fabius Quintilianus (95-35 B.C.) was a Spanish-Roman teacher and writer. His *Institutio oratoria* was a major contribution to educational theory and literary criticism.

[530] Penn has noted the following in the margin:

Making the same point: "The wise are innocent. The wise are free, the wicked are slaves" and "Only the wise are perfect, lacking no virtue. The wicked are imperfect and have no virtue."

We can see that the wisdom to which they referred was virtue in opposition to vice which they considered to be folly, as do the Scriptures. In other words, only those who are good can be considered wise.

Again: "The wise never lie. The wise are peaceable, meek, modest, diligent, virtuous, faithful, and can only act virtuously. Fools are none of these things."

Here, it is obvious that by 'fools' he meant wicked and unteachable people – those who are stiff-necked, who rebel against God, and do not crave knowledge of God.

XII.   Clement of Alexandria quotes Plato as saying, "To be like God is to be holy, just and wise. This is why each person was born and should be the goal in studying philosophy. Virtue and honesty are one and the same."[531]

This was the doctrine, Reader, the study and (best of all) the practice of many of the virtuous heathens. They became a law unto themselves, restricting their mental and physical appetites to bounds set by an inward holy guide. Like careful sailors, they set the course of their lives by the light of a heavenly star, rising in their consciences to guide them through the Gentile night to a blessed immortality. This is the last point in their understanding of the divine – with it, we will close this portion of our discourse.

Ps. 111:10. ["The fear of the LORD *is* the beginning of wisdom: a good understanding have all they that do *his commandments*: his praise endureth for ever."]

Ps. 2:2. ["The kings of the earth set themselves, and the rulers take counsel together, against the LORD, and against his anointed."]

James 3:17. ["But the wisdom that is from above is first pure, then peaceable, gentle, *and* easy to be intreated, full of mercy and good fruits, without partiality, and without hypocrisy."]

[531] Penn has noted Lev. 11:44-45 ["For I *am* the LORD your God: ye shall therefore sanctify yourselves, and ye shall be holy; for I *am* holy: neither shall ye defile yourselves with any manner of creeping thing that creepeth upon the earth. For I *am* the LORD that bringeth you up out of the land of Egypt, to be your God: ye shall therefore be holy, for I *am* holy."] in the margin.

Chapter XI

Gentile beliefs about immortality and eternal rewards.

The following few authorities are quoted to prove that the Gentiles believed in an afterlife and that all would be held accountable for their deeds during their lives (a point not clearly stated among the Jews).

I.   Pythagoras and the Pythagoreans all believed in the immortality of the soul. Consider his, and their, statements on this point:

First, he said, "The soul is immortal."

Next, "The soul is incorruptible – it never dies. When it leaves the body, it goes into another world, the pure go to God while the impure are bound by the furies[532] in unbreakable chains."[533] Immorality and rewards are clearly stated.

"When people die who have lived justly, their souls ascend to the pure ether (or heaven) and live in the happy aevum (or everlasting age) with the blessed."[534]

II.   Heraclites: "When my body is finished, it must descend to its destined place. Nevertheless, my soul will not descend, but being an immortal thing, it will fly up to heaven."

---

[532] In Greek mythology, the furies (Tisiphone, Megæra, and Alecto) were avenging goddesses with snakes twined in their hair that were sent from Tartarus to avenge wrongs and punish crimes.

[533] Penn has noted Rev. 20:12-14&21:7-8 ["And I saw the dead, small and great, stand before God; and the books were opened: and another book was opened, which is *the book* of life: and the dead were judged out of those things which were written in the books, according to their works. And the sea gave up the dead which were in it; and death and hell delivered up the dead which were in them: and they were judged every man according to their works. And death and hell were cast into the lake of fire. This is the second death. ... He that overcometh shall inherit all things; and I will be his God, and he shall be my son. But the fearful, and unbelieving, and the abominable, and murderers, and whoremongers, and sorcerers, and idolaters, and all liars, shall have their part in the lake which burneth with fire and brimstone: which is the second death."] in the margin.

[534] Penn has noted 2 Cor. 5:8 ["We are confident, *I say,* and willing rather to be absent from the body, and to be present with the Lord."] in the margin.

III.   Euripides,[535] a serious tragedian, who worked to undo the harm that the shameless comedians had done to the people, says, "Who knows if death is not really living, and living, really death?"[536] Surely, he does not doubt immortality, but believes in it and in the reward that good people will achieve.

Socrates' great faith and the lofty faith of the Pythagoreans described.

IV.   Socrates: "The body is an assemblage of parts that is scattered by death. The soul is a unity that can never be divided and that passes from one life to another."[537]

"The souls of the good are taken to a happy place after death, united with God in a blessed unapproachable place; the wicked suffer well-deserved punishment in convenient places."[538] This proves beyond all doubt the ability of the Light to reveal immorality even to heathens – and beyond that, eternal rewards, too. Here, we see that they believed that the righteous will be saved and the wicked damned. This sustained Socrates at the time of his death:

"Truly," he says, "if I did not believe that I would be with the just God, and with people better than any now living, I would not disdain death. But I am sure that I am going to God, a very good master, and hope to meet with good people. I am confident that something survives death and that it is then much better for the good than the bad."[539]

---

[535] Euripides (480-406 B.C.) was a Greek tragic playwright.

[536] Penn has noted Phil. 1:21 ["For to me to live *is* Christ, and to die *is* gain."] in the margin.

[537] Penn has noted Eccles. 12:7 ["Then shall the dust return to the earth as it was: and the spirit shall return unto God who gave it."] in the margin.

[538] Penn has noted Matt. 25:31-33 ["When the Son of man shall come in his glory, and all the holy angels with him, then shall he sit upon the throne of his glory: And before him shall be gathered all nations: and he shall separate them one from another, as a shepherd divideth *his* sheep from the goats: And he shall set the sheep on his right hand, but the goats on the left."] in the margin.

[539] Penn noted 1 Cor. 15:28-31 ["And when all things shall be subdued unto him, then shall the Son also himself be subject unto him that put all things under him, that God may be all in all. Else what shall they do which are baptized for the dead, if the dead rise not at all? why are they then baptized for the dead?

When he was done speaking, Crito, one of his followers, asked him what directions he wanted to leave concerning his sons or other affairs. He asked Socrates if there was anything more that they could do for him.

Socrates replied, "I want nothing more than what I have often told you. If you take care of yourselves, whatever you do will be acceptable to me – although you promise nothing. If you neglect yourselves and virtue, you can do nothing acceptable – even if you promise everything."

"That," promised Crito, "we will do, but how do you wish to be buried?"

"However you think best," was the reply. "If you can catch me and I don't give you the slip." Then with a smile he said, "I cannot persuade Crito that I am anything more than the carcass you will soon see. He, therefore, worries about my burial. He seems unaffected by what I just told him – that as soon as I take the poison I will be transported to the joys of the blessed. He posted my bail, promising the judges that I would appear, but when I am gone, the rest of you must watch over him. Do not let him say that Socrates has been carried to his grave or laid to rest under the ground. Dear Crito, to say such things would unjustly disregard my soul.[540] Do not be sad – however you put it, tell the world that only my body is buried. Even so, I can and will pray to God to grant that my final passage will be happy." With that, he serenely drank the hemlock.

"This was the end," said Plato, "of the best, the wisest, and the most just of all." Cicero reports that he could never read this story without tears.

This concludes what Socrates has to say on the present subject. He was a happy man to meet such a happy end, dying for the one true God. He had good reason to believe that despite the envy and uncharitableness of some, God would reward him. Just as surely on the day of the Lord, some so-called Christians will hear, "Depart from me, I do not know you.[541] As you have sown, so shall you reap."

And why stand we in jeopardy every hour? I protest by your rejoicing which I have in Christ Jesus our Lord, I die daily."] in the margin.

[540] Penn noted in the margin, "Note the distinction Socrates makes between being dead and being departed."

[541] Luke 13:27: "But he shall say, I tell you, I know you not whence ye are; depart from me, all *ye* workers of iniquity."

I do not need to tell the world that Plato and other heathens have written accurately on this subject. Therefore, I will present only two short passages, one from Virgil[542] and the other from the Pythagoreans to bring my testimonies on this topic, and the whole subject of what the Gentiles believed about God, to a close.

> Until at last that long day has come about
> And gone is all filth and foul desire
> And leaves the soul celestial throughout
> Bathing its senses in pure liquid fire

This corresponds to the Golden Couplet of the Pythagoreans:

> Once, after death they reach the heavenly plain,
> They become like God and never die again.

In the Greek, it reads 'immortal gods.' Hierocles[543] interprets these verses as meaning, "All good people will resemble God and, like God, they will be immortal."

Thus, Reader, I have given you an accurate account of Gentile beliefs about God; what their faith was, what their practices were, and what many Gentiles hoped to achieve through the Light within. Each of those I have quoted had numerous followers.

You will notice that they began at the same starting point as Jews and Christians – with God – and they end with what they claim for themselves – a state of immortality in which each is rewarded according to the works of his or her life. But in this they are more remarkable than many of the Jews or Christians of our own times. These Gentiles were more certain, plainer, and truer in their acknowledgment of a Divine Light, Law, or Principle in each person, which, if it is obeyed, provided them daily with guidance and strength and, in the end, led them to God. Likewise, they lived lives that were more faithful in their virtue and self-denial than many alive today. Certainly, on that great and terrible day, when according to Paul's gospel

---

[542] Publius Vergilius Maro (70-19 B.C.), most often called Virgil, was the greatest Roman poet. His greatest work was the *Aeneid*.

[543] Hierocles of Alexandria (fifth century A.D.) was a non-Christian, Neoplatonist philosopher. His principal work is a commentary on the *Golden Verses* attributed to Pythagoras.

God, by Jesus Christ, will judge the secrets of all,[544] these pious Gentiles – who knew God, glorified God, and conscientiously did all that was contained in God's law – will ultimately be acquitted and rewarded.

Chapter XII

The heathens had some understanding that Christ was coming. That, and their refusal to swear, proves the sufficiency of the Light.

Over and above what I promised – and being willing to err on the side of completeness – I will briefly review two things that greatly support our defense of the Light. This should satisfy the questions of our adversaries – if indeed they really want to be satisfied.

1. The testimony of Socrates and Xenocrates about swearing is sufficient to prove that they saw by the Light that there was a state superior to swearing. Such a state of righteousness exceeds the legalisms of the Jews and obviously corresponds with what Christ taught hundreds of years later to be gospel righteousness, "Swear not at all."

2. Although the Light did not tell them the actual names that Christ should be called, they still foresaw and prophesized his coming, that he would be born of a virgin, and both who he was and what work he was to do. These were plainly communicated by the names given by the Holy Spirit, but it is not merely knowing so many letters, syllables, or words that gives true knowledge or gains salvation, but experiencing Christ to be what he is and knowing why he is called the Christ. Christ is the anointed one and he came into the world to save his people from their sins. The name Emmanuel signifies that he is God with us. In this sense, he was prophesized by the Gentiles, although only to the degree that they were enlightened. Listen to what Plato and Virgil have to say:

Marsilius Ficinus,[545] in his biography of that great Gentile, tells us of a time when some people visited Plato. In great seriousness, they asked him

---

[544] Rom. 2:16: "In the day when God shall judge the secrets of men by Jesus Christ according to my gospel."

[545] Marsilio Ficino (Oct. 19, 1433-Oct. 1, 1499) was an Italian philosopher, theologian, and linguist whose translations and commentaries on the writings of Plato and other classical Greek authors generated the Florentine Platonist Renaissance that influenced European thought for two centuries.

was how long people should study his writings. This question made him cautious, since he lived and died believing what he recommended to others, and he solemnly answered, "Until that holier and more divinely inspired person, whom all are to follow, visits this world." It is clear from this that Plato expected such a person to appear and that he did not want anyone to hold on to his own inferior teachings instead of the greater revelations that this divine person would bring. It is as if he had answered, "My teachings will help this generation to know and do their duty and will point toward what is to come. But, I am not he, nor do I believe my words to be the ultimate revelations. The lesser light can lead to the greater one and is then swallowed up in it. I can only point to the one who is to come and, when he has come, all that I have done must give way to him. All ought to follow him, because in doing so, they will obtain eternal blessedness."

Let us see what Virgil can add to this, (as translated by Eusebius[546]):

Ye muses with a lofty wing
Let us of higher matters sing.

And what are these matters?

Who lives this age, will clearly see,
Cumaea's verses accomplished be.

This Cumaea was a Sybil or prophetess of her city who lived about six hundred years before Christ and prophesized his coming. Virgil wrote these verses about forty years before Christ's birth. I wonder if the Jews had so clear a sense of the Messiah's coming. But to continue:

The integrity of times shall now renew again,
A virgin also shall bring back old Saturn's reign.
Now is from heaven high
Descended a new progeny.[547]

---

[546] Eusebius Of Caesarea (c. 260-c. 340), also called Eusebius Pamphili, was an early Christian bishop and author of *Ecclesiastical History*, an account of the first centuries of the church.

[547] Penn has noted the following in the margin:

Isa. 7:14-15. ["Therefore the Lord himself shall give you a sign; Behold, a virgin shall conceive, and bear a son, and shall call his name Immanuel. Butter and honey shall he eat, that he may know to refuse the evil, and choose the good."]

This is a direct prophesy of the miraculous conception, the virgin birth, and the good that would come into the world by it, as he adds:

The birth of that most happy child, by whom
The Iron Age shall end, and golden come,
Chaste Lucina favor
He shall the power of wickedness destroy,
And free the world from fear and all annoy.[548]

…

The goats shall bring their udders milk-filled home,
And the gentle flocks great lions shall not shun.[549]

Isa. 2:2-5. ["And it shall come to pass in the last days, *that* the mountain of the LORD'S house shall be established in the top of the mountains, and shall be exalted above the hills; and all nations shall flow unto it. And many people shall go and say, Come ye, and let us go up to the mountain of the LORD, to the house of the God of Jacob; and he will teach us of his ways, and we will walk in his paths: for out of Zion shall go forth the law, and the word of the LORD from Jerusalem. And he shall judge among the nations, and shall rebuke many people: and they shall beat their swords into plowshares, and their spears into pruninghooks: nation shall not lift up sword against nation, neither shall they learn war any more. O house of Jacob, come ye, and let us walk in the light of the LORD."]

[548] Penn has noted Isa. 9&10, which describe the righteous reign of the coming king, the judgment that will come on the arrogant and on oppressors, and the faithful remnant of Israel, and 1 John 3:5-6 ["And ye know that he was manifested to take away our sins; and in him is no sin. Whosoever abideth in him sinneth not: whosoever sinneth hath not seen him, neither known him"] in the margin.

[549] Penn has noted Isa. 11:6-11 ["The wolf also shall dwell with the lamb, and the leopard shall lie down with the kid; and the calf and the young lion and the fatling together; and a little child shall lead them. And the cow and the bear shall feed; their young ones shall lie down together: and the lion shall eat straw like the ox. And the sucking child shall play on the hole of the asp, and the weaned child shall put his hand on the cockatrice' den. They shall not hurt nor destroy in all my holy mountain: for the earth shall be full of the knowledge of the LORD, as the waters cover the sea. And in that day there shall be a root of Jesse, which shall stand for an ensign of the people; to it shall the Gentiles seek: and his rest shall be glorious. And it shall come to pass in that day, *that* the Lord shall set his hand again the second time to recover the remnant of his people, which shall be left, from Assyria, and from Egypt, and from Pathros, and from Cush, and from Elam, and from Shinar, and from Hamath, and from the islands of the sea."] in the margin.

...

Thy cradle fairest flowers shall send forth still,
Which shall have power, the poisonous herbs to kill,
The serpent he shall to destruction bring,
Assyrian amomum[550] shall each where spring.[551]

...

When thou shalt attain at length
To years of manhood and firm strength.

Is there anyone who would doubt that this is a very moving account of the power and virtue of Christ and of the purpose of his coming into the world? Comparison with the Scriptures makes this plain.[552]

From the hard oak there shall
Sweet honey sweat forth and fall

...

The sea shall then be quiet, no ship shall range

---

[550] It is not clear what plant the ancients meant by amomum. It may be related to cardamom.

[551] Penn has noted Jer. 2:3 ["Israel *was* holiness unto the LORD, *and* the firstfruits of his increase: all that devour him shall offend; evil shall come upon them, saith the LORD."] in the margin.

[552] Penn has noted the following in the margin:

Ps. 2.

Ps. 45.

Isa. 9:6-7. ["For unto us a child is born, unto us a son is given: and the government shall be upon his shoulder: and his name shall be called Wonderful, Counsellor, The mighty God, The everlasting Father, The Prince of Peace. Of the increase of *his* government and peace *there shall be* no end, upon the throne of David, and upon his kingdom, to order it, and to establish it with judgment and with justice from henceforth even for ever. The zeal of the LORD of hosts will perform this."]

Isa. 11:1-3&9. ["And there shall come forth a rod out of the stem of Jesse, and a Branch shall grow out of his roots: And the spirit of the LORD shall rest upon him, the spirit of wisdom and understanding, the spirit of counsel and might, the spirit of knowledge and of the fear of the LORD; And shall make him of quick understanding in the fear of the LORD: and he shall not judge after the sight of his eyes, neither reprove after the hearing of his ears ... They shall not hurt nor destroy in all my holy mountain: for the earth shall be full of the knowledge of the LORD, as the waters cover the sea."]

Abroad, her wares with others to exchange.
Then every land shall everything produce,
And then to plow the earth they shall not use.
Vines by hook shall not be rectified,
Nor wool with divers colors shall be died;
Fair fleeces, voluntary, shall proceed,
And clothe the lambs, while they do gently feed.
Oh might my days be lengthened, so that I
Might sing of thy great deeds before I die.[553]

Although much more might be said, this is enough to show that the heathens, by the Light we have been defending, not only foretold Christ's appearance, but the purpose of his coming for which he was called the

---

[553] Penn has noted the following in the margin:

Isa. 40.

Isa. 61:1-3. ["The Spirit of the Lord GOD is upon me; because the LORD hath anointed me to preach good tidings unto the meek; he hath sent me to bind up the brokenhearted, to proclaim liberty to the captives, and the opening of the prison to them that are bound; To proclaim the acceptable year of the LORD, and the day of vengeance of our God; to comfort all that mourn; To appoint unto them that mourn in Zion, to give unto them beauty for ashes, the oil of joy for mourning, the garment of praise for the spirit of heaviness; that they might be called trees of righteousness, the planting of the LORD, that he might be glorified."]

Matt. 1:21-25. ["And she shall bring forth a son, and thou shalt call his name JESUS: for he shall save his people from their sins. Now all this was done, that it might be fulfilled which was spoken of the Lord by the prophet, saying, Behold, a virgin shall be with child, and shall bring forth a son, and they shall call his name Emmanuel, which being interpreted is, God with us. Then Joseph being raised from sleep did as the angel of the Lord had bidden him, and took unto him his wife: And knew her not till she had brought forth her firstborn son: and he called his name Jesus."]

Luke 2:10-33.

1 John 3:5&8. ["And ye know that he was manifested to take away our sins; and in him is no sin ... He that committeth sin is of the devil; for the devil sinneth from the beginning. For this purpose the Son of God was manifested, that he might destroy the works of the devil."]

Christ, Jesus, Emmanuel, the Restorer of Breaches,[554] Redeemer, Savior, etc. I hope that our adversaries will either disprove these writings or admit that the Light that God gave to the Gentiles and obeyed by them was sufficient for some of them to gain a glimpse of Christ.

I have skipped some Sybils that Justin Martyr, Tertullian, Clement of Alexandria, and other ancients so admired. The reason for this is that David Blondel,[555] a careful Frenchman, has shown that many of the books attributed to them are not genuine, having been written by Christians who hoped to use them to convert the Gentiles. Although he admits that there were Sybils in ancient times and that they wrote some amazing things, their books were burnt in Rome several hundred years before Christ and only scattered remnants survived. Even so, as Virgil's reference to the Cumaean shows, enough existed to prove that some of the Gentiles foresaw Christ's conception by the Holy Spirit, virgin birth, and coming into the world to bring salvation.

---

[554] Isa. 58:12: "And *they that shall be* of thee shall build the old waste places: thou shalt raise up the foundations of many generations; and thou shalt be called, The repairer of the breach, The restorer of paths to dwell in."

[555] David Blondel (1591-1655) was a French Protestant clergyman who specialized in debunking popular myths. He is best remembered for proving that the story of Pope Joan (i.e., the claim that a woman had been elected pope) was false. What Penn fails to mention is that Blondel also refuted the theory that Virgil had been writing about Christ.

Chapter XIII

Although Jews, and even more so Christians, have an advantage over Gentiles, the Gentiles had enough to gain salvation.

But, in the course of dispelling ignorance, I have no desire to help the malicious. Let no one infer that I prefer the spiritual state of the Gentile to that of the Christian. Nor do I equate their status with that of the Jews, the adopted children of God, heirs of the divine glory, the covenants, and the law. They are the patriarchs, the human ancestors of Christ, who is God (the only God) over all, forever praised! Amen.[556]

Everyone should know that the spiritual privileges of both the Jews and the Christians are far greater than those of the ancient Gentiles. God gave the Jews everything that the Gentiles had, but the Gentiles did not receive everything that was freely bestowed on the Jews. Even so, it is beyond doubt that they received enough to achieve Godliness. The differences were not at the core of the two dispensations, but in the additional help that the Jews received and in their outward worship, which prepared the way for later glory.

The Word close within the heart of which Moses testified[557] was not restricted to the Jews, but available to the Gentiles as well. The Spirit of God worked within the Gentile as well as in the Jew. And God declared the Jew's new moons, Sabbaths, and solemn assemblies to be an abomination[558] – instructing them to cleanse themselves of their evil ways so that they

---

[556] Rom. 9:4-5: "Who are Israelites; to whom *pertaineth* the adoption, and the glory, and the covenants, and the giving of the law, and the service *of God*, and the promises; Whose *are* the fathers, and of whom as concerning the flesh Christ *came*, who is over all, God blessed for ever. Amen."

[557] Deut. 30:14: "But the word *is* very nigh unto thee, in thy mouth, and in thy heart, that thou mayest do it."

[558] Penn has noted Isa. 1:12-15 ["When ye come to appear before me, who hath required this at your hand, to tread my courts? Bring no more vain oblations; incense is an abomination unto me; the new moons and sabbaths, the calling of assemblies, I cannot away with; *it is* iniquity, even the solemn meeting. Your new moons and your appointed feasts my soul hateth: they are a trouble unto me; I am weary to bear *them*. And when ye spread forth your hands, I will hide mine eyes from you: yea, when ye make many prayers, I will not hear: your hands are full of blood."] in the margin.

might gain a new heart and a new spirit.[559] In this way God let them know that although they would receive much help in their spiritual childhood – help denied to any other nation – in return they owed purity, righteousness, love, reverence, and awe. And more than these, they owed obedience to the Spirit of God within. This was recognized not just by the Jews, but by many Gentiles, too. They knew that they were led by the same Spirit which, as Job says, is in all – the inspiration of the Almighty that gives understanding.[560] I cannot in good conscience say that they lacked the basis for salvation any more than the Jews. In summary, what I am arguing is this: God gave more to the Jews than to the Gentiles and now, in the Christian dispensation, we have the perfection of the Divine Light, Life, and immortality that they had dimly seen. But make no mistake, God granted the Gentiles a sufficient measure of Divine Light and Spirit to gain – if it was attended to and faithfully followed – salvation from sin in this world and from wrath in the next world. They believed, taught, lived, and died full of hope and assurance of eternal reward in a state of immortality.

I am not so rigid as to deny that good training, education, or other circumstances might have also benefited the best of the Gentiles, but I stand firm in declaring that the Light they received was alone sufficient to bring them to salvation as their lives and stated doctrines amply demonstrate. Some of them had a glimmering vision and as bold a belief in a state of purity, glory, and immortality as any living person is capable of achieving. This is enough on the universality and sufficiency of the Light of Christ within – whether some are pleased with it or not – at least as respects the Gentiles' beliefs. This is a full answer to the questions and accusations of our adversaries regarding the ability of the Light to reveal sin and turn any person away from it.

---

[559] Penn has noted Eze. 18:31-32 ["Cast away from you all your transgressions, whereby ye have transgressed; and make you a new heart and a new spirit: for why will ye die, O house of Israel? For I have no pleasure in the death of him that dieth, saith the Lord GOD: wherefore turn *yourselves*, and live ye."] in the margin.

[560] Job 32:8: "But *there is* a spirit in man: and the inspiration of the Almighty giveth them understanding."

Chapter XIV

The Light is both Law and Gospel. These are not the same, but the Light encompasses both in its nature.

Nevertheless, I expect there are still those who doubt this blessed Light. They would rather oppose it and hold on to their own notions than to believe and obey it and thereby find salvation. I expect that some will offer this objection:

Objection: This Light within is at most the law within the human conscience, a remnant of the old covenant. In this whole long essay, you have hardly made any mention of Christ. If, as you Quakers claim, this Light was Christ, then why was he not called Light by the Jews and Greeks of old? And, how could he have been prefigured (that is, foretold as yet to come) when he was already present? Furthermore, you maintain that this Light is the Savior, Messiah, Christ, etc. – if so, how is it that Christ bears our sins and that men and women are saved by his blood?

I think the Reader would agree that this objection is the most serious made against our beliefs. In stating it in the strongest possible terms, I have been more evenhanded with our opponents than they usually have been with us. I will now answer each part of it in the love and awe of God and in the spirit of moderation.

The objection consists mainly of four parts: The first part equates the Light only with the Law and not with the Gospel. The second asks why the Light was not called Christ by the Jews or Greeks. The third asks how Christ can pre-exist and at the same time be prefigured. The fourth relates to Christ's blood and his bearing of our sins – how this can be attributed to the Light without diminishing the holy mission of Jesus.

A way to reconcile the apparent difference between Law and Gospel.

With respect to the first part, I agree that the Light is the Law. This in no way precludes it also being the Gospel. If it was only the Law, it could not free anyone from sin. I claim that it is simultaneously Law and Gospel.

As the Apostle says, "Where there is no law, there are no violations of law."[561] It might just as well have been said (since it is admitted that it is the

---

[561] Rom. 4:15: "Because the law worketh wrath: for where no law is, *there is* no transgression."

Law), that where there is no Light, there can be no violation. And the apostle explicitly states, "Whatever is condemned (or sinful) is revealed by the Light."[562] Therefore, since all have sinned, all have the Light and always have.

If this were all, it would be a law that justified no one – all would be prisoners of sin[563] and children of wrath[564] because all who sin are condemned by the Law and the Light. But, those who genuinely repent and come to obey the Light are justified in two ways (I will be explicit so that all who have a false impression of the word will understand). First, God acquits us for his name's sake[565] – God is merciful, pardoning the iniquity, transgressions, and sins[566] of those who truly repent. Second, God accepts us for our renewed and continuing humble and sincere obedience. But such people are not yet children of God; they are not at the end, but only the beginning of their journey. Each must give proof of enduring faithfulness, diligence, and loyalty as a servant before claiming the status of a child of God who will never leave the Father's house forever.[567]

This is clearly distinguished and seriously expressed by the apostle Paul in his letter to the Galatians: "As long as heirs are children, they have no more rights than servants; they are under the authority of their tutors until they come of age. In the same way, when we were children, we were slaves to the values of this world, but then the Seed came and, by faith in it, our adoption as children of God is known."[568] This is the full brightness of the

---

[562] Eph. 5:13: "But all things that are reproved are made manifest by the light: for whatsoever doth make manifest is light."

[563] Gal. 3:22: "But the Scripture hath concluded all under sin, that the promise by faith of Jesus Christ might be given to them that believe."

[564] Eph. 2:3: "Among whom also we all had our conversation in times past in the lusts of our flesh, fulfilling the desires of the flesh and of the mind; and were by nature the children of wrath, even as others."

[565] 1 John 2:12: "I write unto you, little children, because your sins are forgiven you for his name's sake."

[566] Heb. 8:12: "For I will be merciful to their unrighteousness, and their sins and their iniquities will I remember no more."

[567] John 8:35: "And the servant abideth not in the house for ever: *but* the Son abideth ever."

[568] Gal. 4:1-5: "Now I say, *That* the heir, as long as he is a child, differeth nothing from a servant, though he be lord of all; But is under tutors and governors until the time appointed of the father. Even so we, when we were children, were in

Light, perfect and unchanging in itself, but seen differently by each person. The outward sun is the same when it is dimly seen at dawn and when it is brightly shining at noon. If people – either through their own weaknesses or from the fogs and mists of tradition, education, ignorance, and prejudice – find themselves in shadow, they must not blame the Light, but themselves. Those who follow the holy revelations of the Light – who walk in what has always been the path of the just – will find blessedness at the end of their journey. But those who let the world of wickedness come between themselves and the Light are lost in the night.

It is said that Abraham saw Christ's day.[569] What day is that? It is the day of the dispensation of the Son as heir of all things, the day of perfect restitution. Abraham could never have seen it without the Light. Several of those holy ancients were granted a greater measure of Light than most people and, as a result, enjoyed the benefits of a divine dispensation that, through the weakness of the people, was not generally experienced. By attending to the heavenly Light in their consciences, these few could see beyond the rituals, types, figures, and shadows to the coming inward, spiritual, and substantial state. Undeniably, this was the purpose of all external ministry: to turn humanity's attention inward and point them to the more hidden mystery that their wandering away from God had caused them to neglect. Christ was the saving Light in that state. The Light of the Law was their schoolmaster, leading those who would obey it to a more complete understanding of that same Light that is the Gospel or glad-tidings. And certainly it was glad-tidings that, after such a dark and cold season, the Sun of Righteousness appeared in the blessed body that had been prepared for that purpose. This appearance transcended all earlier revelations of Christ.

Those who had most faithfully lived up to the Law of God, or Light of that dispensation, gladly received Christ, believed in him, became his followers, and were his companions in his sufferings and death. He who was the Light of the Law is also the Light of the Gospel, though not in the same form or degree of revelation. The Light does not at the same time

---

bondage under the elements of the world: But when the fulness of the time was come, God sent forth his Son, made of a woman, made under the law, To redeem them that were under the law, that we might receive the adoption of sons."

[569] John 8:56: "Your father Abraham rejoiced to see my day: and he saw *it*, and was glad."

condemn and justify, although it does both. It does not shine as brightly in infants, children, and parents – but it is still One in itself – the pure, eternal, and unalterable Light of Life and Righteousness. If, therefore, it enlightens some only with knowledge of the Law, we can be sure that those people are still in a state of condemnation for evil and do not yet know the fulfillment of the Law – knowledge that comes to every true follower of Christ and to everyone who seeks to come to Christ.

The Light is further defended.

Christ fulfills the law for us. But how? The Light within us, as we obey it and are led by it, empowers us to do what is good and acceptable in the sight of God. By obeying the Light, we fulfill the law. In this way, Christ works his works in us and for us. Christ did not excuse his followers from the indispensable duty to keep the outward law, rather he set before them a far harder task – how much easier it is to refrain from actions than from thoughts. The dispensation of Moses says, "You shall not commit adultery."[570] But the dispensation of Christ says, "Anyone who looks at a woman lustfully has already committed adultery with her in his heart."[571] Certainly, those people who suppose that they are excused from the law and need not perform good works in order to be justified have utterly shamed themselves and dangerously imperiled their souls. In short, the one who said, "Anyone who looks at a woman lustfully has already committed adultery with her in his heart" is the true Light. And so was the one who said to Moses, "You shall not commit adultery." Should we assume, therefore, that there are two Lights? Or are these just two of many forms or continuing revelations of the same eternal Light?

To conclude, what I am saying is that the Law is the beginning of the Gospel and the Gospel is the completion of the Law. Whoever wishes to be justified must first be condemned, just as those who wish to be healed must first be wounded. The Law is the sword, the Gospel is the balm; one is duty, the other, love. To obtain the greatest revelation only one thing is needed – to be humbly subject and constantly obedient to the least revelation. The faithful servant becomes an heir by adoption. If you wish to know the Word as reconciler, you must first feel it as a hammer, a sword, and a fire. The way to find gospel righteousness is first to perform the law

---

[570] Exod. 20:14: "Thou shalt not commit adultery."

[571] Matt. 5:28: "But I say unto you, That whosoever looketh on a woman to lust after her hath committed adultery with her already in his heart."

righteously. By law, I do not mean the public ceremonies and rituals – the shadows of worship – or the external practices of the Jews, but the moral and eternal law. This was written down by Moses (although it predates Moses), and was fulfilled by Christ. Those who conscientiously keep the first part – who have conquered doing evil – can hope to reach the end. If they are faithful to the Light they have received, it will enable them to overcome evil words, and at last evil thoughts as well. They will see the Scripture fulfilled in themselves, "Judgment (the law) is brought forth into victory (the gospel)."[572] "Whoever follows me (the Light of the world that enlightens all who come into the world[573]) will never walk in darkness, but will have the Light of Life."[574] I do not distinguish the Law from the Gospel to make a distinction in kind, but only in degree, and for the benefit of those who are accustomed to it. "If the Son sets you free, you are truly free."[575] As a condemner, the Light may be said to bring death – by enlightening the conscience, it slays the sinful nature. It is said, "The day of the Lord is a day of darkness"[576] because of the judgments and terrors that will come into the consciences of the sinful. But, to the obedient, it is the "Light of Life," bringing peace and consolation.

This is Christ, the Word-God and Light of the world in every dispensation. He is One, although different in appearance at different times and to different people – not as different lights, but as different revelations of one and the same eternal Light of Life and Righteousness.

---

572 Matt. 12:20: "A bruised reed shall he not break, and smoking flax shall he not quench, till he send forth judgment unto victory."

573 John 1:9: "*That* was the true Light, which lighteth every man that cometh into the world."

574 John 8:12: "Then spake Jesus again unto them, saying, I am the light of the world: he that followeth me shall not walk in darkness, but shall have the Light of Life."

575 John 8:36: "If the Son therefore shall make you free, ye shall be free indeed."

576 Amos 5:18: "Woe unto you that desire the day of the LORD! to what end *is* it for you? the day of the LORD *is* darkness, and not light."

Chapter XV

The second part of the objection, that Christ was not called the Light in ancient times, is answered from Scripture and right reason.

The second part of the objection stated above is, "Why was the Light not called Christ by Jews or Greeks?" My answer is that we do not claim that the Light in every person is Christ, but that it is of Christ or from Christ. He is the fullness of the Light from which all receive a measure or suitable portion of Divine Light and knowledge. No individual has the whole or complete Christ within – if that were the case, Christ would be nowhere else. Such an absurdity never came from us, nor can it be derived from our doctrines, despite what our adversaries have maliciously claimed. Just as light from the external sun falls on physical eyes and allows each person to see the external world, so too the internal Sun of Righteousness shines on the eyes of each soul and allows it to see the invisible things of the spiritual world. The external light is not the sun, nor is the Light within the same as Christ. That said, it is easy to see that we would not expect everyone to call the Light by the name Christ and therefore, feel no obligation to explain why the Greeks and Jews did not do so. Even so, I will say this, Christ was called the Light before he came into the world – although not before he was the Christ. Isaiah's words, "I will give you as a Light to the Gentiles,"[577] are only one example. If there is anyone who says that this Light was not Christ, say so in plain words. And then they can also tell us why John, the prophet of the Holy Spirit, was inspired to call Christ 'Light' as soon as, if not sooner than he was called 'Christ'? It is certainly the case that the Light he spoke of in the first chapter of his gospel as was Christ. He might just as well have said, "I will give Christ as a Light to enlighten the Gentiles" or "He who is the Christ, is the Light" or simply "The Light is Christ." It is obvious that the Gentiles were enlightened by Christ – this is the whole of our claim with respect to the Light within everyone.

Consider too that John explicitly calls the Light with which everyone is enlightened 'the Word' and that the Word became flesh. If the one who

---

[577] Isa. 49:6: "And he said, It is a light thing that thou shouldest be my servant to raise up the tribes of Jacob, and to restore the preserved of Israel: I will also give thee for a light to the Gentiles, that thou mayest be my salvation unto the end of the earth."

became flesh is Christ (as everyone, except Muggleton and his gullible followers, agrees), then Christ is the Light by which all are enlightened.

More to the point, Christ himself says, "I am the Light of the world,"[578] which is the same as saying, "I have lighted or shined forth into the world." The Light that shines in the hearts of all is Christ, although no individual is illuminated by the presence of the entire Christ – to say so would imply that there are many Christs, a statement as absurd as it is blasphemous.

Finally, the apostle calls him Christ before he came into the world – Christ was Christ before his appearance in the flesh. This should completely settle the objection. To re-state the objection, our adversaries seem to say, "Christ did not exist as Christ before he became flesh. Therefore, although the Word-God might have enlightened all, this was not done as the Christ." But, if the Christ did not pre-exist his coming into the world, then should we identify him as Christ only for that brief time when he lived on earth? I would like to hear a good reason for such a claim. Our opponents' dilemma is simply this: those who deny that Christ was Christ before that coming into the world must also deny a text that is as plain as any that can be found in the Scriptures. Under those circumstances, their opposition to our doctrine must be seen as unsound and reprehensible. However, most of our opponents admit that Christ, as the Word-God, enlightened all people prior to his coming in the flesh. Moreover, the apostle has said that Christ (before he came in the flesh) was a rock to Israel in the wilderness.[579] Therefore, unless they wish to claim that Christ and the Word are two distinct beings or that there are two distinct Christs, Christ was that Light that has enlightened all humanity and the Light was the Christ of God. Consequently, the Light has been called, both implicitly and explicitly, Christ before his visible appearance in Jerusalem.

---

[578] John 8:12: "Then spake Jesus again unto them, saying, I am the light of the world: he that followeth me shall not walk in darkness, but shall have the Light of Life."

[579] 1 Cor. 10:1-4: "Moreover, brethren, I would not that ye should be ignorant, how that all our fathers were under the cloud, and all passed through the sea; And were all baptized unto Moses in the cloud and in the sea; And did all eat the same spiritual meat; And did all drink the same spiritual drink: for they drank of that spiritual Rock that followed them: and that Rock was Christ."

It has also been claimed that the scriptural statement, "none of the rules of this world knew"[580] contradicts us. But this text is not relevant to the question, since it is referring to wisdom that had been hidden[581] and not to the physical existence of Christ. But even if we suppose for a moment that it did, then we would say that those who rejected him, and much more those who crucified his outward body, first despised and crucified him within themselves. These were people who, as Job said, "Rebel against the Light and do not love its ways."[582] I boldly declare, in the face of any opponent, that it was the inward sight of this Light that allowed Simeon, Peter, Nathaniel, and all the others who believed in him, to recognize, acknowledge, and suffer for him. Those who had not by sin and wickedness hardened their hearts – but who, through the Light of the Lord, kept their consciences clear – received and embraced him. The Light knew its own. The lesser light is naturally attracted to the greater Light and is led to it.

To conclude this section, let me note that it was not "the princes of this world" who put him outwardly to death, but Pilate, the governor of one small province, acting in response to the envious and wicked accusations of a broken and conquered people. Since I believe what the apostle said is true, I can only infer that he meant that the princes of this world crucified Christ mystically, not physically. In any case, this part of our adversaries' objection – that the Light was not called Christ before he came into the world – has clearly been refuted.

---

[580] 1 Cor. 2:8: "Which none of the princes of this world knew: for had they known *it*, they would not have crucified the Lord of glory."

[581] 1 Cor. 2:7: "But we speak the wisdom of God in a mystery, *even* the hidden *wisdom*, which God ordained before the world unto our glory."

[582] Job 24:13: "They are of those that rebel against the light; they know not the ways thereof, nor abide in the paths thereof."

Chapter XVI

An answer to the third part of the objection, that if Christ was known under the Law (which he was if the Light was Christ), then why is he prefigured? The type and anti-type may, in some respects, co-exist.

At first sight, the third part of the objection might appear to have some weight: "If the Light within is Christ, and the Jews and Gentiles had it from the beginning of the world, how can you say that Christ was prefigured and prophesied as coming when he had already come?" In some respects, this part of the objection is based on the same mistake at the second part; that is, that the Light within is the whole of Christ. On this point, I have plainly and completely expressed myself above. To be fair to our opponents, I will therefore re-state their objection: "If, as you say, Christ enlightened the Jews and Gentiles before his visible coming, then didn't he come while at the same time being promised for the future? Isn't that a contradiction?" In response, I say that the supposed contradiction arises from a misunderstanding of the differences between the old and new dispensations. It seems to assume that the degree to which the Light illuminated the world was the same before and after the birth of Jesus. Let me be clear, when I speak of the Light before and after that event, I mean one and the same Light. But, we acknowledge that there has been a greater manifestation of that same Light since the birth of Jesus. And what does this imply? That the lesser luminance of Light was appropriate to the spiritual state of the Jews at the time and that, by prefigurings and prophesies, God provided glimpses of the far more excellent and glorious dispensation of the Light and love of God still to come.

The purpose of God giving the Israelites the outward prophet and leader, Moses, was to bring them eventually to the inward leader, Christ Jesus. Though they were not aware of him and therefore could not attend to him, Moses prophesized about him. Indeed, all the external dealings of God with humanity have been to some degree to bring them to Christ, the seed within, who can "bruise the serpent's head."[583] With good reason, we

---

[583] Gen. 3:14-15: "And the LORD God said unto the serpent, Because thou hast done this, thou *art* cursed above all cattle, and above every beast of the field; upon thy belly shalt thou go, and dust shalt thou eat all the days of thy life: And

can assert truthfully that Christ the Light was the rock that followed Israel in the wilderness. (Christ is the rock of ages and foundation of all generations[584] – lighting all, the same yesterday, today, and tomorrow.) The promised greater manifestation of the Light was preached to those who knew only the lesser light.

We are not without support for this claim in the Scripture. Despite all the outward washings of those times, God frequently urged the essence of those ceremonies on them, e.g., "a clean heart and a new spirit."[585] All outward forms of worship were described as no better than "cutting a dog's neck or offering the blood of pigs."[586] When Christ offered the bread and wine to his disciples, didn't he ask them to do it only until he came?[587] The Catholics say that the bread and wine are the actual body and blood of Christ. On this basis, they claim that he comes bodily to them every time they receive it. I cannot believe that my opponents agree with that. Therefore, they must believe (with us) that Christ, when he said these words, was prefiguring the Christ who was to come. In this instance, we can see that a prefiguring of Christ and Christ already existing are not incompatible. We need also to keep in mind the distinction between a lesser and a greater manifestation. This does not divide the Light – it remains one, pure and eternal; the Sun of Righteousness throughout all dispensations. Likewise, the passage from Paul (cited above) plainly answers their objection. Christ was the Israelite's rock, or the rock of that age, even though the signs of his coming were also present. The type and the anti-type co-existed. It is in this way that I wish to be understood.

I will put enmity between thee and the woman, and between thy seed and her seed; it shall bruise thy head, and thou shalt bruise his heel."

[584] Isa. 58:12: "And *they that shall be* of thee shall build the old waste places: thou shalt raise up the foundations of many generations; and thou shalt be called, The repairer of the breach, The restorer of paths to dwell in."

[585] Ps. 51:10: "Create in me a clean heart, O God; and renew a right spirit within me."

[586] Isa. 66:3: "He that killeth an ox *is as if* he slew a man; he that sacrificeth a lamb, *as if* he cut off a dog's neck; he that offereth an oblation, *as if he offered* swine's blood; he that burneth incense, *as if* he blessed an idol. Yea, they have chosen their own ways, and their soul delighteth in their abominations."

[587] 1 Cor. 11:26: "For as often as ye eat this bread, and drink this cup, ye do shew the Lord's death till he come."

Before I conclude, please consider the following saying from Christ to the Jews and consider how it relates to our doctrine: "Before Abraham was born, I am! Abraham foresaw my day and rejoiced."[588] Briefly, although he was not to come visibly for more than nineteen hundred years, Abraham saw him and his time. I don't know any other way to interpret this passage. Those Jews who did not believe him to be the Messiah thought it highly presumptuous of him to compare himself with Abraham. They asked, "Are you greater than our father Abraham? He died, and so did the prophets. Who do you think you are?"[589] To that he answered (showing himself to be the true Messiah and the Christ of God), "Abraham foresaw my day and rejoiced." They could not see beyond the physical body of the outward man and replied, "You, who are not yet fifty, have seen Abraham?"[590] To this he responded, "This is the truth – before Abraham was even born, I am." Then they picked up stones to throw at him, etc.[591] Unless our adversaries deny Christ's words, he clearly distinguished his physical body – then not even fifty years old – from the Christ of God, the Messiah and Savior of the world. Christ existed long before Abraham's time and the holy ancients had at least a glimpse of him and of his glorious coming into the world. You need look no further than the many clear and heavenly prophesies in the Scriptures of Truth that so often foretold and introduced the coming gospel dispensation.

This is unquestionably confirmed by Paul's statement to the Romans, "They are the ancestors – through them is traced the human ancestry of Christ, who is God over all, for ever praised! Amen."[592] Here, Christ is both

---

[588] John 8:56-58: "Your father Abraham rejoiced to see my day: and he saw *it*, and was glad. Then said the Jews unto him, Thou art not yet fifty years old, and hast thou seen Abraham? Jesus said unto them, Verily, verily, I say unto you, Before Abraham was, I am."

[589] John 8:53: "Art thou greater than our father Abraham, which is dead? and the prophets are dead: whom makest thou thyself?"

[590] John 8:57: "Then said the Jews unto him, Thou art not yet fifty years old, and hast thou seen Abraham?"

[591] John 8:58-59: "Jesus said unto them, Verily, verily, I say unto you, Before Abraham was, I am. Then took they up stones to cast at him: but Jesus hid himself, and went out of the temple, going through the midst of them, and so passed by."

[592] Rom. 9:5: "Whose *are* the fathers, and of whom as concerning the flesh Christ *came*, who is over all, God blessed for ever. Amen."

distinguished from the body that he took and, at the same time, declared to be one with God, ever blessed forever. Paul might just as well have written, "From their flesh, his body came." Christ existed before he took flesh, the birth of that body did not mark the beginning of Christ – who is God. And, as God (not merely flesh or the bodily descendent of any people), he pre-existed all things.

To conclude, God promised the outward and natural Abraham, the father of the outward and natural Jews, that his seed would be blessed with earthly blessings (such as the land of Canaan) and that they foreshadowed the one seed – Christ. Since one outward thing cannot prefigure another outward thing, it follows that the descendents of Christ, through his spiritual resurrection, will be spiritual and inward. This is what the Scriptures teach us – the outward lamb prefigures the inward lamb; the outward Jews prefigure the inward Jews. Just as God blessed the Jews above all other nations with many remarkable outward kindnesses, God has now blessed the Jews in spirit above all other peoples.

I will offer two more short arguments to further prove what I believe and proclaim regarding the spirituality of the true seed – and consequently, a clearer refutation of our opponents' opinions concerning the true Christ. First, each thing gives birth only to more of its own kind. A natural being cannot give birth to a spiritual being. Material things do not create immaterial ones. The nature or image born in the hearts of true believers is spiritual; it follows therefore that the seed that is conceived and gives birth to it must also be spiritual. Christ's body – what he received from the virgin – could therefore not be the seed.

Second, it is clear from this that the serpent must also be a spirit and that nothing can bruise the head of the serpent within us unless it is also internal and spiritual.[593] If the body of Christ were the only seed, then he could not bruise the head of the serpent within us. The body of Christ is not within anyone (although some have misunderstood or perverted our doctrine of the Christ within and accused us of that). Consequently, the promised seed is a holy and spiritual principle of Light, life, and power – when it is received into the heart, it bruises the serpent's head. The seed

---

[593] Gen. 3:14-15: "And the LORD God said unto the serpent, Because thou hast done this, thou *art* cursed above all cattle, and above every beast of the field; upon thy belly shalt thou go, and dust shalt thou eat all the days of thy life: And I will put enmity between thee and the woman, and between thy seed and her seed; it shall bruise thy head, and thou shalt bruise his heel."

(which in this sense cannot be the body) is Christ and, as the Scriptures testify, that seed is one, that seed is Christ, and Christ is God.[594] From all this, we proclaim that Christ was and is the divine Word of Light and Life that was in the beginning with God and was and is God over all, blessed forever.

To make this even more apparent, consider seriously whether the seed bruised the serpent's head in the holy men and women of all generations prior to the birth of Christ – otherwise, they could not have been holy, but would have been snakelike and wicked. If the one seed existed before the birth of Jesus, and that seed was Christ, it is clear that Christ was Christ before the outward appearance. Consequently, the outward appearance could only be a more excellent and free revelation of the same truth, righteousness, salvation, wisdom, power, glory, and authority.

In that day, this heavenly seed was to some degree known and, when people turned their minds inward to the Word of God near within their hearts, its power and virtue cleansed and redeemed them. Some achieved great things – even coming to know the coming great day of complete redemption when the seed would conquer all its oppressors and become, as the prophet says, the only Son, the wonderful counselor, the mighty God, the everlasting Father, and the Prince of Peace whose authority will grow without limit.[595] Even so, we understand that most people in those times could not see clearly – they were weak, in darkness, and in bondage to earthly and miserable things.[596] God took pity on their weaknesses and allowed them to practice outward forms and rituals to keep them from wandering off the true path in pursuit of the pompous inventions and idols of other nations. God pointed them toward the still hidden glory of

---

[594] Gal. 3:16: "Now to Abraham and his seed were the promises made. He saith not, And to seeds, as of many; but as of one, And to thy seed, which is Christ."

[595] Isa. 9:6-7: "For unto us a child is born, unto us a son is given: and the government shall be upon his shoulder: and his name shall be called Wonderful, Counsellor, The mighty God, The everlasting Father, The Prince of Peace. Of the increase of *his* government and peace *there shall be* no end, upon the throne of David, and upon his kingdom, to order it, and to establish it with judgment and with justice from henceforth even for ever. The zeal of the LORD of hosts will perform this."

[596] Gal. 4:9: "But now, after that ye have known God, or rather are known of God, how turn ye again to the weak and beggarly elements, whereunto ye desire again to be in bondage?"

spiritual revelations that would be disclosed later – that is, the complete redemption of the soul and the reign of the Holy Seed.

From all this, by the absolute force of truth, we must and do conclude:

1. The Seed, which is Christ, was in all ages – with Abraham, the Israelites, and the prophets – and therefore Christ was before he came into the world in the flesh.

2. But, in that time, he was not so clearly revealed, so perfectly made known, or so generally understood. He was known darkly – by types and shadows. Though these could not cleanse or save or redeem, they pointed toward that more hidden and spiritual substance to come that would cleanse, save, and redeem, freeing all who were faithful from sin and wrath.

3. It is, consequently, not at all unreasonable that the more perfect revelation of truth was prefigured and prophesized in that time. Reason and Scripture are clear on this and that concludes our answer to this part of the objection.

Chapter XVII

The fourth part of the objection.

I will now turn to the portion of the objection that seems to most trouble people with respect to the Light within: "If the Light in everyone is Christ, how does that Light take away our sins and transgressions? How can we be justified, redeemed, or saved by its blood – all things promised in the Scripture to come through the man Jesus who was born in Bethlehem? Doesn't your belief in the Light within deny the value of his life, death, resurrection, ascension, and mediation?"

From my reading of the most forceful writings of our adversaries, I take this to be the essence of their argument.

In answering this last part of the objection, it must be considered how to reconcile the work of the Light with those Scriptures that seem to attribute everything to Christ's bodily sufferings. I hope to make it clear how we can honor the Light without in any way slighting the earthly life and death of Christ.

According to Scripture, the Light – or rather that which is the Light within ('light' is, of course, a metaphor for that which reveals our spiritual darkness) – is like a lamb slain since the creation of the world.[597] That is, soon after the world was created, Lucifer the fallen angel tempted humanity into betraying its innocence. By this disobedience, sin came into the world and humanity came to resist, grieve, and slay (this 'slaying' also being metaphorical) the Light or Principle of Life under whose care humanity had been placed. The pure and innocent life was mortally wounded by disobedience and, by that rebellion, the lamb-like image in which Adam and Eve were created was lost. The holy principle that God had placed in their hearts – true Light, Life, and Power – bore the weight of that sin. It was suffering greatly – burdened like a cart weighed down with a full-load of grain.[598] You might say, the Light was overwhelmed with iniquity.

This was the condition of that precious and chosen Seed, Spirit, Light, Life, and Truth – by whatever name people may choose to call it – ever since that first act of rebellion. In the wicked, God's holy Light and Spirit has been deeply wounded – as deeply as if it were slain. Even in the good, who have a sense of the world's atrocities, it feels those many burdens because the Light and Life is One in all, although it is not treated the same by all. Those who have been reformed by it, and joined to it, have been as one spirit with it – they too have felt their share of the Lord's heavy sufferings from an ungodly world. These come as much from the ages before his outward coming as in our own times and in future ages.

In all ages, some of the disobedient have listened to the still, small voice of the Word, the messenger of God in their hearts, and have been affected by it. Like a parent's reprimand, it chastises them and convicts them of their sins. When this is answered with true brokenness of the soul and repentance of the spirit, that same principle and Word of Life has interceded for them and reconciled them and God has accepted them, letting the Light of his face fall upon them[599] and replenishing those humble penitents with divine consolation. Still, Christ, the Word-God who has

---

[597] Rev. 13:8: "And all that dwell upon the earth shall worship him, whose names are not written in the book of life of the Lamb slain from the foundation of the world."

[598] Amos 2:13: "Behold, I am pressed under you, as a cart is pressed *that is* full of sheaves."

[599] Ps. 4:6: "*There be* many that say, Who will shew us *any* good? LORD, lift thou up the light of thy countenance upon us."

200 The Christian Quaker

enlightened all, is grieved and burdened – bearing the iniquities of all who sin and reject his benefits. But, those who hear his knock and let him into their hearts are first wounded and then healed. Afterwards, he reconciles, intercedes, and reinstates each into the holy image from which they fell by sin. Behold! This is the state of restitution! This, in some degree, was experienced by the holy patriarchs, prophets, and servants of God in old time. Christ was to them the same Savior and Seed, bruising the serpent's head, as he is now to us. Any apparent differences are only in the form in which he reveals himself.

Christ's death and sufferings acknowledged and respected as beneficial to salvation.

That same Light and Life later clothed itself with an outward body and, as I have often said, the Divine Life was never as completely present as it was in that sanctified and prepared body. What he suffered and did in that transcendent manifestation may be credited for all the work that he had done before or since for our salvation. Undoubtedly, the very same Light, Life, and Power that dwelled in that fleshly tabernacle was the Convincer, Condemner, Savior, and Redeemer - but not only when confined to that blessed body, but also as revealed in our hearts. He was in Paul's, who never met him in the flesh, but willingly received him – to bind the strong man in his heart and cast him out,[600] so that the one to whom it belonged could take possession of it. Do you doubt that the Divine Light, Life, Spirit, Nature, or Principle within that body was the ultimate cause of salvation? Look at the meaning of his name, i.e., to save his people from their sins.[601] He spoke not one word of wrath except in response to sin. Since sin is in the heart and conscience of a person, nothing but a Divine Light, Spirit, or Power can reach in and fill those inward parts with purity. Consequently, whatever does that must be the Redeemer and Savior from sin. Some claim that salvation is only from the wrath that sin earns and not from the sin itself. To do so is to deny the clear words of Scripture. It may be comforting to believe that one can be saved while still sinning, but there is no support for their rejection of an inherent and achievable holiness.

---

[600] Matt. 12:29: "Or else how can one enter into a strong man's house, and spoil his goods, except he first bind the strong man? and then he will spoil his house."

[601] Matt. 1:21: "And she shall bring forth a son, and thou shalt call his name Jesus: for he shall save his people from their sins."

I further admit that during his righteous life in an earthly body, he was grieved by sin. The weight of the iniquity of the whole world bore down on both his spiritual and his physical natures. He lived under its weight as he went about his labors. No one else knew of the eternal wrath that awaited the impenitent, nor did any other person know that it was his task alone to raise the holy, but oppressed Seed over the iniquities in people's hearts and to bruise the serpent's head in everyone. Outwardly, he gave his outward life for the world, so that he might inwardly diffuse the blood of God in their souls – that is, the holy purifying Life and Virtue in him as the Word-God. In this way, he is the Light and Life of the world.

It was this that that gave the man Jesus the understanding and strength to take on so great a task. It was by this power alone that he fasted, prayed, preached, cast out devils, performed miracles, lived an unblemished life, patiently suffered death, and was raised again – confirming everything he had done – despite all the opposition of the Jews. This divine power accompanied his followers in their ministry and because of it, many were convinced and converted by that ministry. The invisible, spiritual, and divine life, principle, or nature was the root and fountain of all that seems to be ascribed in the scriptures to the body. This common misunderstanding confuses the thing contained, which was the Eternal Power, Wisdom, Life, etc., with the container, which was the body. We would not irreverently rob that blessed body of whatever it deserves, nor separate what God has joined.

The Light of Christ is sufficient for salvation if it is completely followed.

But, with holy fear, I dare not attribute to any external being what is the natural and proper work only of the Divine Light and Life. Certainly there were others called "Savior" in the Scripture for their trials, works, and labors on behalf of the salvation of mankind – the title is even more appropriately bestowed on one who had the Spirit without measure. I freely acknowledge that holy person to have been, in some sense, a co-worker and partner with the Divine Light in those trials and sufferings for mankind. Yet, in all persons, it is the divine power that makes them acceptable for the great work; even in Jesus, it was the Divine Light that made his holy life what it was. Therefore, we attribute salvation to the Christ, the Word-God. To the holy body, we believe only that it was the instrument through which the Christ worked. This was the chosen vessel in which and by which God declared the blessed tidings of love and the message of reconciliation to the world. Through it we have received the most perfect example of purity –

the clearest evidence of truth, goodness, mercy, patience, deep labors for the world, self-denial, holiness, and triumphant martyrdom shined forth through that life, ministry, and death.

No wonder then that he is called a Savior. He came not only on a mission of salvation, but while on it, drew many after himself who were struck by the authority of his words. For a time, he allowed them to have their eyes and hearts upon him. But afterwards, he let his disciples know the benefit that could come only if he left them – not forever and in all ways, but in his outward appearance. Each received a measure of the Light, Power, and Life so that they might know him no more in the flesh, but in their hearts as a Comforter who would not leave his faithful disciples helpless.[602] "He that is now with you," he promised, "will be in you."[603]

Chapter XVIII

Belief in redemption, remission of sins, justification, and salvation by Christ.

*I*n this chapter, I will yet again briefly express our reverence for Christ's appearance as the man born of Mary.

I.   We believe the Eternal Power, Life, and Light that inhabited that holy person who was born at Bethlehem was and is the only Savior: "There is no Savior besides me," says God.[604] The human body taken by the Savior was instrumental, prepared, and chosen for the work that Christ, the Word-God, had to do while in it. This was the actual salvation of some living at that time and the intentional salvation of the whole world in all times. This is confirmed in Scripture, "Here I am – it is

---

[602] John 16:7: "Nevertheless I tell you the truth; It is expedient for you that I go away: for if I go not away, the Comforter will not come unto you; but if I depart, I will send him unto you."

[603] John 14:16-17: "And I will pray the Father, and he shall give you another Comforter, that he may abide with you for ever; *Even* the Spirit of truth; whom the world cannot receive, because it seeth him not, neither knoweth him: but ye know him; for he dwelleth with you, and shall be in you."

[604] Isa. 43:11: "I, *even* I, *am* the LORD; and beside me *there is* no saviour."

written about me in the scroll – I have come to do your will, O God – you prepared a body for me."[605]

II.   It was necessary for one to die for the people so that whoever believed in him then or since, had and has a sign or confirmation of the forgiveness of their sins in his blood. According to the rituals of Jewish sacrifice, that blood utterly blots out the sins and all memory of them – as if they had been carried off to a land of forgetfulness. This assurance of forgiveness and safety from God's wrath is received in the ratifying blood of Christ by all who repent of their sins, believe, and obey the holy Light with which they are enlightened. For Paul, being turned from darkness to the Light within his heart was the same as believing in the Son of God as revealed in his heart.

III.   This glorious appearance ended the need for the less-glorious services of the Jews. The figures were fulfilled – the shadows replaced with substance. He, in the flesh, preached and lived beyond those miserable elements. He drew religion inward, even into the secret of the heart, and founded it in a higher state of righteousness, filled with the spirit of the gospel. He was both the author of a more heavenly dispensation and an example to all, Gentile and Jew alike. A common religion for both was sealed with his blood, forever ending all distinctions and hostility between them and making all one in Christ.[606] By his one most pure and spiritual offering and worship, he brought an end to the Jews' outward rituals and overthrew the Gentiles' idolatries.

IV.   This much is plain: Jesus, whose outward body was slain in Jerusalem, was by our wicked acts crucified for the works done in the streets of Sodom and Egypt – that is, in our polluted hearts and consciences. Unless we come to know the power and benefit of the inward life – corresponding to and expressed by the outward life he gave for the world – his sacrifice will be of no value to us. This is the mystery and the miracle – that the life of the crucified can only save those who may well be called the crucifiers. Those who did not slay him outwardly have slain him

---

[605] Heb. 10:5-7: "Wherefore when he cometh into the world, he saith, Sacrifice and offering thou wouldest not, but a body hast thou prepared me: In burnt offerings and *sacrifices* for sin thou hast had no pleasure. Then said I, Lo, I come (in the volume of the book it is written of me,) to do thy will, O God."

[606] Gal. 3:28: "There is neither Jew nor Greek, there is neither bond nor free, there is neither male nor female: for ye are all one in Christ Jesus."

inwardly when their evil spirits resist and reject his spiritual appearance in their souls. Truly, we must know that divine life raised up and announced to all for sanctification and redemption from sin. Oh! How great was his love for humanity! Truly, it was larger than all our cruelties – in dying at the hands of the wicked, he died for them. And when dead, they could not stop him from rising again to do good for those who had done their worst for his destruction. He showed mercy to those who had no mercy for him or for themselves. "O Jerusalem! Jerusalem! How often have I longed to gather you and you were not willing?"[607]

V.   Give your attention to his words, "I lay down my life for the world."[608] Everything he did was for the good of the world, especially laying down his life in order to express his love and to show us our duty. If he had not desired our salvation, and for that purpose prepared a body in which to visit us, and by his daily labors to further our eternal happiness, he would never have been put to death. But, by coming and being so badly abused, he demonstrated his great love for us. Beyond the burden of sin that he carried inwardly for our eternal well-being, he willingly offered up his bodily life to seal and reveal his love for the forgiveness of sin and as a holy example for us to follow.

But these words can be understood in another way, as can those he spoke to the Jews, "Unless you eat my flesh and drink my blood, you have no life in you." We can plainly see that the Jews misunderstood. Thinking he meant his outward body, they were opposed to it, but, Christ reveals the true meaning to his disciples in a few profound words, "The flesh is useless – the spirit gives life."[609] These words are true and weighty in both senses.

---

[607] Luke 13:34: "O Jerusalem, Jerusalem, which killest the prophets, and stonest them that are sent unto thee; how often would I have gathered thy children together, as a hen *doth gather* her brood under *her* wings, and ye would not!"

[608] This quote combines two passages from John:

John 10:17: "Therefore doth my Father love me, because I lay down my life, that I might take it again."

John 3:16: "For God so loved the world, that he gave his only begotten Son, that whosoever believeth in him should not perish, but have everlasting life."

[609] John 6:51-54&62-63: "I am the living bread which came down from heaven: if any man eat of this bread, he shall live for ever: and the bread that I will give is my flesh, which I will give for the life of the world. The Jews therefore strove among themselves, saying, How can this man give us *his* flesh to eat? Then Jesus said unto them, Verily, verily, I say unto you, Except ye eat the flesh of

VI.   We further acknowledge that in that holy body, the divine principle of Light and Life discovered the depths of Satan's darkness, encountered hell, death, and the grave, and knew every temptation with which the subtle serpent could entice him. In that way, he was made like us in all things except sin[610] so that he might understand our weaknesses. The divine life exerted itself through it all, giving strength to and supporting the outward man so that he could persevere, and in the end utterly defeat and forever overcome the power of the tempter. He bruised the serpent's head for all. He engaged the prince of darkness and god of this world in plain combat, disgracing him and shaking his foundations, dividing his kingdom,[611] chasing away his lying prophets, and delivering a fatal blow to his whole empire. This holy conquest, purchased by a sweat of blood and the deepest agonies,[612] and with holy patience, can be compared to that of a worldly prince who righteously resists an invasion, routing the usurpers in battle (by which I mean his overall victory over sin). But even in victory, many towns and citadels remain in the enemy's hands (by which I mean the men and women who are still enslaved by sin). These do not automatically surrender, although it may be easier to approach them, and they are more accessible than they were before.

The One Seed, who is Christ, is God over all, blessed forever. In defeating the god of this world, he gave as proof of his everlasting authority and brought salvation for all. This was the one great battle fought in garments rolled in blood[613] between the two seeds, two spirits, two natures, and two powers. The enemy of his glory has been weakened, but the god of

---

the Son of man, and drink his blood, ye have no life in you. Whoso eateth my flesh, and drinketh my blood, hath eternal life; and I will raise him up at the last day. ... *What* and if ye shall see the Son of man ascend up where he was before? It is the spirit that quickeneth; the flesh profiteth nothing: the words that I speak unto you, *they* are spirit, and *they* are life."

[610] Heb. 4:15: "For we have not an high priest which cannot be touched with the feeling of our infirmities; but was in all points tempted like as *we are, yet* without sin."

[611] Matt. 12:26: "And if Satan cast out Satan, he is divided against himself; how shall then his kingdom stand?"

[612] Luke 22:44: "And being in an agony he prayed more earnestly: and his sweat was as it were great drops of blood falling down to the ground."

[613] Isa. 9:5: "For every battle of the warrior *is* with confused noise, and garments rolled in blood; but *this* shall be with burning *and* fuel of fire."

this world maintains garrisons in many cities, towns, and strongholds – that is in the souls of the many men and women still possessed and enslaved by him. The prince of darkness still reigns and rules in the hearts of the children of disobedience. Victory over the spirit of darkness has made their hearts more accessible to the Light, but unless those strongholds are besieged and taken – the things of Mammon and Beliel destroyed and all strange gods thrown out of their hearts – they cannot be freed from the yoke of that Pharaoh's taskmaster. Then they will be reclaimed, renewed, sanctified, brought into holy subjection to the Lord of heaven, and become joint-heirs[614] with the true heir of all things.[615]

What we say is that the general victory was achieved and holy privileges claimed for us. The holy body was the instrument, but the preeminent cause was the Divine Light and Life which so clearly revealed and wounded the Mystery of Iniquity.[616] But although the privilege has been claimed, none can benefit from this victory unless they experience the Holy Seed of Life, God's mighty arm,[617] which has been revealed to us to bring salvation from sin in each individual conscience. None can fail if they accept it first as a Light that reveals and condemns every evil thing they have done and who then continue to walk in it.

VII.   There is still another benefit that comes from the blood of Christ – Christ is the reconciler and redeemer of all who have faith in it. Although the individual benefit comes from the Light, Life, and Spirit revealed within each person, the blood shed by the body of Christ (which was offered up through the eternal Spirit) was reconciling. Although this bloody act might have brought down stupendous punishments on the heads of his murders (if they died without repenting), it was the most precious offering in the eyes of God and drew God's love ever more to humanity, or at least to those who believed in his name. For this, we have

---

[614] Rom. 8:17: "And if children, then heirs; heirs of God, and joint-heirs with Christ; if so be that we suffer with *him*, that we may be also glorified together."

[615] Heb. 1:1-2: "God, who at sundry times and in divers manners spake in time past unto the fathers by the prophets, Hath in these last days spoken unto us by *his* Son, whom he hath appointed heir of all things, by whom also he made the worlds."

[616] 2 Thess. 2:7: "For the mystery of iniquity doth already work: only he who now letteth *will let*, until he be taken out of the way."

[617] Ps. 89:13: "Thou hast a mighty arm: strong is thy hand, *and* high is thy right hand."

the words of solemn prayer to the Father that are plainly recorded by the beloved disciple.[618]

How could it be any other way? Since God credited the sufferings of his only begotten son to those who believe in him, how could forgiveness not be offered to all who believe in Christ, the Light of the world? Christ's sacrifice, the last and greatest of all his external acts, undoubtedly earned God's special tenderness and unique care for all who believe in his name. This was the capstone of all his bodily sufferings, earning forgiveness of all sin. For the spiritual good of the world, he resisted evil – even offering his blood and life on the cross through the power of the Eternal Spirit – so that God's great gift to the world would be preached in his name and in his blood. Is it any wonder that the Holy Spirit would find it good that redemption, remission, and reconciliation should be proclaimed and granted in the blood of Christ to all who have faith? As the Apostle said to the Romans, "God sent him as a reconciler, through faith in his blood,"[619] and to the Ephesians, "By him and through his blood, we have redemption and the forgiveness of sins."[620] This implies several things.

1. A firm belief that Christ came in the flesh and that no one could claim him as their reconciler or redeemer who refused to acknowledge and believe in his visible appearance (which, John tells us, some deny[621]).

2. That Christ came for the remission, redemption, and salvation of the world.

3. That his death was both a clear sign of his love and the strongest proof of his message and work.

---

[618] John 17:25-26: "O righteous Father, the world hath not known thee: but I have known thee, and these have known that thou hast sent me. And I have declared unto them thy name, and will declare *it*: that the love wherewith thou hast loved me may be in them, and I in them."

[619] Rom. 3:25: "Whom God hath set forth *to be* a propitiation through faith in his blood, to declare his righteousness for the remission of sins that are past, through the forbearance of God."

[620] Eph. 1:7: "In whom we have redemption through his blood, the forgiveness of sins, according to the riches of his grace."

[621] 1 John 2:22: "Who is a liar but he that denieth that Jesus is the Christ? He is antichrist, that denieth the Father and the Son."

4. That, as the Epistle to the Hebrews tells us, Christ's substitution of himself for temporary and prefiguring sacrifices brought to an end the Jews' outward rituals.

5. That through the holy Light within each person, he brought people to acknowledge and believe in the blood that confirmed all that he did in the flesh. In so doing, people were brought to a more inward and spiritual knowledge of Christ, an understanding consistent with his own words, "It is the Spirit that gives Life,"[622] and the apostle's proclamation, "The Lord from heaven is the life-giving Spirit."[623] By this Eternal Spirit he had offered himself up as an unblemished sacrifice.[624]

No one can reasonably suppose that Christ, when he explained to his disciples those things he had said obscurely and in parables to the crowds,[625] revealed anything hidden or more divine than they or others could understand. What hindered the others was their inability to recognize him for who he was. Without such an acknowledgement, they could not understand or benefit from what he preached nor could they experience his Divine Life in themselves.

In conclusion, that body belonged to the Divine Life ("a body prepared for me"[626]), therefore all that was done by that body for the redemption of humanity is truly the work of the Divine Life. But, an action is frequently credited to an instrument, rather than to the one who uses the instrument. In order to accommodate the understanding of ordinary people, the

---

[622] John 6:63: "It is the spirit that quickeneth; the flesh profiteth nothing: the words that I speak unto you, *they* are spirit, and *they* are life."

[623] 1 Cor. 15:45&47: "And so it is written, The first man Adam was made a living soul; the last Adam *was made* a quickening spirit. ... The first man *is* of the earth, earthy: the second man *is* the Lord from heaven."

[624] Heb. 9:14: "How much more shall the blood of Christ, who through the eternal Spirit offered himself without spot to God, purge your conscience from dead works to serve the living God?"

[625] Matt. 13:10-11: "And the disciples came, and said unto him, Why speakest thou unto them in parables? He answered and said unto them, Because it is given unto you to know the mysteries of the kingdom of heaven, but to them it is not given."

[626] Heb. 10:5: "Wherefore when he cometh into the world, he saith, Sacrifice and offering thou wouldest not, but a body hast thou prepared me."

Scriptures often speak of the inward substance and hidden reality of things in parabolic, hyperbolic, and metaphoric terms (as is the proper form in both Hebrew and Greek) – observable and obvious things are used to give a sense of unobservable mysteries. The Divine Life acting in that body was the origin and ultimate Redeemer, but with the following qualification. That body was essential for proclamation and revelation, and its physical sufferings helped to procure and secure salvation. Only those who acknowledge Christ's presence in that body – an understanding sparked by a measure of that same Divine Life in themselves – can enjoy the benefits that were obtained through it.

This is the main point of the passages: "whom God has sent as a reconciler"[627] and "in whom we have redemption through his blood."[628] Who is this that God has sent? Who is the redeemer? Certainly, it is the same one that was before Abraham, who (long before that body was conceived and born) cried, "Lo, I have come to do your will, O God! You have prepared a body for me."[629] But some say, then how can it be his blood? I answer, just as it is his body.

Those who had faith in that blood believed in the reality of his visible appearance. They acknowledged that the one who came to save the world shed his own blood as the seal and confirmation of that work. He is the only reconciler, redeemer, and savior of all who had or have faith in his life, message, and revelations. Only by the inward revelations and work of the Light – Christ, the Word-God who took flesh – was it possible for anyone in that day to recognize and believe in the Divine Light and Life that appeared in that body.

As true and spiritual witnesses, the apostles described the heavenly visitation as it was made visible through that prepared body. They commended to us the great love of Christ as revealed by the cruel sufferings

---

[627] Rom. 3:25: "Whom God hath set forth *to be* a propitiation through faith in his blood, to declare his righteousness for the remission of sins that are past, through the forbearance of God."

[628] Eph. 1:7: "In whom we have redemption through his blood, the forgiveness of sins, according to the riches of his grace."

[629] Heb. 10:5&7: "Wherefore when he cometh into the world, he saith, Sacrifice and offering thou wouldest not, but a body hast thou prepared me... Then said I, Lo, I come (in the volume of the book it is written of me,) to do thy will, O God."

of both his body and his spirit, but they did not intend us to stop there. It was their desire that those who know Christ in the flesh would press on and seek a more spiritual knowledge of Christ beyond that body – not denying the body, but looking through it to the heavenly life that had suffered in it. Those who had known Christ in the flesh were urged to go deeper and achieve a more spiritual understanding of him. It was necessary for those who had been most devoted to him in his outward appearance to be weaned of it, so that the more interior and more beneficial revelation of Christ might be witnessed by the soul.

The great question for the Jews of that day was whether God had truly been present in the earthly body they had seen. Faith in his blood was necessary for people to recognize him as the Christ, who is God over all and blessed forever. This is the essential point, God came in human flesh and died for us. In summary, we believe that Christ, who came into the world, was and is the only reconciler with God, and all who have true faith in his blood obtain their redemption through him. Still, for a soul to be redeemed from the pollution of sin, it must, to some degree, witness to the Light, Life, and Power within.

VIII.   "No one is justified by the law."[630] The law was given to humanity because of its transgressions. It cannot condemn people as sinners and justify them before God while they remain sinners. Allow me to distinguish between two understandings of justification. The first understanding sees it as merely the remission, pardon, or forgiveness of past and repented sins. The second views justification of a person as the reconciliation with and acceptance by God. That is to say, God recognizes that person as a keeper of the law of the spirit of life[631] and God makes him or her inherently just, righteous, or holy.

If we use the word only in the first sense, no one can be justified by the very law that he or she has broken (and since all have sinned,[632] no one can be justified). Moreover, "by the works of the law no one is justified"[633] – all

---

[630] Gal. 3:11: "But that no man is justified by the law in the sight of God, *it is* evident: for, The just shall live by faith."

[631] Rom. 8:2: "For the law of the Spirit of life in Christ Jesus hath made me free from the law of sin and death."

[632] Rom. 3:23: "For all have sinned, and come short of the glory of God."

[633] Gal. 2:16: "Knowing that a man is not justified by the works of the law, but by the faith of Jesus Christ, even we have believed in Jesus Christ, that we might

the righteous acts a person can do will never cancel out the penalties for his or her unrighteousness ones – righteousness is simply what we owe God. But still, those who keep the law must be justified – a just God would not condemn both those who break the law and those who keep it. How do we say explain this? Since the time of Adam and Eve, justification (in the first sense) has been God's love freely granted in response to repentance. And since Christ's visible appearance and suffering, the message of remission, pardon, and forgiveness – available to all who believed in his name – has been preached to the whole world.

In the second sense, no one is justified unless he or she is made just and is actually doing the will of God. This is what gains access to and acceptance from God. It was in this sense that the apostle said that "those who do the law will be justified."[634] This is more than freedom from the guilt for what they had formerly done – that comes from the free love of God, given to anyone who repents. This has been true in all ages, but never widely proclaimed to the whole world as it has been since the coming of our Lord Jesus Christ in the flesh.

So far, we can approach the more honest of those who claim to be religious – or rather, we were never far from them – in saying that people can be completely reconciled and, in a sense justified, even though sin has not been completely destroyed. God, on seeing their repentance from past sins (although they are not clear of all evil), can and (we believe) does remit, pardon, and forgive those offenses. In that way, some reconciliation is achieved – God ceases to be angry or distant from them as when they were disobedient to the Light. But this is not the same as becoming a child of God. For that, a new birth, regeneration, and recovery of the divine and heavenly image is required – taking off the old self along with its ways[635] and being baptized by the Holy Spirit and fire[636] into the one holy body,[637]

---

be justified by the faith of Christ, and not by the works of the law: for by the works of the law shall no flesh be justified."

[634] Rom. 2:13 "For not the hearers of the law *are* just before God, but the doers of the law shall be justified."

[635] Col. 3:9: "Lie not one to another, seeing that ye have put off the old man with his deeds."

[636] Matt. 3:11: "I indeed baptize you with water unto repentance: but he that cometh after me is mightier than I, whose shoes I am not worthy to bear: he shall baptize you with the Holy Ghost, and *with* fire."

of which Christ, the immaculate lamb of God,[638] is the head and Lord.[639] All those who claim for themselves or for others that which was promised to those who are reborn – without being regenerated themselves – are liars and God will so judge them. Let everyone seriously consider whether or not our claim is more consistent with the Scriptures – and even more so with the Light of Truth in their own consciences.

IX.   This is not all of the good that came from the life and sufferings of that blessed person. Having been enabled to completely live according to the will of God, and to suffer and die so patiently at the hands of the wicked, he earned great and priceless gifts. As each person comes to believe in the Light with which Christ Jesus enlightens, and is led by it, he or she will gain a share in those great benefits.

In short, we acknowledge him as the savior who came in that prepared body. He visited the world with his marvelous Light and Truth to turn people's minds from error and darkness. In so doing, he converted and reclaimed many. He bestowed his own heavenly Light, Life, and Power on his followers so that they could carry forward a lively, piercing, and effective ministry in his outward absence and continue his work in each succeeding generation. We recognize all this as the work of the Divine Light, Life, and Power – poured out and revealed for the salvation of the world – first through the physical body of our Lord and then through his servants.

Many were reached in their hearts and consciences at that time. Great and mighty things were obtained for all. Christ in the flesh was the source of salvation[640] for many. But we do not (as has been darkly hinted by our opponents) attribute the salvation of any individual to the appearance of that Light either in the Lord or in his servants. Rather, Christ is the Light within each person individually. Then, as now, he appears in each heart and

---

[637] 1 Cor. 12:13: "For by one Spirit are we all baptized into one body, whether *we be* Jews or Gentiles, whether *we be* bond or free; and have been all made to drink into one Spirit."

[638] John 1:29: "The next day John seeth Jesus coming unto him, and saith, Behold the Lamb of God, which taketh away the sin of the world."

[639] Col. 1:18: "And he is the head of the body, the church: who is the beginning, the firstborn from the dead; that in all *things* he might have the preeminence."

[640] Heb. 5:9: "And being made perfect, he became the author of eternal salvation unto all them that obey him."

each conscience, awakening them and turning their minds away from the darkness of tradition, ritual, and sin, which had overcast and darkened the soul, concealing it from that blessed Light within. This is the real and true cause of salvation. All exterior assistance or outward ministry, even though originating in the same Light, is secondary to and supportive of the work of the Light within each man or woman.

In this sense, Christ as revealed and obeyed in the conscience is the only effective means of salvation – both his physical appearance and the ministry of his servants are mere instruments by which he is known. So, the question is not whether Quakers deny the benefits that come from Christ's bodily sufferings, but whether our opponents admit and acknowledge the primacy of the work of the Divine Light and Life?

In short, he was the Savior of all by his appearance in Jerusalem, doing many great and good things for mankind, but is the Savior of each individual only when that person finds him in their heart – a holy Light revealing sin, condemning it, and turning him or her away from it. Then they are taken into the holy nature of the Light, Jesus Christ, to be flesh of his flesh and bone of his bone.[641]

This, I declare in love and humility, is my understanding – grounded in my experience and the illumination that God has given me – of the truth, importance, and reason for the outward coming of Christ and for his deep sufferings at the hands of, and on behalf of, the world. Likewise, it is my understanding of the nature of his coming into the soul – to expel the darkness that has taken up residence there and to give each person the Light of Life. In these acts, I know him to be the Savior of the world in general and the Savior of each person individually. But the benefit that comes from him as Savior of all is only known and received by those who know him to be their individual Savior – this I know to be true. Christ within becomes the hope of glory[642] and, by the Spirit of the Lord, we can

---

[641] Gen. 2:23: "And Adam said, This *is* now bone of my bones, and flesh of my flesh: she shall be called Woman, because she was taken out of Man."

[642] Col. 1:27: "To whom God would make known what *is* the riches of the glory of this mystery among the Gentiles; which is Christ in you, the hope of glory."

be transformed into God's image, with ever-increasing glory.[643] This is the salvation and perfection of every true Christian.

Chapter XIX

Christ is the Light, or the Light is Christ, proved from Scripture.

What remains in order to complete our scriptural discourse on the Divine Light is to show that it is what our enemies hate to call it – and because we do, they undervalue both it and us – I mean Christ. This is not to say that the Light within each conscience is the whole of Christ, but that Christ, the Word-God, is the Light of Righteousness that enlightens all. The Scripture is quite explicit in that well-known but little believed passage that the beloved disciple has given us, "This is the true Light that enlightens all who come into the world."[644] Of all his disciples, John knew the Lord best and had little need for others to tell him how best to describe or name our Lord. Even so, our opponents and others implicitly accuse him of weakness and obscurity, if not outright error and blasphemy. They accuse the poor Quakers of all this (and would if possible, more) for believing this weighty passage to mean all that it says on pure conviction.

I have thoroughly discussed our belief that Christ is the universal and sufficient Light – and that the Light is Christ – in my recent book, *The Spirit of Truth Vindicated*. I refer the reader to that book and feel little need to add to what I said there. However, in order to demonstrate that this belief is on as firm a foundation as possible, I will briefly comment on two things that are commonly assumed and are contrary to our understanding of the first nine verses of the gospel of John.

1. Some say that the Light spoken of in these verses is human reasoning and therefore, has no saving power. Others call it a natural illumination of the soul, degenerated by the fall of Adam and Eve, which all people share in, both before and after Christ came in the flesh.

---

[643] 2 Cor. 3:18: "But we all, with open face beholding as in a glass the glory of the Lord, are changed into the same image from glory to glory, *even* as by the Spirit of the Lord."

[644] John 1:9: "*That* was the true Light, which lighteth every man that cometh into the world."

2. Others say that this is indeed a universal and saving Light, but limit it to the time of Christ's visible appearance. They also restrict "all" to mean only those who believe and "the world" to be the new spiritual world that Christ came to create by the knowledge of salvation that his believers came to possess.

I will briefly answer each of these claims.

Those who make the first claim agree that, at the beginning of this gospel, Christ's eternal divinity is declared by the evangelist. Some of them, agreeing with Eusebius, tell us that it was written to answer Cerinthus[645] on that very point.

"The Word was with God and was and is God."[646] This God, the same writer tells us in his first epistle, "is Light."[647] "By him, all things were made"[648] – including mankind. He then tells us that this Word had life and what the Word was relative to humanity: "In him (the Word) was life, and that life was the Light of all"[649] and, as such, "He was the true Light (that is, John the Baptist was not, but came only to bear witness to that true Light)[650] that lights all who come into the world."[651]

I will now prove that this Light was divine and in no way natural – other than it was Christ's nature or natural for the Word.

In these verses, people are presumed to exist before they are enlightened. Therefore, anything that is a proper or natural part of being human is within them before they are enlightened – i.e., each person has a

---

[645] Cerinthus (first century A.D.) was the leader of a Christian-Jewish sect, probably in Egypt. According to Irenaeus, the Gospel of John was written to answer his heretical errors.

[646] John 1:1: "In the beginning was the Word, and the Word was with God, and the Word was God."

[647] 1 John 1:5: "This then is the message which we have heard of him, and declare unto you, that God is light, and in him is no darkness at all."

[648] John 1:3: "All things were made by him; and without him was not any thing made that was made."

[649] John 1:4: "In him was life; and the life was the light of men."

[650] John 1:8: "He was not that Light, but *was sent* to bear witness of that Light."

[651] John 1:9: "*That* was the true Light, which lighteth every man that cometh into the world."

reasonable soul[652] endowed with intelligent abilities and is clothed with a living body having the proper sense organs. This body distinguished them from inanimate objects and the soul, from irrational creatures. But the Light, with which the soul is enlightened regarding God and things related to its eternal well-being, is not theirs by nature as human beings. That Light is conferred over and above the components that are required to make up a mere understanding creature and must consequently come from above. In this sense, it is supernatural. Thus, the Word created all things and among them was humanity; and alone of all created things, the Word enlightened humanity with a supernatural Light.

This Light was not only over and above human nature, but is also divine and saving in itself. There is no need to look at the effects of the Light to prove it Divine – the proof is simply that it is the Life of the Word.[653] If the Life of the Word is the Light of mankind, then that Light is divine because the Word is divine. The Life does not create the Light or cause the Light (i.e., the Light is not a product of the Life) – the Life is the Light. Hence, unless they consider the Life of the Word to be natural (that is, a created thing), they cannot conclude that the Light, which is the same as the Life, is merely a natural light. On the contrary, it is necessarily supernatural, divine, and infinite.

Consequently, I have no need to separately prove that the Light can save, unless those who oppose us wish to propose that salvation can somehow be divided from divinity. However, let me say briefly, that the Light within an individual shares in the true Light – so-called that because of its excellence, greatly rising above that of John the Baptist and it was through John that all could believe in him.[654] Moreover, we are told that "the power to become children of God"[655] was given to all those who received him as the universal enlightener or true Light. Indisputably, this shows that the Light has the power to save. I have previously, by multiple arguments and testimonies, shown from Scriptures the universality and

---

[652] In the seventeenth century, the mind was considered to be a faculty of the soul, not the brain.

[653] John 1:4: "In him was life; and the life was the light of men."

[654] John 1:7: "The same came for a witness, to bear witness of the Light, that all *men* through him might believe."

[655] John 1:12: "But as many as received him, to them gave he power to become the sons of God, *even* to them that believe on his name."

sufficiency of that Divine Light. Those who say that it is a degenerated thing (because they are degenerated themselves) are like those at sea who think they see the shore move when the ship gets underway. The problem is in those eyes that have been blinded by the god of this world,[656] not in that blessed Light that shines to no effect on blind eyes – especially when the blindness is the product of their own disobedience. Let the scales fall from their eyes[657] by sincere repentance and the sun will prove that it gives light. Darkness cannot blame the Light, but only itself, for being blind.

Some accept that all are enlightened, but deny that the Light is sufficient by itself to save them. They refuse to be ruled by it or to live up to it. But, before they deny it, let them first obey it. Before they discard it, let them prove that they don't need it. When they exceed all of its requirements and nothing in their lives is condemned by it, then they can call it impotent or imperfect and hold up their experience as proof that it is insufficient. It is foolhardy to underestimate that which can both charge them with failure to do their duty and reveal the sins they have committed. Happy are those who put aside their prejudices and follow the Light within!

This I can be sure of: the Life of the Word is the Light of all and consequently is Divine. With that, I will leave the first kind of objectors, with all their absurdities and fruitless opposition, and turn my attention to the second objection to our interpretation of this text.

The Light of all is the Life of the Word and the Word was God by whom all things were created. "All" are specified in the text and "all" are to receive the Light without any qualification beyond being born into the world. There are no grounds for claiming that this gift is linked in any way to Christ's coming in the flesh. I must conclude that such a notion is not only false, but injurious.

This passage clearly applies to all of humanity from Adam and Eve in the beginning to the last, yet to be born, humans – I cannot conceive how any other interpretation can be valid. Otherwise, John (who was born before Jesus) would have come before Christ, rather than Christ coming before Abraham. Moreover, we are told that John is not that Light because

---

[656] 2 Cor. 4:4: "In whom the god of this world hath blinded the minds of them which believe not, lest the light of the glorious gospel of Christ, who is the image of God, should shine unto them."

[657] Acts 9:18: "And immediately there fell from his eyes as it had been scales: and he received sight forthwith, and arose, and was baptized."

the true Light was the enlightener of "all," even of John. It was called the true Light, the source of all Light, Light itself, from whom all others are derived, but Christ derives from none.[658]

The miserable spiritual conditions under which mankind labored before Christ came in the flesh will not be mentioned, but consider that these first nine verses in John's gospel do not relate in any way to his physical presence – the event to which these objectors date both Christ's origin and humanity's illumination. They are simply a continued series of proofs of his divinity, so that we can know what he was before he came into the world as well as what he was in the world. These verses are merely an introduction to the description of his life on earth. Nor is it right for these people to use allegory to deny Christ his divinity but refuse to let us use allegory to prove it. If they wish to deny those meanings elsewhere, they should do it here as well. It is hardly proper for intelligent people to use that intelligence to prop up fantasies.

Further, let me add that the one who came into the world was the same one who created that world[659] and existed, therefore, before that coming. Nor can it be claimed that the world into which all come is a new creation. The scripture does not say "all who believe," as is the case when they refer to the new heaven and new earth. For example, Luke refers to those who "believe and are saved,"[660] and Mark to those "who believe and are not damned."[661] Nor can those who do not believe be excluded from enlightenment – the wicked could not rebel against the Light if they did not have it;[662] nor could their evil acts be condemned without it.[663] All of these claims are refuted by the Scripture and contrary to reason.

---

[658] Penn has noted: "See Origen, Chrysostom, Greg., Erasmus, Drusius, Cam., Grot., B. Sand., Dr. Ham." in the margin.

[659] John 1:10: "He was in the world, and the world was made by him, and the world knew him not."

[660] Luke 8:12: "Those by the way side are they that hear; then cometh the devil, and taketh away the word out of their hearts, lest they should believe and be saved."

[661] Mark 16:16: "He that believeth and is baptized shall be saved; but he that believeth not shall be damned."

[662] Job 24:13: "They are of those that rebel against the light; they know not the ways thereof, nor abide in the paths thereof."

[663] John 3:19: "And this is the condemnation, that light is come into the world, and men loved darkness rather than light, because their deeds were evil."

We must conclude then that Christ, the Word-God, is the Light of the world and that all are enlightened by him, the Eternal Sun of Righteousness. The Light of all is Christ. It was to Christ, the true Light, that John testified. Through Christ, the wicked see their unrighteousness and the good are led in the paths of holiness, and unquestionably if they persevere, to eternal happiness. Without obedience to that guide, all the great acts of righteousness performed by Christ will bring us nothing – that righteousness will not be imputed to us on the great and terrible Day of Judgment. On that day, all will be judged for the deeds that they performed in their own mortal bodies, not for those performed by anyone else.

Next, I will finish this topic with a few reasons supporting the universality and sufficiency of the Light within. In so doing, you will see that in addition to the Scriptures of Truth and other authorities, we have reason (which is more universal) on our side.

Chapter XX

The universality of the Light within proved by reason.

There has been plentiful testimony in all ages that there is a universal Light. There is nothing else that can claim such general support or such antiquity. There is no nation at any time that does not report the revelations of an internal Light that allowed people to distinguish good from evil – virtue has always been praised and vice damned. This is a matter of fact, which I have already proved, and even the most barbarous of nations provide clear evidence of what I say. By the inward revelations of the Divine Light of Christ, the wicked have known their wickedness and the good their goodness in every age. I conclude, therefore, that no one is exempt from this illumination.

This is also completely consistent with the goodness of God and the order of creation. It seems unreasonable that humanity should have the benefit of a natural sun, shining on the just and the unjust,[664] to guide their steps and transact their temporal affairs in security, but not have a spiritual luminary or Sun of Righteousness to guide their souls. Compared to the

---

Eph. 5:13: "But all things that are reproved are made manifest by the light: for whatsoever doth make manifest is light."

[664] Matt. 5:45: "That ye may be the children of your Father which is in heaven: for he maketh his sun to rise on the evil and on the good, and sendeth rain on the just and on the unjust."

value of a single soul, Christ declares the whole world worthless.[665] The soul has eyes as well as the body. People can see when the sun is in the outward sky – unless they deliberately close their eyes. In the same way, all rational souls can choose to see with the eye of reason how to act and walk spiritually. The spiritual sun gives direction and discernment to the mind as certainly as the outward sun gives it to the body.

If this were not so, people could, in their misery, charge God with neglecting them. We can reasonably assume that God gave every creature the ability to recognize its Creator (in a way appropriate to its nature). Mankind's unique duty in this respect is homage and worship – expressed by a life lived in keeping with the will of God. If so, it is only just for God to endow us with something, which is itself divine, that will allow us to do that duty. Otherwise, we would be unable to fulfill our duty; we could not please or even properly acknowledge God. If all mankind ought to worship, fear, and reverence God, certainly all have received an ability from God to do so; otherwise, something perfectly impossible is expected of poor, impotent creatures. The eternal God, in righteousness and justice, could never expect from us what we never had the power to do – we cannot improve on a talent we never had.[666] In short, if we believe that God must be worshipped and revered, either we must agree that we are endowed with a Divine Light and knowledge or say (with the unfortunate servant in Matthew's account) that God is a hard master who harvests where he did not sow and gathers up what he did not plant.[667] I am afraid that the principles and prejudices of some people predispose them to believe in a harsh and unfeeling God rather than to think favorably about the Light. Don't those who say it is impossible for the Light to bear their iniquities see how shortsighted it is to wound it daily with their rebelliousness?

But, they object, some people deny they have it, and others, by their depraved lives, amply demonstrate that they do not. To that, I say that it is possible for a life of worldliness, pleasure, and utter debauchery to darken, or nearly blind, the inward eye that sees the Light of Truth and, when it is

---

[665] Mark 8:36: "For what shall it profit a man, if he shall gain the whole world, and lose his own soul?"

[666] See the Parable of the Talents (Matt. 24:14-30).

[667] Matt. 25:24: "Then he which had received the one talent came and said, Lord, I knew thee that thou art an hard man, reaping where thou hast not sown, and gathering where thou hast not strawed."

fixed on the Truth, fills the body with Light.[668] This does not change the Light. If through repentance and contrition the scales fall away, the Light will not refuse to again enter the eye that can and will see it. The Light remains unchanged, it is the person who changes. When some run about in madness, does it prove that all of humanity is insane? Neither is the universality of the Light disproved because some have by sin so spiritually deadened themselves that they cannot see it.

Nor does a corrupt life disprove the sufficiency of the Light – although it may prove disobedience to it. Is it logical to say that if a wicked person rejects good advice, the advice was never offered? Does it make any more sense to say that people disobey the Light and therefore they never had it – at least to let them know their wickedness? People may be said to be lighted when they know and do not do their duty; but, I confess, I would rather see them become better because of this illumination. In the first sense, all are illuminated; in the second sense, only those who obey the Light are – they find their understandings illuminated and their hearts mended. This is what others lose by disobedience. In short, all who have not completely blinded themselves have enough Light to condemn their wickedness. But, only those who receive it and love it obtain its benefits as a teacher and guide.

The general agreement of humanity, the goodness and justice of God, and reason all plead strongly for the universality of the Light. I need to say no more and will move on to consider its sufficiency.

Chapter XXI

The sufficiency of the Light proved by reason.

Since the sufficiency of the Light to bring salvation is attacked as often as the universality has been, I hope it will not seem unnecessary for me to respond briefly. Let me note first that much of what I have said above certainly applies to this topic as well.

That the universal Light is also sufficient is a belief so reasonable and necessary that to deny it seems to question the justice of God. Everyone admits that God made us rational and capable (to one degree or another) of knowing our Creator. We would certainly not have been given this ability

---

[668] Luke 11:34: "The light of the body is the eye: therefore when thine eye is single, thy whole body also is full of light; but when *thine eye* is evil, thy body also *is* full of darkness."

unless God wished us to discover something about himself. Surely, God did not want to create a false impression. Since our love, awe, and reverence are expected, God must have made sufficient revelation, and the ability for us to perceive that revelation, by obvious signs and plainly felt touches of the Light on our souls. These are true, clear, and, if they are attended to, effective. For God to require our service, and not give us what is needed to perform that service, would be worse than not giving anything at all. Who can be faulted for failing to correctly follow an imperfect guide? And do we suppose that (out of neglect or unwillingness) God's revelations have been imperfect? Does God expect homage as our sovereign Lord, and that we live uprightly in the world without giving us the ability to do either? Would God condemn us for failing to do the impossible? Reason tells us that no one was made solely to be destroyed, but rather so that God might be glorified by the salvation to which all are invited – God does not intend for anyone to live under the cloud of an impossible demand. Such a dismal situation cannot be the truth, so we are well assured that the Light of which we speak has been sufficient in every age to reveal, condemn, and redeem all who are its diligent disciples from the power and pollution of evil.

It seems completely unreasonable that the spirit of darkness is sufficient to draw someone into sin, but the Spirit and Light of Christ is not sufficient to redeem and save that same person from it. On this basis alone, we deny any insufficiency in the Light within. Otherwise, we would have to believe several things: First, that while we are required to worship God properly, that way has been hidden from us. Second, that the gifts of God are impotent. Third, that humanity is required to do what it has no power to accomplish. Fourth, that God requires our service, but does not show us how to do so. All this is unworthy of God. Rather, we trust that God, who made humanity, has given each person a soul capable of knowing and serving its Maker, endowed each with Divine Knowledge, as well as with the Light and Power necessary to enable each person to live in obedience to that knowledge. God's gift is perfect and sufficient for that task and, since the Divine Light attends to and is naturally drawn toward God (from whom it came), those who are follow it will be led to a state of blessed immortality.

In short, Reader, accept these few arguments as comprehensive not only of these two chapters, but of most of what I have said so far:

1. God does not require anything without giving first the Light to know it and the power to do it. God requires love, reverence, and righteousness from all. Therefore, each person has been given both a revelation of God's will and the power to do it.

2. No one should worship God ignorantly, but all have been commanded to worship God. Therefore, all must do it knowingly.

3. No one can know anything about God unless God chooses to disclose it, and that revelation cannot be seen without Light. Therefore, everyone has Light.

4. Unless God's gifts are imperfect or inadequate to accomplish their purposes, this Light must be sufficient. All of God's gifts are perfect and perfectly suited to fulfill their purposes, and the Light is a gift from God, therefore it must be sufficient.

In summary, everyone should love, revere, worship, and obey God. No one can do it correctly who does not know God, and no one can know God except by divine revelation. Nothing is visible without Light. Nor could imperfect or insufficient Light reveal anything. Therefore, all must have a sufficient Light for this purpose: to love, revere, worship, and obey God. This Light is Christ.

Chapter XXII

Who are those that obey this Divine Light? What is their true character?

I have now come to my final question: "Who are they that obey this Light and, by obeying, obtain salvation?" What are the characteristics of those who obey this Light? I am not asking for names, but what kind of people are they? In short, what does it mean to obey the Light?

I think that I have so completely answered these questions that an honorable and candid Reader would excuse me from further consideration. But just be sure that no one will think I have avoided answering directly because the question is unanswerable, I will answer from my own experience. The easy answer is that it is those who obey the Light, who refrain from all that the Light shows to be evil, and who strive to do all that it requires to be done. For example, the Light shows that it is inconsistent to love God and to be immoral, easily angered, proud, covetous, backbiting, envious, wrathful, unmerciful, revengeful, blasphemous, drunken, pleasure-seeking, or unclean – in other words, those things that the Scriptures call "the unfruitful works of darkness"[669] – and that those who practice them

---

[669] Eph. 5:3-5, 11: "But fornication, and all uncleanness, or covetousness, let it not be once named among you, as becometh saints; Neither filthiness, nor foolish

are "children of wrath"[670] who see no reason to acknowledge God.[671] When the Light reveals these things to be inconsistent with a proper reverence and love for God, those who obey the Light turn their backs on them and give them up forever no matter how difficult or costly it may be – even if their families threaten and beg them; or the world mocks them; or they become the subject of drunken songs and are taunted by their dearest and oldest friends. No, they no longer dare to follow the passing fashions of the world that draw them into vain and harmful delights – the very things that had previously dragged them down. They can no longer gratify lusts of the eye, the lusts of the flesh, or their own pride[672] – these do not come from God, who created them with better desires and convictions. They reject the way of life they once enjoyed and, in the eyes of the children of the world, seem to be depraved and troubled. They take up the cross, not feeling any shame in it,[673] they are baptized with the baptism of terrible trials, and willingly drink the cup of bitter mocking from which Christ Jesus, their Lord, drank and was baptized with.[674]

---

talking, nor jesting, which are not convenient: but rather giving of thanks. For this ye know, that no whoremonger, nor unclean person, nor covetous man, who is an idolater, hath any inheritance in the kingdom of Christ and of God. ... And have no fellowship with the unfruitful works of darkness, but rather reprove *them*."

[670] Eph. 2:3: "Among whom also we all had our conversation in times past in the lusts of our flesh, fulfilling the desires of the flesh and of the mind; and were by nature the children of wrath, even as others."

[671] Rom. 1:28: "And even as they did not like to retain God in *their* knowledge, God gave them over to a reprobate mind, to do those things which are not convenient."

[672] 1 John 2:15-16: "Love not the world, neither the things *that are* in the world. If any man love the world, the love of the Father is not in him. For all that *is* in the world, the lust of the flesh, and the lust of the eyes, and the pride of life, is not of the Father, but is of the world."

[673] Heb. 12:2: "Looking unto Jesus the author and finisher of *our* faith; who for the joy that was set before him endured the cross, despising the shame, and is set down at the right hand of the throne of God."

[674] Mark 10:38-39: "But Jesus said unto them, Ye know not what ye ask: can ye drink of the cup that I drink of? and be baptized with the baptism that I am baptized with? And they said unto him, We can. And Jesus said unto them, Ye shall indeed drink of the cup that I drink of; and with the baptism that I am baptized withal shall ye be baptized."

They reject conventional religions as merely the cares and pleasures of this world.[675] These people can have nothing to do with those who practice a religion that they know only from the teachings of other people or that they have decided on themselves after reading the Scriptures – attempting to take up the practices of prophets and apostles and trying to understand external and shadowy things without the leading of that same Spirit who inspired those prophets and apostles. They see all such faith and worship as mere human imaginings or lifeless imitations. They prefer to hear one sigh that was inspired by a sense of God's work in the heart to the longest humanly prepared prayers. They have parted company from others and follow their own path, fearing to offer any sacrifice that God has not specified. They declare that all other faiths and worships are insufficient and of merely human power – not held or performed in a holy conviction, prepared by the angel of God, the Light within their hearts and consciences. In the strength of God, they go forth against the merchants of Babylon, crying woe and plagues against those buyers and sellers of souls.[676] They are devoted to and protective of the name of the Lord, and therefore do not dare to befriend others,[677] but testify against all their ways. Freely they received and freely they give.[678]

Thus they are free of the complications, religiosity, and foundations of their former states in which they were religious according to the letter, rituals, human traditions, education, and their own imaginations. They were completely undone so that they could be re-done as the Lord would have them be. They are convinced of sin and of righteousness, too. The joy they had when they went wherever and did whatever they wanted is now turned to sorrow – where they once rejoiced, now they weep and howl. They have seen God in the Light of Christ and detest who they once were. Sin, which was once pleasant in their mouths, is now bitter in their bellies. The things

---

[675] This is an allusion to the Parable of the Sower in Luke 8, in particular to verse 14: "And that which fell among thorns are they, which, when they have heard, go forth, and are choked with cares and riches and pleasures of *this* life, and bring no fruit to perfection."

[676] Penn is drawing on imagery from the fall of Babylon as described in Revelation 18.

[677] Ps. 28:3: "Draw me not away with the wicked, and with the workers of iniquity, which speak peace to their neighbours, but mischief *is* in their hearts."

[678] Matt. 10:8: "Heal the sick, cleanse the lepers, raise the dead, cast out devils: freely ye have received, freely give."

that the world chases after they flee as they would from a mother bear robbed of her cubs. Sin seems overwhelmingly sinful and they cry out, "Who will rescue me?"[679] Though they are weary and very heavily burdened,[680] they do not seek to escape this spiritual winter,[681] but are resolved to stand the trial. They not only bring their former deeds to the Light and accept the judgments that are passed on them, but they patiently join in judging what they had so recently done. Nor does their obedience end with the sentence passed on their past sins and on them; they patiently endure the hand of God[682] until the Lord's righteous anger has passed and the root of sin has been utterly removed from deep within their hearts and all its fruits utterly destroyed. Then, the same Spirit of judgment that condemned sin comes forth in perfect victory over the nature and power of sin. This judgment is found and felt in the Light, and therefore, the children of the night reject all knowledge of its ways, while the children of the day rejoice in its appearance.[683]

This is not all that makes up those who obey the Light. A complete child of the Light is one who has conquered and expelled the darkness. It is true – once they were in darkness, but now they are in the Light[684] because they have been turned from darkness to the Light and from Satan's power to God,[685] who is Light itself.[686] They are in God's fellowship always.

---

[679] Rom. 7:24: "O wretched man that I am! who shall deliver me from the body of this death?"

[680] Matt. 11:28: "Come unto me, all *ye* that labour and are heavy laden, and I will give you rest."

[681] Mark 13:18: "And pray ye that your flight be not in the winter."

[682] 1 Pet. 5:6: "Humble yourselves therefore under the mighty hand of God, that he may exalt you in due time."

[683] 1 Thess. 5:5: "Ye are all the children of light, and the children of the day: we are not of the night, nor of darkness."

[684] Eph. 5:8: "For ye were sometimes darkness, but now *are ye* light in the Lord: walk as children of light."

[685] Acts 26:18: "To open their eyes, *and* to turn *them* from darkness to light, and *from* the power of Satan unto God, that they may receive forgiveness of sins, and inheritance among them which are sanctified by faith that is in me."

[686] 1 John 1:5-7: "This then is the message which we have heard of him, and declare unto you, that God is light, and in him is no darkness at all. If we say that we have fellowship with him, and walk in darkness, we lie, and do not the truth:

These are people who follow the Light of the Lamb[687] of God to find an inward cleansing. Having been cleansed by the Spirit of Judgment and the Spirit of Burning[688] (also called the severe condemnation, reprimand, and terror of the Light in the conscience), they set a guard within their hearts. Not a single thought is admitted unless it has the password – when it appears, they cry out, "Friend or foe!" If a friend, and acknowledged as such by the Light (the great leader who was given by God for that purpose), then it is accepted. Otherwise, they bring it before the Commander of the Conscience[689] to judge it. This is Christ the Light, King, Judge, and Lawgiver. By this they grow strong and grow with gifts of God. They often read the blessed Scriptures with great delight, marveling at God's abundant love to former ages and seeing it in their own time. In this refreshment, the meanings of many passages are opened to them – as is the Light, the Path of the Just, that in every age shines brighter and brighter[690] and in which the blood of Jesus Christ is felt to wash away all sin.[691] In this way, they restrain their thoughts so that their words and actions will give no offense.[692] Above all, they love fellowship with God, often withdrawing to be alone with the Lord and waiting for their daily bread. This time is not filled with their own words, wants, or wishes. Rather they empty themselves of thoughts, and in

---

But if we walk in the light, as he is in the light, we have fellowship one with another, and the blood of Jesus Christ his Son cleanseth us from all sin."

[687] Rev. 21:23: "And the city had no need of the sun, neither of the moon, to shine in it: for the glory of God did lighten it, and the Lamb *is* the light thereof."

[688] Isa. 4:4: "When the Lord shall have washed away the filth of the daughters of Zion, and shall have purged the blood of Jerusalem from the midst thereof by the spirit of judgment, and by the spirit of burning."

[689] Isa. 55:4: "Behold, I have given him *for* a witness to the people, a leader and commander to the people."

[690] Prov. 4:18: "But the path of the just *is* as the shining light, that shineth more and more unto the perfect day."

[691] 1 John 1:7: "But if we walk in the light, as he is in the light, we have fellowship one with another, and the blood of Jesus Christ his Son cleanseth us from all sin."

[692] James 3:1-3: "My brethren, be not many masters, knowing that we shall receive the greater condemnation. For in many things we offend all. If any man offend not in word, the same *is* a perfect man, *and* able also to bridle the whole body. Behold, we put bits in the horses' mouths, that they may obey us; and we turn about their whole body."

that peace and comfort, silently wait to feel the heavenly substance enter their souls directly from the hand of the Lord.

True peace does not come from remembering an old thought or some passage from Scripture or from carefully calling to mind something that another person taught, but from every word that comes directly from the mouth of God.[693] Only this will satisfy them. In short, those who obey the Light have been "taught to renounce ungodliness and worldly desires,"[694] and to be serious, righteous, patient, humble, meek, upright, merciful, long-suffering, forgiving, peaceable, gentle, self-denying, loyal, faithful, and holy because the Lord God is holy.

Thus, Reader, I have told you who they are not, as well as who they are – obedient to the Light within, Christ's spiritual appearance within their hearts. They know and feel Christ's holy blood cleansing, reconciling, and saving all who believe and obey from the guilt and pollution of sin.

Chapter XXIII

A Summary and Conclusion with a Plea to All who claim to be religious, especially our opponents.

I will sum up this whole discourse in a few main points:

I.   Salvation consists of first being saved from sin and, as a result, from wrath. "He will save his people from their sins."[695]

II.   Christ, the Word-God, has lighted all – not only after coming in the flesh, but before. The Light has always been universal and sufficient to lead all who obey it to God. These properties and effects have been demonstrated.

III.   The difference generally made between the law and the gospel was more one of form than content. God's gifts to mankind might have

---

[693] Matt. 4:4: "But he answered and said, It is written, Man shall not live by bread alone, but by every word that proceedeth out of the mouth of God."

[694] Titus 2:12: "Teaching us that, denying ungodliness and worldly lusts, we should live soberly, righteously, and godly, in this present world."

[695] Matt. 1:21: "And she shall bring forth a son, and thou shalt call his name JESUS: for he shall save his people from their sins."

been greater and more bountiful in more recent than in earlier times, but God gave each person, in every age, a sufficient measure of the same Divine Light to lead him or her through this world and to eternal blessedness.

IV.   Jews and Greeks, heathens and Christians, all agree in this.

V.   Christ's appearance in the flesh is the pre-eminent event. Both in general and in every particular, Christ was the fullness of time and the fullness of revelation, putting an end to all types and figures and outward commandments. Christ was the true substance that abolished and fulfilled them all. In their time, these were an outward guide by which weak people could find a scrap of the mystical glory, but they are now unneeded, weak, and beggarly elements.[696]

VI.   The Eternal Light did not only use that body to preach the purpose of all things. It is the origin of a more plain and perfect way – though less easy for flesh and blood to follow – that stressed the need for all to come to gospel righteousness. In that specially prepared body, Christ became our first minister and perfect example. In and by his life, preaching, miracles, death on the cross, and resurrection, the Savior of all gained a name above all other names.[697]

VII.   Nevertheless, that most excellent body was only the instrument by which the Holy Light of Life brought salvation. It was the Eternal Light and Life that gave meaning and significance to the actions and sufferings of the body.

VIII.   The benefit of that sacrifice is only witnessed by those who believe in Christ the Light as he appears in their hearts and consciences to save them from sin, destroy the works of the devil, end wrongdoing, and bring in everlasting righteousness. Those who imagine that they are entitled to salvation, while still in rebellion against the Light within – who ignore Christ's inward knocking and appearance – suffer from a deadly delusion that will destroy their souls.

---

[696] Gal. 4:9: "But now, after that ye have known God, or rather are known of God, how turn ye again to the weak and beggarly elements, whereunto ye desire again to be in bondage?"

[697] Phil. 2:9: "Wherefore God also hath highly exalted him, and given him a name which is above every name."

IX.   On the whole, it is determined and concluded that Christ is that Light that shines in the conscience.

X.   By reason, it has been proven that the Light is universal and sufficient. The first is demonstrated by the compliance of humanity and the goodness and rectitude of God. The second is obvious both in our experience and in being consistent with the goodness and wisdom of God to give all a Light sufficient to lead them to salvation.

This is, in ten points, most of the matter about the Light presented above. I urge our adversaries to seriously consider the whole before they attempt either reject it or attempt to reply to it. Let them try the power of the Light before they declare it to have none. In the love of God, consider whether there is something within themselves that condemns them for evil and, among other things, for their attacks on it and their unthinking undervaluation of it.

Why, oh why, would people want to know so much more than they faithfully practice! Before they show such disrespect for the Light, let them first try to exceed its just and holy requirements. They wickedly call it a "Will o' the wisp," "an unlit lantern," "natural," "insufficient," "ignis fatuus,"[698] "the Quakers' idol," and an abundance of similar, profane, and indeed blasphemous epithets, as if these were its proper name. The Scriptures they quote in their attacks plainly tell them that the whole work of the apostolic ministry was "to turn people from darkness to the Light, from the power of Satan to God, so that they might receive forgiveness for their sins."[699] In other words, those who turn to the Light have turned to God who is Light, and those who wait there expectantly will have both remission of punishment and cleansing from the defilement of sin.

Whatever anyone thinks of us, we believe, assert, and will maintain against humans and devils that God is Light and in the darkness that is out of that Light no one can know God or truly worship any God except the unknown God.[700] Those who receive this illumination and do not rebel

---

[698] Swamp gas.

[699] Acts 26:18: "To open their eyes, *and* to turn *them* from darkness to light, and *from* the power of Satan unto God, that they may receive forgiveness of sins, and inheritance among them which are sanctified by faith that is in me."

[700] Acts 17:23: "For as I passed by, and beheld your devotions, I found an altar with this inscription, TO THE UNKNOWN GOD. Whom therefore ye ignorantly worship, him declare I unto you."

against it, but work to increase this heavenly talent within themselves, have fellowship with the pure eternal God and feel the blood of Jesus Christ cleansing them of all unrighteousness.[701]

As to those who think glory can be obtained in another way and resist any attempts to admonish them, let them go. We say only what we know to be true and can do no more than to declare what we have felt of the work of God in our hearts. We value the Scriptures highly, but we do not believe the things we quote from them to be true only because they are found there. We have personally witnessed the work of God and, from our own experiences, we testify to and confirm the truth in that book. Only in this way can anyone truly honor the Scriptures – all others are at best empty Scribes and babbling Pharisees.

So I leave my labors on this matter with God, hoping that the heavenly Light may rise more abundantly within the dark hearts of humanity and awaken them to repentance. It has shined too long uncomprehended in darkness and the darkness has grown impudent, putting it in people's minds that their inability to see is because the Light is insufficient. God would be pleased to cause it to shine out of the darkness in the consciences of men and women so that it might demonstrate its superiority to the scorn and slanders that so-called Christians sling at it. This only proves to me how little they truly possess of the true, pure, and undefiled religion regardless of how important they may seem to weak and ignorant people. Their unprincipled and unchristian opposition makes my soul ache and fear for the consequences of their resistance. I desire only that they might see the futility of their work against the Light, that they repent, and be converted so that God can heal them. This sincere prayer is my answer to all their cruel speeches and ungodly words against us in general and myself in particular.

W. Penn

---

[701] 1 John 1:9: "If we confess our sins, he is faithful and just to forgive us *our* sins, and to cleanse us from all unrighteousness."

A DISCOURSE

ON THE

GENERAL RULE OF FAITH AND PRACTICE,

AND THE JUDGE OF CONTROVERSY.

Greatly importing all those who desire to take right Measures of Faith, and to determine (at least to themselves) the numerous Controversies now on foot in the World.

—*oooo*—

An appendix to the first part of the *Christian Quaker* by the same author.

—*oooo*—

For in Christ Jesus neither circumcision availeth any thing, nor uncircumcision, but a new creature. And as many as walk according to this rule, peace be on them, and mercy, and upon the Israel of God.
Galatians *6:15-16*

But God hath revealed them unto us by his Spirit: for the Spirit searcheth all things, yea, the deep things of God. ... The things of God knoweth no man, but the Spirit of God. ... He that is spiritual judgeth all things.
1 Corinthians *2:10, 11, 15*

But ye have an unction from the Holy One, and ye know all things.
1 John *2:20*

THE UNIVERSAL RULE OF FAITH AND PRACTICE

There are many faiths in the world, and many perplexing controversies about them. If a person wishes to advocate one, it would seem necessary first to truly know the true faith that overcomes the world.[702] I will, therefore, say something about the general rule of faith and life and the judge of controversy at this time. Indeed, I feel it is essential that I do so, since people who do not have that rule may perish spiritually. Indeed, it is easier for a sailor to find port without a compass or a star to guide him than for an individual to find truth without it.

To be clear, I will begin with an explanation of the terms 'rule' and 'faith.' This will serve as a general introduction to this section.

We understand a general rule of faith and practice to be an unvarying standard measure that people in all ages have used to judge whether doctrines are true or false and whether thoughts, words, and actions are good or evil.

We understand faith as acceptance by an individual of the revelations made by God in these matters. That is, in resigning one's own will and depending entirely on God as the Great Creator and Savior of all people. This is inseparable from good works.

In all ages, people have had a belief in and some knowledge of God – although it is clear from history that some people received greater revelations than others. This has been testified to in ancient times, by the writings of Justin Martyr, Clement of Alexandria, Augustine, and others. In more recent times, their work has been added to by Du Plessy,[703] Grotius,[704] Amiraldus,[705] Herbert,[706] and above all, Dr. Cudworth.[707]

---

[702] 1 John 5:4: "For whatsoever is born of God overcometh the world: and this is the victory that overcometh the world, *even* our faith."

[703] Philippe de Mornay, Seigneur Du Plessis-marly (1549-1623) was a Protestant French diplomat. He wrote a number of tracts defending the Protestant cause during the French Wars of Religion (1562-98).

[704] Huig de Groot (1583-1645), also known as Hugo Grotius, was a Dutch legal and religious scholar. His greatest work is considered to be *The Law of War and Peace*, which advocated the development of international law. He also published *The Truth of the Christian Religion* which attempted to use legal tools to demonstrate the unity of the Christian religion including Catholicism.

[705]. Moise Amyraut (1596-1664), founder of Amyraldianism, a form of Calvinism in which the chief doctrine is not predestination but that faith justifies. He believed that religious belief should not be in a fixed theology, but rather that religious precepts changed and developed over time. Amyraldianism became the theology of the School of Saumer in France which William Penn attended in 1662-63. While there, Penn lived in Amyraut's house.

Indeed, the few scraps we have from the most ancient historians and authors demonstrate this point.

The Scriptures tell us that "no one knows the Father except the Son and those to whom the Son chooses to reveal him"[708] and, "no one knows the human mind except the human spirit, and no one knows God's mind except the Spirit of God."[709] Therefore, we may safely conclude that God has been revealed in all ages by the creating Word that, from the beginning, was with God and was God, in whom was Life and that Life was the Light of all,[710] the life-giving Spirit.[711] Consequently, that Light or Spirit must have been the universal rule for human knowledge of, faith in, and obedience to God. This doctrine is expressed in one of the maxims of Pythagoras, who lived about six hundred years before Christ, "No one can know what God desires unless he or she hears it from God – and that must be within." Both apostle and prophet agree with this doctrine. Paul states that "whatever reveals is Light,"[712] and "whatever might be known about

---

[706] Although Penn has written 'L. Herbert', he probably means Edward Herbert, First Baron of Cherbury (1583-1648), an English courtier, soldier, diplomat, historian, metaphysical poet, and philosopher – called the father of English Deism. In *On Truth*, he argued that there are five religious ideas that are God-given and innate: belief in a Supreme Being, the need to worship God, the pursuit of a pious and virtuous life as the best form of worship, repentance, and rewards and punishments in the next world.

[707] Ralph Cudworth (1617-1688) was an English philosopher and theologian. He was one of the Cambridge Platonists, a seventeenth-century circle which expounded rationalistic theology and ethics.

[708] Matt. 11:27: "All things are delivered unto me of my Father: and no man knoweth the Son, but the Father; neither knoweth any man the Father, save the Son, and *he* to whomsoever the Son will reveal *him*."

[709] 1 Cor. 2:11: "For what man knoweth the things of a man, save the spirit of man which is in him? even so the things of God knoweth no man, but the Spirit of God."

[710] John 1:1-4: "In the beginning was the Word, and the Word was with God, and the Word was God. The same was in the beginning with God. All things were made by him; and without him was not any thing made that was made. In him was life; and the life was the light of men."

[711] 1 Cor. 15:45: "And so it is written, the first man Adam was made a living soul; the last Adam *was made* a quickening spirit."

[712] Eph. 5:13: "But all things that are reproved are made manifest by the light: for whatsoever doth make manifest is light."

God was revealed within; because God (who is Light[713]) has showed it to them."[714] Likewise Micah wrote "God has showed you what is good and what God requires of you,"[715] which could not happen without the Light of God's son shining in the conscience. Therefore, the Light of God in the conscience must have been the general rule. It was by this law that Enoch, Noah, Abraham, Melchizedek, Abimelech, Job, Jethro, etc. walked and were accepted. As Irenaeus and Tertullian wrote, "They were justified by the law written in their hearts." This was the rule that led them to and guided them in a righteous state.

Objection: You seem to deny the Scriptures to be the universal rule.

Answer: How can something be a universal rule that is not universal? The Scriptures were written at particular times, something that existed both before that time and has continued since that time is more universal. The Light in the conscience – which was law and guide for the patriarchs, who lived long before Moses began to write the Scriptures – consequently must be the universal rule.

Objection: Granted, the Light within existed before the Scripture were written. But since the time that they were written, they – and not the Light – have been the universal rule.

Answer: Unless we consider Palestine or Canaan, a tiny province in Asia, to be the whole world and the Jews to be the whole of humanity, this cannot be the case. For much of history, those writings were available to the Jews, while the rest of humanity had only the Light and Law within. The apostle confirms this in the passage, "For the Gentiles, who do not have the law (that is the outward law written on stone tablets), naturally do things that are required by the law, showing that the requirements of the law are written in their hearts."[716] The Gentiles themselves called it the

---

[713] 1 John 1:5: "This then is the message which we have heard of him, and declare unto you, that God is light, and in him is no darkness at all."

[714] Rom. 1:19: "Because that which may be known of God is manifest in them; for God hath shewed *it* unto them."

[715] Mic. 6:8: "He hath shewed thee, O man, what *is* good; and what doth the LORD require of thee, but to do justly, and to love mercy, and to walk humbly with thy God?"

[716] Rom. 2:14-15: "For when the Gentiles, which have not the law, do by nature the things contained in the law, these, having not the law, are a law unto themselves: Which shew the work of the law written in their hearts, their

immutable law and everlasting foundation of virtue; not lifeless precepts, but immortal ones; a sacred good, God who oversees all; the living rule, the root of the soul, the essence of a good person. These were cited above from the works of Thales, Pythagoras, Socrates, Plato, Plotin, Hieron, Philo, and Plutarch. Sophocles said, "God grant that I always observe in my words and deeds the venerable sanctity that these noble precepts (written in each person's heart) require. God is their source and they will never be abolished, because they have a great God within them that never grows old." This is a more reverent statement than our opponents can offer – as can clearly be seen in their books – and yet, they claim to be good Christians.

Thus, it is obvious that the Scriptures have not been a universal rule after they were written.

Objection: But have they not been and are they not now a universal rule?

Answer: There has been since they were written and is now the same obstacle. Before Christ came in the flesh, and since that time, the Light has been known in many places where the Scriptures have not. Some nations have known, but "not glorified God as God,"[717] choosing instead all kinds of iniquity. Their minds may have been veiled, but in no case did they lose all sense of the Light within. Therefore, the Scriptures were not a universal rule among them since at no time can it be shown that all (or even most) of the world has had them. Even if we pretend that there have been times when this was so, it would not convince us – universality needs to be a natural characteristic of a universal rule, that is, it must have been the rule for all humanity from the beginning of the world until our day and on into the future until the end.

Objection: But isn't the Scripture the rule for our day?

Answer: If it is the rule today, then it must be the universal rule. Whatever is the rule for faith and life precludes any other rule from being universal. Any other must be merely a particular example, and therefore *a* rule, but not *the* rule for faith and life.

---

conscience also bearing witness, and *their* thoughts the mean while accusing or else excusing one another."

[717] Rom. 1:21: "Because that, when they knew God, they glorified *him* not as God, neither were thankful; but became vain in their imaginations, and their foolish heart was darkened."

Besides not being universal, I have several reasons why the Scriptures cannot be the rule for faith and life:[718]

First, if something is the rule now, it was always the rule. But nothing other than the Light was ever the rule and therefore cannot be the rule now. Everyone accepts that the Scriptures have not always been the rule, but some deny that that they are therefore not the rule now. I will prove this as follows. If the faith of God's people in all ages is in its essence the same, then its rule must also be the same in essence. From chapter 11 in the Epistle to the Hebrews we can see that true faith has always been essentially

---

[718] Penn has the following note in the margin:

Justin Martyr said that all who live with Christ are Christians – people such as Abraham and Elias or, from among the Greeks, Socrates or Heraclites. Scultetus [Michael Praetorius, 1571-1621, Lutheran theorist and musician] said that some of his day taught that Melchizedek, Abimelech, Ruth, Rachab, the Queen of Sheba, Hiram of Tyre, Naaman the Syrian, and the city of Nineveh should be counted as Christians.

Eusebius Pamphili, in his *Ecclesiastical History*, said that Abraham and the ancient fathers were Christians. He defined a Christian as someone who, by the knowledge and doctrine of Christ, excels at moderation, righteousness, temperance, virtuousness, and godliness toward the one God.

Clement of Alexandria said the law of nature and discipline is one, and that Moses seems to call the Lord, the covenant – a covenant not to be found in the Scripture, since God is the source of all. He also says that you can find the Lord called 'the Word' or 'Reason' and 'the Law' in the preaching of Peter. This is near the end of his first book, *Stromata*. Earlier, on page 353, he said that the law and the gospel are the work of one Lord who is the virtue and wisdom of God. The fear that the law produced helps people to find salvation – 'the fear of the Lord is the beginning of wisdom' [Ps. 111:10]. She (Wisdom) preaches God's care and guidance and is our good guide and benefactor. As a good guide, she tells us when we have strayed from the path to salvation and as benefactor; she gives us everything that we need for salvation. This journey is from darkness to light and we need to listen to Wisdom, as our director and minister, so that we might ascend to the status of her adopted children. The law works to make those immortal who choose to live temperately and justly. Evil people do not know the law, but those who seek the Lord understand every good thing. The whole first book of the *Stromata* was written to prove the antiquity of the one true religion or philosophy, as Clement calls it.

the same,[719] and consequently the rule has as well. In short, if our holy, spiritual ancestors had faith before the Scriptures were written, they also had a rule prior to the Scripture – wherever there is faith, there is a rule of faith. If the faith is essentially unchanged, the rule is as well. Their faith was inward and spiritual – the creation of the immortal Word, which is Life and the Light of all – and that Word of Life and Light was the rule. Therefore, no book, no writing, nothing carved on visible and perishable matter can be the rule now.

To repeat, the rule must be of the same nature as faith. The faith is inward and spiritual, but no mere book can ever be.

Second, if the Scriptures were the rule, they must always have been a perfect rule from when they were first written. But, since they were written over many hundreds of years and have been imperfectly collected, this cannot be the case. How then can they then be a perfect rule?

All will admit that they could not have been a perfect rule before they were all written and likewise, that they took many hundreds of years to write. I will now also prove that they have not been perfectly collected.

Enoch's Prophecy is mentioned by Jude,[720] but this is not included in the Bible. The Book of the Wars of the Lord,[721] the Book of Jasher,[722] the

---

[719] Hebrews 11 begins, "Now faith is the substance of things hoped for, the evidence of things not seen" and proceeds to trace the history of faith from Abel through Abraham and Sarah to Moses and David.

[720] Jude 1:14-15: "And Enoch also, the seventh from Adam, prophesied of these, saying, Behold, the Lord cometh with ten thousands of his saints, To execute judgment upon all, and to convince all that are ungodly among them of all their ungodly deeds which they have ungodly committed, and of all their hard *speeches* which ungodly sinners have spoken against him."

[721] Num. 21:14-15: "Wherefore it is said in the book of the wars of the LORD, What he did in the Red sea, and in the brooks of Arnon, And at the stream of the brooks that goeth down to the dwelling of Ar, and lieth upon the border of Moab."

[722] Josh. 10:13: "And the sun stood still, and the moon stayed, until the people had avenged themselves upon their enemies. Is not this written in the book of Jasher? So the sun stood still in the midst of heaven, and hasted not to go down about a whole day."

2 Sam. 1:18 "Also he bade them teach the children of Judah the use of the bow: behold, it is written in the book of Jasher."

Book of Nathan,[723] the Book of Shemaiah,[724] the Book of Jehu,[725] the Epistle of the Apostle Paul to the Laodiceans,[726] and several others are mentioned in the Scriptures, but are not now known to exist. Lastly, Luke says that many wrote eyewitness accounts of the things that were most surely believed by the primitive Christians.[727]

It is taken for granted that John wrote many years after Luke. When Luke wrote of 'many,' he was not referring only to Matthew and Mark (indeed, some even think that Luke wrote before Mark). But, to this day, there are only four gospels in our Bibles, therefore, many such writings must have been lost. If so, then the Scriptures must be imperfect and, if they are, how can they be the perfect rule of faith?

My third reason is that the Scriptures, although useful for instruction, building faith, and comfort,[728] seem not to be essentially designed or purposely assembled and given to us as the universal rule and complete statement of faith. Rather, they were written on particular occasions and in response to specific emergencies. Doctrines are scattered throughout the Scriptures and religious bodies that have produced explicit statements of faith have had to search here and there, pulling in bits and pieces, in order

---

[723] 2 Chron. 9:29: "Now the rest of the acts of Solomon, first and last, *are* they not written in the book of Nathan the prophet, and in the prophecy of Ahijah the Shilonite, and in the visions of Iddo the seer against Jeroboam the son of Nebat?"

[724] 2 Chron. 12:15: "Now the acts of Rehoboam, first and last, *are* they not written in the book of Shemaiah the prophet, and of Iddo the seer concerning genealogies? And *there were* wars between Rehoboam and Jeroboam continually."

[725] 2 Chron. 20:34: "Now the rest of the acts of Jehoshaphat, first and last, behold, they *are* written in the book of Jehu the son of Hanani, who *is* mentioned in the book of the kings of Israel."

[726] Col. 4:16: "And when this epistle is read among you, cause that it be read also in the church of the Laodiceans; and that ye likewise read the *epistle* from Laodicea."

[727] Luke 1:1-2: "Forasmuch as many have taken in hand to set forth in order a declaration of those things which are most surely believed among us, Even as they delivered them unto us, which from the beginning were eyewitnesses, and ministers of the word."

[728] 1 Cor. 14:3: "But he that prophesieth speaketh unto men *to* edification, and exhortation, and comfort."

to come to agreement on one or another principle. Even then, they have found it difficult to produce a statement in something close to scriptural language. If the Scriptures were as plain and direct as a rule (by its nature) must be, all this would be unnecessary – all they would have needed to do is to endorse what was already written. Besides which, the Scriptures are in some places literal and in others metaphorical; sometimes, plain and other times, mystical. Most often, the truth of a point must be tested by comparing and weighing different passages. Some allusions may be appropriate, while others distort the plain sense of the text – careful discernment is required despite the claims that they are infallible. What is most plain is that the Scriptures are not plain, except to the spiritual person. On the contrary, as Peter said of Paul's writings, they are hard in many places to understand.[729] A rule must be exact, plain, and easily understood – the Scriptures are not.

A fourth reason the Scriptures cannot be the rule of faith is that it cannot give faith. It tells us that faith is a gift from God[730] that overcomes the world.[731] Nor is it a guide to practice – it cannot tell us what should be practiced and what should not, since both are contained within it.

This was the case for Christ's disciples. They had no particular rule in the Old Testament that abolished part of the religion of the Old Testament. On the contrary, they could have argued for the continuance of it since Christ commanded them to do what those who sat in Moses' chair told them.[732] Certainly, this would be a more reasonable claim than that of our contemporaries when they plead for their newly invented forms of worship.

---

[729] 2 Pet. 3:15-16: "And account *that* the longsuffering of our Lord *is* salvation; even as our beloved brother Paul also according to the wisdom given unto him hath written unto you; As also in all *his* epistles, speaking in them of these things; in which are some things hard to be understood, which they that are unlearned and unstable wrest, as *they do* also the other Scriptures, unto their own destruction."

[730] Eph. 2:8: "For by grace are ye saved through faith; and that not of yourselves: *it is* the gift of God."

[731] 1 John 5:4: "For whatsoever is born of God overcometh the world: and this is the victory that overcometh the world, *even* our faith."

[732] Matt. 23:1-3: "Then spake Jesus to the multitude, and to his disciples, Saying, The scribes and the Pharisees sit in Moses' seat: All therefore whatsoever they bid you observe, *that* observe and do; but do not ye after their works: for they say, and do not."

What guided the disciples in declaring old ways void and giving them up? For example, God said that circumcision was a sign forever,[733] but Paul tells the Galatians that if they let themselves be circumcised, Christ will be of no value to them.[734] Wasn't it the Spirit of Truth, that guides us to all truth,[735] that the apostles took as the judge of and rule for their doctrines and practices? James and the assembly of the apostles said as much when they told the believers, "it seemed good to the Holy Spirit and to us."[736]

Fifth, those who say that the Scriptures are the rule of faith and life contradict themselves in making that claim – the Scriptures nowhere say that it is true. In answer, they hide behind their explanations and interpretations. The question is not about the truth of the text – that is agreed by all – but about the meaning of them. Should I follow the letter of the text or someone's interpretation? If I accept interpretation, then is my rule the Scripture or is it someone's understanding of the Scripture? Consider the person interpreting the Scripture –he or she doesn't take the Scripture as a rule, but his or her own understanding of them, despite whatever is said to others in support the claim. By consenting to that interpretation, I accept that person's conceptions as my rule.

Sixth, how can I be sure that these particular Scriptures came from God? I am required by the Scriptures to test all things.[737] If all things are to be tested, then the Scriptures are included. But what am I to use to test them? The Scriptures? Then they become the basis for examining themselves – this hardly seems to be proper. If I test the Scriptures with the Spirit that gave them forth – which searches even the deep things of God[738]

---

[733] Gen. 17:13: "He that is born in thy house, and he that is bought with thy money, must needs be circumcised: and my covenant shall be in your flesh for an everlasting covenant."

[734] Gal. 5:2: "Behold, I Paul say unto you, that if ye be circumcised, Christ shall profit you nothing."

[735] John 16:13: "Howbeit when he, the Spirit of truth, is come, he will guide you into all truth: for he shall not speak of himself; but whatsoever he shall hear, *that* shall he speak: and he will shew you things to come."

[736] Acts 15:28: "For it seemed good to the Holy Ghost, and to us, to lay upon you no greater burden than these necessary things."

[737] 1 Thess. 5:21: "Prove all things; hold fast that which is good."

[738] 1 Cor. 2:10: "But God hath revealed *them* unto us by his Spirit: for the Spirit searcheth all things, yea, the deep things of God."

and a degree of which is given to me for my benefit[739] – then it seems that the Spirit, and not the Scriptures, is the rule.

Seventh, if the Scriptures are the rule, then either they were in the original manuscripts or they are in the existing copies. If the originals are required, then no rule currently exists – the last known original manuscript was a piece of John's history at Ephesus and that has not been seen for nearly one thousand years. If a copy is the rule, we need to know which of the thirty or more different versions that we know about is closest to the originals. This question is currently unanswered and, for all I know, may be unanswerable.[740] When the various copies of these versions are carefully examined, we find thousands of differences – further proving my point. If we cannot depend on the copies to provide a universal rule, how can translations from them be any better? These may not only differ from the truest sense of the oldest copies, but also with each other.

I would like those in our current age who promote the Scriptures as the universal rule (instead of the Spirit) to tell me the basis for their claim of authority. Is it by tradition or revelation? I mean, is it by the internal testimony of the Spirit or by human, external determination? If they say by the Spirit, then they must join with us because then the Spirit must be both the judge and the rule. If they choose a human source, I have to ask how they can be sure that they have not been badly misguided either by carelessness or even deliberately. Surely we can see that, even with the greatest care and diligence, translation, transcription, and printing are each subject to numerous mistakes – some of which are serious and against which the Scriptures provide no protection.

But even if this objection is set aside, I still demand that our adversaries tell us if they have complete confidence in those men who first collected them together and publicly decreed them to be authentic? We have read that this was done at the Council of Laodicea, held in 360 A.D.,[741] and that

---

[739] 1 Cor. 12:7: "But the manifestation of the Spirit is given to every man to profit withal."

[740] Penn is referring to those ancient manuscripts that were known to exist in the seventeenth century. Many more have been found since that time. Determining which of several variant wordings to accept as most accurate continues to be a problem for Bible scholars.

[741] A fourth century council of bishops, held in Laodicea, issued sixty decrees or canons. Canon 60 listed the books of the Bible. It does not list all the books now included in the Bible. The date of this council is not well established.

their canon does not agree with our current Bible. During those first three centuries, there was extensive debate, many judgments, and countless opinions. Some books were accepted and some rejected and all undoubtedly were transcribed thousands of times. It is not unlikely that in the process, some were also intentionally altered. If a mistake in judgment was made in the early church councils, it has not been corrected in the years since. How do our opponents know that these men discerned the status of each book correctly? Either they were infallible or not. If they were, then we must admit that there has been a source of infallibility since the days of the apostles – a claim that would contradict what our opponents say elsewhere.[742] Even supposing that they were infallible, how could anyone know for sure? Surely not by inspiration, which our opponents call a dangerous doctrine. How else then? Not by tradition.[743] Was it by the Scripture? In other words, could the Scripture tell us that those who collected it together and declared it closed were right? I do not know of any such scriptural statement, and if there were, it would just beg the question. I can see no other possible grounds for this belief except to accept what our opponents call popery – that is, to believe what the church believes. But if those men were fallible, as our opponents' beliefs require and as the council's flawed decisions prove, what is left? Undoubtedly, our adversaries' situation is very uncertain.

It must be remembered that some of the Scriptures that were accepted by one council as canonical were rejected by another as apocryphal, while some that the first one rejected, the second accepted. It is obvious that they contradicted one another and equally obvious that both differed from our contemporary beliefs. The current Protestant canon disagrees with the one held by the church of Rome that came from those councils and, let me say without giving offense, from any number of other lists that can be produced. Behold! You run into a labyrinth of uncertainty when you flee the heavenly gift within yourselves. That is the only way by which the Holy Scriptures can be truly discerned, enjoyed, and distinguished from human imaginings and inventions.

Eighth, suppose the Scriptures were the rule of faith and life in their original manuscripts and that the ancient copies were exact. Even so, only

---

[742] Protestants uniformly rejected the papal claim of infallibility, saying that no one since the days of the apostles was infallible.

[743] Protestants also rejected the validity of the Roman Catholic claim that church tradition is a source of religious authority.

the well-educated could depend on them since translations can never be exact – by far the greatest part of humanity would be denied clear access to that universal rule. This fails to fulfill either the promise of the gospel or the need for all humanity to have a rule for faith and life.

Nineth, that the Scriptures are not the rule of faith and life is further proved by the many volumes of cases of conscience that have been published among us. If the Scriptures were sufficient as a rule of faith and life, there would have been no need for such books. Each person would have seen his or her own condition laid out in the Scripture without any need for these numerous supplements. Don't your own words and deeds prove the inadequacy of the Scriptures? You urge people to seek to know the mind of God by studying this or that important affair – if the Scriptures are the universal rule, why not simply open it to the proper chapter and verse? And words that are so commonly spoken, "God direct you" (which implies inspiration and revelation – that is direct guidance and assistance from God), are never seen, much less acknowledged in your writings. Rather, they are scorned and branded the alarming products of possession, familism,[744] fanaticism, or Quakerism. There are, in short, a thousand cases – not a few occurring each day – in which the Scripture cannot be our plain and distinct rule and guide.[745] But God is not left without a witness in each person. The grace that brings salvation has appeared to all, teaching those who believe in it to deny ungodliness and worldly desires and to live soberly, righteously, and devoutly in the present world.[746] Christ Jesus, the Eternal Word, has enlightened everyone coming into the world[747] to reveal, guide, and instruct each person about faith and practice.

Objection: If the Law and Light in the conscience is enough, what need is there for the Scriptures?

---

[744] Familists were members of the Family of Love, a religious sect that held that religion consisted chiefly in the exercise of love.

[745] In the margin, Penn has noted, "Scripture does not specify any general rule regarding how to conduct yourself in court or to act in times of suffering."

[746] Titus 2:11-12: "For the grace of God that bringeth salvation hath appeared to all men, Teaching us that, denying ungodliness and worldly lusts, we should live soberly, righteously, and godly, in this present world."

[747] John 1:9: "*That* was the true Light, which lighteth every man that cometh into the world."

Answer: One could make the same argument with respect to God, Christ, the Holy Spirit, or Grace. Each of these is sufficient without the addition of Scripture. This is the situation. Through its wanderings after outward and perishable things, humanity's mind becomes estranged from the Light and Spirit. In this way, the Light becomes obscured, the Spirit suppressed, and the Law distorted. In keeping with the covenant with Abraham, God showed extraordinary mercy to the Jews by repeating (to use Ursin's[748] term) the law that was within by declaring it outwardly. This provided each person with both an outward witness and an inward one. Although they had lost much of their inward feeling and wandered away from the Law and the Light within, this outward witness was available to their outward senses – meeting them in the places to which spiritually they had strayed.

God provided the Scriptures and other outward assistance in response to humanity's foolishness and blindness – the products of their rebellion against the Law and the Light within. It is a weak and futile argument to infer from God's generosity that the Light is insufficient. Would our opponents require that God's Light and Spirit appear to and communicate with people through their outward senses? Such a thing cannot happen. God is too spiritual and people too earthly for it to happen. Or, are the Light and Spirit insufficient when they communicate with humanity through outward things that are suited to our earthly nature? The greatest part of the Scriptures is description of the knowledge and experience of those who had achieved a higher spiritual state through the teachings of the Light and Spirit. This was put into words so that those who lagged behind might be awakened and encouraged to be like them and follow the Lord in the Light of his Spirit. Certainly, the Scripture could never accuse the Light of being insufficient since the Scripture is simply the mind and teachings of the Divine Light as it was known and recorded by others. Can a faithful description of a thing be out of harmony with, or deny the reality of, the thing described? Should we remove the Light and Spirit from the offices of rule and judge because God for a time allowed outward supplements to it? Some ignorant people have claimed that we are putting aside the instituted religion when we earnestly seek for the Truth that came before (and eliminates any need for) those temporary external things. The outward Law was a guide only from the time of Moses until the Son came: the servant

---

[748] Zacharias Ursinus (1534-1583) was the principle author of the Heidelberg Confession and one of the founders of the German Reformed tradition.

does not have a permanent place in the house.[749] The written Law had a place until the inward Law rose in its glory and brightness – or rather, until people became more capable of being turned to it and to living with it and in it. "In those days, said the Lord, I will write my Laws in their hearts."[750] Those who claim that the Scriptures say anything else are perverting and abusing them – there is nothing more clearly stated in them than the rule and reign of the Spirit. Christ said, "My kingdom is not of this world,"[751] and "The kingdom of God is within."[752] "I will write my laws in their hearts and place my fear in their inward parts," "All your children will be taught by the Lord and they will be rooted in righteousness."[753] "I will pour out my Spirit on all."[754] "The grace of God that brings salvation has appeared to all, teaching us, etc."[755]

Objection: If the written law that was given to Moses was a rule to the Jews, why isn't the law delivered by Christ and written down by the apostles the rule for Christians?

Answer: Christ left nothing in writing as the rule for faith and practice, and we cannot believe that Christ was less careful in fulfilling his duties than was Moses. Undoubtedly, if he had intended his followers to have a

---

[749] John 8:35: "And the servant abideth not in the house for ever: *but* the Son abideth ever."

[750] Jer. 31:33: "But this *shall be* the covenant that I will make with the house of Israel; After those days, saith the LORD, I will put my law in their inward parts, and write it in their hearts; and will be their God, and they shall be my people."

[751] John 18:36: "Jesus answered, My kingdom is not of this world: if my kingdom were of this world, then would my servants fight, that I should not be delivered to the Jews: but now is my kingdom not from hence."

[752] Luke 17:21: "Neither shall they say, Lo here! or, lo there! for, behold, the kingdom of God is within you."

[753] Isa. 54:13-14: "And all thy children *shall be* taught of the LORD; and great *shall be* the peace of thy children. In righteousness shalt thou be established: thou shalt be far from oppression; for thou shalt not fear: and from terror; for it shall not come near thee."

[754] Joel 2:28: "And it shall come to pass afterward, *that* I will pour out my spirit upon all flesh; and your sons and your daughters shall prophesy, your old men shall dream dreams, your young men shall see visions."

[755] Titus 2:11-12: "For the grace of God that bringeth salvation hath appeared to all men, Teaching us that, denying ungodliness and worldly lusts, we should live soberly, righteously, and godly, in this present world."

written rule, he would have left one for them. We can be sure that he would have wasted no time in telling what needed to be done or believed. Nor did his followers write the New Testament in the form of a rule, as parts of the Old Testament were, nor did they call it a rule or recommend it to others as a rule.

And this leads me to my eighth reason why the Scriptures cannot be the rule under the new covenant. Even admitting (as I do) that the law written by Moses on tablets of stone was an outward rule for the Jews, Christ, as the spiritual leader of a spiritual Israel, has written a spiritual law in the heart. This was God's promise – the privilege and blessing of the *new covenant* – that just as the outward Jews had an outward law as a guide, the inward Jews would have an inward law as a guide. And just as the outward Jews had an outward priest from whose mouth they could hear the law, the inward Jews (those who have been circumcised in the spirit[756]) has an inward and spiritual high priest[757] whose lips preserve knowledge[758] and from whose mouth they receive the Law of Life. This is the rule of the ruler of God's people, who reigns in righteousness and whose heavenly government will never end. As the Scriptures tell us, the King, Ruler, Judge, Lawgiver,[759] High Priest, Law, rule, and temple are all spiritual. "My kingdom is not of this world."[760] "The kingdom of God is within."[761] "I will write my law in their hearts and put reverence in their inner parts."[762] "All

---

[756] Rom. 2:29: "But he *is* a Jew, which is one inwardly; and circumcision *is that* of the heart, in the spirit, *and* not in the letter; whose praise *is* not of men, but of God."

[757] Heb. 3:1: "Wherefore, holy brethren, partakers of the heavenly calling, consider the Apostle and High Priest of our profession, Christ Jesus."

[758] Prov. 22:12: "The eyes of the LORD preserve knowledge, and he overthroweth the words of the transgressor."

[759] Isa. 33:22: "For the LORD *is* our judge, the LORD *is* our lawgiver, the LORD *is* our king; he will save us."

[760] John 18:36: "Jesus answered, My kingdom is not of this world: if my kingdom were of this world, then would my servants fight, that I should not be delivered to the Jews: but now is my kingdom not from hence."

[761] Luke 17:21: "Neither shall they say, Lo here! or, lo there! for, behold, the kingdom of God is within you."

[762] Jer. 31:33: "But this *shall be* the covenant that I will make with the house of Israel; After those days, saith the LORD, I will put my law in their inward parts, and write it in their hearts; and will be their God, and they shall be my people."

will be taught by me and rooted in righteousness."[763] "The tabernacle of God is among humanity – God will live among them."[764] "I will pour out my spirit on all flesh."[765] "Grace has come to all, teaching them, etc."[766] "All receive the Spirit for the common good."[767] "The inspiration of the Almighty gives understanding."[768] "Whatever can be known about God is revealed within."[769] "Walk in the Spirit."[770] "If we walk in the Light, etc."[771] "Come and walk in the Light of the Lord."[772] "There was no need for the sun or moon to shine because the Glory of God illuminates it and the Lamb lighted it."[773] "Peace and mercy will come to those who follow this rule and on the Israel of God."[774] What rule? Not that of the old, legal

---

[763] Isa. 54:13-14: "And all thy children *shall be* taught of the LORD; and great *shall be* the peace of thy children. In righteousness shalt thou be established: thou shalt be far from oppression; for thou shalt not fear: and from terror; for it shall not come near thee."

[764] Rev. 21:3: "And I heard a great voice out of heaven saying, Behold, the tabernacle of God *is* with men, and he will dwell with them, and they shall be his people, and God himself shall be with them, *and be* their God."

[765] Joel 2:28: "And it shall come to pass afterward, *that* I will pour out my spirit upon all flesh; and your sons and your daughters shall prophesy, your old men shall dream dreams, your young men shall see visions."

[766] Titus 2:11: "For the grace of God that bringeth salvation hath appeared to all men, Teaching us that, denying ungodliness and worldly lusts, we should live soberly, righteously, and godly, in this present world."

[767] 1 Cor. 12:7: "But the manifestation of the Spirit is given to every man to profit withal."

[768] Job 32:8: "But *there is* a spirit in man: and the inspiration of the Almighty giveth them understanding."

[769] Rom. 1:19: "Because that which may be known of God is manifest in them; for God hath shewed *it* unto them."

[770] Gal. 5:16: "*This* I say then, Walk in the Spirit, and ye shall not fulfil the lust of the flesh."

[771] 1 John 1:7: "But if we walk in the light, as he is in the light, we have fellowship one with another, and the blood of Jesus Christ his Son cleanseth us from all sin."

[772] Isa. 2:5: "O house of Jacob, come ye, and let us walk in the light of the Lord."

[773] Rev. 21:23: "And the city had no need of the sun, neither of the moon, to shine in it: for the glory of God did lighten it, and the Lamb *is* the light thereof."

[774] Gal. 6:16: "And as many as walk according to this rule, peace *be* on them, and mercy, and upon the Israel of God."

creation that has passed away, but the rule of the new creation – as it is properly understood and as Drusius also interprets it. This is the way of life that Isaiah spoke of, "There will be a highway called the way of holiness; the unclean will not walk on it and travelers, even if they are fools, will not go astray. There will be no lions of other ferocious beasts there – only the redeemed will walk there."[775] This Way, Teacher, Guide, Rule, Light, Spirit, and Holy Unction who directs us and keeps us in the steady paths of truth is Christ Jesus our Lord.

Objection: Don't you remove the Scriptures from their rightful place – as being open to doubt and not particularly useful writings – essentially rejecting and denying them completely?

Answer: Some, in an attempt to discredit us, have made this claim, but we do not.

The Scriptures are uncertain when placed on an uncertain foundation – ours is solid. When we reveal that others have put their faith in their own ideas or in human tradition does that make the Scriptures uncertain or invalid? By no means! We merely ask that they be accepted based on the testimony and evidence of the Spirit that brought them forth. Although in the gospel dispensation (which is power and life itself) we do not accept them as the rule for faith and life, they are still to be read reverently, believed, and fulfilled. Remember that the law written on stone was not Paul's law after the Son of God was revealed to him,[776] but the Son taught Paul to fulfill the righteous requirements proclaimed by that law.[777] Would those who have accused us of denying and rejecting the Scripture – because we cannot accept it as a rule – accuse Paul of the same thing? He took the Law of the Spirit of Life in Christ Jesus as his rule.[778] There is a great

---

[775] Isa. 35:8-9: "And an highway shall be there, and a way, and it shall be called The way of holiness; the unclean shall not pass over it; but it *shall be* for those: the wayfaring men, though fools, shall not err *therein.* No lion shall be there, nor *any* ravenous beast shall go up thereon, it shall not be found there; but the redeemed shall walk *there.*"

[776] 2 Cor. 3:3: "*Forasmuch as ye are* manifestly declared to be the epistle of Christ ministered by us, written not with ink, but with the Spirit of the living God; not in tables of stone, but in fleshy tables of the heart."

[777] Rom. 8:4: "That the righteousness of the law might be fulfilled in us, who walk not after the flesh, but after the Spirit."

[778] Rom. 8:2: "For the law of the Spirit of life in Christ Jesus hath made me free from the law of sin and death."

difference between declaring that the Spirit is the rule and casting aside or vilifying the Scriptures. Indeed, it is an old trick of the devil to pretend to honor the letter of the law in order to resist, without raising suspicion, the Spirit[779] to which the letter testified. Those who are led by the Spirit achieve the goal for which the Scriptures were written. The apostle John said nearly the same thing when he wrote that his readers did not need anyone to teach them because the anointing they had received and which lived within them[780] would lead them into all truth.[781] This is as plain as anything in the whole Scripture. To claim that those Christians had one rule and we another – they the Spirit and we the letter – is unreasonable. Did John's writings invalidate the Scriptures or nullify his own epistle? It's hard to believe that anyone would say such a thing. How does our exaltation of the Light and Spirit of Christ reject or vilify the Scriptures? We follow a higher rule that leads us to live up to what they require and to enjoy the good things that they describe. How does that deny them? Erasmus and Grotius think that they are most obviously valued by people who are examples of their truth (see in particular what they have written about 2 Peter 1:19). I freely acknowledge that they contain an account of heavenly prophesies, divine warnings, instructions, and several examples that should be obeyed and followed.

Objection: If that is so, then how are they not a rule for faith and life?

Answer: A *rule* and *the rule* are two different things. I understand *the rule* of faith and practice to be the living, close, omnipresent, revealing, and ordering Spirit of God. On the other hand, I understand *a rule* to be some device by which or through which the great and universal rule can convey its directions. We recognize various parts of the Scriptures to be such secondary, subordinate, and proclaiming rules. The reason for our obedience to them is not merely because they are written there (which would be mere legalism), but because they are eternal precepts of the Spirit,

---

[779] 2 Cor. 3:6: "Who also hath made us able ministers of the new testament; not of the letter, but of the spirit: for the letter killeth, but the spirit giveth life."

[780] 1 John 2:27: "But the anointing which ye have received of him abideth in you, and ye need not that any man teach you: but as the same anointing teacheth you of all things, and is truth, and is no lie, and even as it hath taught you, ye shall abide in him."

[781] John 16:13: "Howbeit when he, the Spirit of truth, is come, he will guide you into all truth: for he shall not speak of himself; but whatsoever he shall hear, *that* shall he speak: and he will shew you things to come."

which are also found, repeated, and proclaimed in our consciences. It is the Spirit's testimony that is the true rule for believing and understanding the Scripture, and therefore, the Spirit of Truth, and not the Scripture, must be our rule for belief and understanding. As can be seen in the following, this was clearly the belief of the ancients.

Tertullian: "The Lord calls worldly wisdom foolishness.[782] Putting philosophy (which is concerned with worldly wisdom) in its rightful place, God has chosen the foolish things of the world.[783] A Divine interpreter is needed to understand the Divine nature and order."

Justin Martyr: "The interpretation of the Scriptures must be done according to the will of the Spirit, not to human reasoning."

Hieron: "The Scriptures must be opened by spiritual exposition."

Epiphanius:[784] "The Scriptures are plain and clear only to the children of the Holy Spirit."

Nor do the leading Protestants disagree. The Council of Trent's[785] fourth article against the Lutherans says, in essence, that it is an erroneous doctrine to believe that no sophisticated guide or commentary is necessary to understand the Scripture, but only to have the Spirit of a Sheep in Christ's pasture.

Erasmus: "What a human produces by human means can be understood by a human mind. But whatever is produced by the inspiration of the Holy Spirit requires an interpreter inspired by the same Spirit. Without such inspiration, the secrets of God cannot be known."

Luther: "The Scriptures can be understood only by the Spirit by which they were written."

---

[782] 1 Cor. 3:19: "For the wisdom of this world is foolishness with God. For it is written, He taketh the wise in their own craftiness."

[783] 1 Cor. 1:27: "But God hath chosen the foolish things of the world to confound the wise; and God hath chosen the weak things of the world to confound the things which are might."

[784] Epiphanius of Salamis (c. 310-403) was bishop of Constantia on Cyprus. He compiled a compendium of eighty heresies of the early church.

[785] The Council of Trent (1545-63) was the founding event of the Counterreformation. At this Roman Catholic council, dogma was clarified and reforms instituted in reaction to the Reformation.

Peter Martyr:[786] "The Spirit is the means by which we must secure ourselves from error in understanding the Scriptures. By the Spirit, we can discern the difference between Christ's words and a stranger's." He quotes Christ's words, "My sheep know my voice"[787] and other places in Scripture. He also has said, "The Spirit of God reveals the truth in the Scriptures."

Heinrich Bullinger:[788] "People can only acquire understanding of heavenly things and knowledge of the Holy Spirit from the same Spirit."

John Bradford (in answer to the Archbishop of York):[789] "As Christ's sheep, we know the Scriptures by the same Spirit that wrote and spoke them. Of this, we are assured."

Calvin (in his *Institutes*): "It is necessary for the same Spirit that spoke from the mouths of the prophets to pierce our hearts and persuade us that they have faithfully delivered what was given to them by God."

Beza[790] (commenting on 2 Peter 1:19[791]): "The way of understanding prophesies and correctly comprehending them must be sought or attained from the same Spirit that dictated them to the prophets.

William Tyndale[792] (called the English apostle by John Foxe[793]): "It is impossible to understand the Scriptures better than a Muslim unless the law of God is written in the heart."

---

[786] Pietro Martire Vermigli (1500-1562) was an Italian religious reformer. Accused of heresy, he fled to England, where he became Regius Professor of Divinity at Oxford.

[787] John 10:4: "And when he putteth forth his own sheep, he goeth before them, and the sheep follow him: for they know his voice."

[788] Heinrich Bullinger (1504-1575) was a Swiss reformer and disciple of Zwingli.

[789] John Bradford (1510-1555) was a Protestant Lancashire evangelist and fellow of Cambridge University. He was one of the Marian martyrs, burnt at the stake in 1555.

[790] Theodore Beza (1519-1605) was a French Protestant theologian. He worked with and succeeded Calvin as the leader of the Genevan Protestant reformers. He produced Greek and Latin translations of the New Testament that were instrumental in the production of the Geneva and King James Version Bibles.

[791] 2 Pet. 1:19: "We have also a more sure word of prophecy; whereunto ye do well that ye take heed, as unto a light that shineth in a dark place, until the day dawn, and the day star arise in your hearts."

Bishop John Jewel[794] (in response to Harding[795]): "The Spirit of God is revealed neither by a sharp mind nor by abundant learning. Flesh and blood cannot understand the holy will of God without special revelation. No matter how wise and well educated a reader may be, without this special help and prompting, the Scripture is a sealed book."

Dr. William Ames[796] (in response to Bellarmin[797]): "The anointing of the Holy Spirit teaches the faithful so that they can understand what they have received from the apostles and can, therefore, understand the things in Scripture that are necessary for salvation."

Vatablus (on Job 32:8[798]), Drusius Clarius, and others say much the same thing.

Walter Cradock:[799] "The Scripture is a speechless thing without the Spirit."

---

[792] William Tyndale (1490-1536) attempted to translate the Bible into English – an activity that was then illegal. He had not finished the task when he was captured and executed. The New Testament and pieces of the Old Testament that he had produced at the time of his death influenced the translators of the Geneva Bible.

[793] John Foxe (1516-1587) was an English Puritan preacher. He is best known for his *Book of Martyrs* that listed those who suffered for Protestantism.

[794] John Jewel, Bishop of Salisbury (1522-1571), has been called the father of the Church of England, because his tract, *The Apologie of the Church of England*, contrasted the positions of the Church of England and the Roman Catholic Church.

[795] Thomas Harding (1516-1572) was initially favorable to the Reformation, but returned to the Catholic Church when Queen Mary took the throne. He engaged in a long controversy with John Jewel.

[796] William Ames (1576-1633) was an English Independent (Congregational) theologian who fled to the Netherlands in 1610. He engaged in numerous debates and an extended pamphlet controversy with the Arminians.

[797] Robert Bellarmin (1542-1621) was a Jesuit priest, bishop, theologist for Popes Clement VIII and Paul V, and an active spokesman for the Counterreformation. In 1586, he published a point-by-point answer to Protestant theses. He was responsible for an updating of the Vulgate Bible.

[798] Job 32:8: "But *there is* a spirit in man: and the inspiration of the Almighty giveth them understanding."

[799] Walter Cradock (c. 1610-1659), was a Welsh Puritan minister.

Thomas Goad:[800] "There is no knowledge of Christ, nor of the Scripture, except by revelation."

Dr. John Owen:[801] "The public, authentic, and infallible interpreter of the Holy Scriptures is the author of them. From breathing in that Spirit they derive all their truth, clarity, and authority."

Thus, we see that in the judgment of many prominent people, the Scripture is not a rule for believing and understanding in itself and, therefore, not the rule of the faith and practice for the things that they describe.

I will give a short example of Christ's words concerning regeneration. He taught (probably to the amazement of wise Nicodemus) that "no one can see the kingdom of God without being born again."[802] This is as plain a statement as can be found, and we can trust its accuracy. But what is our trust compared to the knowledge and experience of the new birth itself? And that knowledge and experience are not likely to be found in a book. Nor can that Scripture (or any other writing) guide me in meeting the many trials that come as I seek the kingdom of God. We are born again only by the Immortal Word and Spirit. What, other than the same Spirit, can be my rule – to inform, order, strengthen, and lead me?

All doctrines in the Scriptures were experienced before they were written – otherwise, the writers would not have been faithful witnesses. Only that which was their rule can guide us into the same experiences. And only by experience can we come to truly know them. Christ says, "If anyone does God's will, they will know the doctrines."[803] I have read the story, but that will not save me. Neither can the story be my guide to the mysteries –

---

[800] Thomas Goad was an English theologian, Precentor of St. Paul's in London, chaplain to George Abbot (Archbishop of Canterbury), and chosen by King James I as a delegate to the Synod of Dordt in 1618-19.

[801] John Owen (1616-1683) was an English Independent (Congregational) clergyman and theologian. He was an aide and chaplain to Oliver Cromwell from 1653 to 1658.

[802] John 3:3: "Jesus answered and said unto him, Verily, verily, I say unto thee, Except a man be born again, he cannot see the kingdom of God."

[803] John 7:17: "If any man will do his will, he shall know of the doctrine, whether it be of God, or *whether* I speak of myself."

that can only be the Spirit that searches the deep things of God.[804] Consequently, the Spirit, and not the Scriptures, is the rule for believing and living.

Objection: But doesn't this run contrary to the Protestant principle that the Scriptures are the rule of faith and practice?

Answer: Not at all. The issue that Protestants raised against the Roman Catholics was not whether the Spirit of Christ or the Scripture was the rule. Rather, it was whether God's tradition, the Scriptures, or the Pope's traditions were to be used to test the truth of doctrines and practice. We grant that particular Scriptures – rightly understood – may be used to judge particular claims. That is to say that doctrines and practices that are contrary to a part of the Scriptures – specifically, those relating to observing so-called holy days – are called into question by the Scriptures. All contend that what they do and say follows Scripture. Even so, this does not make the Scriptures the universal rule.

Objection: If God has not revealed those things that are in Scripture, how could they have been known to us?

Answer: They were known by the Light and Spirit of Christ before they were written – it is only after they were written down that they are called Scripture. It was said that the prophets carefully searched what and when the Spirit of Christ, that was within them, revealed when it foretold the sufferings of Christ.[805] Nor are they more accessible to a blind or darkened mind, just because they have been written down – the mysteries of rebirth remain just as puzzling to the natural mind and to earthly wisdom as they did before. This was all well said by Epiphanius: "The Scriptures are plain and clear only to the children of the Holy Spirit." Humanity's intellectual efforts to work out principles without this infallible guide have been the cause of the tremendous confusion that has ruled in religion right up to the current day.

---

[804] 1 Cor. 2:10: "But God hath revealed *them* unto us by his Spirit: for the Spirit searcheth all things, yea, the deep things of God."

[805] 1 Pet. 1:10-11: "Of which salvation the prophets have enquired and searched diligently, who prophesied of the grace *that should come* unto you: Searching what, or what manner of time the Spirit of Christ which was in them did signify, when it testified beforehand the sufferings of Christ, and the glory that should follow."

Objection: Prophesies are not a matter of witness, but of foretelling – how else could we have known them to be true?

Answer: By extraordinary revelations, far beyond what is necessary for our salvation, God shows his power and faithfulness and demonstrates that he can foretell things and cause what was foretold to happen. But is an extraordinary Light or Spirit required to make an extraordinary revelation? Rather, doesn't it require an extraordinary sight and sense of the same Light and Spirit? Something coming from the Spirit, which leads me to believe (rather than forcing me to believe) and to be glad of it – this is my rule for believing. As Calvin and Beza have told us, it is necessary for the same Spirit that spoke from the mouths of the prophets to pierce our hearts and persuade us that they have faithfully delivered the message given to them by God.

Objection: But this Light could not tell you how sin came into the world – that there was an Adam and an Eve or how they sinned and let sin into the world; that Christ was born of a virgin, suffered death, and rose again; or that you ought not to swear. The Scriptures are needed to tell you those things.

Answer: True enough, but consider it carefully. Moses, according to popular opinion, wrote the account of creation we find in Genesis more than two thousand years after it occurred – by revelation. Everyone must admit that there could be no revelation without this Divine Light or Spirit, which is the Light of the Eternal, Creating Word. As the apostle Paul says, "The things of God are known only by the Spirit of God"[806] and "Whatever reveals is Light."[807] It has already been shown that Light and Spirit are merely two names for one and the same thing. It was the Light of the Eternal Word that revealed those past things to Moses and let the prophets see things yet to happen. If the Scriptures are believable, then to say that the Light or Spirit could not have done so is both blasphemous and absurd.

To argue that the Light is inadequate because it does not reveal every detail of history to each individual is unreasonable. Let us suppose that we

---

[806] 1 Cor. 2:11: "For what man knoweth the things of a man, save the spirit of man which is in him? even so the things of God knoweth no man, but the Spirit of God."

[807] Eph. 5:13: "But all things that are reproved are made manifest by the light: for whatsoever doth make manifest is light."

did lack an account of the life of Christ and of his followers (just as before Moses there was no description of Adam and Eve or of their descendants) and that the Lord saw that such an account was needed. No doubt, the same Light and Spirit, that revealed the story of creation to Moses and foretold events in life of Christ hundreds of years before they happened, would also have provided us with the story of Christ. But the gospels already exist, so the objection is purely hypothetical.

Remember, that each person has a share or portion of the Light to inform and guide him or her – they do not need to know all that the Light knows or all that it could reveal to them. Let me turn this argument back on our adversaries. They say that they have 'the Spirit of God' – should we conclude they know all that the Spirit knows or can reveal to them? If such a conclusion is absurd, then so is the premise on which it is based.

They also say that the Light did not reveal Christ to the Gentiles or that Christ would be born of a virgin – and therefore, it is inadequate. My answer is that the Spirit of God, given to the children of Israel,[808] did not tell them that Christ would be born of a virgin, nor much more about his life – does that make the Spirit of God inadequate? The same accusation could be made against the Spirit in the prophets; it is obvious from 1 Peter 1:10-11[809] that the Spirit had not revealed to all the prophets the time of Christ's coming and his sufferings. Was the Spirit inadequate for them?

But what is most difficult for our opponents is that the Scriptures themselves are imperfect, telling less than one percent of what happened. Therefore, the Scriptures seem to be as inadequate in revealing to each individual what has already happened as the Light and Spirit are in revealing all that will happen up to the end of the world, although in time, it may be necessary to know that.

Likewise, history is not and cannot be the rule of faith and life that is absolutely essential for salvation. God, not history, gives faith; and God works by love and overcomes the world. Millions who believed in history

---

[808] Neh. 9:20: "Thou gavest also thy good spirit to instruct them, and withheldest not thy manna from their mouth, and gavest them water for their thirst."

[809] 1 Pet. 1:10-11: "Of which salvation the prophets have enquired and searched diligently, who prophesied of the grace *that should come* unto you: Searching what, or what manner of time the Spirit of Christ which was in them did signify, when it testified beforehand the sufferings of Christ, and the glory that should follow."

have been overcome by the world – they are mired in the spirit of the world and the practices of the world. The rule must be compatible with and meet the needs of the faith. It must guide me in my duty. History tells me about others' actions, but those actions may not provide a guide to me. Some of those events are unique, such as those of Adam and Eve or Christ's virgin birth and death on the cross for the sins of all – it cannot be my duty to repeat such unique events and therefore they are not my guide. The same may be said of the history of the Jewish people, which recounts the particular concerns and actions of that people.

Objection: But these things should be believed.

Answer: I agree. As cited above, D. John Owen says that when that history has reached (and the Spirit of God has awakened) the conscience, it gives authority, clarity, and truth. But, as Bishop Sanderson[810] has said, people in those places that have never heard this history and individuals who die without ever hearing it are not required to believe it.

It is one thing to say that the Scriptures ought to be read, believed, and fulfilled, and another to say that they are the universal rule of faith and life. When I read, believe, and experience them, I need a rule by which to read, understand, believe, and witness them. That rule must be the Divine Light and Spirit of Christ, not the Scriptures themselves.

Furthermore, it is granted by all that the Sybils had insight into the divine, proving that the Light and Spirit within the heathens was sufficient to reveal these things. I don't mean the false reports created by some Christians that Blondel has refuted, but those that are acknowledged as true – those in which they prophesized that a virgin would give birth to a son, that he would destroy the serpent, and fill the earth with righteousness. This was cited above from the works of Virgil, who quoted it from verses spoken by the Sybil of Cumaea.

Let me now respond to the second part of the objection above: how would we have known that it was unlawful to swear without Matthew 5:34 to guide us? This is of importance because it is a matter of duty and is called by some a gospel precept, which is to say, a step beyond the outward laws of the Jews. Before Christ came, there were people, the Essenes, among the

---

[810] Robert Sanderson (1587-1662) was an early English Protestant moralist and Bishop of Lincoln following the Restoration of King Charles II. He is best remembered today for the fact that Izaak Walton wrote his biography.

Jews who did not swear. "They keep their promises," wrote Josephus, "and treat every word they speak as if they had bound themselves to it with an oath. They shun oaths as worse than perjury and consider anyone who would require one to be a liar."

Philo taught that it was best to abstain from swearing so that one's word would be believed without an oath.

And Pythagoras, in his speech to the Crotonian Senators, urged them, "Let no one testify with an oath, even when in a court, but only say what can be believed without the need for an oath."

The Scythians are said to have told Alexander that they could not confirm their friendship with an oath, but only swear by keeping their word.

Clinias, a Greek Pythagorean, chose to pay a fine of three talents (which was approximately three hundred pounds of gold) rather than to impugn his own truthfulness by taking an oath. This act was contrasted by Basilius[811] with the practice of Christians in his time. If we were to follow the example of our opponents, we would say that Basilius preferred the Light of the Gentiles to that of the Christians. But the Light is always One in itself, and what he was saying was that Christians did not live up to it as well as the Gentiles

I ask our opponents if the Light that preached the Sermon on the Mount was the same as the Light that shined in the consciences of those Gentiles who so plainly believed, practiced, and taught the same message many hundreds of years earlier. Perhaps some, out of an excess of envy, pride, and passion, will continue to deny it, but the more reasonable among them will accept the evidence presented and conclude that the attacks on us come from ignorance and foolishness. Truly, the voice that cried out, "To you, O people, I call, and my voice is to all humanity; hear me, for I will tell you wonderful things"[812] was also heard by the Gentiles. What was necessary for holy living – as revealed in Matthew's account of the Sermon on the Mount – was obviously not hidden from them. Their writings overflow with a chorus of "Amen!"

---

[811] St. Basil (329-379) was an early church Father and bishop of Caesarea who defended orthodox Christianity against the Arian heresy.

[812] Prov. 8:4&6: "Unto you, O men, I call; and my voice *is* to the sons of man. ... Hear; for I will speak of excellent things; and the opening of my lips *shall be* right things."

We admit that the voice was so soft and the revelations of the Light so dim that it did not reveal many of those things mentioned above. Does that give reasonable people grounds to conclude that the Divine Wisdom or Light was insufficient? Or, that therefore the Divine Wisdom or Light was not then (and could never become) the rule and guide for all mankind? Such false consequences have been the cornerstone and foundation of our opponents' charges against us. I believe that no reasonable person can deny that they are building their case on a sandy foundation.

THE JUDGE OF ALL CONTROVERSY

*L*et me start by explaining what I mean by these terms.

A judge is someone that has both the power to decide an issue and the discernment to do it correctly.

Controversy is a debate between two parties about the truth or falsehood of a proposition to be decided by a judge.

From this, I am led to assert that the judge of a controversy must be certain and unerring.

Although this might seem strange to some, it is nevertheless true in itself. A judge who is fallible might, by an exercise of authority, succeed in silencing the contending parties, but not in resolving the controversy, since the ruling may be true or false. Therefore a fallible judge cannot be a true judge of a controversy – it is absurd and a contradiction in terms to think otherwise – someone who is uncertain cannot decide with certainty. And an uncertain decision is no decision at all. Nor would people, who are sure of the truth of their position, give it up on such shaky grounds. People will not accept a judgment without conviction – especially one against their own convictions – just because they are required to submit to it. The most contemptible people are those who make much of religious belief, even using coercion to enforce their chosen orthodoxy, but who acknowledge that they are not certain in their own faith.

If therefore the judge must be unerring, it is worthwhile to ask where such an infallible judge can be found. Christ said, "No one is good but

God"[813] – that is, no one else is good by nature – and just as surely, no one is infallible but God. But to a degree, individuals can share in that ultimate good and in the same way, as Bishop Latimer[814] has told us, infallibility, certainty, or confidence in the truth of things is given to people according to their abilities. Otherwise, people would be required to believe things and obey commands (at the risk eternal damnation) with no hope of knowing whether for sure whether they are true or false.

He is called "Emmanuel, God with us"[815] because he is our rule and therefore our judge. He is the lawgiver and therefore the best interpreter of any point of that law. People can be certain, or infallible, only to the degree to which they are subject to his Voice, Light, or Spirit within themselves – and no further, because *humanum est errare*, to err is human. Only one thing can keep us from making errors or protect us from the costs of those errors – the sound and certain judgment that God, by the Light of his Spirit, has given to us.

Objection: But isn't the Scripture the judge of controversy?

Answer: How can that be when most often the question is about the meaning of Scripture? Is there any place where, without interpretation, the Scriptures tell us whether the Socinians or the Trinitarians are correct in their very different understandings of "three that bear record, etc."?[816] Or decide between the Homousians[817] and Arians?[818] Or between Papists and

---

[813] Mark 10:18: "And Jesus said unto him, Why callest thou me good? *there is* none good but one, *that is*, God."

[814] Hugh Latimer (1492-1555) was an influential preacher in the first generation of English Protestants. He was named Bishop of Worcester in 1535, but later forced to resign when he fell out of royal favor. When Mary became queen, he refused to give up his beliefs and was burned at the stake.

[815] Matt. 1:23: "Behold, a virgin shall be with child, and shall bring forth a son, and they shall call his name Emmanuel, which being interpreted is, God with us."

[816] 1 John 5:7: "For there are three that bear record in heaven, the Father, the Word, and the Holy Ghost: and these three are one."

[817] This is a synonym for Trinitarian. *Homoousios* is the Greek term used in Trinitarian doctrine to indicate that Christ was of the same essence or substance as God the Father.

[818] Arius (c. 256-336) taught that Christ was the highest created being, having a substance or essence similar to but not the same as that of God the Father. His followers were referred to as Arians.

Protestants on transubstantiation?[819] If the Scripture leaves things literally and expressly undefined and undetermined, and the question is about the meaning of the words in the Scripture, how can it determine which of the interpreters is correct? This is certainly not reasonable, and it must therefore be acknowledged that it is not the thing being interpreted that is the judge, but person who acts as interpreter.

This interpreter can interpret by his or her own wisdom or spirit – what the apostle called "the human spirit"[820] – by investigating the text, considering the intent of the writer, comparing various passages, and producing a judgment that the Scripture does not state for itself. Or, the interpreter may depend on the Spirit of God, which gives understanding,[821] and, as the same apostle says in the same place, "searches even the depths of God."[822] The first way is fallible, the second, infallible.

Was it the Scripture or the Holy Spirit that presided over the apostles when they sat together and said, "It seemed good to the Holy Spirit and to us, etc."[823] If you agree that it was the Holy Spirit, then please show us a plain Scripture passage that says we are now to have any other judge. If that cannot be done, then we must stick with the same, infallible judge, the Spirit of Truth, which leads Christians into all Truth,[824] and was given to us by Christ, for just this purpose.

Objection: It is true that the Spirit is infallible. But how can we know that anyone is judging by the Spirit and not merely giving his or her own beliefs?

---

[819] To Catholics, when the bread and wine are consecrated in the mass, they become the actual body and blood of Christ, although they differ in their outward appearance. Protestants deny this.

[820] 1 Cor. 2:11: "For what man knoweth the things of a man, save the spirit of man which is in him? even so the things of God knoweth no man, but the Spirit of God."

[821] Job 32:8: "But *there is* a spirit in man: and the inspiration of the Almighty giveth them understanding."

[822] 1 Cor. 2:10: "But God hath revealed *them* unto us by his Spirit: for the Spirit searcheth all things, yea, the deep things of God."

[823] Acts 15:28: "For it seemed good to the Holy Ghost, and to us, to lay upon you no greater burden than these necessary things."

[824] John 16:13: "Howbeit when he, the Spirit of truth, is come, he will guide you into all truth: for he shall not speak of himself; but whatsoever he shall hear, *that* shall he speak: and he will shew you things to come."

Answer. By the same Spirit. As Walter Craddock has said so well, "The way to know whether the Spirit is in us is by its own evidence and that is the way to know it in others, too. The person who has the Spirit may know the Spirit in another. ... There is a kind of wisdom in true Christians for this purpose." This opinion is shared by a large number of Protestant writers. Just as they believe that the Scriptures cannot be known except by the Spirit that inspired them, they also believe that only that Spirit can guarantee the truth of an interpretation. Peter Martyr, who was quoted above, tells us, "The Holy Spirit is the arbiter or judge." Also Dr. John Owen says, "The Holy Spirit is the only genuine interpreter of the Scriptures." If that is the only genuine interpreter, then it is the only infallible judge. That is to say, the judge of the meaning of the Scriptures is both the only judge and an infallible judge. But putting all this aside, couldn't the same objection be made against the Scripture itself since one person says it means this and another, that? To know God's mind, people must look to God's Spirit – otherwise, these difficulties are insurmountable.

In short, it would be very nice if people would refrain from hotly debating things for which they have no assurance from the Holy Spirit. Without such certification, they are just beating the air to no good purpose. God does not subordinate his secrets to the ideas of disobedient minds. Let all do what they know to be their duty and avoid searching for foolishness and unknown matters. The apostle's words were and are worth particular consideration, "Let us live up to what we have already learned."[825] This passage both limits us to the knowledge that we have already been given and urges us to live up to it. If we need to know anything more, it will, in due time, be revealed by God's Spirit. Only in this way can we know, discern, and judge which are the things of God.

Objection: How can this settle the controversy and end the furious debates that so fill the world?

Answer. If people would follow this guide, there would be nothing like it; but if they do not, there is nothing left for them except the wrath to come.[826] But, from the Light and Witness that God has placed in their consciences, most religions agree on the absolute necessities. These are, that

---

[825] Phil. 3:16: "Nevertheless, whereto we have already attained, let us walk by the same rule, let us mind the same thing."

[826] Luke 3:7: "Then said he to the multitude that came forth to be baptized of him, O generation of vipers, who hath warned you to flee from the wrath to come?"

God is; that God rewards those who diligently seek him;[827] the way to God is by purity, patience, humility, etc; without which no one can see the Lord.[828] Indeed, they agree in many things beyond these basics, for example, that God was revealed in the flesh; that God died for the world; that those who believe and obey God's grace in their hearts would receive forgiveness for their sins and life everlasting. Now I say, since people generally agree on these things, let them all live up to them and give up their meaningless scurrying after things or notions that lead them into strife and contention – leaving mankind worse, rather than better off – and the world would soon be free of controversy. Holy living, not disputing, would be the business of mankind. What better situation could there be than for people to give up their debates about notions and opinions and take up the practice of the good that God has already shown them. Listen to the prophet Micah and the apostle Paul: "God has shown you, O people, what is good – to act justly and to love mercy and to walk humbly with your God."[829] "What may be known about God is revealed within them, because God has shown it to them."[830] And if one person claims that anything was revealed more to him or her than to others, let the rest judge that claim in the Spirit or wait silently until God reveals more to them so that they can make a true judgment.

It is good to "test all things,"[831] but we must have something to test them with and what could that be other than the "Spirit that searches[832] and the anointing that teaches all things."[833] This is Truth itself. Here, mankind

---

[827] Heb. 11:6: "But without faith *it is* impossible to please *him*: for he that cometh to God must believe that he is, and *that* he is a rewarder of them that diligently seek him."

[828] Heb. 12:14: "Follow peace with all *men*, and holiness, without which no man shall see the Lord."

[829] Mic. 6:8: "He hath shewed thee, O man, what *is* good; and what doth the LORD require of thee, but to do justly, and to love mercy, and to walk humbly with thy God?"

[830] Rom. 1:19: "Because that which may be known of God is manifest in them; for God hath shewed *it* unto them."

[831] 1 Thess. 5:21: "Prove all things; hold fast that which is good."

[832] 1 Cor. 2:10: "But God hath revealed *them* unto us by his Spirit: for the Spirit searcheth all things, yea, the deep things of God."

[833] 1 John 2:20&27: "But ye have an unction from the Holy One, and ye know all things. ... and ye need not that any man teach you: but as the same anointing

can live in love, with at least a natural affection (now lost by the barbarity of some of their cruel religions and by their heated arguments). Judgment will be based on the Eternal Light and Spirit that has never erred, rather than on the rash, biased, short-sighted, and perverse human mind. No matter how much the Protestants of this age might dislike it, this was the principle of John Philpot[834] and Bishop Latimer, two of the great founders of the Reformation in England.

When Bishop of Chichester commented, "These heretics take it upon themselves to be sure of everything they accept as true," Philpot replied, "Let those who wish to, doubt. May God grant that I will always be sure of true faith and favor in Christ."

John Foxe, in his *Book of Martyrs*, reports that Latimer gave the following answer to an objection by Sir Edward Baynton: "Your friends do not deny that certain truths are communicated to each person in one degree or another. But as to my presumption and arrogance, either I am certain or uncertain about what I preach. If it is truth, why not say so? If I am uncertain, how could I dare preach it? If your friends are preachers, ask them after their sermons whether or not they are certain and sure that they have preached the truth – and send me their answers. If they say they are sure, you know what that means. But, if they say that they are not sure, how can you be sure of what so doubtful and unsure a teacher has taught?"

It would be shameful for Protestants to condemn us for accepting a doctrine that is confessed and confirmed by some of the most prominent of our spiritual ancestors. An unerring, certain, and infallible judgment of the things essential to salvation is both possible and necessary and God communicates it to our souls by his Spirit.

---

teacheth you of all things, and is truth, and is no lie, and even as it hath taught you, ye shall abide in him."

[834] John Philpot (died 1555) was the archdeacon of Winchester when Queen Mary took the throne. He stayed when others fled to safety and debated the Catholic Bishops that Mary appointed. He was arrested, tried, and executed as a heretic.

CONCLUSION

*T*o conclude, Emmanuel – God near us or with us – is a word that is not only suited to Christ's appearance in the flesh, but to the whole gospel dispensation. "God is among humanity, living in them and walking with them."[835] "They will all be taught by the Lord and rooted in righteousness."[836] That is, they will be taught by the Spirit of God's Son. This does not permit any book or literal rule or judge to be the soul's rule of faith and practice or to come between that indwelling Spirit of Light, Life, and Wisdom from God and the soul.

Because it is the unutterable goodness of God to people in these days, as the culmination of Scripture prophesy, to make himself known in this way, we are unceasing in our cries to all – that they turn their minds inward and listen for the heavenly voice and for the knock at their door – to let Christ in so that he can teach them to know and do his will, and so that they will become experienced and expert in the school of Christ. No one has ever spoken or taught as Christ can speak and teach today in the consciences of those who listen and are willing to learn his ways. The priest was outward, now he is inward. The law was outward, now it is within. Now, "No one is a Jew who is only one outwardly, nor is circumcision merely outward and physical. No, a person is a Jew who is one inwardly; and circumcision is circumcision of the heart, by the Spirit, not by the letter. Such a person is praised not by other people, but by God."[837] This in no way diminishes the authority of the Scriptures of Truth, unless they are taken to be the ultimate guide and judge – in that case, they can never be correctly understood or faithfully followed. Indeed, as I have said before, I must say again when unregenerated people try, by their own minds and

---

[835] Rev. 21:3: "And I heard a great voice out of heaven saying, Behold, the tabernacle of God *is* with men, and he will dwell with them, and they shall be his people, and God himself shall be with them, *and be* their God."

[836] Isa. 54:13-14: "And all thy children *shall be* taught of the LORD; and great *shall be* the peace of thy children. In righteousness shalt thou be established: thou shalt be far from oppression; for thou shalt not fear: and from terror; for it shall not come near thee."

[837] Rom. 2:28-29: "For he is not a Jew, which is one outwardly; neither *is that* circumcision, which is outward in the flesh: But he *is* a Jew, which is one inwardly; and circumcision *is that* of the heart, in the spirit, *and* not in the letter; whose praise *is* not of men, but of God."

wisdom, to understand the intentions of the Holy Spirit in those writings, they give rise to the confusion, darkness, and perplexed controversy that so lamentably pesters the world. While they remain in that degenerate state, despite all the external similarities between their worship and the outward worship of the ancients, they will never be accepted by the Spirit of the Lord God.

The sum-total of that literal knowledge, historical faith, and outward religion is, at best, only the old heavens that are to be rolled up like a scroll.[838] It is the old wine and old bottles that do not belong to the kingdom of God.[839] Such believers may flatter themselves and in the end cry out "Lord, Lord!"[840] But alas! They will never enter into the rest[841] that God has reserved for his reborn and redeemed children. Envy, wrath, malice, persecution, pride, passion, covetousness, worldly-mindedness, etc. can and do reign under that faith and religion. Truly, they are hidden from God's Spirit, so much so, that when the Lord moves anyone to condemn these hypocritical displays of religion, they are denounced as rash and censorious. This is followed by a plea: Don't we follow the commands of the Scriptures? Don't we do the same as those in the Scripture did? But at best, these are merely the ceremonial duties, not the call to obedience. Nor do they seem to notice whether their activities are those of the old creature or of the new.[842] They abuse and malign us for making such distinctions, as if the prayers, preaching, singing, outward baptisms, etc. – all coming from their own unsanctified spirits, strength, and wills – are required and accepted by God as gospel worship. This is the deepest darkness and most

---

[838] Isa. 34:4: "And all the host of heaven shall be dissolved, and the heavens shall be rolled together as a scroll: and all their host shall fall down, as the leaf falleth off from the vine, and as a falling *fig* from the fig tree."

[839] Mark 2:22: "And no man putteth new wine into old bottles: else the new wine doth burst the bottles, and the wine is spilled, and the bottles will be marred: but new wine must be put into new bottles."

[840] Luke 13:25: "When once the master of the house is risen up, and hath shut to the door, and ye begin to stand without, and to knock at the door, saying, Lord, Lord, open unto us; and he shall answer and say unto you, I know you not whence ye are."

[841] Heb. 3:18: "And to whom sware he that they should not enter into his rest, but to them that believed not?"

[842] 2 Cor. 5:17: "Therefore if any man *be* in Christ, *he is* a new creature: old things are passed away; behold, all things are become new."

dangerous presumption! They have lost their way in faith and practice, and in knowing the true rule and judge of them. They pervert faith to agree with their own understandings and imitate the practice of the old covenant, taking up things that were only signs of the good things to come and the duties of sacrifice (so far from the Emmanuel state!). They elevate the Scriptures – an account of things that others were directed to do by the Holy Spirit – to be their rule and judge. But only that Holy Spirit who came before any words were written can be our rule and judge and guide to faith and practice.

God, by his Spirit, creates faith. God, by his Spirit, rules faith and governs the lives of his children. "All who are led by the Spirit of God are the children of God."[843] Much of the Scripture is merely a declaration of faith and experience – therefore not a rule or judge. Faith and experience came before Scripture, because (as I said before), wherever there is faith, there must be a rule and judge. Therefore, the Scripture is not that rule and judge. Before that declaration can be accepted or fulfilled by anyone, they must come to the faith, rule, and judge that it declares. Faith is surrendering to the requirements of God's Spirit within us, with complete assurance of the forgiveness of past sins through the Son of God's love, and of life everlasting. From that flows daily acts of holiness that are pleasing to God. This is more than mere words, more than agreeing to something – however true it may be. The life of a true Christian is not found in physical exercises, which, the apostle says provide little benefit.[844] Nor is it found in imitating

---

[843] 2 Cor. 5:17: "Therefore if any man *be* in Christ, *he is* a new creature: old things are passed away; behold, all things are become new."

[844] Penn has noted the following in the margin:

1 Tim. 4:8. ["For bodily exercise profiteth little: but godliness is profitable unto all things, having promise of the life that now is, and of that which is to come."]

Col. 2:20-23. ["Wherefore if ye be dead with Christ from the rudiments of the world, why, as though living in the world, are ye subject to ordinances, (Touch not; taste not; handle not; Which all are to perish with the using;) after the commandments and doctrines of men? Which things have indeed a shew of wisdom in will worship, and humility, and neglecting of the body; not in any honour to the satisfying of the flesh."]

Gal. 5:16, 22-23. ["*This* I say then, Walk in the Spirit, and ye shall not fulfil the lust of the flesh ... But the fruit of the Spirit is love, joy, peace, longsuffering, gentleness, goodness, faith, Meekness, temperance: against such there is no law."]

the ancients' temporary and shadowy practices – this a hypocrite can do as easily as a saint – but in self-denial and walking in the Spirit to bring forth the fruits of the Spirit. This is the pure and spiritual obedience that results from the living and spiritual faith of God's chosen. The Spirit of Truth – which alone gives true understanding, faith, and obedience and which searches the depths of God[845] – is its source and creator.

Oh! You who claim to be religious! Seriously consider these things and examine yourselves in God's sight. God is not impressed by outward appearances. Is this saving faith your faith? Is this heavenly life your life? Is the Holy Spirit your ruler and leader? If not, you are merely legal and formal worshippers; living by the letter of the law; worshipping as you desire, not as God desires. In that state, your rule is not the wisdom of the new creature from above, but that from the old creature below. You read the Scripture and interpret it, pray, preach, sing, and perform all the legal duties, but you do not walk as a new creature. You hope to follow the gospel in that legal spirit, but I must tell you, it will end in a bed of sorrows.

Do not resist the Light and Spirit within, but listen to its condemnations. Then, every day, you will walk in the Way of Life.[846] Then, you will be alive to God in all your duties and live in that life which is hidden with Christ in God.[847] Being born again, and inwardly renewed, you can offer that pure and spiritual worship that is a sweet delight to the Lord. Then God will bless you with heavenly blessings and daily replenish your souls with unspeakable joys of love and salvation. This I heartily desire, and through all difficulties unceasingly work for, in body, soul, and spirit, so that the All-wise, Good, Omnipotent God may be known, served, and obeyed by you. This will be your comfort and God's eternal honor, who alone is worthy to receive it, now and forever. Amen.

William Penn

---

[845] 1 Cor. 2:10: "But God hath revealed *them* unto us by his Spirit: for the Spirit searcheth all things, yea, the deep things of God."

[846] Prov. 6:23: "For the commandment *is* a lamp; and the law *is* light; and reproofs of instruction *are* the way of life."

[847] Col. 3:2-3: "Set your affection on things above, not on things on the earth. For ye are dead, and your life is hid with Christ in God."

Primitive Christianity

REVIVED

IN THE

Faith and Practice

Of the PEOPLE called

QUAKERS.

Written, in *Testimony* of the present Dispensation of God, *through Them*, to the World: that Prejudices may be removed, the Simple informed, the Well-enclined Encouraged, and the *Truth* and its Innocent *Friends, Rightly* Represented.

By *William Penn*

This People have I formed for my self: They shall shew forth my Praise, Isaiah *43:21*

LONDON,

Printed and Sold by *T. Sowle*, near the *Meeting-house* in *White-Hare-Court* in *Gracious-Street*, and at the *Bible* in *Leaden-Hall-Street* near the *Market, 1696.*

An Epistle to the Reader

R eader,

By this short treatise, you will come to understand that the Light of Christ in Each Person is the manifestation of God's love for us and for our happiness. This is the unique testimony and characteristic of the people called Quakers. It is their most fundamental principle – distinguishing them from all other Christians of this time – and, in their ministry and writing, is basis their faith, worship, and practice. They hold that just as fingers grow naturally out of the hand or branches out of the trunk of a tree, so all aspects of true religion grow out of this Divine Principle.

There are some who are greatly prejudiced against this people. Others admire Quakers for their seriousness and principled lives, but out of misunderstanding or ignorance believe them to be wrong on important points of doctrine. But there are many more, within every other denomination, who earnestly desire to know and delight in God directly, as these people describe it. They long for a state of holiness and acceptance by God, but despair of ever attaining it. Because they have not felt the inward power that God has given them or experienced it working within them, enabling them to attain that state, they doubt its reality.

For these reasons, Reader, I have decided to write a short tract about the nature and power of the Inward Light of Christ, explaining what and where it is, and the purposes it serves. In so doing, I will describe the religion of the people called Quakers so that everyone may know their true character, what true religion is, and how to practice that true religion in this age of hypocrisy and perverted belief. I am writing so that the merciful visitations of the God of Light and Love, which efficiently and directly promote piety (which is true religion), will no longer be ignored in our nations. Rather, all may come to believe with their hearts and confess with their mouths,[848] that this is the dispensation of Love and Life from God to the whole world. Moreover, you will see that this poor people called Quakers – so despised, so often maligned and treated as the scum of the earth – are the people of God and children of the Most High.

---

[848] Rom. 10:9: "That if thou shalt confess with thy mouth the Lord Jesus, and shalt believe in thine heart that God hath raised him from the dead, thou shalt be saved."

Bear with me, Reader, I know what I am saying – I am not arrogant, but truly God-fearing. Though I write with confidence toward you, it is with humility toward God. But don't take my word alone – don't act on trust, but on knowledge. Judge what I write carefully. That is all I ask and all I need to convince you and to vindicate myself. Take this tract as a spiritual inquiry to and for your soul. It requires no faith in outward authority, but is obvious to anyone who honestly examines it.

Reader, when you become familiar with this Divine Principle, and its plain and joyful teachings, like us, you will be amazed that you did not long ago see the truth of something so close to you. In the past, you thought us strange for believing; soon you will wonder why others are so blind to it. The time, I believe, is at hand when all will accept this unquestionable evidence and declare the absolute authority of this principle.

Let me finish this preface with a brief description of my plan. First, I will state the Divine Principle and demonstrate to you (as God has enabled me) its nature and power in religion. In doing so, the common doctrines and principles of Christianity will be presented and explained for your benefit in a straightforward manner. In this, I have tried to use only plain and simple terms – not figurative, allegorical, or ambiguous phrases – so that there is no room for misunderstanding, equivocation, or double meanings. The truth of this matter will be evident and easily understood by everyone. Second, each point will be supported by Scripture, reason, and the effects it has had on the lives of so many people. Their consistent faithfulness, at all times and despite sufferings on its account, may challenge the beliefs of serious readers. Third, I have written briefly so that this book will be inexpensive and quickly read. Putting as much as possible into a few words seemed best – as people grow richer, they seem to have less time and money for God or religion. Perhaps those who would not buy a large book will find it in their hearts to purchase and give away such little and cheap ones for their neighbors' benefit.

Be serious, Reader, be impartial, and then be as inquisitive as you are able – as much for your own soul as for the credibility of this most misunderstood and abused people. And may God the Father of Lights[849]

---

[849] James 1:17: "Every good gift and every perfect gift is from above, and cometh down from the Father of lights, with whom is no variableness, neither shadow of turning."

and Spirits[850] bless you as you read this short treatise, so that you may receive real benefit from it, to God's glory and to your spiritual comfort. This is my only desire or reason for writing it. In the bonds of Christian charity, I am very much, and very ardently,

Thy real Friend,

William Penn

Chapter 1

Friends' Fundamental Principle

For the people called Quakers, the foundation of all religious belief is this: God, through Christ, has placed a guide in each person to show them their duty and provided each with the ability to follow that guide. In every nation, race, and religion, there are those who follow this guide – these are the people of God – and those who live in disobedience to it and are not God's people regardless of what they say. This is the Friends' ancient, first, and unchanging principle. This is the testimony they have made and will continue to make to the whole world.

The Nature of this Principle

Friends understand that this guide is Divine. While it is found within all people, it does not belong to them. It is from God and of God. For those who will let it, it will lead them back to God.

The Names Given this Principle

There are many names for this Divine Principle. By some, it is called the Light of Christ or the Light within.[851] This is the oldest, most common, and familiar phrase. Others call it the Revelation[852] or Appearance of

---

[850] Heb. 12:9: "Furthermore we have had fathers of our flesh which corrected *us*, and we gave *them* reverence: shall we not much rather be in subjection unto the Father of spirits, and live?"

[851] Penn has noted John 1:9 ["*That* was the true Light, which lighteth every man that cometh into the world."] in the margin.

[852] Penn has noted the following in the margin:

Rom. 1:19. ["Because that which may be known of God is manifest in them; for God hath shewed *it* unto them."]

Christated,[853] the Witness of God,[854] the Seed of God[855] or the Seed of the Kingdom.[856] Still others identify it as Wisdom,[857] the Word in the Heart,[858]

Titus 3:4. ["But after that the kindness and love of God our Saviour toward man appeared."]

[853] Penn has noted the following in the margin:

Acts 17:28. ["For in him we live, and move, and have our being; as certain also of your own poets have said, For we are also his offspring."]

2 Pet. 4 [no such chapter, perhaps 1 Pet. 4:13-14 is intended: ["But rejoice, inasmuch as ye are partakers of Christ's sufferings; that, when his glory shall be revealed, ye may be glad also with exceeding joy. If ye be reproached for the name of Christ, happy *are ye*; for the spirit of glory and of God resteth upon you: on their part he is evil spoken of, but on your part he is glorified."]

[854] Penn has noted the following in the margin:

Rom. 8:16. ["The Spirit itself beareth witness with our spirit, that we are the children of God."]

1 John 5:10&12. ["He that believeth on the Son of God hath the witness in himself: he that believeth not God hath made him a liar; because he believeth not the record that God gave of his Son. ... He that hath the Son hath life; *and* he that hath not the Son of God hath not life."]

[855] Penn has noted the following in the margin:

1 Pet. 1:23. ["Being born again, not of corruptible seed, but of incorruptible, by the word of God, which liveth and abideth for ever."]

1 John 3:9. ["Whosoever is born of God doth not commit sin; for his seed remaineth in him: and he cannot sin, because he is born of God."]

[856] Penn has noted Matt. 13:19&23 ["When any one heareth the word of the kingdom, and understandeth *it* not, then cometh the wicked *one*, and catcheth away that which was sown in his heart. This is he which received seed by the way side. ... But he that received seed into the good ground is he that heareth the word, and understandeth *it*; which also beareth fruit, and bringeth forth, some an hundredfold, some sixty, some thirty."] in the margin.

[857] Penn has noted the following in the margin:

Prov. 1:20-23. ["Wisdom crieth without; she uttereth her voice in the streets: She crieth in the chief place of concourse, in the openings of the gates: in the city she uttereth her words, *saying*, How long, ye simple ones, will ye love simplicity? and the scorners delight in their scorning, and fools hate knowledge? Turn you at my reproof: behold, I will pour out my spirit unto you, I will make known my words unto you."]

Prov. 8:1-4. ["Doth not wisdom cry? and understanding put forth her voice? She standeth in the top of high places, by the way in the places of the

the Grace Available to All,[859] the Spirit sent for Each Person's Benefit,[860] the Truth Within,[861] or the Leaven that Transforms the Lump of Humanity.[862] Many of these are figurative expressions, but all have been

---

paths. She crieth at the gates, at the entry of the city, at the coming in at the doors. Unto you, O men, I call; and my voice *is* to the sons of man."]

[858] Penn has noted the following in the margin:

Deut. 30:12[-14]. ["It *is* not in heaven, that thou shouldest say, Who shall go up for us to heaven, and bring it unto us, that we may hear it, and do it? Neither *is* it beyond the sea, that thou shouldest say, Who shall go over the sea for us, and bring it unto us, that we may hear it, and do it? But the word *is* very nigh unto thee, in thy mouth, and in thy heart, that thou mayest do it."]

Rom. 10:6-8. ["But the righteousness which is of faith speaketh on this wise, Say not in thine heart, Who shall ascend into heaven? (that is, to bring Christ down *from above*:) Or, Who shall descend into the deep? (that is, to bring up Christ again from the dead.) But what saith it? The word is nigh thee, *even* in thy mouth, and in thy heart: that is, the word of faith, which we preach."]

Ps. 119:10. ["With my whole heart have I sought thee: O let me not wander from thy commandments."]

[859] Penn has noted Titus 2:11-12 ["For the grace of God that bringeth salvation hath appeared to all men, Teaching us that, denying ungodliness and worldly lusts, we should live soberly, righteously, and godly, in this present world"] in the margin.

[860] Penn has noted 1 Cor. 1 [possibly verses 3-5, "Grace *be* unto you, and peace, from God our Father, and *from* the Lord Jesus Christ. I thank my God always on your behalf, for the grace of God which is given you by Jesus Christ; That in every thing ye are enriched by him, in all utterance, and *in* all knowledge."] in the margin.

Later editions have identified this as 1 Cor. 12:7. ["But the manifestation of the Spirit is given to every man to profit withal."]

[861] Penn has noted the following in the margin:

Ps. 51:6. ["Behold, thou desirest truth in the inward parts: and in the hidden part thou shalt make me to know wisdom."]

Isa. 26:2. ["Open ye the gates, that the righteous nation which keepeth the truth may enter in."]

John 14:6. ["Jesus saith unto him, I am the way, the truth, and the life: no man cometh unto the Father, but by me."]

[862] Penn has noted Matt. 13:33 ["Another parable spake he unto them; The kingdom of heaven is like unto leaven, which a woman took, and hid in three measures of meal, till the whole was leavened."] in the margin.

used by the inspiration of the Holy Spirit. They will be used in this Treatise since they are frequently found in Friends' writings and ministry. But, Reader, do not be misled or confused by the diversity of terms – please remember that when you see any of these terms, it always refers to the one, unchanging Divine Principle that I have mentioned above. As I have said, it is in us, but not of us but of God; and although inspired writers have called it by many names, in relating its various manifestations and actions, it is one.

Faith and Practice, Ministry and Worship

It is to this Principle of Light, Life, and Grace that Friends entrust themselves. They identify it as the single great active force in religion, without which there is no conviction, no conversion, no re-birth,[863] and consequently, no entry into the Kingdom of God. By conviction, I mean a true recognition of one's own sinfulness or sorrow for it. This is necessary to spur people to conversion – that is, giving up a sinful life and overcoming evil. Without conviction and conversion, people can expect no forgiveness of sin and no justification from it – that is, acceptance by God and peace within the soul – no sanctification or becoming virtuous, holy, or good. Without justification and sanctification, there is no salvation.

Indeed, the reason there is so little true religion among those who call themselves Christians – so much superstition instead of devotion, so little enjoyment in practicing their faith, and so little real change in their hearts – is that people overlook and neglect this principle in their religious lives. They claim to be faithful without it, and to be Christians without it, but without it, they are neither.

In this degenerate state, it is natural for people to prefer ritual over obedience, to believe that rote words are prayer, and to hope that outward ceremonies will reconcile them with God. In that corrupt state, it is only natural that people will excuse themselves from the requirements of this principle: taking up their cross, giving up their bodily comforts, and doing whatever God requires of them. This is true religion – to be holy, humble, patient, meek, merciful, just, kind, and charitable. Everyone who acts these ways is truly religious, but they cannot achieve this by their own efforts, only by embracing what the Light reveals and teaches them. This Divine

---

[863] Penn has noted John 3:5 ["Jesus answered, Verily, verily, I say unto thee, Except a man be born of water and *of* the Spirit, he cannot enter into the kingdom of God."] in the margin.

Principle is the root of all true religion, and the good seed from which all good fruit grows.

To sum up what Friends have said about the nature and qualities of the Light, this Principle is Divine, Universal, and Effective in granting humanity:

1. Knowledge of God and of themselves, and consequently an understanding of themselves, their duty to God, and of their disobedience to it.

2. A true sense of and sorrow for sin in those who seriously consider what it shows them.

3. The ability to give up sin, and be sanctified from it.

4. Through God's mercy in Christ, forgiveness of past sins and justification for all who offer sincerely repentance and obedience.

5. The ability for the faithful to persevere, leading them to perfection, and the assurance of everlasting blessedness.

Friends offer three things in evidence of the truth of this claim:

1. The ample witness of the Scriptures, especially the New Testament.

2. The self-evident reasonableness of it.

3. The spiritual experience of all people and, in particular, their own. The truth of this experience has been demonstrated in the fruits of their ministry and the results God has granted in answer to that ministry.

These are acknowledged by all impartial observers. In the rest of this work, I will take the occasion to briefly outline their history to illustrate these points.

Chapter 2

Evidence in Scripture

I will begin with the evidence in the blessed Scriptures of Truth for this Divine Principle. The foremost and most common name used in them to express and name this Principle is 'Light' – a most apt and proper word given the current dark state of the world.

> In the beginning was the Word, and the Word was with God, and the Word was God. ...Through him, all things were and without him nothing was made that has been made. In him was Life; and that Life was the Light of all. ... the true Light, which lights everyone that comes into the world.[864]

The Divinity of the Light

I have begun with the apostle John, the most beloved Disciple of Jesus and the last of the apostles to die. Because of his pre-eminent knowledge and wisdom of heavenly things, he is properly called John the Divine.

His gospel starts with the beginning of creation by God. He tells us that in the beginning, he was the Word and, although that should make it apparent who that Word would be, he goes on to explain that the Word was with God and was God.[865] This should remove any doubt about the divinity of the Word or any underestimation of its importance. The Word is Divine and the evangelist chose that term because it so clearly expresses the wisdom and power of God.

All Things Created by it

"All things were made by him." If that is so, then there is no lack of power. And if we were made by the Word, we must be re-made by that same Word or we will never come into joyful union with God. The power of the Word shows its dignity and demonstrates that nothing is impossible

---

[864] John 1:1, 3-4, 9: "In the beginning was the Word, and the Word was with God, and the Word was God. ...All things were made by him; and without him was not any thing made that was made. In him was life; and the life was the light of men. ...*That* was the true Light, which lighteth every man that cometh into the world."

[865] John 1:1: "In the beginning was the Word, and the Word was with God, and the Word was God."

for the one who made all things, and without which nothing was made.[866]
Just as our Maker is our spouse,[867] so our Creator is our redeemer.[868]

What the Light has to do with Salvation

"In him was Life, and that Life was the Light of all." This is precisely our point. John starts with the nature of existence of the Word and continues on to the works of the Word. Then, he tells us how the Word is connected to humanity beyond the rest of creation – the Word was Life, and the Life was the Light of all.[869] This relationship must be very close and intimate, if the Life of the Word (which was with God, and was God) is the Light of all humanity. This is said of no other creature – as if humanity were next to the Word and above the rest of creation.

Accordingly, humanity does not lack Light – a Divine Light (if the Life of the Divine Word is not divine or supernatural, then nothing can be). And, this text proves not only the Divinity of the Light, but also its Universality – applying to all humanity. This is most directly stated in the ninth verse, "the true Light, which lights everyone that comes into the world." This implies that anything that fails to enlighten all of humanity is not that true Light. Therefore, John was not that Light, but only testified to the one who was[870] – the one who enlightens everyone[871] and the Word that became flesh.[872] In this way, the divine nature and the universality of the Inward Light of Christ are proved together.

---

866 John 1:3: "All things were made by him; and without him was not any thing made that was made."

867 Isa. 54:5: "For thy Maker *is* thine husband; the LORD of hosts *is* his name; and thy Redeemer the Holy One of Israel; The God of the whole earth shall he be called."

868 Isa. 44:24: "Thus saith the LORD, thy redeemer, and he that formed thee from the womb, I *am* the LORD that maketh all *things*; that stretcheth forth the heavens alone; that spreadeth abroad the earth by myself."

869 John 1:4: "In him was life; and the life was the light of men."

870 John 1:8: "He was not that Light, but *was sent* to bear witness of that Light."

871 John 1:9: "*That* was the true Light, which lighteth every man that cometh into the world."

872 John 1:14: "And the Word was made flesh, and dwelt among us, (and we beheld his glory, the glory as of the only begotten of the Father,) full of grace and truth."

Chapter 3

How this Scripture is Distorted

No passage or proposition to be found in the Scriptures is of greater interest to humanity or more clearly set down by the Holy Spirit than the one I have reported. But, there is also none that has been more ingeniously distorted from its true and plain meaning – especially since Quakers began to stress it in defense of their testimony of the Light within. Some claim that John was writing about a natural light, or of some part of our own human nature. But, it was the true Life of the Word by which the world was made, and these verses are embedded in a section concerned with God's eternal power and the Word's place within the Godhead. So that I can be clearly understood, I will state each objection as clearly as I can, and then give an answer to it.

The Claim that it is a Natural Light

If by 'natural' they mean a created thing, as a person or anything that makes up a person is, then I reject their contention. The text expressly refutes it, saying that the Light with which all humanity is lighted is the Life of the World, which was with God and was God.

On the other hand, they may mean simply that the Light comes along with us into the world, or that we have it as sure as we are born. That is to say that it is the light of our nature – of our minds and understandings – not the result of any revelation from outside ourselves by other people or by angels. Then we mean the same thing since it is *natural* for each person to have a *supernatural* Light and for creation to be lighted by an *uncreated* Light – this is the Life of the *Creating Word.*

If people would simply acknowledge their own nature, it would do much to dispel any confusion about this. A person can no more be a Light to his or her own mind than to his or her own body. People can see things with the help of light, but are not themselves the light that makes those objects visible. Just as the sun in the sky is the light of the body, allowing us to see in our everyday lives, the Life of the Word is the glorious Light and sun of the soul. It illuminates our intellects, enlightening our minds and granting us true judgment and discernment about of those things that most immediately concern our better, inward, and eternal selves.

The Claim that not All are Enlightened

Others assert that the text says that all "who are enlightened" are enlightened by the Word. This not only distorts the text by narrowing its meaning, but portrays God as unfair and unjust, leaving the greatest part of the world in darkness, without any means or opportunity to find salvation. But the Scriptures assure us that all have the Light;[873] that Christ is the Light of the World;[874] and that he died for all[875] – even for the ungodly;[876] that God does not desire the death of any, but rather that all should repent, come to know the Truth, and be saved;[877] and that the Grace of God has appeared to all, etc.[878]

The Claim that it is the Doctrine and the Example of Christ's Life that Enlighten

There is still a third group, who claim that humanity in not enlightened and saved by the Light of Christ, but by the doctrine that Christ preached, the life he led in the world, and the example he set for us. Yet, not even one-thousandth of humanity has heard these doctrines or knows about his life. Moreover, this claim directly contradicts John's clear message at the beginning of his gospel. This consists entirely of the story of Christ before he became flesh, or at least, of what Christ is to the soul by his direct enlightenment and influence.

---

[873] Penn has noted John 1:4, 9 ["In him was life; and the life was the light of men. ...*That* was the true Light, which lighteth every man that cometh into the world."] in the margin.

[874] Penn has noted John 8:12 ["Then spake Jesus again unto them, saying, I am the light of the world: he that followeth me shall not walk in darkness, but shall have the light of life."] in the margin.

[875] Penn has noted 2 Cor. 5:15 ["And *that* he died for all, that they which live should not henceforth live unto themselves, but unto him which died for them, and rose again."] in the margin.

[876] Penn has noted Rom. 5:6 ["For when we were yet without strength, in due time Christ died for the ungodly."] in the margin.

[877] Penn has noted 1 Tim. 2:4 ["Who will have all men to be saved, and to come unto the knowledge of the truth."] in the margin.

[878] Penn has noted Titus 2:11-12 ["For the grace of God that bringeth salvation hath appeared to all men, Teaching us that, denying ungodliness and worldly lusts, we should live soberly, righteously, and godly, in this present world"] in the margin.

It is true that Christ was a Light to the World – 'shining forth' in his heavenly doctrine, his many miracles, and his self-denying life and death – but this does not diminish the fact that he was, and is, that Spiritual Light, which shines in one degree or another in the hearts of all of mankind's sons and daughters. Remember Christ told his disciples, "You are the lights of the world."[879] In the same (although more powerful) way, his life and teachings are a Light to the world. But Christ the Word enlightened those disciples, enlightens us, and enlightens everyone who comes into the world.[880] It is not his personal and outward life at a time long since past that continually illuminates those who come into the world. In the flesh, he is remote from us; but in Truth, he is present and immediate. Otherwise, the scriptural text would be, "That was the true Light that used to enlighten all," rather than "the Light that enlightens all." Indeed, the evangelist uses this as evidence that Christ, not John the Baptist for whom many had great reverence, is the Messiah. In verse 8, he writes of John, "He himself was not the Light, but he came as a witness to the Light." Going on, the next verse provides the proof (and our testimony), "That was the true Light, which lights everyone who comes into the world." Not John nor any other person, but the Word that was with God, and was God.[881]

John does not describe Christ as a man who fasted for forty days, preached so many sermons, worked so many miracles, lived a holy life, and after all that, patiently suffered death (as Christ did), in order to prove that he was the Light of the World. No. John begins by writing that was the true Light, the Word made flesh,[882] the Messiah, and that neither John the Baptist, nor any other person lighted everyone who comes into the world. Right from the start, Christ alone is distinguished and revealed by giving Light. What is more, his followers are distinguished from all other people by receiving and obeying that Light.

---

[879] Matt. 5:14: "Ye are the light of the world. A city that is set on an hill cannot be hid."

[880] John 1:9: "*That* was the true Light, which lighteth every man that cometh into the world."

[881] John 1:1: "In the beginning was the Word, and the Word was with God, and the Word was God."

[882] John 1:14: "And the Word was made flesh, and dwelt among us, (and we beheld his glory, the glory as of the only begotten of the Father,) full of grace and truth."

There are many other relevant passages in both testaments that refer implicitly and explicitly to the Light within. For brevity, I will not recite them all, but the reader will find directions to some of them in the margin.[883]

---

[883] Penn has noted the following in the margin:

Job 18:5-6. ["Yea, the light of the wicked shall be put out, and the spark of his fire shall not shine. The light shall be dark in his tabernacle, and his candle shall be put out with him."]

Job 21:17. ["How oft is the candle of the wicked put out! and *how oft* cometh their destruction upon them! *God* distributeth sorrows in his anger."]

Job 25:3. ["Is there any number of his armies? and upon whom doth not his light arise?"]

Job 38:5. ["Who hath laid the measures thereof, if thou knowest? or who hath stretched the line upon it?"] Penn probably intended Job 38:15, "And from the wicked their light is withholden, and the high arm shall be broken."

Ps. 18:28. ["For thou wilt light my candle: the LORD my God will enlighten my darkness."]

Ps. 27:1. ["The LORD *is* my light and my salvation; whom shall I fear? the LORD *is* the strength of my life; of whom shall I be afraid?"]

Ps. 34:5. ["They looked unto him, and were lightened: and their faces were not ashamed."]

Ps. 36:9. ["For with thee *is* the fountain of life: in thy light shall we see light."]

Ps. 118:27. ["God *is* the LORD, which hath shewed us light: bind the sacrifice with cords, *even* unto the horns of the altar."]

Ps. 119:105. ["Thy word *is* a lamp unto my feet, and a light unto my path."]

Prov. 13:9. ["The light of the righteous rejoiceth: but the lamp of the wicked shall be put out."]

Prov. 20:20&27. ["Whoso curseth his father or his mother, his lamp shall be put out in obscure darkness. ... The spirit of man *is* the candle of the LORD, searching all the inward parts of the belly."]

Prov. 24:20. ["For there shall be no reward to the evil *man*; the candle of the wicked shall be put out."]

Isa. 2:5. ["O house of Jacob, come ye, and let us walk in the light of the LORD."]

Isa. 8:20. ["To the law and to the testimony: if they speak not according to this word, *it is* because *there is* no light in them."]

Chapter 4

The Power of the Light Within to Give Discernment

Consider the power and effectiveness of the Light to achieve the purpose for which God has given it – that is, to lead and guide human souls to Blessedness. The first thing it does, in accomplishing this, is to give a person true insight into, or discernment of, themselves – the ability to know who they truly are and what they do – so that they may see and know their own spiritual condition. By this, they know what judgment to make of themselves with respect to religion and a future state. As the unerring Word says, and John reports, everyone who does evil hates the Light and avoids the Light, so that their wicked deeds will not be exposed. But those who live by the Truth come to the Light so that all might see that everything they do has been done in God.[884] A most compelling expression of the power and authority of the Light!

First, the Light is identified as that by which we must examine ourselves. Second, it allows us to accurately discern the differences between good and evil – what is of God and what is not of God. Third, it is a judge who acquits or condemns – rejecting those who reject it and comforting the souls of those who obey it. Only something that is itself divine can reveal to us what comes of God and what does not or permit us to see what within ourselves has been fashioned by the hand of God and what has not. This

---

Isa. 42:6. ["I the LORD have called thee in righteousness, and will hold thine hand, and will keep thee, and give thee for a covenant of the people, for a light of the Gentiles."]

Isa. 49:6. ["And he said, It is a light thing that thou shouldest be my servant to raise up the tribes of Jacob, and to restore the preserved of Israel: I will also give thee for a light to the Gentiles, that thou mayest be my salvation unto the end of the earth."]

1 Pet. 2:9. ["But ye *are* a chosen generation, a royal priesthood, an holy nation, a peculiar people; that ye should shew forth the praises of him who hath called you out of darkness into his marvellous light."]

1 John 2:8. ["Again, a new commandment I write unto you, which thing is true in him and in you: because the darkness is past, and the true light now shineth."]

[884] John 3:20-21: "For every one that doeth evil hateth the light, neither cometh to the light, lest his deeds should be reproved. But he that doeth truth cometh to the light, that his deeds may be made manifest, that they are wrought in God."

passage is not only concerned with revealing a person's inner state, but, what is much more, with an understanding of God and the works of God. It tells us that each person who is obedient can also come to know, to some degree, which acts are the performed by the power of God and according to the will of God and which are the products of their own wills.

If the Light did not reveal God, it could not tell us what God's will is for us, nor give us a well-grounded sense and discernment of the origin, nature, and tendencies of our own minds and of our innermost being. Certainly, this is both explicitly expressed and abundantly implied by our Savior in this passage. And if the Light reveals God, we can be sure that it makes Christ, who flows from and comes from God, known to us. Who then would oppose or rebuff this blessed Light?

The Light Reveals God

That this Light reveals God is evident in Romans 1:19, "For what can be known about God is plain to them, because God has shown it to them." This is a universal proposition and we have the Apostle's word for it – the word of a man who was one in a thousand and inspired by the Holy Spirit to tell us Truth. Let us grant it is due importance. If what can be known about God "is plain to them," then the people called Quakers certainly cannot be going astray when they extol the Light within. Without that Light, nothing can be made known to our minds.

Remember that the same Apostle wrote to the Ephesians, "Everything that is condemned is revealed by the Light – whatever reveals is Light."[885] Since the Light within reveals in us and to us everything that may be known of God, it is rightly called a revelation or appearance of God. Similarly, the Prophet Micah tells us, "God has shown you, O mortal, what is good; and what does the Lord require of you but to do justice, and to love mercy, and to walk humbly with your God?"[886] I repeat: "God has shown you, O mortal!" This is very emphatic. And how has God shown us? By God's Light in our consciences, "against which the wicked rebel" – those who,

---

[885] Ephesians 5:13: "But all things that are reproved are made manifest by the light: for whatsoever doth make manifest is light."

[886] Mic. 6:8: "He hath shewed thee, O man, what is good; and what doth the LORD require of thee, but to do justly, and to love mercy, and to walk humbly with thy God?"

"for what ever cause, do not know its ways, and do not stay in its paths."[887] But, to those who do obey, "its ways are ways of pleasantness, and all its paths are peace."[888]

The Light Gives Life to the Soul

The Light gives the Light of Life – in other words, it grants eternal life to those who receive it and obey it. For this, we have the word of the blessed Savior of the World, "I am the Light of the World. Whoever follows me will never walk in darkness but will have the Light of Life."[889] Christ is the Light of the World, because he enlightens everyone who comes into the world[890] and those who obey that Light obey him and therefore have the Light of Life. That is to say, the Light becomes eternal life to the soul. Just as it is the Life of the Word, which is the Light in humanity, so God's heavenly Light becomes Eternal Life in humanity, through our obedience to it.

The Light is the Apostolic Message

Furthermore, this Light was the foundation of the Apostolic Message. As the Beloved Apostle assures us, "This is the message we have heard from him and proclaim to you: God is Light and in him there is no darkness at all. If we say that we have fellowship with him while we are walking in darkness, we lie and are not doing the Truth; but if we walk in the Light as he himself is in the Light, we have fellowship with one another, and the blood of Jesus his Son cleanses us from all sin."[891] This passage so amply demonstrates the surpassing value and power of the Light, as it applies to humanity, that there is little need to say any more. It says, first, that the Light reveals God and that God is Light. Second, it distinguishes

---

[887] Job 24:13: "They are of those that rebel against the light; they know not the ways thereof, nor abide in the paths thereof."

[888] Prov. 3:17: "Her ways *are* ways of pleasantness, and all her paths *are* peace."

[889] John 8:12: "Then spake Jesus again unto them, saying, I am the light of the world: he that followeth me shall not walk in darkness, but shall have the light of life."

[890] John 1:9: "*That* was the true Light, which lighteth every man that cometh into the world."

[891] 1 John 1:5-7: "And the light shineth in darkness; and the darkness comprehended it not. There was a man sent from God, whose name *was* John. The same came for a witness, to bear witness of the Light, that all *men* through him might believe."

darkness from Light and the fact that the two have nothing in common.[892] Third, it tells us that we should walk in the Light. Fourth, that it is the way to obtain forgiveness for sin and sanctification from sin. Fifth, that it is the instrument of peace and fellowship with God and with God's people – the true church, which is saved from all the pollutions of the world.

An Objection About Two Lights Answered

Perhaps some will object, as has happened more than once before, that this is another light, not the Light with which all are enlightened. But, the same Apostle, in his evangelical history, tells us that in the Word was Life, and the Life was the Light of all people – the Light being the Life of the Word – and that Light was the true Light, which enlightens all who come into the world. Could there be a plainer text to support the sufficiency and universality of the Light within? Is there a plainer statement of any article of faith in the whole of the Book of God? If the Beloved Disciple had intended to indicate that there were two Lights, in either his gospel or epistles, we can be sure that he would have made the distinction – but we find none and, from the properties attributed to the Light in each of his writings, we have good reason to conclude that he intended only one.

Natural and Spiritual Light – There are not Two Darknesses nor Two Lights

Still, there may be those who object that John writes of a spiritual Light, but ours is only a natural one. I ask them just two things: First, prove that a natural light, as they put it, can reveal God. Whatever is part of our own being and nature, especially in our fallen state, is so far from God, that it cannot rightly reveal or reject those things that offend God. But the Light we have written about, which we call divine, and others mistakenly call natural, can do both.

Second, if this Light is natural, it still seems to show us our duty and to rebuke us for disobedience to God. That being the case, those who object need to identify the means by which we can correctly discern and distinguish between the revelations and reproofs of a natural light within and those of the Divine Light within – since they propose that both are capable of discovering God and condemning evil. Let them show us one

---

[892] 2 Cor. 6:14: "Be ye not unequally yoked together with unbelievers: for what fellowship hath righteousness with unrighteousness? and what communion hath light with darkness?"

passage in Scripture that distinguishes between a natural and a spiritual Light within. They might as well talk about a natural and a spiritual darkness within. There is, of course, a natural and proper darkness – the night of the outward world – and a spiritual darkness – the clouded and benighted human conceptions that result from disobedience to the Light and Spirit of God. But, there is no third form of darkness. People improperly used to say the blind were dark, and some have also used that term to describe the mentally retarded, but is there another kind of darkness in understanding the things of God?

Neither Christ nor his disciples ever distinguished between one kind of darkness and another nor, in any sense, between two kinds of Light. Yet, all spoke of Light and darkness. The Scriptures often address darkness,[893] but

---

[893] Penn has listed the following texts in the margin:

Luke 1:79. ["To give light to them that sit in darkness and *in* the shadow of death, to guide our feet into the way of peace."]

Matt. 4:16. ["The people which sat in darkness saw great light; and to them which sat in the region and shadow of death light is sprung up."]

John 1:5. ["And the light shineth in darkness; and the darkness comprehended it not."]

John 3:19. ["And this is the condemnation, that light is come into the world, and men loved darkness rather than light, because their deeds were evil."]

John 8:12, 31, 46. ["Then spake Jesus again unto them, saying, I am the light of the world: he that followeth me shall not walk in darkness, but shall have the light of life. ... Then said Jesus to those Jews which believed on him, If ye continue in my word, *then* are ye my disciples indeed ... Which of you convinceth me of sin? And if I say the truth, why do ye not believe me?"]

1 Thess. 5:4. ["But ye, brethren, are not in darkness, that that day should overtake you as a thief."]

1 John 1:6. ["If we say that we have fellowship with him, and walk in darkness, we lie, and do not the truth."]

Acts 26:18. ["To open their eyes, *and* to turn *them* from darkness to light, and *from* the power of Satan unto God, that they may receive forgiveness of sins, and inheritance among them which are sanctified by faith that is in me."]

Rom. 13:12. ["The night is far spent, the day is at hand: let us therefore cast off the works of darkness, and let us put on the armour of light."]

on the closest examination of these verses, there is no distinction made between different kinds. There is only one spiritual darkness. Nor is there a single verse that distinguishes different forms of the Light within, or that there are really two Lights from God with respect to religion.[894]

---

2 Cor. 6:14. ["Be ye not unequally yoked together with unbelievers: for what fellowship hath righteousness with unrighteousness? and what communion hath light with darkness?"]

2 Cor. 6:22 (no such text)

Ephesians 5:8. ["For ye were sometimes darkness, but now *are ye* light in the Lord: walk as children of light."]

Col. 1:13. ["Who hath delivered us from the power of darkness, and hath translated *us* into the kingdom of his dear Son."]

[894] Penn has listed the following texts:

Matt. 4:16. ["The people which sat in darkness saw great light; and to them which sat in the region and shadow of death light is sprung up."]

Luke 2:32. ["A light to lighten the Gentiles, and the glory of thy people Israel."]

Luke 15:8. ["Either what woman having ten pieces of silver, if she lose one piece, doth not light a candle, and sweep the house, and seek diligently till she find *it*?"]

John 1:4-9. ["In him was life; and the life was the light of men. And the light shineth in darkness; and the darkness comprehended it not. There was a man sent from God, whose name *was* John. The same came for a witness, to bear witness of the Light, that all *men* through him might believe. He was not that Light, but *was sent* to bear witness of that Light. *That* was the true Light, which lighteth every man that cometh into the world."]

John 3:19-21. ["And this is the condemnation, that light is come into the world, and men loved darkness rather than light, because their deeds were evil. For every one that doeth evil hateth the light, neither cometh to the light, lest his deeds should be reproved. But he that doeth truth cometh to the light, that his deeds may be made manifest, that they are wrought in God."]

John 8:12. ["Then spake Jesus again unto them, saying, I am the light of the world: he that followeth me shall not walk in darkness, but shall have the light of life."]

Acts 26:18. ["To open their eyes, *and* to turn *them* from darkness to light, and *from* the power of Satan unto God, that they may receive forgiveness of sins, and inheritance among them which are sanctified by faith that is in me."]

Rom. 13:12. ["The night is far spent, the day is at hand: let us therefore cast off the works of darkness, and let us put on the armour of light."]

And we believe that the most skilled of our opponents will not be able to sever Light from Light, or to find two Lights within, in the passages I have listed, or in any other passage that directs us in our duties to God or to our neighbors. If so, then we ask them to give up their unworthy thoughts and words about the Light of Christ within all and acknowledge that the Light reveals evil and condemns it. As Christ himself teaches, "All who do

---

2 Cor. 4:6. ["For God, who commanded the light to shine out of darkness, hath shined in our hearts, to *give* the light of the knowledge of the glory of God in the face of Jesus Christ."]

2 Cor. 6:14. ["Be ye not unequally yoked together with unbelievers: for what fellowship hath righteousness with unrighteousness? and what communion hath light with darkness?"]

Ephesians 5:8&13. ["For ye were sometimes darkness, but now *are ye* light in the Lord: walk as children of light ... But all things that are reproved are made manifest by the light: for whatsoever doth make manifest is light."]

Col. 1:12. ["Giving thanks unto the Father, which hath made us meet to be partakers of the inheritance of the saints in light."]

1 Thess. 5:5. ["Ye are all the children of light, and the children of the day: we are not of the night, nor of darkness."]

1 Tim. 6:16. ["Who only hath immortality, dwelling in the light which no man can approach unto; whom no man hath seen, nor can see: to whom *be* honour and power everlasting. Amen."]

1 Pet. 2:9. ["But ye *are* a chosen generation, a royal priesthood, an holy nation, a peculiar people; that ye should shew forth the praises of him who hath called you out of darkness into his marvellous light."]

1 John 1:5&7. ["This then is the message which we have heard of him, and declare unto you, that God is light, and in him is no darkness at all. ... But if we walk in the light, as he is in the light, we have fellowship one with another, and the blood of Jesus Christ his Son cleanseth us from all sin."]

1 John 2:8. ["Again, a new commandment I write unto you, which thing is true in him and in you: because the darkness is past, and the true light now shineth."]

Rev. 21:23-24. ["And the city had no need of the sun, neither of the moon, to shine in it: for the glory of God did lighten it, and the Lamb *is* the light thereof. And the nations of them which are saved shall walk in the light of it: and the kings of the earth do bring their glory and honour into it."]

Rev. 22:5. ["And there shall be no night there; and they need no candle, neither light of the sun; for the Lord God giveth them light: and they shall reign for ever and ever."]

evil hate the Light and do not come to the Light, so that their deeds may not be exposed."[895] And, as the Apostle Paul wrote, "all things that are condemned are exposed by the Light."[896] There are not two distinct Lights within, but one, exposing, condemning, and teaching Light within. And the Apostle John, in his first epistle, makes this plain, beyond all question, to any reasonable person: First, he declares God Light, saying there is no darkness within God.[897] Second, there is no middle way between Light and darkness[898] – we must walk either in Light or in darkness, there is no other alternative. Everyone must agree that whatever reveals and condemns darkness cannot be darkness itself.

The Objection is Fully Answered by the Apostle John

It is as if John had anticipated their next objection, i.e., that while the Light within reveals evil, it is not necessarily the divine Light, which leads us to higher things and which comes by the gospel. The Apostle wrote, "The darkness is passing away and the true Light is already shining. Anyone who says, 'I am in the Light,' while hating a brother or sister, is still in the darkness."[899] The Light is here shown in opposition to darkness and the darkness to Light. This is the same Light John mentioned in the previous chapter.[900] The darkness is the same; the Light is also the same. Plainly, there is one Light that rebukes a person for hating a brother or sister and that brings us into fellowship with God and to the cleansing blood – this is Light of a divine and effective nature. In short, the Light which is opposite

---

[895] John 3:20: "For every one that doeth evil hateth the light, neither cometh to the light, lest his deeds should be reproved."

[896] Ephesians 5:13: "But all things that are reproved are made manifest by the light: for whatsoever doth make manifest is light."

[897] 1 John 1:5: "This then is the message which we have heard of him, and declare unto you, that God is light, and in him is no darkness at all."

[898] 1 John 1:6: "If we say that we have fellowship with him, and walk in darkness, we lie, and do not the truth."

[899] 1 John 2:8-9: "Again, a new commandment I write unto you, which thing is true in him and in you: because the darkness is past, and the true light now shineth. He that saith he is in the light, and hateth his brother, is in darkness even until now."

[900] 1 John 1:7: "But if we walk in the light, as he is in the light, we have fellowship one with another, and the blood of Jesus Christ his Son cleanseth us from all sin."

to, and condemns spiritual darkness in a man or a woman, is a spiritual Light. This is what the Quakers believe, testify, and maintain.

It is also worth noticing that the Apostle uses the same expression here, "The true Light is shining," as he does in the first chapter of his gospel, "That was the true Light."[901] This indicates that the same divine Word or true Light now shines. The Light that calls to account those who hate a brother or sister is the same true Light that enlightens all. Is it not remarkable that Christ and his disciples – most especially his beloved one – would so often equate the Light that reveals to us our least indiscretion and condemns our grossest evil with the divine life itself? That Light, revealed more and more, calls us to follow it to the Light of Life, to the cleansing blood, and to fellowship with God and with one another. Beyond that, the apostle declares that to be a child of God we must answer this Light in an obvious and ordinary way: by not hating our brothers or sisters. How could anyone shut their eyes so tightly that they cannot see the power that such a Light must have? How could anyone describe this Light as natural or insufficient for salvation? To do so is unreasonable and unscriptural.

Is it dismissed as unimportant because it is so familiar, so ordinary, and so abundantly available to us? Do we underestimate its immeasurable mercy simply because of that abundance? What could be more common than light, air, and water? Should we distain them or prize them? No doubt, we prize them, knowing that we cannot live without them. The more widely mercy is offered, the greater it is, and consequently, the greater our obligation to be grateful and to live humbly in return. To those who do so, its divine secrets are revealed.

---

[901] John 1:9: "*That* was the true Light, which lighteth every man that cometh into the world."

Chapter 5

The Light is the Same as the Spirit of God

Some may object that everything we have attributed to the Light is properly the work of the Spirit and Grace of God. These, they say, are the unique blessings of the new and second covenant and are the fruits of the coming of Christ. Unless, they say, the Light has the same nature as the Spirit and Grace of God, they cannot bring themselves to believe what we have said.

At first glance, this objection seems to carry some weight, but on careful reflection, it will be seen to have more appearance than substance. Even so, because it provides the opportunity to remove some stumbling blocks that may be thrown in the way of the unsophisticated, I will answer it thoroughly. If it can be shown that the properties of the Light within are the same as those of the Holy Spirit and Grace of God, then it will be obvious that we are only using different names to describe the various manifestations or operations of one and the same ultimate Divine Principle. Following the objectors' logic, this will prove our claim that the Light is Divine and is sufficient to lead people to salvation.

Let us examine the claim that the Light within is of the same nature as the Spirit and Grace of God and produces the same result, that is, to bring people to God. First, the Light originates in the One Word and the One Life of that Word, which was with God and was God.[902] Second, it is universal – enlightening all.[903] Third, it gives knowledge of and communion with God.[904] Fourth, it reveals and condemns evil.[905] Fifth, it is named as

---

[902] John 1:1&4: "In the beginning was the Word, and the Word was with God, and the Word was God. ... In him was life; and the life was the light of men."

[903] John 1:9: "*That* was the true Light, which lighteth every man that cometh into the world."

[904] Penn has noted the following in the margin:

Rom. 1:1. ["Because that which may be known of God is manifest in them; for God hath shewed *it* unto them."]

John 3:21. ["But he that doeth truth cometh to the light, that his deeds may be made manifest, that they are wrought in God."]

1 John 1:5-6. ["This then is the message which we have heard of him, and declare unto you, that God is light, and in him is no darkness at all. If we say

the rule and guide for Christian behavior.[906] Sixth, it is the path for God's people to follow and the nations of those who are saved will walk in the Light of the Lamb.[907] Lastly, it is the armor of the Children of God against Satan.[908]

---

that we have fellowship with him, and walk in darkness, we lie, and do not the truth."]

[905] Penn has noted the following in the margin:

John 3:20. ["For every one that doeth evil hateth the light, neither cometh to the light, lest his deeds should be reproved."]

Ephesians 5:13. ["But all things that are reproved are made manifest by the light: for whatsoever doth make manifest is light."]

[906] Penn has noted the following in the margin:

Ps. 43:3. ["O send out thy light and thy truth: let them lead me; let them bring me unto thy holy hill, and to thy tabernacles."]

John 8:12. ["Then spake Jesus again unto them, saying, I am the light of the world: he that followeth me shall not walk in darkness, but shall have the light of life."]

Ephesians 5:13&15. ["But all things that are reproved are made manifest by the light: for whatsoever doth make manifest is light. ... See then that ye walk circumspectly, not as fools, but as wise."]

[907] Penn has noted the following in the margin:

Ps. 119:105. ["Thy word *is* a lamp unto my feet, and a light unto my path."]

Prov. 4:18. ["But the path of the just *is* as the shining light, that shineth more and more unto the perfect day."]

Isa. 2:5. ["O house of Jacob, come ye, and let us walk in the light of the LORD."]

1 John 1:7. ["But if we walk in the light, as he is in the light, we have fellowship one with another, and the blood of Jesus Christ his Son cleanseth us from all sin."]

Rev. 21:23-24. ["And the city had no need of the sun, neither of the moon, to shine in it: for the glory of God did lighten it, and the Lamb *is* the light thereof. And the nations of them which are saved shall walk in the light of it: and the kings of the earth do bring their glory and honour into it."]

[908] Penn has noted the following in the margin:

Ps. 27:1. ["The LORD *is* my light and my salvation; whom shall I fear? the LORD *is* the strength of my life; of whom shall I be afraid?"]

The Properties of the Light and the Spirit Compared

If all this is compared with the properties of the Holy Spirit, the agreement will be immediately obvious. First, it originates in God, because it is the Spirit of God.[909] Second, it is universal. It struggled to help us in the old world of the Law[910] and again in the new world of grace in which everyone has received a measure of it.[911] Third, it reveals God.[912] Fourth, it condemns sin.[913] Fifth, it is a rule and guide for the Children of God to follow.[914] Sixth, it is also the path they are to walk in.[915] "Walk in the Spirit."

Rom. 13:12. ["The night is far spent, the day is at hand: let us therefore cast off the works of darkness, and let us put on the armour of light."]

[909] Penn has noted Rom. 6:11 ["Likewise reckon ye also yourselves to be dead indeed unto sin, but alive unto God through Jesus Christ our Lord"] which seems to have nothing to do with the point just made, whereas John 15:26 ["But when the Comforter is come, whom I will send unto you from the Father, *even* the Spirit of truth, which proceedeth from the Father, he shall testify of me"] is more to the point.

[910] Penn has noted Gen. 6:3 ["And the LORD said, My spirit shall not always strive with man, for that he also *is* flesh: yet his days shall be an hundred and twenty years"].

[911] Penn has noted 1 Cor. 12:7 ["But the manifestation of the Spirit is given to every man to profit withal"].

[912] Penn has noted the following in the margin:

Job 32:8. ["But *there is* a spirit in man: and the inspiration of the Almighty giveth them understanding."]

1 Cor. 2:10-11. ["But God hath revealed *them* unto us by his Spirit: for the Spirit searcheth all things, yea, the deep things of God. For what man knoweth the things of a man, save the spirit of man which is in him? even so the things of God knoweth no man, but the Spirit of God."]

[913] Penn has noted John 16:8 ["And when he is come, he will reprove the world of sin, and of righteousness, and of judgment"].

[914] Penn has noted Rom. 8:14 ["For as many as are led by the Spirit of God, they are the sons of God"].

[915] Penn has noted the following in the margin:

Rom. 8:1. ["*There is* therefore now no condemnation to them which are in Christ Jesus, who walk not after the flesh, but after the Spirit."]

Gal. 5:16. ["This I say then, Walk in the Spirit, and ye shall not fulfil the lust of the flesh."]

And this is not all – it is lastly the spiritual weapon of a true Christian.[916] "Take the sword of the Spirit, which is the Word of God." After this, I hope that no one will deny that this Light and this Spirit must be of one and the same nature, that they produce one and the same effect, and that they clearly point to one and the same holy end.

Demonstration that the Light and the Spirit Flow from the Same Source

What is said of the Light and the Spirit may equally be said of the Light and Grace of God. First, Grace, like the Light, flows from Christ, the Word that became flesh. Just as in him was Life and that Life was the Light of humanity, he was also full of Grace and Truth, and from that fullness we have all received one blessing after another.[917] Second, it is Universal – as can be seen both in this text and in the epistle to Titus, where Paul taught that the Grace of God that brings salvation has appeared to all.[918] Third, it reveals evil. If it teaches us to turn away from ungodliness and worldly desires, it must make those things visible to us. Fourth, it reveals godliness and consequently must show us God. Fifth, it is a teacher and guide, providing us with a rule of life – as Paul's letter to Titus has declared. Sixth, to those who accept it, it is all that they require or desire.[919] "My Grace is sufficient for you." This is strong testimony from heaven of the power of this teaching and saving grace in the face of the greatest temptations.

An Objection Answered

The objection is raised that there is little mention of the Spirit and none of Grace before Christ's coming. From this, it is claimed that the Spirit, as

---

[916] Penn has noted Ephesians 6:17 ["And take the helmet of salvation, and the sword of the Spirit, which is the word of God"].

[917] Penn has noted John 1:4, 9, 14, 16 ["In him was life; and the life was the light of men. ... *That* was the true Light, which lighteth every man that cometh into the world. ... And the Word was made flesh, and dwelt among us, (and we beheld his glory, the glory as of the only begotten of the Father,) full of grace and truth. ... And of his fulness have all we received, and grace for grace"].

[918] Penn has noted Titus 2:11-12 ["For the grace of God that bringeth salvation hath appeared to all men, Teaching us that, denying ungodliness and worldly lusts, we should live soberly, righteously, and godly, in this present world"].

[919] Penn has noted 2 Cor. 12:9 ["And he said unto me, My grace is sufficient for thee: for my strength is made perfect in weakness. Most gladly therefore will I rather glory in my infirmities, that the power of Christ may rest upon me"].

spoken of in the New Testament, and even more so, Grace, must be something separate and better than the Light within.

This is easily answered. Grace and the Spirit are by no means another thing, but merely other names, given to different manifestations or actions of the same eternal Principle. It is called Light because of its property of revealing and the resultant discerning. In the beginning of the old world, God said, "Let there be Light," and there was Light.[920] In the same way, Light is present at the beginning of God's new creation in humanity. It is called Spirit, because it gives life, senses, motion, and vigor. And, every reader can see in a concordance that it is often mentioned in the Old Testament, just as it is in the New. For example, God's Spirit struggled with the old world[921] and with Israel in the wilderness.[922] Likewise, David asked in the agony of his soul, "Where can I go from your Spirit?"[923] And the prophets often felt it.

It is called Grace, not because it is a different thing, but because it was a more complete pouring out of the virtue and power of God's favor and mercy. Something that we are not worthy of should to be called grace or favor or God's goodwill when dispensed to an undeserving people. The wind does not always blow fresh, nor the rain fall freely, nor the sun shine brightly. Do we say that it is not the same kind of wind, rain, or sunshine when it blows softly, rains gently, or shines only a little rather than blowing powerfully, raining hard, or shining brightly? Certainly each is the same in kind and nature – and so is this Blessed Principle, in each of its manifestations and in all its actions for the benefit of souls since the world began.

---

[920] Gen. 1:3: "And God said, Let there be light: and there was light."

[921] Penn has noted Gen. 6:3 ["And the LORD said, My spirit shall not always strive with man, for that he also *is* flesh: yet his days shall be an hundred and twenty years"] in the margin.

[922] Penn has noted Neh. 9:30 ["Yet many years didst thou forbear them, and testifiedst against them by thy spirit in thy prophets: yet would they not give ear: therefore gavest thou them into the hand of the people of the lands"] in the margin.

[923] Penn has noted Ps. 139:7 ["Whither shall I go from thy spirit? or whither shall I flee from thy presence?"] in the margin.

An Illustration of the Differences in Appearance or Action

We freely, humbly, and thankfully acknowledge that the gospel dispensation was the best, clearest, and fullest of all – both as expressed in Christ's life and his sacrifice as the one Holy Offering to God for sin, and in the fuller breaking forth of his Light, the bountiful pouring out of his Spirit, and the abundant appearance of his Grace, in and to humanity, after his ascension into heaven. Though it was not a different Light or Spirit than God had given to humanity in earlier times, it was given in greater measure than ever before. That is the advantage of the gospel over the earlier dispensations – what had previously shone only dimly, now shines with great glory. Before it appeared darkly, but now it is unveiled for all to see.[924] Types, figures, and shadows hid its appearances and made them look low and faint, but in the gospel time, the veil is torn and the hidden glory is hidden no more.[925] Under the law, it was available to us like dew or a light rain, but under the gospel, it has been poured out on everyone as the Prophet Joel told us that God had promised. "Afterward, I will pour out my Spirit on all people."[926] Thus we say, when it rains, look how it pours. This is how God has expanded Light, Grace, and Spirit in these days. We shall not receive it sparingly in dribs and drabs, but fully and freely, even to overflowing. On Pentecost, Peter refers to the promise in Joel, declaring that day to be the beginning of its fulfillment. This is Grace, Favor, and

---

[924] Penn has noted 2 Cor. 3:18 ["But we all, with open face beholding as in a glass the glory of the Lord, are changed into the same image from glory to glory, *even* as by the Spirit of the Lord"] in the margin.

[925] Penn may be referencing Heb. 10:20 ("By a new and living way, which he hath consecrated for us, through the veil, that is to say, his flesh"). He has noted the following in the margin:

John 1:5. ["And the light shineth in darkness; and the darkness comprehended it not."]

John 1:17. ["For the law was given by Moses, *but* grace and truth came by Jesus Christ."]

[926] Penn has noted Joel 2:28 ["And it shall come to pass afterward, *that* I will pour out my spirit upon all flesh; and your sons and your daughters shall prophesy, your old men shall dream dreams, your young men shall see visions"] in the margin. This text is also quoted in Acts 2:17 ("And it shall come to pass in the last days, saith God, I will pour out of my Spirit upon all flesh: and your sons and your daughters shall prophesy, and your young men shall see visions, and your old men shall dream dreams") by Peter in his sermon to the crowds on Pentecost.

Goodness indeed. This greater illumination and greater pouring forth of the Spirit is rightly called Grace. Just as the appearance of the Son exceeded that of the servant, the appearance of the Light and Spirit of God, since the coming of Christ, exceeds that of all previous dispensations.[927] It is sufficient to lead all who follow it to salvation. This is our understanding of the Light, Spirit, and Grace of God. By what has been said in the Scriptures, it is obvious that these are all one and the same Divine Principle. Anyone who with love accepts the Light will not lack the Spirit or Grace of God. All are one: Light to guide us, Spirit to give us life, and Grace to teach, help, and comfort us. To those who diligently follow and obey it, it is sufficient for every circumstance of our lives.

Chapter 6

All are not Good, Although All are Enlightened

Some may still say that if it is as we have described, why is it that all who are enlightened are not as good as they should be or, as good as we have said this would make them?

The answer is that not all people receive and obey it. All have the ability to reason, but not all are reasonable. Is it the fault of grain stored in the granary that it does not grow or of money hidden in a napkin that it does not earn interest?[928] It is obvious when a gift has been given and just as obvious when it has been used profitably – both because others have used a similar gift to their advantage and because the just judge expects the loan to be repaid with interest.[929] So, if those who object will tell us whose fault it was that some have wasted their gift, we are prepared to tell them why the unprofitable servant was not as good as he should have been. The blind must not blame the sun for their blindness, nor should sinners accuse Grace of being inadequate. It is sin that darkens the spiritual eyes, hardens the heart, and obstructs all good things. Christ has told us that if we do

---

[927] This may be a reference to the Parable of the Wicked Tenants in Luke 20.

[928] The reference is to the third servant in the parable of the three servants, in particular to Luke 19:20, "And another came, saying, Lord, behold, *here is* thy pound, which I have kept laid up in a napkin."

[929] Luke 19:23: "Wherefore then gavest not thou my money into the bank, that at my coming I might have required mine own with usury?"

God's will, we will know God's doctrines.[930] Those who do not live up to
what they already have been given cannot blame God for not giving them
more. The unfruitfulness is in them, not in the gift.[931] It would be good if
they would take this to heart, but unfortunately, people are too inclined to
follow their sensual appetites, rather than their reasonable minds. This turns
them into dumb brutes, rather than rational creatures. The reasonable part
in us is our spiritual part – the part guided by the divine *Logos*, or Word.
Tertullian[932] interprets Reason, in this most exalted sense, as that which
makes people truly reasonable and allows them to offer themselves up to
God in spiritual worship.[933] Then they are as God first made them – in
God's own image – and gave them a paradise for their home.[934]

Gospel-truths were known before Christ

Others object that if mankind always had access to this Principle, why
is it that those who were obedient to it did not know the gospel-truths
before the coming of Christ?

The answer is simply that a beginning is not the same as an end. A child
is not a fully grown adult, but the child at the beginning of a life is the same
person as the adult at the end of it. The underlying reality remains the same,
although its appearance changes. Just as the world has and will have many
stages or periods in its history, so does humanity in its progress to
perfection. Those who are faithful to God's dispensation in their own time
will hear the happy welcome of "Well done, good and faithful servant."[935]

---

[930] John 7:17: "If any man will do his will, he shall know of the doctrine, whether it
be of God, or *whether* I speak of myself."

[931] Mark 4:19: "And the cares of this world, and the deceitfulness of riches, and the
lusts of other things entering in, choke the word, and it becometh unfruitful."

[932] Tertullian (c. 155-after 220) was an early Christian theologian and moralist.

[933] Rom. 12:1: "I beseech you therefore, brethren, by the mercies of God, that ye
present your bodies a living sacrifice, holy, acceptable unto God, *which is* your
reasonable service."

[934] Gen. 1:26: "And God said, Let us make man in our image, after our likeness:
and let them have dominion over the fish of the sea, and over the fowl of the
air, and over the cattle, and over all the earth, and over every creeping thing that
creepeth upon the earth."

[935] Matt. 25:23: "His lord said unto him, Well done, good and faithful servant; thou
hast been faithful over a few things, I will make thee ruler over many things:
enter thou into the joy of thy lord."

Even so, many of God's people in those times anticipated the glory of later times – the growth and development of religion and the happiness to come in the church of God. This can be seen in the prophesies of Jacob and Moses concerning the restoration of Israel by Christ.[936] David, in many of his excellent Psalms, expresses palpable and extraordinary joys as well as prophesies, especially in Psalms 2, 15, 18, 22, 23, 25, 27, 32, 36, 37, 42, 43, 45, 51, and 84. The prophets are similarly full of such anticipation, and it is for that reason that they are called prophets, particularly Isaiah in chapters 2, 9, 11, 25, 28, 32, 35, 42, 49 – 54, 59 – 61, 63, 65, and 66; Jeremiah in chapters 23, 30, 31, and 33; Ezekiel in chapters 20, 34, 36, and 37; Daniel in chapters 8 – 12; Hosea in chapters 1 and 3; Joel in chapters 2 and 3; Amos in chapter 9; Micah in chapters 4 and 5; Zachariah in chapters 6, 8, 9, 11, 13, and 14; and Malachi in chapters 3 and 4. They did not write about different things, but always about the same Divine Principle – although it had different appearances at different times. Nor did they prophesy in general terms – what they wrote was specific and extraordinary.

The same Spirit that came on Moses came on John the Baptist. The Spirit that came over Gideon and Sampson was the same as the one that fell on Peter and Paul. This doesn't make it the same dispensation of that Spirit – God visits and appears to people in ways that are appropriate to their spiritual states and conditions and in ways in which they are prepared to receive him. For some it has been outward and sensibly; for others inward and spiritually. There is no human capacity that is too great, or too small, to be touched by this Divine Principle – it made and knows all, so it reaches out to each person in the manner most appropriate. It touches the lowly, and the highest cannot live without it. This is what made David call out in distress to God, "Where can I hide from your Spirit? Where can I flee from your presence?"[937] He implies that God is everywhere – not that God is the

---

[936] Gen. 49:10: "The sceptre shall not depart from Judah, nor a lawgiver from between his feet, until Shiloh come; and unto him *shall* the gathering of the people *be*."

    Deut. 18:15&18: "The LORD thy God will raise up unto thee a Prophet from the midst of thee, of thy brethren, like unto me; unto him ye shall hearken … I will raise them up a Prophet from among their brethren, like unto thee, and will put my words in his mouth; and he shall speak unto them all that I shall command him."

[937] Penn has noted Ps. 139:7-10 ["Whither shall I go from thy spirit? or whither shall I flee from thy presence? If I ascend up into heaven, thou *art* there: if I make my bed in hell, behold, thou *art there. If* I take the wings of the morning,

same at all times and in all places. "If I go to heaven, you are there; to hell, or beyond the seas, even there your hand will guide me and your right hand will hold me." In other words, "Wherever I am and wherever I go, this Divine Word, this Light, this Spirit of God, will find me, lead me, help me, and comfort me. It is with me always in one form or another."[938] David knew this and therefore held that knowledge very precious. "In your Light we see Light,"[939] in other words, we will be enlightened by your Light. Or "You light my candle; the Lord, my God, lights up my darkness,"[940] and "The Lord is my Light; whom shall I fear?[941] It was his armor against all danger. It took away his fear and he was undaunted, because he was safe in it. Of the same blessed Word he says elsewhere, "It is a lamp to my feet and a light for my path."[942] In short, it was a Light that led him in the way of blessedness.

The Gentiles had the Same Light, but Without the Same Advantages

The objectors say that just because the Jews had this Light does not mean that the Gentiles had it too, whereas our doctrine declares that all have it.

We answer yes, our doctrine is exactly that, and it is the glory of our doctrine that it proclaims that God's love is offered to all. Besides the general texts cited above, the Apostle Paul is very specific in the second chapter of his Epistle to the Romans. There he states, "Gentiles, who do

---

and dwell in the uttermost parts of the sea; Even there shall thy hand lead me, and thy right hand shall hold me"] in the margin.

[938] Penn has noted the following in the margin:

Prov. 6:22. ["When thou goest, it shall lead thee; when thou sleepest, it shall keep thee; and *when* thou awakest, it shall talk with thee."]

Isa. 43:2. ["When thou passest through the waters, I *will be* with thee; and through the rivers, they shall not overflow thee: when thou walkest through the fire, thou shalt not be burned; neither shall the flame kindle upon thee."].

[939] Ps. 36:9: "For with thee *is* the fountain of life: in thy light shall we see light."

[940] Ps. 18:28: "For thou wilt light my candle: the LORD my God will enlighten my darkness."

[941] Ps. 27:1: "The LORD *is* my light and my salvation; whom shall I fear? the LORD *is* the strength of my life; of whom shall I be afraid?"

[942] Ps. 119:105: "Thy word *is* a lamp unto my feet, and a light unto my path."

not have the law, do naturally things required by the law, they are a law for themselves." That is to say, they did not have an outward law, as the Jews did, but "the requirements of the law are written on their hearts," which is to say that they had the law within themselves to guide them. And the Jews did too, but they had greater outward help to assist them in obeying – help not given to any other nation. Therefore the obedience of the Gentiles, or uncircumcised, is said to be by nature only, because they did not have the extra, external, and extraordinary ministries and supports available to the Jews. This does not diminish in any way the obedient Gentiles, but exalts them in the Apostle's judgment. Although they did not have those advantages, even so "the requirements of the law written on their hearts" were apparent in the good lives they lived in the world. He adds that everyday their consciences witnessed to them and their own thoughts will accuse them or excuse them for their actions on the Day of Judgment.[943]

This presents us with four things related to our point that are worthy of serious reflection. First, the Gentiles had the law written in their hearts. Second, their consciences were an acceptable witness to their faithfulness in doing their duty. Third, the judgment made on that evidence will be confirmed on the Day of Judgment and is therefore valid and irreversible. Fourth, this could not be the case unless their consciences were illuminated by a divine and sufficient Light. Conscience is nothing more than the sense we have, or judgment we make, of our faithfulness to God's will – as God gives us an understanding of that will. To ensure that only a true and scriptural use is made of this word 'conscience,' I limit it to judgments about our duty to live a virtuous and holy life. We cannot miss or dispute that the Apostle evidently does the same. Read verses 7 to 9.[944] Indeed, it was the judgment of conscience that guided the apostles in preaching the gospel and urging it on all people. The Beloved Disciple, calling it 'heart,'

---

[943] Rom. 2:14-16: "For when the Gentiles, which have not the law, do by nature the things contained in the law, these, having not the law, are a law unto themselves: Which shew the work of the law written in their hearts, their conscience also bearing witness, and *their* thoughts the mean while accusing or else excusing one another; In the day when God shall judge the secrets of men by Jesus Christ according to my gospel."

[944] Rom. 2:7-9: "To them who by patient continuance in well doing seek for glory and honour and immortality, eternal life: But unto them that are contentious, and do not obey the truth, but obey unrighteousness, indignation and wrath, Tribulation and anguish, upon every soul of man that doeth evil, of the Jew first, and also of the Gentile."

also holds it up as the judge of a person's present and future state, "If our hearts condemn us, God is greater than our hearts, and knows everything; but if our hearts do not condemn us, we can be confident before God."[945] Plain and strong words! And what are they about? Just this: Do we love God in Truth and in deed? And how do we show that? The answer: By keeping his commandments,[946] which is simply living up to the duty we all know.

If anyone desires to further satisfy themselves of the divinity available to the Gentiles, let them read Plato, Seneca, Plutarch, Epictetus, Marcus Aurelius Antonius, and the Gentile writers.

They will also find many of their sayings collected in the first part of a book called *The Christian Quaker*. There, they are compared with the testimony of Scripture and their agreement with it is demonstrated. In these Gentile writings, they may find many excellent truths and taste great love of and devotion to Virtue – a fruit that grows only on the Tree of Life, in every age and in every nation. Some of the most eminent early Christian writers, such as Justin Martyr, Origen, and Clemens Alexandrinus, had great respect for these Gentiles and did not fear that a defense of Christianity based on their works would harm Christianity's reputation. The early Christians used these sources to assist their followers in finding Truth, just as Paul had when he called on the Athenians to listen to the words of their own poets.[947]

---

[945] 1 John 3:20-21: "For if our heart condemn us, God is greater than our heart, and knoweth all things. Beloved, if our heart condemn us not, *then* have we confidence toward God."

[946] John 14:15: "If ye love me, keep my commandments."

[947] The reference is to Paul's argument with the Athenians in Acts 17:16-34.

Chapter 7

The Various Dispensations of God

B ut, it may be asked, if there is only one Divine Principle, then why have there been so many different religions since the world began? The religions of the patriarchs, the Law of Moses, and the early Christians have great differences – not to mention what has happened to Christianity since it was first introduced.

I cannot properly call religions 'different' if they claim the one, true God as their object of worship, whether that one God is called the only Savior, the Lord Jesus Christ, or the Light or Spirit of Christ, the agent and means of our conversion and eternal bliss. That would be like calling infant, child, and adult three persons, rather than three stages in growth, or periods of time, in a single life. As was noted above, the various modes or ways in which God has appeared to different people have been appropriate to the various states of each of those people. In each case, it seems to have been God's primary purpose to prevent idolatry and depravity by directing their minds to the true object of worship and by encouraging virtue and holiness.

To the Patriarchs, he added to their enlightenment by sending angels in the guise of travelers, and they in turn conveyed the message to their families. To the Prophets, revelation came most often by the Holy Spirit, sending them to preach to the Jews. In the gospel dispensation, the message has been delivered by the Son – both externally in the flesh and internally by his spiritual appearance in the soul as the Light to the world. Yet all of these flowings of the Spirit, each suited to a particular people at a particular time, have sprung from the same source.

Truth is the Same in Every Shape

It is of great importance for our information and encouragement to remember that God's work with humanity is all of a single piece. In itself, that work has been sharply focused. In every dispensation, God's eye has been set on the same goal: To make us truly good by planting holy awe and love of God in our hearts. At times, he has accommodated our hardness of heart and darkness of mind by spelling out his Holy Mind in ways that, to our more enlightened understandings, are simplistic and worldly. God has allowed Truth to put on various garments so that it can better reach people in their lowly states and persuade them to give up false gods and wasted lives. At times, humanity has sunk far below the state that God intended for it, and people have become little more than brute beasts, forgetting their own strength and nobility.

Why Idolatry Abounds

Consider the prevalence of idolatry in earlier and darker times of the world, as described so well in the Scriptures. This is because idols are outward and visible, more sensual and attuned to please our senses than a more spiritual object of worship – and therefore seem more within the power of humanity.[948] These gods, being the product of their own hands, could not really help them. This was an argument that most galled their worshippers and, for that reason, they were willing to ignore. But still, the fact that it was outward and sensual – that they could see the object of their devotion and address it whenever they wished – was what gave it any advantage over true religion. In addition to being better suited to their dark and brutal state, it was often more fashionable.

Therefore God, by many great afflictions and even greater deliverances, brought forth a people who might remember the hand that saved them and worship God only. God raised up the Jews in order to root out idolatry and plant the knowledge and love of God in their minds, so that they would be an example to all other nations. Anyone who reads Deuteronomy, which is a summary of the other four books of Moses,[949] cannot help but notice that good man's frequent and earnest care and concern for Israel on this very point. Nor can the reader miss how often that, despite God's love, care, and patience for them, people slipped and lapsed into the idolatrous customs of the people around them. Numerous other Scriptures further inform us of this, especially those of the Prophets, in Isaiah 44 and 45, in Psalms 37 and 115, and in Jeremiah 10, where the people are proven wrong and rebuked by the Holy Spirit, who mocks their idols, treating them with holy disdain.

The Quakers' Testimony is the Best Antidote: Walking by a Divine Principle

That which is furthest from idolatry, and the best antidote to it, is the Divine Principle we have proclaimed. The more people's minds are turned and brought to it, and the more that they conform their faith, worship, and

---

[948] Penn has noted Gen. 31 and 35, Exod. 20, Lev. 21, Deut. 29-32, and Josh. 22-24 in the margin.

[949] According to tradition, Moses was the author of the first four books of the Bible: Genesis, Exodus, Leviticus, Numbers, and Deuteronomy.

obedience to that Holy Illumination and Power, the nearer they grow to knowing the purpose of their creation and closer consequently to their Creator. They become more spiritually qualified, and better able, to worship God as God is – as we are told by our Lord Jesus Christ, a Spirit to be worshipped in Spirit and in Truth.[950] These are the kind of worshippers that God is calling to worship him in the gospel times. "The time is coming," he said, "and is now here."[951] This is to say, "Some already do so, but more will." This is a plain assertion of the present time and a promise or prophesy of more true worshippers to come in the future. This makes clear the intended change away from ceremonial worship and an outward state of the church to a spiritual one. The clear meaning of this text is the time is here and coming when worship will be more inward than outward – that is, when worship will be more suited to the nature of God and to our own better selves and natures. Worship will be offered in Spirit and in Truth. 'In Spirit' meaning through the power of the Spirit. 'In Truth' meaning in reality – not in shadows, ceremonies, or forms – but in sincerity, with and in the Life, that is, divinely prepared and enlivened. This enables us not only to offer right worship, but also to enter into intimate communion and fellowship with God, who is a Spirit.

The Purpose of All God's Manifestations: That Humanity Might be God's Image and Delight

If all is given its proper weight, it will be seen that God, in each manifestation, has come nearer and nearer to the insides of humanity. In this way, God reaches into our understandings and opens our hearts, bringing us to a simpler and closer communion with himself in the Spirit. It is there that each of us must seek and find the knowledge of God for our eternal happiness.

All of creation testifies to the power and wisdom of God and of God's goodness toward humanity. Indeed, many point to creation as evidence for the existence of God, but above all else, it is humanity itself that is the proof. We are the precious stone in the ring, the most glorious jewel in the universe – the whole of which seems to have been made and dedicated to

---

[950] John 4:24: "God *is* a Spirit: and they that worship him must worship *him* in spirit and in truth."

[951] John 4:23: "But the hour cometh, and now is, when the true worshippers shall worship the Father in spirit and in truth: for the Father seeketh such to worship him."

our reasonable use, service, and satisfaction. "But God's delight" (by whom, the Holy Spirit tells us, we were made) "is in the inhabited world, with the human race"[952] and with those that are "contrite in spirit."[953]And why are we God's delight? Because of all creation, only humanity is made in God's likeness.[954] This is how intimate humanity's relationship is to God, for of all creatures, only we have the honor of being in God's image. By this resemblance to God, I might say, came our kindred to God and our knowledge of God. Thus, the closest and best way for us to know and to truly understand God, is to seek within ourselves that which is within God's image. As we find that image within ourselves, we will find God and know God.

We are God's image in two respects. The first is in our immortal nature and the second, in that our nature possesses qualities such as wisdom, justice, mercy, holiness, and patience, in a small way (proportional to our capacity) that are infinitely and incomparably to be found in our Creator. As we become more holy, just, merciful, and patient in ourselves, we will come to know the original by analogy – by observing the workmanship within ourselves, we can become acquainted with the Holy Workman.

This, Reader, is the regeneration and new creature that we urge. We say that all ought to be religious and walk in this world according to this rule of peace and mercy.[955] As I have said, we share in two worlds. Our bodies are of this world; our souls are of the other world. The body is the temple of the soul, the soul is the temple of the Word, and the Word is the great

---

[952] Penn has noted Prov. 8:31 ["Rejoicing in the habitable part of his earth; and my delights *were* with the sons of men"] in the margin.

[953] Penn has noted Isa. 66:1-2 ["Thus saith the LORD, The heaven *is* my throne, and the earth *is* my footstool: where *is* the house that ye build unto me? and where *is* the place of my rest? For all those *things* hath mine hand made, and all those *things* have been, saith the LORD: but to this *man* will I look, *even* to *him that is* poor and of a contrite spirit, and trembleth at my word"] in the margin.

[954] Gen. 1:26: "And God said, Let us make man in our image, after our likeness: and let them have dominion over the fish of the sea, and over the fowl of the air, and over the cattle, and over all the earth, and over every creeping thing that creepeth upon the earth."

[955] Penn has noted Gal. 6:15-16. ["For in Christ Jesus neither circumcision availeth any thing, nor uncircumcision, but a new creature. And as many as walk according to this rule, peace *be* on them, and mercy, and upon the Israel of God"] in the margin.

temple and revelation of God. Through the body, the soul looks into and sees the physical world; through the Word, it can behold God and the world that is without end. Much more could be said about how God has ordered things and their respective qualities, but I must be brief.

Chapter 8

The Doctrines of Satisfaction and Justification According to the Scriptures

*A*lthough we have many good things to say about how Christ appears in and works in the soul, to awaken, convict, and convert it, it is objected that Quakers neglect the death and sufferings of Christ. Our adversaries say that Quakers have little reverence for the doctrine of Christ's satisfaction to God for our sins and that we do not believe that the active and passive obedience of Christ, when he lived in the world, is the only basis for a sinner's justification before God.

The Doctrines of Satisfaction and Justification, when truly understood, are so completely intertwined, that each is the necessary consequence of the other. What we say about them is only what has the sanction of the Scriptures and what, for the most part, can be stated in words taken from Scripture. We believe that whenever any difficulty arises, whether from obscure language, mistranslation, or the dust stirred up by squabbles among partisan writers or over-educated critics, it is always best to stay as close as possible to the actual words of the text and to view anything else charitably.

I will first speak negatively, telling what we do not accept. Some, who are more hasty than wise, have used these things to accuse us of belittling the efficacy of the sufferings and death of Christ.

Notions That We Cannot Believe

First, we cannot believe that Christ is the cause of God's Love. Rather we hold that Christ is the effect of that love. This is testified to by the beloved Disciple, John stated in his third chapter, "God so loved the world that he gave his only Son, so that everyone who believes in him will not perish but have eternal life."[956]

---

[956] John 3:16: "For God so loved the world, that he gave his only begotten Son, that whosoever believeth in him should not perish, but have everlasting life."

Second, we reject the idea that God could use no other way to save sinners except by requiring the death and sufferings of his Son to satisfy his offended honor. Nor do we accept that Christ's death and sufferings were necessary and unavoidable to achieve satisfaction for the eternal death and misery that people deserved for their sin and transgression of the laws of God. These notions portray God's mercy as unconcerned about our salvation. Indeed, we stand too far from God's infinite wisdom and power to pretend that we could ever judge whether God acted freely or out of necessity.

Third, we cannot say that Jesus Christ was the greatest sinner in the world (because he bore our sins on his cross[957] or because he, who was sinless, was made sin for us[958]). This statement, though grossly insulting and scripturally unsound, is often spoken by great preachers and professors of religion.

Fourth, we cannot believe that Christ's death and sufferings so completely satisfy God, or justify us, that we are thereby accepted by God. Christ's acts indeed make it possible for people to be accepted by God, but it is only with the obedience of faith and the sanctification of the Spirit that they can attain and maintain that state of acceptance. We cannot imagine that a person would be justified before God who stands self-condemned, or that anyone can be in Christ who has not become a new creature,[959] or that God would look upon anyone as anything but what they truly are. We term it a state of presumption, not a state of salvation, for anyone to call Jesus 'Lord' unless he or she is led to that declaration by the Holy Spirit; or to call him 'Master' when he is not the master of their minds; or 'Savior' when they are not saved from sin by him; 'Redeemer' when they are not redeemed from their passion, pride, covetousness, wantonness, vanity, arrogance, or from the honors, friendships and glories of this world. Those who do so deceive themselves, because God will not be mocked. They will

---

[957] 1 Pet. 2:24: "Who his own self bare our sins in his own body on the tree, that we, being dead to sins, should live unto righteousness: by whose stripes ye were healed."

[958] 2 Cor. 5:21: "For he hath made him *to be* sin for us, who knew no sin; that we might be made the righteousness of God in him."

[959] 2 Cor. 5:17: "Therefore if any man *be* in Christ, *he is* a new creature: old things are passed away; behold, all things are become new."

reap whatever they sow."[960] Even though Christ died for us, we must, with the assistance of his grace, "continue to work out our own salvation with fear and trembling."[961] Just as he died for sin, we must die to sin. Otherwise, we cannot claim to be saved by the death and sufferings of Christ, or to be thoroughly justified and accepted by God.

What has been said so far has been the negative. Now I will tell you what we claim and accept with regard to justification.

Christ, a Sacrifice and a Mediator

We do believe that Jesus Christ was our holy sacrifice, atonement, and propitiation; that he bore our iniquities and by his wounds we are healed[962] of the wounds Adam and Eve gave us in their fall. We believe that God is right to forgive those who are true penitents because of the holy offering that Christ made of himself to God for us. We believe that what he did and suffered, satisfied and pleased God, and was offered for the sake of a fallen humanity that had displeased God. We believe that through the offering up of himself once for all,[963] through the Eternal Spirit, he has forever perfected those in all times who are sanctified, those "who follow not their passions, but the Spirit."[964]

The Two Parts of Justification: From the Guilt of Sin and from the Power and Pollution of Sin

Justification consists of two parts: justification from the guilt of sin and justification from the power and pollution of sin – in this sense, it provides clear and complete acceptance by God. Without the second part, many

---

[960] Gal. 6:7: "Be not deceived; God is not mocked: for whatsoever a man soweth, that shall he also reap."

[961] Phil. 2:12: "Wherefore, my beloved, as ye have always obeyed, not as in my presence only, but now much more in my absence, work out your own salvation with fear and trembling."

[962] Isa. 53:5: "But he *was* wounded for our transgressions, *he was* bruised for our iniquities: the chastisement of our peace *was* upon him; and with his stripes we are healed."

[963] Heb. 10:10: "By the which will we are sanctified through the offering of the body of Jesus Christ once *for all.*"

[964] Penn has noted Rom. 8:1 ["*There is* therefore now no condemnation to them which are in Christ Jesus, who walk not after the flesh, but after the Spirit"] in the margin.

religiously inclined souls are left in doubt, conscience-ridden, and despondent despite all that their teachers have told them of the extent and effectiveness of the first part of justification. And it is a source of widespread unhappiness among those who profess to be Christians that they have been too willing to hide their own active and passive disobedience under the cloak of Christ's active and passive obedience.

We reverently and humbly acknowledge that the first part of justification is the result only of the death and sufferings of Christ – nothing we can do ourselves, even by the work of the Holy Spirit, is sufficient to cancel our debts or wipe out old scores. It is the power and consequence of that propitiatory offering, if met with faith and repentance, which justifies us from the sins that are past. It is the power of Christ's Spirit in our hearts that purifies and makes us acceptable before God. Until our hearts have been purged of sin, God will not accept them. God rightly accuses, denounces, and condemns those that entertain sin there, and such people are not in a justified state. Condemnation and justification are in opposition – those who believe themselves to be justified by the active and passive obedience of Christ, while they are not themselves actively and passively obedient to the Spirit of Christ Jesus, are powerfully and dangerously deluded.

For crying out against this sin-pleasing notion (which we cannot call a doctrine), we are publicly scorned and denounced as deniers and despisers of the death and sufferings of our Lord Jesus Christ. But let those who walk unrighteously under that pretended justification know that they add to Christ's sufferings – they crucify afresh the Son of God and trample the blood of the covenant under their feet. "God will not acquit the guilty nor justify the disobedient and unfaithful."[965]

These people deceive themselves and, at the Great and Final Judgment, they will not hear, "Come you that are blessed,"[966] because it cannot be said of them, "Well done, good and faithful servant."[967] Rather, those who live

---

[965] Job 8:20: "Behold, God will not cast away a perfect *man*, neither will he help the evil doers."

[966] Matt. 25:34: "Then shall the King say unto them on his right hand, Come, ye blessed of my Father, inherit the kingdom prepared for you from the foundation of the world."

[967] Matt. 25:23: "His lord said unto him, Well done, good and faithful servant; thou hast been faithful over a few things, I will make thee ruler over many things: enter thou into the joy of thy lord."

and die in a contemptible and condemnable state will hear, "Depart from me, you who are cursed..."[968]

Exhortation to the Reader

Therefore, Oh my Reader! Rest not, thinking that you are completely saved by what Christ has done for you in his blessed person without you, but strive to know his power and kingdom within you. The strong man, who has for too long lived within you, must be bound, his belongings removed,[969] his works destroyed, and sin ended. As 1 John 3:7 tells us, "Little children, let no one deceive you. Those that do righteousness are righteous."[970] "To that end," says that beloved Disciple, "Christ came so that all things may become new – new heavens and a new earth, in which righteousness dwells."[971] In this way, you will come to glorify God in your body and your Spirit – both of which are God's – and live for God and not for yourself. Your love, joy, worship, and obedience – your very life and all you do in it – your studies, meditations, and devotions will be spiritual. The Father and the Son will make their home in you,[972] and Christ will reveal himself to you, for "the Lord confides in those who love and revere him."[973] You will have a blessing, or Holy Unction, that leads you into all Truth, and you need not human teachings.[974] You will be better taught,

---

[968] Matt. 25:41: "Then shall he say also unto them on the left hand, Depart from me, ye cursed, into everlasting fire, prepared for the devil and his angels."

[969] Mark 3:27: "No man can enter into a strong man's house, and spoil his goods, except he will first bind the strong man; and then he will spoil his house."

[970] 1 John 3:7: "Little children, let no man deceive you: he that doeth righteousness is righteous, even as he is righteous."

[971] Penn seems to have combined Rev. 21:5 ("And he that sat upon the throne said, Behold, I make all things new. And he said unto me, Write: for these words are true and faithful") with 2 Pet. 3:13 ("Nevertheless we, according to his promise, look for new heavens and a new earth, wherein dwelleth righteousness").

[972] John 14:23: "Jesus answered and said unto him, If a man love me, he will keep my words: and my Father will love him, and we will come unto him, and make our abode with him."

[973] Ps. 25:14: "The secret of the LORD *is* with them that fear him; and he will shew them his covenant."

[974] Penn seems to be drawing on several things attributed to the Apostle John:

   1 John 2:20. ["But ye have an unction from the Holy One, and ye know all things."]

instructed directly by the Divine Oracle. You will not depend on hearsay or the words of traditional Christians, but on a fresh and living witness from those who have seen with their own eyes, heard with their own ears, and touched with their own hands the Word of Life in all its works for their souls' salvation.[975] In this they meet. In this they preach. In this they pray and praise.

Behold the new covenant fulfilled – the church and worship of Christ, the great anointed of God and the great anointing of God – in God's Holy Priesthood and in the work of God's Church!

Chapter 9

A Confession of Belief in Christ and His Work, Both in Doing and Suffering

Some say that Quakers are ambiguous in what we profess regarding Christ's coming in the flesh or that we allegorize that event – so as to mean only our own flesh – and that as often as we mention Christ, we mean only a mystery or some mystical sense of him, whether we are speaking of his coming, birth, miracles, sufferings, death, resurrection, ascension, mediation, or judgment.

To eliminate any misunderstanding among those who may be like-minded, and to inform and reclaim for Christ those who are under the power and prejudice of our attackers, let me speak plainly: We thank God that we do religiously believe and confess, to the glory of God the Father and the honor of his dear and beloved Son, that Jesus Christ took our

---

John 16:13. ["Howbeit when he, the Spirit of truth, is come, he will guide you into all truth: for he shall not speak of himself; but whatsoever he shall hear, *that* shall he speak: and he will shew you things to come."]

1 John 2:27. ["But the anointing which ye have received of him abideth in you, and ye need not that any man teach you: but as the same anointing teacheth you of all things, and is truth, and is no lie, and even as it hath taught you, ye shall abide in him."]

[975] 1 John 1:1: "That which was from the beginning, which we have heard, which we have seen with our eyes, which we have looked upon, and our hands have handled, of the Word of life."

nature on himself[976] and was like us in all things excepting sin;[977] that he was born of the virgin Mary, suffered under Pontius Pilate, the Roman governor, was crucified, died, and buried in the sepulcher of Joseph of Arimathea. He rose again on the third day and ascended into heaven, where he sits at the right hand of God, in the power and majesty of his Father. One day, the world will be judged by that blessed man, Christ Jesus – each according to his or her own deeds.

Our Belief and Testimony of Christ's Inward and Spiritual Appearance in the Soul

Because we believe all this, must not we also believe the rest that Christ said? "He that is with you will be in you."[978] "I in them and they in me."[979] "When God was pleased to reveal his Son in me..."[980] "The mystery that has been hidden for ages is Christ among the Gentiles, Christ within you, the hope of glory."[981] "Unless you have failed the test, Christ is within you!"[982] Or are we to be misrepresented as denying Christ in the flesh and the holy purpose of his taking it – in each particular of his work and

---

[976] Heb. 2:17: "Wherefore in all things it behoved him to be made like unto *his* brethren, that he might be a merciful and faithful high priest in things *pertaining* to God, to make reconciliation for the sins of the people."

[977] Heb. 4:15: "For we have not an high priest which cannot be touched with the feeling of our infirmities; but was in all points tempted like as *we are, yet* without sin."

[978] John 14:17: "*Even* the Spirit of truth; whom the world cannot receive, because it seeth him not, neither knoweth him: but ye know him; for he dwelleth with you, and shall be in you."

[979] John 17:23: "I in them, and thou in me, that they may be made perfect in one; and that the world may know that thou hast sent me, and hast loved them, as thou hast loved me."

[980] Gal. 1:15-16: "But when it pleased God, who separated me from my mother's womb, and called *me* by his grace, To reveal his Son in me, that I might preach him among the heathen; immediately I conferred not with flesh and blood."

[981] Col. 1:26-27: "*Even* the mystery which hath been hid from ages and from generations, but now is made manifest to his saints: To whom God would make known what *is* the riches of the glory of this mystery among the Gentiles; which is Christ in you, the hope of glory."

[982] 2 Cor. 13:5: "Examine yourselves, whether ye be in the faith; prove your own selves. Know ye not your own selves, how that Jesus Christ is in you, except ye be reprobates?"

suffering – because we believe, and urgently preach the necessity that others believe, receive, and obey Christ's inward and spiritual appearance and manifestation? Is it because we preach that his Light, Grace, and Spirit in the hearts and consciences of men and women can expose, convict, convert, and reform them? This is cruel and unrighteous treatment! Nor would our harsh and heated adversaries accept such treatment from others – but to do to others as you would have them do to you too often is not part of their practice, regardless of what they preach.

It is Impossible to be Saved by Christ While We Reject His Work and Power within Us

Moreover, we declare to the whole world that we cannot expect men and women to be saved by their belief in one form of justification without knowing and living the other. That is what we oppose, not the Blessed Manifestation of Christ in the flesh. We say that Christ overcame our common enemy, defeated him in the open field, and in our nature conquered the one who had overcome and triumphed over Adam and Eve and all their descendants. Just as Christ himself overcame that one in our nature, so he overcomes the enemy within us when we receive and obey his divine grace. Christ by his Light in our consciences reveals the enemy and enables us to resist him and all his fiery darts,[983] to fight the good fight of faith, to overcome him ourselves, and to lay claim to eternal life.[984]

The Dispensation of Grace: Its Nature and Extent

This is the Dispensation of Grace, which we declare has in one degree or another come to all, teaching those who will receive it "to renounce ungodliness and worldly passions and to live self-controlled, upright, and godly lives in this world while we wait for the blessed hope (which no one else can justly do) – we wait for the glorious appearance of our great God and Savior Jesus Christ."[985] We minister to others from the teaching,

---

[983] Ephesians 6:16: "Above all, taking the shield of faith, wherewith ye shall be able to quench all the fiery darts of the wicked."

[984] 1 Tim. 6:12: "Fight the good fight of faith, lay hold on eternal life, whereunto thou art also called, and hast professed a good profession before many witnesses."

[985] Titus 2:11-13: "For the grace of God that bringeth salvation hath appeared to all men, Teaching us that, denying ungodliness and worldly lusts, we should live soberly, righteously, and godly, in this present world; Looking for that blessed

experience, and direction of this grace with the goal of turning people's minds to that grace in themselves so that all will be doing "the good and pleasing will of God,[986] working out their salvation with fear and trembling,[987] and confirming their high and heavenly calling and election."[988] Nothing else can do that, no matter what religion they profess, which church they attend, or the quality of their personal character, because "you will reap what you sow,"[989] and "you are the servant of the one you obey."[990] We cannot be children of God and heirs of eternal glory, if we are not regenerated. To be born again, another Spirit and Principle must win over, transform, instruct, and govern us – not the Spirit of this world or our own depraved Spirits,[991] but only the Spirit that lived in Christ. Unless that Spirit lives within us, we cannot be Christ's.[992] This Spirit begins by awaking the soul to its sin and ends in conversion and perseverance. One follows the other, with conversion being the consequence of an awakening that is accepted and perseverance being the natural fruit of conversion and being born of God. These "do not sin, because God's seed lives within them."[993]

---

hope, and the glorious appearing of the great God and our Saviour Jesus Christ."

[986] Rom. 12:2: "And be not conformed to this world: but be ye transformed by the renewing of your mind, that ye may prove what *is* that good, and acceptable, and perfect, will of God."

[987] Phil. 2:12: "Wherefore, my beloved, as ye have always obeyed, not as in my presence only, but now much more in my absence, work out your own salvation with fear and trembling."

[988] 2 Pet. 1:10: "Wherefore the rather, brethren, give diligence to make your calling and election sure: for if ye do these things, ye shall never fall."

[989] Gal. 6:7: "Be not deceived; God is not mocked: for whatsoever a man soweth, that shall he also reap."

[990] Rom. 6:16: "Know ye not, that to whom ye yield yourselves servants to obey, his servants ye are to whom ye obey; whether of sin unto death, or of obedience unto righteousness?"

[991] 1 Cor. 2:12: "Now we have received, not the spirit of the world, but the spirit which is of God; that we might know the things that are freely given to us of God."

[992] Penn has noted Rom. 8:9 ["But ye are not in the flesh, but in the Spirit, if so be that the Spirit of God dwell in you. Now if any man have not the Spirit of Christ, he is none of his"] in the margin.

[993] 1 John 3:9: "Whosoever is born of God doth not commit sin; for his seed remaineth in him: and he cannot sin, because he is born of God."

They are faithful to the end and receive what was promised,[994] which is everlasting life.

Further Acknowledgment of the Death and Sufferings of Christ

But let my Readers take this with them, that we do acknowledge that Christ, through his holy works and sufferings ("being a Son, he learned obedience"[995]), has obtained his Father's mercy for mankind. His obedience affects every piece and part of our salvation, since in it he became a conqueror and "held even captivity as a captive and obtained gifts for all – great and precious promises – that by them we might first escape the corruptions of the world caused by evil desires and become participants in the divine nature."[996] We do believe and confess that the active and passive obedience of Christ Jesus has brought about our salvation from the power and pollution of sin as well as from the guilt of sin. He has given this gift to all so that they may see their transgressions, and the sinfulness of them, so that they can repent and turn away from it, and do so no more. By this gift, they will each day depend on God for the strength to resist the fiery darts of the enemy and find comfort in the obedience of faith in, and faithfulness to, the leading of this divine grace from the Son of God.

Christ is both a conqueror and a sacrifice through suffering, and those who reject the divine gift he obtained in this way do not please God, do not truly believe in God, nor are they truly Christians or truly saved. "Woman," said Christ to the Samaritan, "If you knew the gift of God and who it is that speaks to you ..."[997] People do not know Christ or God, "who to know is

---

[994] Heb. 6:15: "And so, after he had patiently endured, he obtained the promise."

[995] Heb. 5:8: "Though he were a Son, yet learned he obedience by the things which he suffered."

[996] Ephesians 4:7-8: "But unto every one of us is given grace according to the measure of the gift of Christ. Wherefore he saith, When he ascended up on high, he led captivity captive, and gave gifts unto men."

2 Pet. 1:4: "Whereby are given unto us exceeding great and precious promises: that by these ye might be partakers of the divine nature, having escaped the corruption that is in the world through lust."

[997] John 4:10: "Jesus answered and said unto her, If thou knewest the gift of God, and who it is that saith to thee, Give me to drink; thou wouldest have asked of him, and he would have given thee living water."

life eternal"[998] because they are ignorant of the gift of God, that is, that "each will receive a share in the Spirit of God for the common good"[999] – it is this that reveals Christ and God to the soul.[1000]

Flesh and blood alone cannot do it. Oxford and Cambridge cannot do it. Learning languages and philosophy cannot do it. Those who do not know God by God's Wisdom take these things for their wisdom.[1001] Although they are clear, careful, and correct in their understandings of those things, alas! it is all in vain and misguided. Because they put their trust in these things and seek God there, they fall further and further from the inward and saving knowledge of God.

The key of David is quite another thing: "What it shuts, no one can open; what it opens, no one can shut."[1002] All who receive and accept the gift of God into their hearts have this key. It opens to them the knowledge of God and of themselves. It gives them new senses of sight and taste, and a new way of understanding things that their educations and traditional knowledge cannot provide. This is the beginning of God's new creation; through it we come to be new beings.

We boldly declare that there is no other way than this one for people to come into Christ, or to be true Christians, or to receive the advantages that come from the death and sufferings of the Lord Jesus Christ. Therefore, on the authority of our own experience as well as of Scripture, we say that Christ is not a saving sacrifice for any who refuse to follow his example.

---

[998] Penn has noted John 17 probably especially 17:3 ("And this is life eternal, that they might know thee the only true God, and Jesus Christ, whom thou hast sent") in the margin.

[999] Penn has noted 1 Cor. 12:7 ["But the manifestation of the Spirit is given to every man to profit withal"] in the margin.

[1000] Penn has noted chapter 2 probably especially, 1 Cor. 2:7&10 ("But we speak the wisdom of God in a mystery, *even* the hidden *wisdom*, which God ordained before the world unto our glory ... But God hath revealed *them* unto us by his Spirit: for the Spirit searcheth all things, yea, the deep things of God") in the margin.

[1001] 1 Cor. 1:21: "For after that in the wisdom of God the world by wisdom knew not God, it pleased God by the foolishness of preaching to save them that believe."

[1002] Rev. 3:7: "And to the angel of the church in Philadelphia write; These things saith he that is holy, he that is true, he that hath the key of David, he that openeth, and no man shutteth; and shutteth, and no man openeth."

Those who reject the gift, deny the giver – instead of denying their own desires for the giver's sake.

Oh! That people were only wise! If people would only consider the end they are approaching and what is required for that end to be a peaceful one! Why should they die clutching vain hopes for eternal life while death reigns in their hearts? Why do they anticipate a future life with God, but do not live up to him or walk with him in this one!

Awake, you who sleep in sin! Awake, you who rest in self-righteousness! Christ will give you Life! Only he is "the Lord from heaven, the life-giving Spirit,"[1003] and we can receive that Life if we do not resist his Spirit or reject it by disobedience.

Receive, love, and obey all the Holy Leadings and Teachings of Christ's Spirit![1004] To that Holy Spirit, I entrust my Readers, so that they can better see where they truly are and come to have true belief in and take full advantage of the works and sufferings of our Dear and Blessed Lord and Savior Jesus Christ. From the power and pollution of sin (as much as from its guilt), he saves all who hear his knock and open the door of their hearts to him, so he can come in and bring about real and thorough reformation in them and for them.[1005] Only in this way can the real benefit, power, and effect of his works and sufferings come into our lives and let us know, according to the doctrine of the apostle, fellowship with Christ in his sufferings and death.[1006] Those who live in sin do not know this spiritual communion, though they claim to be saved by that death and those sufferings. Much more might be said about this matter, but I must be brief.

[1003] 1 Cor. 15:45&47: "And so it is written, The first man Adam was made a living soul; the last Adam *was made* a quickening spirit …The first man *is* of the earth, earthy: the second man *is* the Lord from heaven."

[1004] Penn has noted Rom. 8:14-15 ["For as many as are led by the Spirit of God, they are the sons of God. For ye have not received the spirit of bondage again to fear; but ye have received the Spirit of adoption, whereby we cry, Abba, Father"] in the margin.

[1005] Rev. 3:20: "Behold, I stand at the door, and knock: if any man hear my voice, and open the door, I will come in to him, and will sup with him, and he with me."

[1006] Phil. 3:10: "That I may know him, and the power of his resurrection, and the fellowship of his sufferings, being made conformable unto his death."

Our Adversaries' Unreasonableness

To conclude this chapter, we are not surprised that we are misunderstood, misconstrued, and misrepresented in what we believe and what we do to achieve salvation – better people than us were so treated in primitive times. Nor is it only our religious doctrines – our practices in worship and discipline have been mishandled in similar ways. This is what I sincerely desire, no matter how unfairly people treat us, that they not deceive themselves with respect to their own salvation. While they seem to credit Christ with everything, they risk being discredited by him on the last day. Read the seventh chapter of Matthew's Gospel: Everyone who hears Christ, the Word of God, and does what he commands, following his blessed example, is a wise builder. They have positioned their house well and built with good materials. When the last shock and judgment comes, that house will stand.[1007]

For this reason, we are often plain, direct, and serious with people: Christ did not come to save you in your sins, but from them! Do not believe that Christ has done it all for you – that you are released from his yoke and burden,[1008] or from his cross and example. If he has changed nothing within you and you have given up nothing for the love of him, you will awaken in dreadful surprise at the sound of the last trumpet, and hear this sad and irrevocable sentence: "Depart from me, you evildoers, I do not know you!"[1009]

All may yet avoid that terrible end by attending to Wisdom's voice, turning at her reproach, following her in the ways of righteousness and

---

[1007] Matt. 7:24-25: "Therefore whosoever heareth these sayings of mine, and doeth them, I will liken him unto a wise man, which built his house upon a rock: And the rain descended, and the floods came, and the winds blew, and beat upon that house; and it fell not: for it was founded upon a rock."

[1008] Matt. 11:29-30: "Take my yoke upon you, and learn of me; for I am meek and lowly in heart: and ye shall find rest unto your souls. For my yoke *is* easy, and my burden is light."

[1009] Matt. 7:23: "And then will I profess unto them, I never knew you: depart from me, ye that work iniquity."

along the paths of justice, so that your souls will inherit the substance, the riches and righteousness, of the kingdom of the Father.[1010]

Chapter 10

The True Worship of God

*A*s the Lord, by divine grace, worked in the hearts of God's people, he led them to a divine worship and ministry. They came to experience Christ's words, "God is a Spirit, and his worshipers must worship in Spirit and Truth – these are the kind of worshipers the Father seeks.[1011] They accept what the Spirit has revealed in them. By it, they were taught to give up that which is evil and to do that which is good[1012] in their daily lives. When they gather, they sit down and wait for the Holy Spirit, both to let them see their Spiritual states and conditions before God and to direct them in proper worship. As they became aware of their shortcomings and spiritual infirmities, in the secret of their hearts, prayer would spring to God through Jesus Christ for help, assistance, and sustenance. They dare not "awake their beloved too soon;"[1013] nor "approach the throne of the King of Glory until the scepter was extended to them;"[1014] nor "worry what they would say;"[1015] nor carefully choose

---

[1010] Prov. 1:20&23: "Wisdom crieth without; she uttereth her voice in the streets ... Turn you at my reproof: behold, I will pour out my spirit unto you, I will make known my words unto you"

Prov. 8:20-21: "I lead in the way of righteousness, in the midst of the paths of judgment: That I may cause those that love me to inherit substance; and I will fill their treasures."

[1011] John 4:23-24: "But the hour cometh, and now is, when the true worshippers shall worship the Father in spirit and in truth: for the Father seeketh such to worship him. God *is* a Spirit: and they that worship him must worship *him* in spirit and in truth."

[1012] 3 John 1:11: "Beloved, follow not that which is evil, but that which is good. He that doeth good is of God: but he that doeth evil hath not seen God."

[1013] Song of Sol. 8:4: "I charge you, O daughters of Jerusalem, that ye stir not up, nor awake *my* love, until he please."

[1014] Esther 4:11: "All the king's servants, and the people of the king's provinces, do know, that whosoever, whether man or woman, shall come unto the king into the inner court, who is not called, *there is* one law of his to put *him* to death, except such to whom the king shall hold out the golden sceptre, that he may live: but I have not been called to come in unto the king these thirty days."

words of their own; nor adopt another's careful forms and phrases. To pray in any way that was not as led by the Spirit would be offering God an unholy fire.[1016] It is like asking for something, but not in the name and power of our Lord Jesus Christ, who prayed and spoke as a person with authority[1017] – that is, with the power and strength to reach and pierce the heavens. This authority is granted to all that obey his Light, Grace, and Spirit in their solemn waiting on him. It is the Quakers' principle that fire must come from heaven.[1018] Life and power must come from above, if the soul is to acceptably pour itself out before God.

Only when a coal from God's Holy Altar touches our lips[1019] can we pray and praise as we ought to do. This principle, drawn from Scripture, is our experience and our practice. Blessed be God! Because of this principle, we have turned away from all human forms of worship. These are not based on the direction, instruction, and assistance of the Spirit of Christ, but on human times, designs, and forms. It is not our own wills or desires that lead us to worship as we do, but the will of the One who has called us and brought us into God's own spiritual worship. We are who we are out of obedience to God.

True Ministry by Inspiration

Just as our worship is based on the workings of the Spirit and of Truth within us, so too is our ministry. The Holy Testimonies of the servants of God have always been directed by the workings of his blessed Spirit, and so they must be today. Ministry that does not drink from the spring of the

---

[1015] Luke 12:11: "And when they bring you unto the synagogues, and *unto* magistrates, and powers, take ye no thought how or what thing ye shall answer, or what ye shall say."

[1016] Lev. 10:1: "And Nadab and Abihu, the sons of Aaron, took either of them his censer, and put fire therein, and put incense thereon, and offered strange fire before the LORD, which he commanded them not."

[1017] Matt. 7:29: "For he taught them as *one* having authority, and not as the scribes."

[1018] 1 Chron. 21:26: "And David built there an altar unto the LORD, and offered burnt offerings and peace offerings, and called upon the LORD; and he answered him from heaven by fire upon the altar of burnt offering."

[1019] Isa. 6:6-7: "Then flew one of the seraphims unto me, having a live coal in his hand, *which* he had taken with the tongs from off the altar: And he laid *it* upon my mouth, and said, Lo, this hath touched thy lips; and thine iniquity is taken away, and thy sin purged."

Spirit of Christ is merely from the speaker, not from Christ. Christian ministers are called to deliver what they receive – this is the teaching of Scripture – what we receive is not our own, much less another person's, but the Lord's. Not only do we not steal the thoughts of our neighbors, we do not study nor speak our own words. And, if we are not to study what we are to say on our own behalf before a judge,[1020] then we ought not to study what we are to say for and from God before other people. We are called to minister as the oracles of God.[1021] To do so, we must receive the words of ministry from Christ, God's great oracle. If we are to speak only what we receive, then we must put aside all that we study, collect, and create in our own minds, because that does not come from not the mind of Christ, but from our own imaginings, and will not benefit the people.

Plain Scriptural Support

In the fourteenth chapter of his first epistle to the Corinthians, the apostle Paul recommended that all speak and all may prophesy as they were moved or as anything was revealed to them by the Spirit for the edification of the church.[1022] That is, all may preach as anything is revealed to you and as the Spirit gives you the words, to instruct and benefit others. If the Spirit must give Christ's ministers their words, then those that belong to the Spirit must be careful not to say anything beyond what they have received. One good consequence of this is that those who go beyond their guide and speak without waiting for the words of the Spirit are easily seen as not being among Christ's ministers. They run where God has not sent them and cannot benefit the people. Indeed, how could they? It is impossible for ordinary people, no matter their learning or degrees or artful style, to "turn

---

[1020] Matt. 10:19: "But when they deliver you up, take no thought how or what ye shall speak: for it shall be given you in that same hour what ye shall speak."

[1021] 1 Pet. 4:11: "If any man speak, *let him speak* as the oracles of God; if any man minister, *let him do it* as of the ability which God giveth: that God in all things may be glorified through Jesus Christ, to whom be praise and dominion for ever and ever. Amen."

[1022] 1 Cor. 14:3, 6, 31: "But he that prophesieth speaketh unto men *to* edification, and exhortation, and comfort. ...Now, brethren, if I come unto you speaking with tongues, what shall I profit you, except I shall speak to you either by revelation, or by knowledge, or by prophesying, or by doctrine? ...For ye may all prophesy one by one, that all may learn, and all may be comforted."

people from darkness to Light and from the power of Satan to God."[1023]
That is the purpose of gospel ministry and only those who are inspired –
gifted by God, taught and directed by God's heavenly Spirit – can be
qualified for so great, so inward, and so spiritual a work.

Christ's Ministers are True Witnesses, Speaking What they Know Directly

The ministers of Christ are his witnesses, and witnesses are valuable for
their ability to report that they themselves have heard, seen, or touched.
Thus, the Beloved Disciple states the Truth and authority for their mission
and ministry in his first epistle: "That which we have heard, which we have
seen with our eyes, which we have looked at and our hands have touched –
this we proclaim to you, so that you also may have fellowship with us. And
our fellowship is with the Father and with his Son, Jesus Christ."[1024] If
Christ's ministers are his witnesses, then they must know for themselves
what they preach about. They must have fully experienced the spiritual
states and conditions they describe and know directly those truths they
declare – otherwise, they have not come in through the door, but over the
wall, and are thieves and robbers.[1025] Those with the key of David come in
through the door (Christ Jesus[1026]). Christ acknowledges and approves
them. They have been anointed by the high priest of the gospel
dispensation,[1027] who breathes on them, and lays his hands on them. He
anoints and strengthens them for their journey. He renews their horn with

---

[1023] Acts 26:18: "To open their eyes, *and* to turn *them* from darkness to light, and
from the power of Satan unto God, that they may receive forgiveness of sins,
and inheritance among them which are sanctified by faith that is in me."

[1024] 1 John 1:1&3: "That which was from the beginning, which we have heard,
which we have seen with our eyes, which we have looked upon, and our hands
have handled, of the Word of life ... That which we have seen and heard
declare we unto you, that ye also may have fellowship with us: and truly our
fellowship *is* with the Father, and with his Son Jesus Christ."

[1025] John 10:1-2: "Verily, verily, I say unto you, He that entereth not by the door
into the sheepfold, but climbeth up some other way, the same is a thief and a
robber. But he that entereth in by the door is the shepherd of the sheep."

[1026] John 10:7: "Then said Jesus unto them again, Verily, verily, I say unto you, I am
the door of the sheep."

[1027] Heb. 3:1: "Wherefore, holy brethren, partakers of the heavenly calling, consider
the Apostle and High Priest of our profession, Christ Jesus."

oil,[1028] so it is pure and fresh for every task and every occasion to which he calls them or places them in.

Free Ministry is the Mark of Christ's Ministers

Nor is this all – true ministers received without payment and give without payment.[1029] They do not teach for a salary, prophesy for money, nor preach for gifts and rewards. It was Christ's holy command to his ministers to give freely, and that is our practice. Truly, we cannot help but be amazed that our ministry has been reviled but that preaching for pay is not. Indeed, that is the mark of a false prophet and has been frequently and severely condemned by the true prophets of God.[1030] I do not wish to be uncharitable, but do the guilty remember who it was that offered money to be made a minister so that he could make a living at it? And what Peter's answer was?[1031]

We pray that the Lord will touch the hearts of those who pay to become ministers and who make a living as a preacher, so that they will see what ground they are building on. We pray they will repent and turn to the Lord, receiving God's mercy and becoming living witnesses to God's power and goodness in their souls. They may then be able to tell others what God has done for them – this is the root and ground of true ministry and this ministry, God will bless.

I could say much more on this subject, but what I have already said is sufficient for now. Except for this: I cannot help but notice that when a religion lures people with lucre to entice them to ministry, there is great

---

[1028] David and Solomon were anointed as Kings of Israel with a horn of oil (David in 1 Sam. 16:13 and Solomon in 1 Kings 1:39).

[1029] Matt. 10:8: "Heal the sick, cleanse the lepers, raise the dead, cast out devils: freely ye have received, freely give."

[1030] Mic. 3:11: "The heads thereof judge for reward, and the priests thereof teach for hire, and the prophets thereof divine for money: yet will they lean upon the LORD, and say, *Is* not the LORD among us? none evil can come upon us."

[1031] Penn has noted Acts 8:18-20 ["And when Simon saw that through laying on of the apostles' hands the Holy Ghost was given, he offered them money, Saying, Give me also this power, that on whomsoever I lay hands, he may receive the Holy Ghost. But Peter said unto him, Thy money perish with thee, because thou hast thought that the gift of God may be purchased with money"] in the margin.

danger that they will run faster to that calling than is good for a true gospel minister.

It may has been suggested that our form of ministry and worship might make some people careless and to promote spiritual pride in others. Might, our adversaries ask, this be the cause of great mischief and of false or perverted religion?

By no means! When people come of age, they have a right to receive their inheritance. Our purging of words is designed to bring people to the great Word. Then, the promise of God will be fulfilled: "All will be taught by the LORD, from the least to the greatest. In righteousness they will be established, and great will be their peace."[1032] To these words of the Evangelical Prophet, the Beloved Disciple (providing a full answer to this objection) adds: "I am writing to you about those who are trying to lead you astray. The anointing you received remains in you. You do not need anyone to teach you – this anointing teaches you all things. It is true and not a lie. Remain in Christ, as it has taught you."[1033]

There are three things to be noted in this passage. First, this epistle was written under extraordinary circumstances, in order to prevent the apostle's readers from being deluded. Second, he acknowledges a closer and superior minister than himself – the anointing or grace that they had received – not only for the immediate situation, but for all cases and all times. Third, if his readers only followed the instruction of it, they would have no need for any earthly directions. Nor should they fear that they could be led astray by any ministry that was not inspired by the power of that anointing (indeed, I believe the truest meaning of this message is that those who are faithful

---

[1032] Isa. 54:13-14: "And all thy children *shall be* taught of the LORD; and great *shall be* the peace of thy children. In righteousness shalt thou be established: thou shalt be far from oppression; for thou shalt not fear: and from terror; for it shall not come near thee."

Jer. 31:34: "And they shall teach no more every man his neighbour, and every man his brother, saying, Know the LORD: for they shall all know me, from the least of them unto the greatest of them, saith the LORD: for I will forgive their iniquity, and I will remember their sin no more."

[1033] 1 John 2:26-27: "These *things* have I written unto you concerning them that seduce you. But the anointing which ye have received of him abideth in you, and ye need not that any man teach you: but as the same anointing teacheth you of all things, and is truth, and is no lie, and even as it hath taught you, ye shall abide in him."

should have no fear). Look also to Paul's Epistle to the Thessalonians, "Concerning love among you, you do not need me write to you, for you yourselves have been taught by God to love one another."[1034] Even so, a little help is sometimes useful and can be a great blessing if it comes from God – such was John the Baptist's message when he pointed all to Christ, "Behold the Lamb of God![1035] I baptize you with water, but he will baptize you with the Holy Spirit and with fire."[1036] This is what true ministry does! When people are wrapped up in their day-to-day concerns and lost in the shadows cast by sin and Satan, God is pleased to send enlightening servants to awaken them and turn them from the darkness to the Light within themselves. Through obedience to that Light, they can become "children of the Light"[1037] and find fellowship with one another in it,[1038] and in the end, share the inheritance of the saints in the Light forever.[1039]

Since this is the way God has chosen to call and gather people, a living and holy ministry is of great advantage. It watches over and strengthens the young. It comforts and protects the weak and simple-minded. But still, the more inward that the ministry is, the more people will come to be taught directly by God – by the Light of God's Word and Spirit in their hearts – and the less need they will have for outward ministry. Read Isaiah 60:19-20,[1040] which all agree is a gospel promise. The references to sun and moon

---

[1034] 1 Thess. 4:9: "But as touching brotherly love ye need not that I write unto you: for ye yourselves are taught of God to love one another."

[1035] John 1:29: "The next day John seeth Jesus coming unto him, and saith, Behold the Lamb of God, which taketh away the sin of the world."

[1036] Matt. 3:11: "I indeed baptize you with water unto repentance: but he that cometh after me is mightier than I, whose shoes I am not worthy to bear: he shall baptize you with the Holy Ghost, and *with* fire."

[1037] Penn has noted John 12:36 ["While ye have light, believe in the light, that ye may be the children of light. These things spake Jesus, and departed, and did hide himself from them"] in the margin.

[1038] 1 John 1:7: "But if we walk in the light, as he is in the light, we have fellowship one with another, and the blood of Jesus Christ his Son cleanseth us from all sin."

[1039] Col. 1:12: "Giving thanks unto the Father, which hath made us meet to be partakers of the inheritance of the saints in light."

[1040] Isa. 60:19-20: "The sun shall be no more thy light by day; neither for brightness shall the moon give light unto thee: but the LORD shall be unto thee an everlasting light, and thy God thy glory. Thy sun shall no more go down;

are generally understood to mean the outward practices of the church. Compare this passage with John 1:13,[1041] Romans 1:19,[1042] 1 Corinthians 2:11, 15,[1043] 1 Thessalonians 4:9,[1044] 1 John 2:20, 27,[1045] and Revelation 21:22-24.[1046] All of these passages demonstrate the complete sufficiency and glorious advantages of inward and spiritual teachings that we assert. It is certain that as people grow in grace and come to feel the anointing of the Spirit within themselves, that the action of the Holy Spirit will be less as words (although it may be felt as words) and more as sharing directly in the Life and Power of the Holy Spirit. Then their preaching will change increasingly to praising and their worship will more and more be walking with, rather than talking of, God. That is worship in Truth – bowing to God's will at all times and in all places – the purest and truest worship that those in this world can offer. It is in conforming to God's will as it is revealed by the Light in our hearts that we achieve communion with God and each other. Without obedience to that will and faithfulness to God's Word, there is no fellowship with God; there is no Light from the face of God to be enjoyed; there is no peace or assurance of salvation.

---

neither shall thy moon withdraw itself: for the LORD shall be thine everlasting light, and the days of thy mourning shall be ended."

[1041] John 1:13: "Which were born, not of blood, nor of the will of the flesh, nor of the will of man, but of God."

[1042] Rom. 1:19: "Because that which may be known of God is manifest in them; for God hath shewed *it* unto them."

[1043] 2 Cor. 2:11&15: "Lest Satan should get an advantage of us: for we are not ignorant of his devices ... For we are unto God a sweet savour of Christ, in them that are saved, and in them that perish."

[1044] 1 Thess. 4:9: "But as touching brotherly love ye need not that I write unto you: for ye yourselves are taught of God to love one another."

[1045] 1 John 2:20&27: "But ye have an unction from the Holy One, and ye know all things ... But the anointing which ye have received of him abideth in you, and ye need not that any man teach you: but as the same anointing teacheth you of all things, and is truth, and is no lie, and even as it hath taught you, ye shall abide in him."

[1046] Rev. 21:22-24: "And I saw no temple therein: for the Lord God Almighty and the Lamb are the temple of it. And the city had no need of the sun, neither of the moon, to shine in it: for the glory of God did lighten it, and the Lamb *is* the light thereof. And the nations of them which are saved shall walk in the light of it: and the kings of the earth do bring their glory and honour into it."

I have called this the purest and truest state of worship. Contrast it with the customary days and places, and all the accompanying solemnity, that were the mark of the old covenant and dispensation. Altars, ark, and temples, Sabbaths and festivals, etc. are not to be found in the writings of the New Testament! As Paul wrote, every day is alike and every place the same – all must be dedicated to the Lord.[1047] He directed our attention to a state beyond this world, saying, "To live is Christ and to die is gain."[1048] The life he lived was "the faith of the Son of God and therefore, it was not Paul who lived, but Christ who lived in him"[1049] or who ruled, directed, and guided him. That is the true Christian life – a life that rises above the body and its senses, a life of conversion and regeneration – to which all God's dispensations and the ministries of all God's servants have pointed. This is the goal of God's work with humanity. Here, everyone is a temple and every family a church. Every place is a meeting-place and every visit an opportunity for worship. Wait just a little while and you will see it coming

---

[1047] Penn has noted the following in the margin:

Rom. 14:5-8, 17. ["One man esteemeth one day above another: another esteemeth every day *alike*. Let every man be fully persuaded in his own mind. He that regardeth the day, regardeth *it* unto the Lord; and he that regardeth not the day, to the Lord he doth not regard *it*. He that eateth, eateth to the Lord, for he giveth God thanks; and he that eateth not, to the Lord he eateth not, and giveth God thanks. For none of us liveth to himself, and no man dieth to himself. For whether we live, we live unto the Lord; and whether we die, we die unto the Lord: whether we live therefore, or die, we are the Lord's ... For the kingdom of God is not meat and drink; but righteousness, and peace, and joy in the Holy Ghost."]

1 Cor. 8:6. ["But to us *there is but* one God, the Father, of whom *are* all things, and we in him; and one Lord Jesus Christ, by whom *are* all things, and we by him."]

Col. 2:16-17. ["Let no man therefore judge you in meat, or in drink, or in respect of an holyday, or of the new moon, or of the sabbath *days*. Which are a shadow of things to come; but the body *is* of Christ."]

[1048] Penn has noted Phil. 1:21 ["For to me to live *is* Christ, and to die *is* gain"] in the margin.

[1049] Penn has noted Gal. 2:20 ["I am crucified with Christ: nevertheless I live; yet not I, but Christ liveth in me: and the life which I now live in the flesh I live by the faith of the Son of God, who loved me, and gave himself for me"] in the margin.

more and more. Even now, the Lord is preparing a people to enter into this Sabbath, this state of rest.

But, do not think that we undervalue public and solemn meetings – we hold them all over the nation, wherever the Lord has called us. Even if there are only two or three in a corner of a county, we meet as the apostle urged the saints of his time and condemned those who neglected to assemble themselves.[1050] What we are showing you, dear Reader, is simply a better way to worship. Many go to those public meetings and come away still governed by their human nature – spiritually dead and dry. But worshippers in Spirit and Truth, whose hearts bow to the will of God and whose minds adore the eternal God, are the true, acceptable, constant, and living worshippers – whether in meetings or out of them. They know God, who is a Spirit, in and by that Spirit. They conform to God's will and walk with God in a spiritual life. For them, all outward assemblies are a great comfort and so, we meet for public testimony of religion and worship, for the education and encouragement of those who are still young in the Truth, and to call and gather others (who are now going astray) to the knowledge of that Truth. Blessed be God! That work is not in vain – by it, many are added to the church that we hope and believe will be saved.[1051]

[1050] Heb. 10:25: "Not forsaking the assembling of ourselves together, as the manner of some *is*, but exhorting *one another*: and so much the more, as ye see the day approaching."

[1051] Acts 2:47: "Praising God, and having favour with all the people. And the Lord added to the church daily such as should be saved."

Chapter 11

Against Tithes

Since God has called us away from a human ministry, we cannot in good conscience do anything to support and sustain such a ministry. For that reason, and not because we are greedy or grasping, we refuse to pay tithes or any similar so-called obligations. Many books have been written about this matter in our defense. We simply cannot support what we cannot approve and testify against. If we did so, we would contradict ourselves.

Against All Swearing

We do not dare to swear because God forbids it in Matthew 5: 34, 37, "I tell you: Do not swear at all ... but let your 'Yes' be 'Yes,' and your 'No,' 'No'."[1052] and James, a true disciple, affirms, "Above all, my beloved, do not swear, either by heaven or by earth or by any other oath, but let your 'Yes' be 'Yes' and your 'No' be 'No'."[1053] To swear is not only unnecessary, but evil. The reason for requiring swearing oaths is lying – for some, 'Yes' was not 'Yes.' It was thought that swearing would frighten liars into telling the truth and assure others that what they heard under oath was true. But for the true Christian, 'Yes' is 'Yes', and there is no need for an oath to ensure it. Such use, therefore, is unnecessary, superfluous, and comes only from evil. This is what James taught, what the primitive Christians practiced, and, as can be seen in the *Book of Martyrs*,[1054] what the earliest and best of the Protestant reformers followed.

[1052] Matt. 5:34&37: "But I say unto you, Swear not at all; neither by heaven; for it is God's throne ... But let your communication be, Yea, yea; Nay, nay: for whatsoever is more than these cometh of evil."

[1053] James 5:12: "But above all things, my brethren, swear not, neither by heaven, neither by the earth, neither by any other oath: but let your yea be yea; and *your* nay, nay; lest ye fall into condemnation."

[1054] John Foxe (1516-1587) compiled *The Book of Martyrs*, the full title of which is *A History of the Lives, Sufferings and Triumphant Deaths of the Early Christian and the Protestant Martyrs*. It was first published in 1554, but updated in many subsequent editions. Of particular importance to Penn and his readers is the extensive description in the book of the persecution of English Protestants under Queen Mary (1553-58).

Against All War among Christians

We also believe that war ought to cease among the followers of the Lamb, Christ Jesus, who taught his disciples to forgive and love their enemies, not to fight against and kill them. The weapons of Christ's true followers are not physical, but spiritual, made mighty by God to destroy sin and wickedness and to overthrow the author of sin.[1055] Not only is this the most Christian way, it is also the most rational – love and persuasion have more force than the weapons of war. Even the worst of humanity cannot easily bring themselves to harm those that they really think love them. In the end, love and patience must have the victory.

Against the Greetings of the Times

We dare not offer worldly honor or use the frequent and fashionable greetings of these times. We see plainly that these are signs of vanity, pride, and pretentiousness. Christ also forbade them in his day[1056] and called the love of them a sign of decline from the simplicity of purer times.[1057] His disciples and their followers were observed to obey their Master's decree. We do not do this to set ourselves apart from others or out of pride, poor manners, or spite, but in obedience to the sight and sense we have received from the Spirit of Christ of the evil in it.

For Plainness in Speech

For the same reason, we have returned to the original plainness in our speech, that is, in using 'thou' and 'thee' when referring to a single person. Although people will say nothing else when speaking to God, they can hardly endure it when they hear it from us. It has been a great trial to their pride and has shown the deceit and weakness of many. Whatever people may think or say about us, we do this purely for conscience sake. We may be despised, and certainly have been badly treated for it, but because of it we are now better known and others are better informed about us. In short,

---

[1055] 2 Cor. 10:3-4: "For though we walk in the flesh, we do not war after the flesh: (For the weapons of our warfare *are* not carnal, but mighty through God to the pulling down of strong holds)."

[1056] Luke 10:4: "Carry neither purse, nor scrip, nor shoes: and salute no man by the way."

[1057] Mark 12:38: "And he said unto them in his doctrine, Beware of the scribes, which love to go in long clothing, and *love* salutations in the marketplaces."

both Scripture and grammar direct us to this practice, and we are at peace with ourselves in obeying.

Against Mixed Marriages

We cannot allow mixed marriage, which is to join with any who are not of our society. We oppose and disown any of our members who reject this rule and enter into such a marriage. They can be restored to membership if they sincerely repent – we do not ask them to divorce. This topic is covered more completely and directly in my book, *The Rise and Progress of the People Called Quakers.*

For Plainness in Apparel and Simplicity in Our Lives

Plainness in dress and furniture is another testimony in which, to the degree we practice it, we are alone. We use few words when we speak, but stand by each one. Likewise, we are temperate in our food and abstain from the recreations and pastimes of the world. This, the Spirit of our Lord Jesus Christ has taught us, is required of those who wish to be godly. "Let everyone know your moderation, for the Lord is near"[1058] – God is near to see and to judge every overindulgence or excess. We hope that we have not been a bad example or caused any scandal.

On Observing Days

We cannot in conscience observe the so-called holy days, public fasts or feasts. These were invented and instituted by humanity, not by God; they are the product of a human will, not of a divine command.

On the Care of the Poor, Peace, and Behavior

Lastly, we have been led by this good Spirit of our Lord Jesus Christ (which is the subject of this discourse) to care for one another according to the practices of the primitive Christians. We do this for the preservation of the whole society, calling all to behavior that is consistent with their professed Christianity.

First, with respect to our behavior toward both those within and those outside our society, we are called to act blamelessly. We, likewise, call on others to be careful in their dealings with the world and faithful in their dealings with the church.

[1058] Phil. 4:5: "Let your moderation be known unto all men. The Lord *is* at hand."

Second, we require that collections be made to meet the needs of the poor, so that widows, orphans, and the helpless are cared for. We see to it that advice and counsel is offered as well as material things.

Third, all within our religious society who intend to marry are required first to declare their intentions to, and seek the approval of, their parents or guardians – even before one proposes to the other – and only then to bring their request to their meeting. The meeting is careful to examine whether they are free to marry and, if so, allows them to solemnize their marriage in a public meeting that is called for that purpose. By this procedure, we prevent all secret or fraudulent marriages among us.

Fourth, and with the aim of maintaining good order, comforting and instructing all within the society, and keeping us in the ways of truth, meetings of our members are called to provide care and conduct business. These are held monthly in each district, quarterly within each region, and yearly for the whole nation. These are held to ensure accurate communications with each other on those things that sustain us in piety and charity.

By God's grace, we have been called to be a people, giving praise through God's beloved Son, our ever-blessed and only Redeemer, Jesus Christ, now and forever. Amen.

Thus, Reader, you can see the character of the people called Quakers in their doctrine, worship, ministry, practice, and discipline. Compare what you have read with Scripture and the example of the primitive church, and we hope that you will find that this short discourse has lived up to its title: *Primitive Christianity Revived, in the Faith and Practice of the People Called Quakers.*

A BRIEF

ACCOUNT

OF THE

Rise and Progress

Of the People called

Q U A K E R S.

In Which their *Fundamental* Principle, Doctrines, Worship, Ministry and Discipline are Plainly Declared to prevent the Mistakes and Perversions that Ignorance and Prejudice may make to abuse the Credulous.

With a Summary Relation of the former Dispensations of God in the World, by way of *Introduction*.

An unknown, and yet well known, 2 Corinthians *6:9*

By *W. Penn*

London, Printed and Sold by *T. Sowle*,
near the *Meeting-house* in *White-Hare-Court*
in *Grace-Church-Street*, and at the *Crooked-Billet*
in *Holy-well-Lane* near *Shore-ditch, 1694.*

To The Reader

This account of the people called Quakers was written, in the love of God, for several reasons. First, it is a lasting testimony to that ever blessed, inward Truth which God, in my youth, placed within my soul. My understanding and love of that Truth made me extraordinarily willing to give up all my worldly honors and interests. Second, it is a testimony on behalf of that despised people whom a merciful God has gathered and united by the Holy Spirit so that they might take up the cause of Truth. I value that fellowship more than any worldly distinction. Third, it is written in love and honor of the memory of that worthy servant of God, George Fox – God's instrument in this work and, I believe, the greatest and most blessed apostle of our day.

What is presented here was originally prepared as a Preface to the first edition of George Fox's excellent *Journal*.[1059] In light of a number of unjust allegations, recently published by former members of our society, I have consented to have it republished in this small volume. I know very well that, especially these days, large books are burdensome, both on the pocket and on the minds of many readers, but I know equally well that there are many who want an easy way to learn about this often denounced people. But, blessed be God the Father of our Lord Jesus Christ, every thoughtful and sincere Reader will see that the attacks have been no worse than those that were directed against the primitive Christians in ancient times.

Our great concern, despite all the abuse we have endured, is religious Truth. We hope in our lifetimes to achieve real change in the world, so that through the work of the Light and Spirit of Christ, everyone may come to experience an inward, direct, and clear knowledge of God – a sufficient and blessed means given to all. We hope that by this, all may, to their everlasting benefit, come to know the only true God and to know Jesus Christ, whom God sent to enlighten and redeem the world. Without a doubt, that

---

[1059] As originally published in George Fox's *Journal*, this work was titled, 'The Preface; Being A Summary Account of the Divers Dispensations of God to Men, From the Beginning of the World to That of out Present Age, by the Ministry and Testimony of his Faithful Servant, George Fox, As an Introduction to the Ensuing Journal.'

knowledge is life eternal.[1060] Reader, this is the earnest desire of the author for you.

I am yours in this good work,

William Penn.

Chapter 1

A Brief Account of the Dispensations of God in the World up to the Time When God Raised Up this Despised People Called Quakers

Since the creation of the world, God has used a variety of means to communicate with humanity, but the purpose of each of these dispensations has been to glorify his own blessed name and to bring about reconciliation with mankind. In the beginning, humanity, made in God's image and likeness, was like a god on earth and the greatest of all created things. The world was created innocent – everything in it was good that the good God had made.[1061] And, as God blessed the works of his hands, by their very existence and by the harmony in which they lived together, all things praised their Creator. The morning stars sang together for joy[1062] and all creation said 'Amen!' to God's law. There were no quarrels, no disputes, no conflicts. All – humanity in paradise, the beasts in the fields, the birds in the air, the fishes in the sea, the lights in the heavens, the fruits of the earth, even the air, earth, water, and fire – worshipped, praised, and exalted God's power, wisdom, and goodness, crying: 'O, Holy Sabbath! O, Holy Day of the Lord.'

But this happy state did not last long, because humanity – the crown and glory of the whole – was tempted to become like gods.[1063] Unhappily, they gave in to that temptation – against the command of God and their duty to God, and against their own happiness and best interests – and in so

---

[1060] John 17:3: "And this is life eternal, that they might know thee the only true God, and Jesus Christ, whom thou hast sent."

[1061] Gen. 1:31: "And God saw every thing that he had made, and, behold, *it was* very good. And the evening and the morning were the sixth day."

[1062] Job 38:7: "When the morning stars sang together, and all the sons of God shouted for joy?"

[1063] Gen. 3:5: "For God doth know that in the day ye eat thereof, then your eyes shall be opened, and ye shall be as gods, knowing good and evil."

doing, they fell from the position they had held. They lost the divine image – the wisdom, power, and purity in which they were made. No longer being fit for paradise, they were expelled from God's garden, their proper home and residence. They became vagabonds, driven out of paradise, deprived of God's presence, and left to wander in the habitat of the beasts.

And yet even then, the God who had made them had pity on them. God saw that they had been deceived – they had not sinned out of malice or arrogance, but the cunning serpent (who had already fallen from his own original state) had beguiled the woman and, through her, the man. Out of infinite goodness and wisdom, God provided humanity with a way to repair the breach, to recover what was lost, and to restore fallen humanity. A nobler and more perfect Adam[1064] was born of a woman – so that just as the evil one had used a woman to cause their fall, Christ would come into the world through a woman to prevail over the evil one – bruising his head[1065] and releasing all from his power. In the fullness of time[1066] and in the most remarkable ways, all this was personally and fully accomplished in and by the Son of God, our Savior and Redeemer.

But the Son's power was not limited to the time when he lived on the earth. Both before and since, he has been the Light and Life,[1067] the Rock and Strength,[1068] of all who loved God. He has been with them in their temptations, walked beside them through trials and afflictions, supported them in their difficulties, and accompanied them in their earthly pilgrimage. By this power, Abel's heart exceeded Cain's, and Seth inherited his

---

[1064] 1 Cor. 15:22&45: "For as in Adam all die, even so in Christ shall all be made alive. … And so it is written, The first man Adam was made a living soul; the last Adam *was made* a quickening spirit."

[1065] Gen. 3:15: "And I will put enmity between thee and the woman, and between thy seed and her seed; it shall bruise thy head, and thou shalt bruise his heel."

[1066] Gal. 4:4-5: "But when the fulness of the time was come, God sent forth his Son, made of a woman, made under the law, To redeem them that were under the law, that we might receive the adoption of sons."

[1067] Ps. 27:1: "The LORD *is* my light and my salvation; whom shall I fear? the LORD *is* the strength of my life; of whom shall I be afraid?"

[1068] Ps. 18:2: "The LORD *is* my rock, and my fortress, and my deliverer; my God, my strength, in whom I will trust; my buckler, and the horn of my salvation, *and* my high tower."

birthright.[1069] By it, Enoch walked with God.[1070] It struggled with the old world against which mankind rebelled – blessing and guiding Noah to salvation.[1071]

But the outward dispensation to the Patriarchs that followed the fall of mankind was generally through angels – the scriptures report angels appearing to Abraham,[1072] Jacob,[1073] and others of that age. The next dispensation was that of the Law of Moses, which the apostle tells us was also delivered by angels.[1074] This was very much outward in its form and therefore well suited to humanity's degenerated condition. Paul calls it a schoolmaster who directs and prepares people to look for, and long for, the Messiah,[1075] who would deliver all from dependence on that ceremonial and imperfect dispensation by revealing that the Truth underlying all the mysterious signs and outward acts was within each person.

[1069] Seth is the third son of Adam and Eve and is given Cain's rights as the first-born when Cain kills Abel.

[1070] Enoch was believed to have been so righteous that he was taken up into heaven without dying. This belief is based on Genesis 5:24 ("And Enoch walked with God: and he *was* not; for God took him") and Hebrews 11:5 ("By faith Enoch was translated that he should not see death; and was not found, because God had translated him: for before his translation he had this testimony, that he pleased God").

[1071] 2 Pet. 2:5: "And spared not the old world, but saved Noah the eighth *person*, a preacher of righteousness, bringing in the flood upon the world of the ungodly."

[1072] For example, Gen. 22:11: "And the angel of the LORD called unto him out of heaven, and said, Abraham, Abraham: and he said, Here *am* I."

[1073] For example, Gen. 32:1 "And Jacob went on his way, and the angels of God met him."

[1074] Acts 7:35: "This Moses whom they refused, saying, Who made thee a ruler and a judge? the same did God send *to be* a ruler and a deliverer by the hand of the angel which appeared to him in the bush."

[1075] Gal. 3:24-25: "Wherefore the law was our schoolmaster *to bring us* unto Christ, that we might be justified by faith. But after that faith is come, we are no longer under a schoolmaster."

At that time, the Law was written on stone;[1076] the temple was built by hands;[1077] and external rituals and ceremonies were performed by an outward priesthood.[1078] These were only the shadows of the good things that were to come,[1079] and were only to be used until the Seed came, that is until the full and universal revelations of Christ. The promise was made to Christ[1080] – in whom all the promises of God are answered 'Yes!' and 'Amen!'[1081] – and to all people through him,[1082] even the promises of life from death,[1083] immortality, and eternal life.[1084]

The prophets up to John the Baptist foresaw this and comforted the believing Jews with the certainty that it would come. John, the forerunner of the Messiah, was the final prophet of the Dispensation of Moses, finishing its revelation. Then God, who had spoken many times and in various ways to our ancestors through the prophets, spoke to all through

---

[1076] 2 Cor. 3:3: "*Forasmuch as ye are* manifestly declared to be the epistle of Christ ministered by us, written not with ink, but with the Spirit of the living God; not in tables of stone, but in fleshy tables of the heart."

[1077] Mark 14:58: "We heard him say, I will destroy this temple that is made with hands, and within three days I will build another made without hands."

[1078] Heb. 9:1&6: "Then verily the first *covenant* had also ordinances of divine service, and a worldly sanctuary ... Now when these things were thus ordained, the priests went always into the first tabernacle, accomplishing the service *of God.*"

[1079] Heb. 10:1: "For the law having a shadow of good things to come, *and* not the very image of the things, can never with those sacrifices which they offered year by year continually make the comers thereunto perfect."

[1080] Gal. 3:16&19: "Now to Abraham and his seed were the promises made. He saith not, And to seeds, as of many; but as of one, And to thy seed, which is Christ... Wherefore then *serveth* the law? It was added because of transgressions, till the seed should come to whom the promise was made; *and it was* ordained by angels in the hand of a mediator."

[1081] 2 Cor. 1:20: "For all the promises of God in him *are* yea, and in him Amen, unto the glory of God by us."

[1082] Gal. 3:26: "For ye are all the children of God by faith in Christ Jesus."

[1083] John 5:24: "Verily, verily, I say unto you, He that heareth my word, and believeth on him that sent me, hath everlasting life, and shall not come into condemnation; but is passed from death unto life."

[1084] Rom. 2:7: "To them who by patient continuance in well doing seek for glory and honour and immortality, eternal life."

his Son, Christ Jesus, who is the heir of all things.[1085] This is the gospel dispensation, bringing a new testament and surer hope of salvation. This marked the beginning of God's rule on earth and the reconciliation of all creation with God, even the restoration of the kingdom to Israel.[1086]

The Spirit, which had communicated only sparingly in the earlier dispensations, began to be poured out on all people as had been promised by the prophet Joel.[1087] The Light that shined in darkness[1088] (or had shined dimly), now blazed brightly out of darkness, and the morning star began to arise in the hearts of believers,[1089] showing them the knowledge of the glory of God shining in the face of Christ Jesus.[1090]

Now, the Lord thought especially about the poor in spirit, the meek, those who truly mourn, those who hunger and thirst for righteousness, the peacemakers, the pure in heart, the merciful, and the persecuted.[1091] These

---

[1085] Heb. 1:1-2: "God, who at sundry times and in divers manners spake in time past unto the fathers by the prophets, Hath in these last days spoken unto us by *his* Son, whom he hath appointed heir of all things, by whom also he made the worlds."

[1086] Acts 1:6: "When they therefore were come together, they asked of him, saying, Lord, wilt thou at this time restore again the kingdom to Israel?"

[1087] The prophesy of Joel, in Joel 2:28 ("And it shall come to pass afterward, *that* I will pour out my spirit upon all flesh; and your sons and your daughters shall prophesy, your old men shall dream dreams, your young men shall see visions"), was fulfilled on Pentecost (Acts 2:17).

[1088] John 1:5: "And the light shineth in darkness; and the darkness comprehended it not."

[1089] 2 Pet. 1:19: "We have also a more sure word of prophecy; whereunto ye do well that ye take heed, as unto a light that shineth in a dark place, until the day dawn, and the day star arise in your hearts."

[1090] 2 Cor. 4:6: "For God, who commanded the light to shine out of darkness, hath shined in our hearts, to *give* the light of the knowledge of the glory of God in the face of Jesus Christ."

[1091] Matt. 5:1-10: "And seeing the multitudes, he went up into a mountain: and when he was set, his disciples came unto him: And he opened his mouth, and taught them, saying, Blessed *are* the poor in spirit: for theirs is the kingdom of heaven. Blessed *are* they that mourn: for they shall be comforted. Blessed *are* the meek: for they shall inherit the earth. Blessed *are* they which do hunger and thirst after righteousness: for they shall be filled. Blessed *are* the merciful: for they shall obtain mercy. Blessed *are* the pure in heart: for they shall see God. Blessed *are* the peacemakers: for they shall be called the children of God.

were sought out and blessed by Israel's true shepherd. Old Jerusalem and her children fell out of favor, while the New Jerusalem, the mother of the gospel-children,[1092] was in demand. God is not worshipped better in old Jerusalem or on the mountain of Samaria than in other places, for, behold, God's own Son has declared and preached that God is a Spirit who can only be known and truly worshipped in the Spirit and in the Truth![1093] God has now come nearer to us than in the old times, and will write the law in our hearts[1094] and, as promised, put Love and the Holy Spirit within us.[1095] Then, with the dawning of the new day, the failure of all the old signs and types and shadows to clean the inside of the cup[1096] – that is, to cleanse the conscience – was revealed. All the old services were made void in and by him who is the fulfillment of all.

The apostles, whom he had chosen and anointed by his Spirit, testified that this was the great and blessed purpose of the gospel dispensation – to turn the Jews from their prejudice and superstition, and the Gentiles from their vanity and idolatry, to Christ's Light and Spirit shining within them. Then all could live again, free from their deadly sins and trespasses,[1097] to

---

Blessed *are* they which are persecuted for righteousness' sake: for theirs is the kingdom of heaven."

[1092] Gal. 4:26: "But Jerusalem which is above is free, which is the mother of us all."

[1093] John 4:21&23-24: "Jesus saith unto her, Woman, believe me, the hour cometh, when ye shall neither in this mountain, nor yet at Jerusalem, worship the Father ... But the hour cometh, and now is, when the true worshippers shall worship the Father in spirit and in truth: for the Father seeketh such to worship him. God *is* a Spirit: and they that worship him must worship *him* in spirit and in truth."

[1094] Jer. 31:33: "But this *shall be* the covenant that I will make with the house of Israel; After those days, saith the LORD, I will put my law in their inward parts, and write it in their hearts; and will be their God, and they shall be my people."

[1095] Eze. 36:27: "And I will put my spirit within you, and cause you to walk in my statutes, and ye shall keep my judgments, and do *them*."

[1096] Luke 11:39: "And the Lord said unto him, Now do ye Pharisees make clean the outside of the cup and the platter; but your inward part is full of ravening and wickedness."

[1097] Ephesians 2:1: "And you *hath he quickened*, who were dead in trespasses and sins."

serve the living God[1098] in a new life of the Spirit,[1099] and to walk in the Day of Holiness as Children of the Light and of the Day.[1100] They have clothed themselves with Christ,[1101] the Light of the World, and no longer worry about how they will satisfy their bodily desires.[1102] The apostles ministered from, and turned people's minds to, the Light, Spirit, and Grace that come through Christ and are found within each person. By that divine principle they gathered and built up Christ's churches in their day.

They pleaded with the people not to quench the Spirit,[1103] but to wait for the Spirit,[1104] speak by the Spirit,[1105] pray by the Spirit,[1106] and walk in the Spirit[1107] – to do God's will and not their own; to drink of Christ's cup and be baptized with Christ's baptism of self-denial.[1108] This would prove them to be the truly begotten children of God, born not by flesh or blood,

---

[1098] 1 Thess. 1:9: "For they themselves shew of us what manner of entering in we had unto you, and how ye turned to God from idols to serve the living and true God."

[1099] Rom. 6:4: "Therefore we are buried with him by baptism into death: that like as Christ was raised up from the dead by the glory of the Father, even so we also should walk in newness of life."

[1100] 1 Thess. 5:5: "Ye are all the children of light, and the children of the day: we are not of the night, nor of darkness."

[1101] Gal. 3:27: "For as many of you as have been baptized into Christ have put on Christ."

[1102] Rom. 13:14: "But put ye on the Lord Jesus Christ, and make not provision for the flesh, to *fulfill* the lusts *thereof*."

[1103] 1 Thess. 5:19: "Quench not the Spirit."

[1104] Gal. 5:5: "For we through the Spirit wait for the hope of righteousness by faith."

[1105] 1 Cor. 12:8: "For to one is given by the Spirit the word of wisdom; to another the word of knowledge by the same Spirit."

[1106] 1 Cor. 14:15: "What is it then? I will pray with the spirit, and I will pray with the understanding also: I will sing with the spirit, and I will sing with the understanding also."

[1107] Gal. 5:25: "If we live in the Spirit, let us also walk in the Spirit."

[1108] Matt. 20:23: "And he saith unto them, Ye shall drink indeed of my cup, and be baptized with the baptism that I am baptized with: but to sit on my right hand, and on my left, is not mine to give, but *it shall be given to them* for whom it is prepared of my Father."

or by the choice of their parents, but of God.[1109] This is the way and the path to blessedness that all the heirs of life have walked.

But alas! Even in the days of the apostles, those bright stars of the first magnitude of gospel light, clouds began to gather, forecasting an eclipse of this primitive glory. Early on, they cautioned that some were falling away from the power of Godliness and the purity of that spiritual dispensation and that more and more would follow – seeking to worship in outward and seemingly faithful ways, but turning their backs on the true meaning of Christ's death on the cross.[1110]

But the apostles saw beyond this state to a time of even greater glory for the true church. Their vision of the future was true, and what they foretold to the churches gathered by the power of and in the name of Jesus came to be. The practices of Christianity degenerated into outward observances: special days and foods and various other ceremonies.[1111] Worse, they fell into fighting among themselves, splitting into warring camps, growing jealous of each other, and whenever they were able, persecuting one another. They brought shame and scandal on Christianity. They were offensive to the heathens from whom God had so long protected them and this behavior was a stumbling block to their conversion. When kings and emperors adopted Christianity, these churches took worldly power into their hands, declaring the Kingdom of Christ (which is not of this world[1112]) to be an earthly dominion – or rather, that the kingdoms of this world that were in their hands to be the kingdom of Christ. They became worldly and no longer true Christians.

[1109] John 1:12-13: "But as many as received him, to them gave he power to become the sons of God, *even* to them that believe on his name Which were born, not of blood, nor of the will of the flesh, nor of the will of man, but of God."

[1110] Penn uses the words 'the offense of the cross ceased' which is taken from Gal. 5:11 ["And I, brethren, if I yet preach circumcision, why do I yet suffer persecution? then is the offence of the cross ceased"]. In this text, a physical act is paired with the image of the cross as a stumblingblock to belief.

[1111] Heb. 9:10: "*Which stood* only in meats and drinks, and divers washings, and carnal ordinances, imposed *on them* until the time of reformation."

[1112] John 18:36: "Jesus answered, My kingdom is not of this world: if my kingdom were of this world, then would my servants fight, that I should not be delivered to the Jews: but now is my kingdom not from hence."

These so-called Christians had long ago abandoned the guidance of God's meek and heavenly Spirit. A door had been opened by their coarse and degenerate behavior, and human inventions and novelties, both in doctrine and in worship, swarmed rapidly through it into that church. They embraced superstition; they followed the guidance of their own minds; they put their faith in the good works they chose to do. Their superstition was as self-righteous and dangerous as it is blind. All were required to bow to its boundless fanaticism or suffer the consequences.

Any evidence of the gifts of the Spirit was persecuted in the name of the Spirit – they suppressed in others what they had rejected in themselves: the Light, Grace, and Spirit of the Lord Jesus Christ. And these persecutions were always justified as opposition to innovation, heresy, schism, or some other plausible enemy. True Christianity allows no religious persecution – no matter what name or pretense is given to it. It is by its very nature meek, gentle, and forbearing, consisting of faith, hope, and charity, and no persecutor can have these while persecuting others – no one can believe the Truth, or trust in it, or have a charitable and tender regard for others while at the same time violating their minds or their bodies over questions of faith or the worship of God.

Thus, the false church sprang up and claimed the chair.[1113] But though it had lost its way, it always claimed to be the bride of the Lamb,[1114] the true church and mother of the faithful. It required all to accept its mark, either on the forehead or on the right hand,[1115] which is to say either publicly or privately. In fact and in truth, this was mystery Babylon, the mother of harlots, [1116] mother of those who, despite their outward displays of religion, were corrupt and turned away from the Spirit, Nature, and Life of Christ.

[1113] The chair of Peter is a symbol of the authority of the papacy to speak for God on matters of faith and morals.

[1114] Rev. 21:9: "And there came unto me one of the seven angels which had the seven vials full of the seven last plagues, and talked with me, saying, Come hither, I will shew thee the bride, the Lamb's wife."

[1115] Rev. 14:9: "And the third angel followed them, saying with a loud voice, If any man worship the beast and his image, and receive *his* mark in his forehead, or in his hand."

[1116] Rev. 17:5: "And upon her forehead *was* a name written, MYSTERY, BABYLON THE GREAT, THE MOTHER OF HARLOTS AND ABOMINATIONS OF THE EARTH."

They had grown vain, worldly, ambitious, covetous, cruel, etc. – these are fruits of the flesh, not of the Spirit.

The true church fled into the wilderness,[1117] away from superstition and violence, to a remote, secluded, and lonely place. It was hidden and out of human sight, but still in this world, which proves that visibility is not a necessary attribute of the true church in the eyes of the Holy Spirit. It was as true a church in the wilderness, although not as splendid or as visible as in its early, magnificent state. Many times, it attempted to return, but the waters were yet too high,[1118] and the way was blocked. Many beloved children, in many centuries and many nations, fell victim to the cruelty of superstition because they would not fall from faithfulness to the Truth.

The Reformation took some steps forward, in doctrine, worship, and practice, but these quickly failed as wickedness soon flowed over the reformers just as it had flowed over those they reformed from, so that, by their fruits, you could not tell one from the other.[1119] Very early, the children of the reformers (if not the reformers themselves) gave up the spiritual weapons with which the work was begun and took for themselves earthly power in order to carry out and sustain their Reformation. This, I have often thought, was one of the greatest reasons that the Reformation made so little real progress in changing the life and soul of religion.

So long as the reformers were humble and spiritually-minded – trusting in, looking to, and living in the love of God – they had no need of earthly counsel. And day by day, the Lord added to their number those who were being saved.[1120] They did not avoid persecution, but responded to it with innocence and faithfulness, being more concerned to spread the Truth by their faith and patience than to wrest worldly power from the hands of their

---

[1117] This is a reference to Rev. 12:6 ("And the woman fled into the wilderness, where she hath a place prepared of God, that they should feed her there a thousand two hundred *and* threescore days.") This was understood to prophesy the 1000 years of apostasy of the Roman Church during which the true church was in hiding.

[1118] Rev. 12:15: "And the serpent cast out of his mouth water as a flood after the woman, that he might cause her to be carried away of the flood."

[1119] Matt. 7:20: "Wherefore by their fruits ye shall know them."

[1120] Acts 2:47: "Praising God, and having favour with all the people. And the Lord added to the church daily such as should be saved."

persecutors. And it will be good if God will keep them and protect them from falling themselves into persecution.

In reforming doctrine, they stopped short of the goal. In other things, they avoided one extreme by running to the opposite extreme. In their worship, there was more of human invention than of God's. They acknowledged the inspiration and revelations of the Spirit. They based their separation from Rome and their reformation of the church on their sense and understanding of the scriptures of Truth. This was their claim: that the Scripture was the text, the Spirit was the interpreter, and that all could understand them by the Spirit. But both praying and preaching still depended too much on human interpretation, tradition, and cleverness. Too much worldly authority and worldly greatness was ascribed to their ministers – especially in England, Sweden, Denmark, and parts of Germany. God was therefore pleased to pour us from vessel to vessel,[1121] humbling the ministers, so that they were more careful in preaching, more devout in praying, more zealous in keeping the Lord's Day and in teaching God's Truth to the children and servants, and in repeating to their families at home what they had heard in public.

As the ministers grew in power, they not only whipped some out of the temple,[1122] but others were whipped into it.[1123] They appeared to be more dogmatic than faithful, more political than pious, and that gave birth to another people that was more separated from the world and more restrictive in their membership.[1124] These people did not invite all into their

---

[1121] The reference is to Jer. 48:11 ("Moab hath been at ease from his youth, and he hath settled on his lees, and hath not been emptied from vessel to vessel, neither hath he gone into captivity: therefore his taste remained in him, and his scent is not changed.") Penn seems to be referring to the succession of changes from Catholic to Protestant to Catholic and back to Protestant that were imposed on the church in England by King Henry VIII, Queen Mary, and Queen Elizabeth I.

[1122] John 2:14-16: "And found in the temple those that sold oxen and sheep and doves, and the changers of money sitting: And when he had made a scourge of small cords, he drove them all out of the temple, and the sheep, and the oxen; and poured out the changers' money, and overthrew the tables; And said unto them that sold doves, Take these things hence; make not my Father's house an house of merchandise."

[1123] Attendance at government-authorized church services was required by law.

[1124] In the sixteenth century, the Puritan movement arose within the English Church. While some Puritans (called 'conforming') continued to consider

communion or join in the worship services of others, but formed churches among themselves, including only those who could attest to being saved or at least to having hope for salvation from the work of God's grace on their hearts. They joined together by mutual agreement in Covenants of Fellowship. In contrast to their predecessors, who tried to frighten people into religion, these people were somewhat gentler – celebrating the love, mercy, and goodness of religion, rather than threatening other with its judgments and punishments.

They also allowed their members greater liberty to prophesy. If called by God, persons of any trade, even menial laborers, had the right to speak or pray, in addition to the pastor that they (not the civil authorities) had chosen. But, alas! This people, too, had their downfall. Getting a taste of worldly empire and the favor of princes,[1125] and the riches that followed, they too degenerated. Although they had denounced the establishment of national churches and ministry, and the enforced tithes to support them, when they achieved power, some fell under the weight of worldly honors and advantages. They took profitable parsonages for themselves – outliving and contradicting their own principles. Worse, some who had been persecuted turned to the persecution of others for God's sake. Among them were some who feared that they had not been 'scripturally baptized' and, hoping and desiring to find the presence and power of God in that watery ordinance, submitted to another Baptism.[1126]

These people also made it a practice to deny (or even to renounce and condemn) the need for and the use of human learning in ministry. They considered the support and gifts of the Holy Spirit, poured out on all, to be the only qualifications needed. For a time, they seemed to be, like John the Baptist, a burning and shining Light to the world.[1127]

---

themselves part of that church, others ('non-conforming Puritans'), withdrew from participation in the established church and its services in order to worship only among those they considered to be believers.

[1125] Penn may be referring to the American colonies founded by religious dissenters and the political dominance held by Dissenters during the Commonwealth.

[1126] Anabaptists rejected the validity of infant baptism and required adults to be re-baptized.

[1127] John 5:35: "He was a burning and a shining light: and ye were willing for a season to rejoice in his light."

They were very diligent, plain, and serious, strong in the scripture and bold in proclaiming their faith, bearing with much hostility and opposition. But what had tripped up others now snared them, as well. Worldly power spoiled them – gaining a little, they began to wonder what they might achieve if they had more. They were content with their watery dispensation, failing to move on to receive the baptism of fire and the Holy Spirit from the one who came with a fan in his hand to clear the floor,[1128] to smelt away the dross and tin of his people,[1129] and make them finer than gold.[1130] Feeling false security, they grew proud, arrogant, and self-righteous, denying the possibility that others might have greater understandings. They forgot the beauty of their own origins and early days. As a result, many left them, and all the other visible churches and religious societies, to wander about like sheep without a shepherd or doves without their mates. They sought their Beloved, but they were unable to find the One that their souls longed to know and loved more than their greatest joy.

These people were called 'Seekers' by some and the Family of Love by others.[1131] As they came to know each other, they sometimes met together – not to pray and preach formally at designated times or places – but simply to wait together in silence. If anyone present felt something arising in his or her mind that seemed to flow from the divine spring, it might be spoken aloud. But some of them, after receiving a revelation, failed to acknowledge their dependence on God for their new understanding. Without humility or fear of God, they mixed their own thoughts in with God's gifts to them.

[1128] Matt. 3:11: "I indeed baptize you with water unto repentance: but he that cometh after me is mightier than I, whose shoes I am not worthy to bear: he shall baptize you with the Holy Ghost, and *with* fire: Whose fan *is* in his hand, and he will thoroughly purge his floor, and will gather the wheat into his garner; but the chaff he will burn with fire unquenchable."

[1129] Isa. 1:25: "And I will turn my hand upon thee, and purely purge away thy dross, and take away all thy tin."

[1130] Isa. 13:12: "I will make a man more precious than fine gold; even a man than the golden wedge of Ophir."

[1131] The Family of Love or Familists were a religious sect, founded by Henry Nicholas in the sixteenth century. They believed in the quest for holiness and the possibility of the perfection of human nature in this life. The term Seekers is generally applied to individuals, rather than an organized religious movement, in the seventeenth century. These were people who were disillusioned with the then-current religious practices and sought a more authentic relationship with God.

This gave birth to an abomination, and scandalized those who loved God and waited daily for the Consolation of Israel[1132] in the temple not made by human hands[1133] – those who are Jews inwardly, circumcised in their hearts.[1134]

These people were called 'Ranters' for their ranting and outrageous practices.[1135] They misinterpreted Christ's fulfillment of the law for us, claiming it discharged us from any and all obligations or duties that the law required of us. They declared that therefore they could no longer sin – even in doing what had been a sin under the law – because Christ had done away with blind obedience to the old law and that, consequently, all things that they did were good, if they sincerely believed them to be. They attempted to distinguish between an action and any evil associated with it, solely on the basis of their intentions. A number of them took up gross and despicable practices, claiming that they could, without sin, commit the same act which was a sin for others.

Thus, they supposed that the abundance of God's grace would permit them to sin just as abundantly – turning from the grace of God to wantonness was proclaimed as the way to salvation. It was as if Christ had come not to save us from our sins, but in our sins; not to take away sin, but to free us to sin without restraint at his cost and with no danger to ourselves. This ensnared many and cost them the utter and lamentable loss of their eternal reward. They grew to be very troublesome for more conscientious people, and gave those who are less conscientious an excuse for wickedness.

[1132] Luke 2:25: "And, behold, there was a man in Jerusalem, whose name *was* Simeon; and the same man *was* just and devout, waiting for the consolation of Israel: and the Holy Ghost was upon him."

[1133] Acts 17:24: "God that made the world and all things therein, seeing that he is Lord of heaven and earth, dwelleth not in temples made with hands."

[1134] Rom. 2:29: "But he *is* a Jew, which is one inwardly; and circumcision *is that* of the heart, in the spirit, *and* not in the letter; whose praise *is* not of men, but of God."

[1135] The name Ranters was applied to various antinomian groups in the seventeenth century. Not a formal organization, they were individuals characterized by a belief in their own perfection and consequently, in the belief that they could not sin, even when they engaged in acts that would be sinful if performed by others.

Chapter 2

The Rise of this People

*I*t was about that time, as you can see in George Fox's *Journal*,[1136] that the eternal, wise, and good God, in his infinite love, honored this benighted and bewildered nation with the breaking of a new, heavenly and glorious dawn.[1137] Through the testimony of one chosen vessel,[1138] the sure and certain Word of Light and Life was heard by many thousands to their real and blessed benefit. For this, they say, "Glory be to the name of the Lord forever!"

The Word sounded in their consciences and broke into their hearts, bringing many to look within and to understand that what they had been seeking outwardly, with much pain and cost, could only be found inwardly. There they found what they had so vainly sought: the way to peace with God. They were pointed to the Light of Jesus Christ within them, the Seed[1139] and Leaven[1140] of the Kingdom of God. The Light is near to all because it is within all and is God's gift to all – a faithful and true witness and honest counselor in every heart – it is the grace that leads to life and salvation, though few appreciate it. Tradition-bound Christians – strong-willed, smugly convinced of their own righteousness and overcome by blind zeal – dismiss this gift as inadequate or commonplace. Even worse, they harshly reject it as a mere human invention – in anger and ignorance denying the possibility of fresh revelations of God's power and Spirit in our

---

[1136] *The Rise and Progress* was originally written as a preface to the first edition of *The Journal of George Fox*.

[1137] Luke 1:78-79: "Through the tender mercy of our God; whereby the dayspring from on high hath visited us, To give light to them that sit in darkness and *in* the shadow of death, to guide our feet into the way of peace."

[1138] The 'chosen vessel' is George Fox (from Acts 9:15: "But the Lord said unto him, Go thy way: for he is a chosen vessel unto me, to bear my name before the Gentiles, and kings, and the children of Israel"), who is portrayed not as the founder of Quakerism, but merely as the carrier of God's message to England.

[1139] Matt. 13:31: "Another parable put he forth unto them, saying, The kingdom of heaven is like to a grain of mustard seed, which a man took, and sowed in his field."

[1140] Matt. 13:33: "Another parable spake he unto them; The kingdom of heaven is like unto leaven, which a woman took, and hid in three measures of meal, till the whole was leavened."

times – insulting and slandering what is more than ever needed to make true Christians out of them. They are not unlike the Jews of Jesus' time, who rejected the Son of God while blindly asserting that they were awaiting the arrival of the Messiah. Alas! He appeared among them, but not in keeping with their worldly plans and expectations.

Many abusive books have resulted, filling some with envy and others with rage, and impeding the spread of the gospel message. For those who received this blessed gospel, the way became straight and very narrow indeed.[1141] But the Lord recognized these as his own and this testimony reached, gathered, comforted, and sustained the weary and heavy laden,[1142] the hungry and thirsty,[1143] the poor and needy,[1144] the mournful and sick who had paid much to physicians without being cured[1145] and waited for relief from heaven – all those who knew that the only true relief comes from above. They had seriously considered all things and had found that nothing would do but Christ himself – the Light from his countenance,[1146] a touch of his garment, or help from his hand[1147] – who healed the poor woman's hemorrhage, the centurion's servant,[1148] and Peter's mother;[1149]

[1141] Matt. 7:14: "Because strait *is* the gate, and narrow *is* the way, which leadeth unto life, and few there be that find it."

[1142] Matt. 11:28: "Come unto me, all *ye* that labour and are heavy laden, and I will give you rest."

[1143] Matt. 5:6: "Blessed *are* they which do hunger and thirst after righteousness: for they shall be filled."

[1144] Ps. 40:17: "But I *am* poor and needy; *yet* the Lord thinketh upon me: thou *art* my help and my deliverer; make no tarrying, O my God."

[1145] Mark 5:25-27: "And a certain woman, which had an issue of blood twelve years, And had suffered many things of many physicians, and had spent all that she had, and was nothing bettered, but rather grew worse, When she had heard of Jesus, came in the press behind, and touched his garment."

[1146] Matt. 28:3: "His countenance was like lightning, and his raiment white as snow."

[1147] Ps. 119:173: "Let thine hand help me; for I have chosen thy precepts."

[1148] Matt. 8:13: "And Jesus said unto the centurion, Go thy way; and as thou hast believed, *so* be it done unto thee. And his servant was healed in the selfsame hour."

[1149] Matt. 8:14-15: "And when Jesus was come into Peter's house, he saw his wife's mother laid, and sick of a fever. And he touched her hand, and the fever left her: and she arose, and ministered unto them."

who raised the widow's son[1150] and the ruler's daughter.[1151] As soon as they felt his power in their souls, they surrendered their wills to him – becoming obedient in their minds and faithful in their hearts – despite frequent mocking, opposition, confiscations, beatings, imprisonments, and other earthly penalties for Jesus' sake.

Truly, these were very many and very great, so that in all human likelihood they should have been quickly pulled under by the proud and noisy waves that rose up and washed over them, but the God of all their tender mercies[1152] was with them. The hills often fled and the mountains melted[1153] before the power that filled them, working mightily for them and in them. The action of this power deeply comforted them and confirmed their beliefs – they saw clearly that all things were possible with God.[1154] And the more that what God required of them seemed to contradict human wisdom and to expose them to human wrath, the more God appeared to help and carry them through it all to his Glory.

If any people could ever say, "You are our sun and our shield,[1155] our rock and sanctuary,[1156] and by you we have leaped over walls, run through a

---

[1150] Luke 7:12-15: "Now when he came nigh to the gate of the city, behold, there was a dead man carried out, the only son of his mother, and she was a widow: and much people of the city was with her. And when the Lord saw her, he had compassion on her, and said unto her, Weep not. And he came and touched the bier: and they that bare *him* stood still. And he said, Young man, I say unto thee, Arise. And he that was dead sat up, and began to speak. And he delivered him to his mother."

[1151] Luke 8:49-50: "While he yet spake, there cometh one from the ruler of the synagogue's *house*, saying to him, Thy daughter is dead; trouble not the Master. But when Jesus heard *it*, he answered him, saying, Fear not: believe only, and she shall be made whole."

[1152] Ps. 119:156: "Great *are* thy tender mercies, O LORD: quicken me according to thy judgments."

[1153] Nah. 1:5: "The mountains quake at him, and the hills melt, and the earth is burned at his presence, yea, the world, and all that dwell therein."

[1154] Matt. 19:26: "But Jesus beheld *them*, and said unto them, With men this is impossible; but with God all things are possible."

[1155] Ps. 84:11: "For the LORD God *is* a sun and shield: the LORD will give grace and glory: no good *thing* will he withhold from them that walk uprightly."

band of marauders,[1157] and routed foreign armies,"[1158] these people had that right. God freed their souls of the wearying burdens of sin and vanity, changed their spiritual poverty to riches, satisfied their hunger and thirst for eternal righteousness, filled them with all the good things of heaven,[1159] and made them the stewards of all God's gifts. In return, they went into every corner of these nations declaring what God had done from them – what and where and how they had found the way to peace with God – and inviting all to come and see and taste for themselves the Truth of what they preached.[1160]

They testified to the Principle of God in mankind – the precious pearl[1161] and leaven of the kingdom[1162] – the only way that God has established to convince people of their need to change, to sanctify them, and to give them spiritual life. They described what this principle was, why it was given to them, and how anyone might distinguish it from their own thoughts or the subtle work of the evil one. They told what it would do for all those who turned away from the vanities of the world, from its empty ways and spiritually lifeless teachers, and held fast to God's Blessed Light

---

[1156] Isa. 8:14: "And he shall be for a sanctuary; but for a stone of stumbling and for a rock of offence to both the houses of Israel, for a gin and for a snare to the inhabitants of Jerusalem."

[1157] Ps. 18:29: "For by thee I have run through a troop; and by my God have I leaped over a wall."

[1158] Heb. 11:34: "Quenched the violence of fire, escaped the edge of the sword, out of weakness were made strong, waxed valiant in fight, turned to flight the armies of the aliens."

[1159] Matt. 7:11: "If ye then, being evil, know how to give good gifts unto your children, how much more shall your Father which is in heaven give good things to them that ask him?"

[1160] Penn is referring to a group of early Quaker ministers, often called the Valiant Sixty or the First Publishers of Truth, who travelled throughout the British Isles, British colonies in the Caribbean and North America, and Northern Europe, bringing the Quaker message.

[1161] Matt. 13:45-46: "Again, the kingdom of heaven is like unto a merchant man, seeking goodly pearls: Who, when he had found one pearl of great price, went and sold all that he had, and bought it."

[1162] Matt. 13:33: "Another parable spake he unto them; The kingdom of heaven is like unto leaven, which a woman took, and hid in three measures of meal, till the whole was leavened."

within themselves, which exposes and condemns sin in all its disguises and, if obeyed, would show them how to overcome it. That Light gives us the power to avoid and resist those things that displease God and to grow strong in love, faith, and good works. To God's eternal praise, those that sin has made into a wilderness that is overrun with briars and thorns, can become like the garden of God – cultivated by the divine power and replenished with virtuous and beautiful plants planted by God's own right hand.

But these new preachers of the glad tidings of God's Truth and Kingdom were not free to go wherever they wished or to pray and preach whenever they pleased, but only as Christ, their redeemer, prepared and directed them. They waited for direction from his blessed Spirit in their services and meetings, speaking only those words that were given to them. It was plain to the serious-minded, whose spiritual eyes had been opened even a little by the Lord Jesus, that when they taught, it was with authority and not like the dry and formal imaginings of the Pharisees – each given a chosen gift by the Holy Spirit – one had been given the word of exhortation, another had the word of reproof, and a third, the word of consolation – to convince and instruct many.

These preachers grew strong and confident through faithfulness and, by the power and Spirit of the Lord Jesus, they became exceedingly fruitful. In a short time, their testimony, both by ministry and by sufferings, turned thousands to the Truth within. In most counties and many of the larger towns of England, meetings were set up and daily more were saved and added to their number.[1163] They were diligent to plant and to water, and the Lord blessed their labors with an overwhelming increase[1164] – despite opposition to their blessed labors by false rumors, defamation, and bitter persecution, from the government and from others who wished to injure and abuse them. They were like sheep, sent to be slaughtered, and as a people facing death all day long.[1165]

[1163] Acts 2:47: "Praising God, and having favour with all the people. And the Lord added to the church daily such as should be saved."

[1164] 1 Cor. 3:6: "I have planted, Apollos watered; but God gave the increase."

[1165] Rom. 8:35-36: "Who shall separate us from the love of Christ? *shall* tribulation, or distress, or persecution, or famine, or nakedness, or peril, or sword? As it is written, For thy sake we are killed all the day long; we are accounted as sheep for the slaughter."

A volume, rather than a preface, would be needed to list the cruel sufferings they suffered from both religious and irreligious people, from the civil authorities and the common rabble. It may truly be said of this abused and despised people that they went forth weeping and sowing their tears, bearing testimony to the precious Seed[1166] – the seed of a kingdom that depends not on words – not even on finest words that human minds can conceive – but on God's power. God the Father has given Christ Jesus all power in heaven and earth[1167] to rule the angels above and humanity below, and, as their work demonstrates, Jesus has in turn empowered these ministers. Through their ministry, many have been turned from darkness to the Light,[1168] away from the broad way and to the narrow way of life and peace.[1169] They have led people to live serious, conscientious, and godly lives, practicing the doctrines that they have been taught.

Without this secret divine power, there is no rebirth or regeneration of spiritually dead souls. The lack of this rebirthing and regenerating power and life is the reason so many former and present ministries bear so little fruit. Oh! If only the ministers and the people were aware of this! My soul is often troubled for them; I am enveloped in sorrow and mourning for their sakes. Oh! If only they were wise! Oh! If only they would really consider and take to heart those things that can truly and significantly give them lasting peace.

Let us touch briefly on two things, the doctrines they taught and the example they set. I have already mentioned their fundamental principle – the cornerstone on which all else depends – the Light of Christ within. This is God's gift for salvation. It is the root out of which the tree of good

---

[1166] Ps. 126:5-6: "They that sow in tears shall reap in joy. He that goeth forth and weepeth, bearing precious seed, shall doubtless come again with rejoicing, bringing his sheaves *with him*."

[1167] Matt. 28:18: "And Jesus came and spake unto them, saying, All power is given unto me in heaven and in earth."

[1168] Acts 26:18: "To open their eyes, *and* to turn *them* from darkness to light, and *from* the power of Satan unto God, that they may receive forgiveness of sins, and inheritance among them which are sanctified by faith that is in me."

[1169] Matt. 7:13-14: "Enter ye in at the strait gate: for wide *is* the gate, and broad *is* the way, that leadeth to destruction, and many there be which go in thereat: Because strait *is* the gate, and narrow *is* the way, which leadeth unto life, and few there be that find it."

doctrines grew and which I will now describe in their natural and experiential order.

The first is repentance from dead works so that we might serve the Living God. This encompasses three operations: an understanding of one's own sins, knowing the meaning of those sins and feeling genuine sorrow for them, and mending one's way of living. This was the repentance they preached and urged on people. It is the natural consequence of turning to the Light, because the Light allows an inner sight; and with that sight comes understanding and sorrow; and from that understanding and sorrow comes a change in life. This doctrine of repentance leads to justification, that is, to forgiveness of past sins through Christ, the only way to reconciliation and it leads to sanctification – to a cleansing of the soul from the defiling nature and habits of sin. This is justification in the complete sense of the word in that it includes both justification from the guilt of past sins (as if they had never been committed) through the love and mercy of God in Jesus Christ, and an inward righteousness through the cleansing and sanctifying power and Spirit of Christ revealed in the soul – commonly called sanctification. But no one can come to know Christ as their sacrifice who rejects him as their sanctifier. The purpose of his life on earth was to save his people from the habit and the defilement, as well as from the guilt, of sin. Therefore, those who resist his Light and Spirit have made his coming and his offer void for themselves.

From this sprang a second doctrine that they were led to declare as the prize that all true Christians are called to,[1170] that is, perfection from sin. The Scriptures of Truth testify that this is the purpose of Christ's coming and the nature of his kingdom. His Spirit was and is given to us so that we might be perfect and holy because God is holy.[1171] This is what the apostles preached, that Christians could be sanctified in body, soul, and spirit. They never argued for perfection in wisdom or glory in this life or from illness or death, as some have imagined and accused them of. They called this a redeemed state, regeneration, or the new birth and they taught it everywhere. This was the foundation – without it, no one could inherit the kingdom of God.

[1170] Phil. 3:14: "I press toward the mark for the prize of the high calling of God in Christ Jesus."

[1171] Matt. 5:48: "Be ye therefore perfect, even as your Father which is in heaven is perfect."

Third, this provides them with good reason to believe in the reality of eternal rewards and punishments – otherwise, they would be the most miserable of all people, after forty years of terrible suffering for their beliefs. Indeed, in some cases, they have been treated worse than the worst, as garbage and rubbish.[1172]

This was the significance of their doctrine and ministry. For the most part, it is much the same as what others who call themselves Christians claim to believe – at least in word and form, but not in the power of godliness. That was long ago lost when humanity abandoned the principle and the seed of life that is within each person, but which has not been valued or understood. Only within it and by it, can our minds be turned to the service of the living God in the newness of life.[1173] As true religion was lost, most people lived and worshipped God as they wanted and not as God would have them worship – nor according to the example of Christ, who relied on the works and fruits of the Holy Spirit. These Quaker ministers called on people to experience the Spirit itself, not mere notions about the Spirit; to know Godliness itself, not just the form of it. Feeling the work of God's righteous judgments within themselves, they knew that without holiness no one would ever find the Lord's consolation.

Their Fundamental Principles, Doctrines, and Practices

Growing like branches from these general doctrines, several particular doctrines spring forth which illustrate and further explain these three general doctrines:

I.   *Fellowship with and loving one another.* This has been noted by all sorts of people concerning these ministers. They meet together – they help and support one another. It is common to hear someone say, 'Look how the Quakers love and care for one another.'[1174] If it is the mark of primitive Christianity to love one another and know intimate religious communion,

---

[1172] Lam. 3:45: "Thou hast made us *as* the offscouring and refuse in the midst of the people."

[1173] Rom. 6:4: "Therefore we are buried with him by baptism into death: that like as Christ was raised up from the dead by the glory of the Father, even so we also should walk in newness of life."

[1174] Penn seems to be echoing a scriptural description of early Christians, e.g., 1 John 3:11 ("For this is the message that ye heard from the beginning, that we should love one another").

to meet frequently to worship God and care for one another, then – bless the Lord! – they have it in abundance.

II.   *Loving Enemies.* This they both taught and practiced. They not only refused take revenge for injuries received, condemning it as unchristian, but they freely forgave those who had been cruel to them – even when vengeance was within their power. Many notable examples of their efforts to overcome injustice and oppression with patience, or of preaching this Christian doctrine for others to follow, could be provided.

III.   *Speaking Truthfully.* Following Christ's own words, they use 'yea, yea' and 'nay, nay' among Christians, without swearing. They do this both because of Christ's explicit prohibition in Matthew 5[1175] and because they live under a covenant of Truth. As such, there is no need for an oath – indeed, it is an insult to Christian truthfulness to believe that honesty can be insured by extraordinary forms of speaking. Simple, uncompounded answers – yea and nay – without solemn affirmations, attestations, or supernatural vouchers are most suited to a gospel righteousness. At the same time, they invite the same punishment for any false speaking as others would receive for perjury. They denounce all true oaths, all false oaths, and all profanity. Remember that for swearing, the whole land itself did and does mourn[1176] and the great God was and is offended.

IV.   *Not Fighting, but Suffering.* This people insists that Christianity teaches people to beat their swords into plowshares and their spears into pruning hooks and never again to train for war,[1177] that the wolf will lie down with the lamb and the lion with the calf,[1178] and nothing that destroys will enter the hearts of the people. They urge all to turn their zeal loose on

---

[1175] Matt. 5:37: "But let your communication be, Yea, yea; Nay, nay: for whatsoever is more than these cometh of evil."

[1176] Jer. 23:10: "For the land is full of adulterers; for because of swearing the land mourneth; the pleasant places of the wilderness are dried up, and their course is evil, and their force *is* not right."

[1177] Isa. 2:4: "And he shall judge among the nations, and shall rebuke many people: and they shall beat their swords into plowshares, and their spears into pruninghooks: nation shall not lift up sword against nation, neither shall they learn war any more."

[1178] Isa. 11:6: "The wolf also shall dwell with the lamb, and the leopard shall lie down with the kid; and the calf and the young lion and the fatling together; and a little child shall lead them."

sin and their anger against Satan, and no longer to make war against each other. All wars and fightings arise in human covetousness, according to the apostle James,[1179] not from the meek Spirit of Christ Jesus. Christ is the captain of a different warfare,[1180] carried out with different weapons.[1181] Just as swearing gave way to speaking truth, fighting yielded to faith and Truth in their doctrines and practices.

This should not cause any difficulty for civil governments – while they cannot fight for the government, they cannot fight against it either. Such a promise will provide any government with a measure of security. Nor is it reasonable to blame them for failing to do more for others than they can do for themselves. Even ignoring the demands of Christianity, peace, with its all inconveniences, is generally preferable to the costs and results of war. Though they can not fight, they do submit to the authority of the government – not out of fear, but for conscience sake, if the government does not interfere with conscience – this, they believe, is God's decree.[1182] They believe that, when governments are just, they are a great benefit to mankind, but due to the blind zeal of some and the self-interest of others, they have felt the weight and severity of civil penalties more than any other religious body of our times – although, religious practices aside, they have given the government the least trouble of any.

V. *Refusal to Pay Tithes.* Another aspect of this people's character is their refusal to financially support the national church's ministers. There are two reasons for this: First, they believe that all compelled payments, even to gospel ministers, is unlawful because it is contrary to Christ's command,

---

[1179] James 4:1: "From whence *come* wars and fightings among you? *come they* not hence, *even* of your lusts that war in your members?"

[1180] Heb. 2:10: "For it became him, for whom *are* all things, and by whom *are* all things, in bringing many sons unto glory, to make the captain of their salvation perfect through sufferings."

[1181] 2 Cor. 10:4 "(For the weapons of our warfare *are* not carnal, but mighty through God to the pulling down of strong holds)."

[1182] Rom. 13:1-3: "Let every soul be subject unto the higher powers. For there is no power but of God: the powers that be are ordained of God. Whosoever therefore resisteth the power, resisteth the ordinance of God: and they that resist shall receive to themselves damnation. For rulers are not a terror to good works, but to the evil."

'You received without paying; give without payment.'[1183] At the very least, support for gospel ministers should be voluntary, not forced. Second, those appointed clerics are not gospel ministers. The Holy Spirit is not the foundation of their work, but human arts and letters. This is not a matter of choice or stubbornness, but purely of conscience toward God. They cannot assist or support the national church's ministers – these positions have too often and too visibly become merely ways to achieve worldly advantage and advancement.

VI.   *Being Deferential to No One.* They were often attacked and abused for refusing to confer flattering titles on people, or to use pretentious gestures and complements as a false show of respect. They insist that such practices are sinful. They are willing to acknowledge the rights of those with power and authority, but – following the example of Mordecai[1184] and Elihu[1185] – only in a plain and simple, sincere and proper manner. Moreover, they follow the command of their Lord and Master, Jesus Christ, who prohibited his followers from calling anyone Rabbi[1186] – that title, meaning Lord and Master – which was a fashionable greeting of those times. Christ warned against flattering others who, in their fallen state, are prone to pretentiousness and self-importance. Although this practice has made conversation with them unpleasant for some, they should remember what Christ said of the Jews, "How can you be a believer if you accept praise from one another?"[1187] If those who are offended would give his doctrine any credit, their resentment would be gone.

[1183] Matt. 10:8: "Heal the sick, cleanse the lepers, raise the dead, cast out devils: freely ye have received, freely give."

[1184] Esther 3:2: "And all the king's servants, that *were* in the king's gate, bowed, and reverenced Haman: for the king had so commanded concerning him. But Mordecai bowed not, nor did *him* reverence."

[1185] Job 32:6: "And Elihu the son of Barachel the Buzite answered and said, I *am* young, and ye *are* very old; wherefore I was afraid, and durst not shew you mine opinion."

[1186] Matt. 23:8: "But be not ye called Rabbi: for one is your Master, *even* Christ; and all ye are brethren."

[1187] John 5:44: "How can ye believe, which receive honour one of another, and seek not the honour that *cometh* from God only?"

VII.   Quaker ministers also use the plain forms of 'thou' and 'thee' when speaking to a single person, no matter what their station in life.[1188] The wisdom of God is apparent in calling this people to so simple an act. It strongly tested their faithfulness, forcing them to live their beliefs publicly – not just to talk about them. The public use of this language seemed exceedingly brash and rude to many people and they did not take it well, saying, "My dog is 'thou.' Use 'thou' with me and I'll thou thy teeth down thy throat!"[1189] They seem to forget what language they use to address God in their own prayers, the forms commonly used in the scriptures, and even proper forms of grammar. One must ask how much good religious belief is for those who are so acutely offended by this plain, honest, and true form of speech.

VIII.   *Taciturnity.* By their example, they recommend silence, having very few words on any occasion. They stand by their word in business dealings; nor can their customers tempt them into haggling. They have more regard for Truth than for standard business practices – to being an example than to making big profits.

They seek solitude, but when in the company of others, they neither engage in nor invite unnecessary chatter, rumors, or gossip. In this way, they maintain the purity of their minds – undisturbed by useless thoughts or unnecessary diversions. Nor do they engage in the custom of wishing others 'Good Night,' 'Good Day,' or 'Go with God' – they know the night is good and the day is good without their wishing it; and, in the last expression, the holy name of God is insincerely and thoughtlessly used, and therefore, taken in vain. Besides, these words and wishes are uttered simply as a matter of habit and are usually not meant – just as the words 'love' and 'at your service' are not meant when some tip their hats or bend their knee. These excesses, as in other things, are oppressive to them, and therefore,

---

[1188] In the seventeenth century, the second person singular pronouns (thee, thou, etc.) were used only when addressing a social equal or inferior. When addressing one's social superiors, it was expected that the plural forms (you, your, and yours) would be used as a sign of respect. It may be difficult for modern readers to understand the degree to which the use of 'plain speech' was a deliberate insult. Saying 'thou' to one's 'betters' was roughly equivalent to using a vulgarity to address someone today.

[1189] The threat of violent reprisal was not an empty one. A seventeenth-century Gentlemen normally carried a sword or at least a heavy cane and could be expected to use it when insulted.

they not only decline to use them, but find themselves obligated to criticize their use by others.

IX.   *Toasting.* For the same reason, they shun drinking toasts to people in the ordinary manner. This practice is not only unnecessary and self-indulgent, but is unworthy of a Christian in that it encourages excessive drinking and drunkenness.

X.   *Their Way of Marriage.* This practice distinguishes them from all other Christian societies. They say that marriage was ordained by God and that only God can properly join a man and a woman in marriage. Therefore, they have no use for either priests or civil authorities to perform a marriage – the man and woman simply take each other as husband and wife in the presence of witnesses, promising to each other, with God's assistance, to be loving and faithful until death shall separate them.

But, before this, they first present themselves to their local Monthly Meeting for Business. There they declare their intentions, if the Meeting does not object, to take one another in marriage. The Meeting asks any necessary questions – for example, have they told parents or guardians of their intentions and have received their consent? – minutes their request, and appoints a number of persons to examine their behavior. These people determine whether they living properly, are clear of promises to any others or have unfulfilled obligations to their parents, and report to the next Monthly Meeting for Business. If at that Meeting, which the man and woman also attend, it is determined that they can proceed, the Meeting approves their proposal and records that approval in the Meeting records. If the woman is a widow with children under her care, the Meeting also makes certain that adequate provision is made for them before approving the marriage. The couple is then directed to set a time and place for the wedding and to inform relatives, friends, and neighbors that they would like them to be witnesses to the marriage.

At that time, they take each other by the hand, and make reciprocal promises of love and faithfulness to each other. A description of all these proceedings is recorded on a certificate to be signed at the wedding, first by the couple as a visible record of their union, and then by all in attendance as witnesses of all that was said and of the couple's signatures. This certificate is afterwards registered in the records of the Meeting at which the marriage was solemnized. As it should be, this procedure has been recognized as valid by courts of law despite the lack of the usual ceremony, priest, ring, etc.

These things were not rejected on a whim, but originate in a well-grounded conscience. The scriptures provide no counter-example to this procedure. Among the Jews, the priest played no part in the marriage other than to act as a witness like all others present. This people, therefore, sees no reason to enhance the apparent power or profit of today's clergy by imposing them on the wedding. As for the ring, it is sufficient to note that this is a meaningless, heathen custom, which was never practiced by the people of God – neither by Jews or primitive Christians. Likewise, the words used in the common form of the ceremony (e.g., 'with my body I thee worship, etc.') are hardly defensible. In short, the practices of this people are more careful, exact, and in keeping with the scriptures than any other form now used and are free from the difficulties that other methods introduce. The care and many checks that they provide prevent the performance of any clandestine weddings among them.

XI.   *Births.* Since births and burials are the occasions of so much pomp and solemnity among too many who call themselves Christians, it seems appropriate to describe what this people do for them. At birth, the parents name their own children – usually several days after they are born – in the presence of the midwife (if she can be present), those who witnessed the birth, and others. All sign a certificate of birth and the name of the child or children is recorded in the records of the Monthly Meeting to which the parents belong. All the other customary ceremonies and festivals surrounding a birth are avoided.

XII.   *Burials.* These are performed with the same simplicity. If the body of the deceased is near to any public meeting place, it is usually carried there. Those who will accompany it to the burial ground gather together, and often one or another may feel called to offer a word of exhortation for the benefit of those present. After this, the body is carried away by the young men – those who were close to the deceased if they are present. The corpse is laid in a plain coffin, without any covering or decoration on it. In the graveyard, they pause some time before they put the body into its grave, again offering those present the opportunity to speak and often they are not disappointed. This allows relatives to kindly and solemnly take their last leave of a departed brother or sister. All present have a sense of mortality and are given the chance to reflect on their own coming end. Beyond this, they have no ceremonies or rituals.

The family of the deceased does not put on mourning clothes – these are seen as worldly ceremony and display. The grief of a Christian at the loss of a beloved friend of relative should be worn in the mind. That is where the loss is experienced, the love is felt, and the memories are carried. Grief is outwardly expressed by faithfulness, by care for those who are left behind, and by love for what the deceased loved. This conduct, although it is plain and unfashionable, leaves nothing of importance neglected or undone, and their purpose is to do no more. They find such simplicity in living to bring great satisfaction – though not without its mockery from the vain world in which they live.

Their Progress and Sufferings

These principles and practices have given them a rough and disagreeable appearance to the others, who thought they were out to turn the world upside down – and in some sense, they were. They are charged, as was Paul, to bring things back to their primitive and correct order again. Their practices are not simply made up or designed to draw attention to themselves, as some may think, but are the fruits of an inward sense which God has instilled in them. They did not set out to contradict the rest of the world or to set themselves apart from it – that was not their concern nor their interest. It was not the result of planning or a carefully designed strategy to provoke schism or propound new ideas. Once God had let them see their true selves, they could see the whole world in that same truthful way – they could clearly see human desires and passions; they understood why things are as they are.

Those beautiful and ostentatious things that satisfy our earthly desires are not from our Heavenly Father, but from the world.[1190] The long dark night of apostasy, which has oppressed the people for so long, grew out of these things. Losing sight of the Light and Spirit of God, people adopted these and many other vain customs. But, when the heavenly day of Christ dawns in the soul, they can see that these should never have been introduced into Christian practice nor should they have allowed their practices to become so distorted over time that they are now harmful. To many people, these things seem trivial and the Quakers' opposition to them unnecessary and even arrogant, but there is more here than meets the eye.

It was not easy for the first Friends to make a public spectacle of themselves – a target for the mockery and ridicule of the world. They easily could see that such was the natural consequence of such unpopular actions,

---

[1190] 1 John 2:16: "For all that *is* in the world, the lust of the flesh, and the lust of the eyes, and the pride of life, is not of the Father, but is of the world."

but the wisdom of God is seen in the foolishness of these things.[1191] First, people's satisfaction in and high regard for the fashionable things of this world, despite a pretense of concern about the other world, was revealed by their great discomfort with any criticism of them. Honesty, virtue, wisdom, and ability were not enough without these things. Second, it appropriately and usefully distinguished their manner of living from ours – when the lives lived by some of their relatives and friends made them uncomfortable, it provided them with an opportunity to withdraw and reflect. In that reflection, they met with better companions, perhaps even the Lord God, their Redeemer, and grew in God's love, power, and wisdom, becoming more capable of service to God. The success of this contemplation in some has been abundantly obvious – Blessed be the name of the Lord!

Although the early Quaker ministers were not respected and well-educated in the eyes of this world, they spoke with authority and had no lack of followers. These generally were drawn from among the most serious and religious members of the various other congregations – many new followers being people of acknowledged ability, substance, and consequence.

Others were intellectuals and people with significant wealth, although as in the earliest times, not many who were wise or noble were called – or perhaps because of the cross that came with a sincere answer, not many of those answered the heavenly call. But wealth and learning do not make people into better Christians – just more accomplished speakers and debaters. It is ignorance about the divine gift that has caused a common and hurtful mistake: Theory is not practice; the thought is not the reality; and mere words are not actions.

[1191] 1 Cor. 1:24-27&3:19: "But unto them which are called, both Jews and Greeks, Christ the power of God, and the wisdom of God. Because the foolishness of God is wiser than men; and the weakness of God is stronger than men. For ye see your calling, brethren, how that not many wise men after the flesh, not many mighty, not many noble, *are called*: But God hath chosen the foolish things of the world to confound the wise; and God hath chosen the weak things of the world to confound the things which are mighty ... For the wisdom of this world is foolishness with God. For it is written, He taketh the wise in their own craftiness."

A Gentle and Sincere Protest

Oh! The penitent, the reformed, the humble, the watchful, the self-denying, and holy souls are Christians. These conditions are the fruits and works of the Spirit as seen in the life of Jesus. That life, though in part concealed by God, has been poured out in the hearts of those who truly believe. Oh! If only people knew that this would purify them, circumcise them, give them new life, and make new creatures of them[1192] – recreating and regenerating them in Christ to do good works[1193] – they might live for God instead of for themselves. Then they would offer living prayer and living praises to the living God through the living Spirit – the only way worship is to be offered in this gospel age.

Oh! If only those who read this could feel what I feel. My heart is filled with love by this merciful gift of the Father of Lights and Spirits to this poor nation and to the whole world. Why do its inhabitants reject this testimony? Why do they pass up the blessed benefit of it? Why don't they turn to the Lord and say with all their hearts, "Speak, Lord, your poor servants are now listening.[1194] Oh! That your will might be done – your great and holy will be done – here on earth as it is in heaven![1195] Do it within us; do it on us; do what you will with us, for we are yours and wish only to glorify our Creator and our Redeemer. You redeem us from the vanities and pollutions of the earth to be God's own people."[1196] Oh! What an extraordinary day it would be for England, if she could say this truthfully! But, alas, this is not the case. For this reason, some of the inhabitants of this, the land of my birth, have mourned with bitter weeping and wailing. Their heads have been like springs of water and their eyes like fountains of tears[1197] because of your sins and stubbornness; because you

---

[1192] 2 Cor. 5:17: "Therefore if any man *be* in Christ, *he is* a new creature: old things are passed away; behold, all things are become new."

[1193] Ephesians 2:10: "For we are his workmanship, created in Christ Jesus unto good works, which God hath before ordained that we should walk in them."

[1194] 1 Sam. 3:10: "And the LORD came, and stood, and called as at other times, Samuel, Samuel. Then Samuel answered, Speak; for thy servant heareth."

[1195] Matt. 6:10: "Thy kingdom come. Thy will be done in earth, as *it is* in heaven."

[1196] Deut. 14:2: "For thou *art* an holy people unto the LORD thy God, and the LORD hath chosen thee to be a peculiar people unto himself, above all the nations that *are* upon the earth."

[1197] Jer. 9:1: "Oh that my head were waters, and mine eyes a fountain of tears, that I might weep day and night for the slain of the daughter of my people!"

will not hear and fear and return to the rock – the rock, Oh England, from which you were made. But be warned, you must receive him into your heart. Behold! He has stood so long at your door, knocking, but you have not let him in![1198] Awake! Before Jerusalem's judgments[1199] swiftly overcome you! Jerusalem's sins flourish in you – Jerusalem was rich in the outward forms of God's law, but she ignored the heart of God's laws, just as you do daily.

She resisted the Son of God in the flesh and you resist the Son of God in the Spirit. He longed to gather her as a hen gathers her chicks under her wings, but she was unwilling.[1200] So would Christ gather you out of your lifeless religion and give you the true substance of religion[1201] – showing you God's power and kingdom. So often, Christ has knocked within, by his Grace and Spirit, and without, by his servants and witnesses, but you would not allow yourselves to be gathered. On the contrary, just as Jerusalem persecuted, crucified, whipped, and imprisoned the servants of the Son of God, so have you. Oh Land! You have again nailed the Lord of Life and Glory to the cross. You have mocked his Spirit of Grace; scorned the Fatherly visitation; and, by your laws and in your courts, persecuted God's blessed messengers. They constantly plead with you in the power and Spirit of the Lord; in love and gentleness, they have begged you to know and serve the Lord, so that you might become the glory of all lands.[1202]

But you have treated them evilly and rejected the good advice they offered. Falsely, you have denied their criticisms. Their example was too

---

[1198] Rev. 3:20: "Behold, I stand at the door, and knock: if any man hear my voice, and open the door, I will come in to him, and will sup with him, and he with me."

[1199] Eze. 14:21: "For thus saith the Lord GOD; How much more when I send my four sore judgments upon Jerusalem, the sword, and the famine, and the noisome beast, and the pestilence, to cut off from it man and beast?"

[1200] Matt. 23:37: "O Jerusalem, Jerusalem, *thou* that killest the prophets, and stonest them which are sent unto thee, how often would I have gathered thy children together, even as a hen gathereth her chickens under *her* wings, and ye would not!"

[1201] Prov. 8:21: "That I may cause those that love me to inherit substance; and I will fill their treasures."

[1202] Eze. 20:6: "In the day *that* I lifted up mine hand unto them, to bring them forth of the land of Egypt into a land that I had espied for them, flowing with milk and honey, which *is* the glory of all lands."

difficult and their requirements too stringent for you to accept. You are like the Jews of old, who cried, "Isn't this the carpenter's son? Aren't his brothers and sisters here with us?"[1203] Which of the scribes or learned (the Orthodox) believe in him?" You predict that they will not last more than a year or two. You pass and enforce severe laws to try and bring about their downfall. You try to terrify them into renouncing their holy way and destroy them for remaining faithful to it. But you have seen how many governments have opposed them and sought their downfall, only to be swept away themselves.[1204] But they have been preserved and have grown to be numerous among the middle classes of your inhabitants. Despite the many difficulties, both from without and from within, with which they have struggled since the Lord gathered first them, they are still increasing in number. In various places, the Lord is still adding more who would be saved, if they persevere to the end. Oh England! The Lord has lifted them up as an example to you and to the nations around you.[1205] They are like a shining city built on a hill,[1206] so that by their light, you may come to the Light of Christ Jesus, the Light of the World. That can be your Light and Life, too, if you would only turn from your many evil ways, receive it, and obey it. As the scriptures testify, the nations that are saved must walk in the Light of the Lamb.[1207]

Remember, Oh Nation of Claimed Religion! The Lord has waited on you since the dawning of the Reformation, imploring with you by many

---

[1203] Mark 6:3: "Is not this the carpenter, the son of Mary, the brother of James, and Joses, and of Juda, and Simon? and are not his sisters here with us? And they were offended at him."

[1204] Quakers were persecuted by a series of governments from the time the first appeared in the 1650s. The Commonwealth was overthrown and replaced by the Stuart Restoration in 1660. It was in turn overthrown in the Glorious Revolution of 1688 and replaced by William and Mary. Only in 1689 was persecution finally ended.

[1205] Jer. 50:2: "Declare ye among the nations, and publish, and set up a standard; publish, *and* conceal not: say, Babylon is taken, Bel is confounded, Merodach is broken in pieces; her idols are confounded, her images are broken in pieces."

[1206] Matt. 5:14: "Ye are the light of the world. A city that is set on an hill cannot be hid."

[1207] Rev. 21:23-24: "And the city had no need of the sun, neither of the moon, to shine in it: for the glory of God did lighten it, and the Lamb *is* the light thereof. And the nations of them which are saved shall walk in the light of it: and the kings of the earth do bring their glory and honour into it."

mercies and judgments: Awake and arise from your deep sleep![1208] Hear God's Word in your hearts so that you may live.[1209]

Do not let this Day of Visitation[1210] pass by unobserved. Oh England! Do not turn your back on the salvation that has come to your house. Why should you die, Oh Land that God wishes to bless? Without a doubt, it is God who is in the midst of this people, in the midst of you – not some delusion, as your mistaken teachers have led you to believe. By their marks and by their fruits you will know them, if you will only judge them in a spirit of equity.

[1208] Ephesians 5:14: "Wherefore he saith, Awake thou that sleepest, and arise from the dead, and Christ shall give thee light."

[1209] John 5:25: "Verily, verily, I say unto you, The hour is coming, and now is, when the dead shall hear the voice of the Son of God: and they that hear shall live."

[1210] The 'Day of Visitation' is central to early Quaker concepts of salvation. During that time (which may come at any time during an individual's life), an offer of salvation is made to each person. This offer may be accepted or rejected, but once the 'Day' has passed (not necessarily 24 hours), there is no chance of being saved: "God .. has given a certain day or time of visitation to everyone, whether Jew or Gentile, Turk or Scythian, Indian or Barbarian, or of whatever nation, country or place. During that day or time of visitation, it is possible for them to be saved, and to partake of the fruit of Christ's death. ... However, many men outlive this day, and after it has passed there is no possibility of salvation for them" (Barclay, pp. 82, 84).

Chapter 3

The Qualifications of their Ministry – Eleven Marks that it is Christian

I.   They were changed themselves before they tried to change others. Their hearts were torn as well as their clothes[1211] and they felt the power and the work of God acting on them.[1212] This was immediately obvious in the changes it caused – in their more faithful way of life and more Godly manner of living.

II.   They did not go where they wished or preach when they wanted, but only as directed by the will of God. Nor did they use carefully chosen words, but only those given them by God's Spirit. They became well acquainted with that Spirit in their own conversion, but that cannot be expressed intelligibly to worldly people – to them, it is as Christ said, "Like the wind, no one knows where it comes from or where it is going."[1213] This is the proof and seal of their ministry: that so many of them were turned from lifeless religion and evil ways to the knowledge of God and a holy life, as thousands can witness. And since they had received what they had to say from the Lord without paying, they gave it to others without being paid.[1214]

III.   The goal and purpose of their ministry was conversion to God – to regeneration and holiness, not to doctrinal systems, the wording of creeds, or new ways of worship. They sought to strip away everything superfluous – trimming away the ceremonious and formal and urging an embrace of the real, the necessary, and the spiritually beneficial – as all, on serious reflection, must do.

IV.   They directed people to look to a Principle within themselves, though not belonging to them. Through direct experience of that principle,

---

1211 Joel 2:13: "And rend your heart, and not your garments, and turn unto the LORD your God: for he *is* gracious and merciful, slow to anger, and of great kindness, and repenteth him of the evil."

1212 Ephesians 3:7: "Whereof I was made a minister, according to the gift of the grace of God given unto me by the effectual working of his power."

1213 John 3:8: "The wind bloweth where it listeth, and thou hearest the sound thereof, but canst not tell whence it cometh, and whither it goeth: so is every one that is born of the Spirit."

1214 Matt. 10:8: "Heal the sick, cleanse the lepers, raise the dead, cast out devils: freely ye have received, freely give."

anyone could know that everything they asserted, preached, or urged was true. Everything could be achieved within them by that principle.

They knew with absolute certainty that what they preached was true, and they were not afraid of it being tested. They were bold, and that boldness depended not on any human authority, but only on the conviction of this principle – the revelations and workings of which were to be found within each person. By it, they urged their listeners to examine and discover the Truth of everything they preached.

This is more than any of the world's many ministries could claim. They use the words of God, Christ, and the Spirit to make fine declarations about holiness and heaven and how all should repent and change their lives or they will go to hell, etc., etc. But, which of them can speak from their own experience or from their own knowledge? Which ever pointed people to the divine principle, placed by God within each person, to help in that work? Which told how to know it – to wait to feel its power working within and turning all to know and do the will of God?

Some have spoken of the Spirit and how it works to bring people to sanctification and to worship God, but not where and how to find it and not to wait for it to act within. This is declared a mystery, reserved for revelation in a later reformation. But this people not only offers words – based on knowledge and their own experience – they also urge repentance, conversion, and holiness. They direct those to whom they preach to a principle that is capable of achieving these things. They point out where it is, by what means they can come to know it, and how they can experience its power and capacity to bring their souls to happiness. This is more than the theories or speculations on which other ministries depend. Here, there is a certainty, a rock on which people can confidently stand before God on the great Final Day.

V. They touch the inward states and conditions of people – clear evidence of the power of their Principle and evidence that their ministry is rooted in that Principle and not in their own imaginations or their own misrepresentations of and commentaries on the Scriptures. Nothing can reach into a heart that does not arise in a heart; nothing can pierce a conscience that does not come from a living conscience. And yet, this has often happened: People have confided their state or condition to a particular Friend for advice or to ease their burden. The ministry they received in return has so pierced them that they have accused their friends with revealing the details of their secrets and accused their preachers of disclosing the state of their affairs. The very thoughts and desires of their hearts have been so plainly detected that they, like Nathanael, have cried out to Christ within themselves, "You are the Son of God; you are the King of Israel."[1215] Those who have embraced this Divine Principle have seen the signs of its Truth and Divinity. Like the Samaritan woman, they have cried out, "He told me everything I ever did;[1216] he showed me the innermost secrets of my heart.[1217] He has made justice the measuring line and righteousness the plumb line."[1218] Thousands today can testify to this in their own lives. Everything claimed by this people about the power and virtue of this Heavenly Principle has turned out to be true and more than true. What they have experienced inwardly of the power, purity, wisdom, mercy, and goodness of God is twice what they have been told outwardly.

VI.   This Principle has completely prepared even the poorest and least-educated people for their work and service. It has furnished them with extraordinary understanding of divine things and a remarkable ability to captivate an audience, which led some to wonder, "Isn't this the laborer's child,[1219] how could this person know so much without an education?"[1220] Some used this as an excuse to accuse them of being Jesuits[1221] (who have for many years had a reputation as scholars) in disguise. A charge that is in no way justified – these ministers, their homes, their families, and their educations are all well known.

[1215] John 1:49: "Nathanael answered and saith unto him, Rabbi, thou art the Son of God; thou art the King of Israel."

[1216] John 4:39: "And many of the Samaritans of that city believed on him for the saying of the woman, which testified, He told me all that ever I did."

[1217] Ps. 44:21: "Shall not God search this out? for he knoweth the secrets of the heart."

[1218] Isa. 28:17: "Judgment also will I lay to the line, and righteousness to the plummet: and the hail shall sweep away the refuge of lies, and the waters shall overflow the hiding place."

[1219] Matt. 13:55: "Is not this the carpenter's son? is not his mother called Mary? and his brethren, James, and Joses, and Simon, and Judas?"

[1220] John 7:15: "And the Jews marvelled, saying, How knoweth this man letters, having never learned?"

[1221] Besides the obvious charge that a person is secretly a Roman Catholic, the term 'Jesuit' also implied a high degree of craftiness and deceptiveness in argument.

VII. They are humble, despised, and hated, as the primitive Christians were. They lacked the advantages of worldly wisdom or earthly power, as some earlier reformers did. But in all things, this people were brought forth by the cross – they are a challenge to the ways, the worship, the conduct, and the customs of this world. Indeed, they would oppose even motions of the wind and tide to prevent anyone boasting before God.[1222]

VIII. They gained no personal benefit from this work that might expose them to scorn and abuse. For the love of God, they gladly spent everything and were spent themselves.[1223] Taking their lives in their hands, they left their husbands, wives, and children, homes and lands, and everything that they held dear. Daily, they risked everything, but – revived in their spirits by the good Spirit and power of God – they proclaimed the primitive message: God is Light and in God there is no darkness at all.[1224] God sent his Son into the world[1225] as a Light to enlighten all[1226] in order that they might be saved.[1227] Those, who say they have fellowship with God and are God's children and people, but who walk in darkness (that is, in disobedience to the Light in their consciences and in pursuit of worldly delights), are liars and do not live by the Truth.[1228] But, all who love the Light and lay their deeds out to the Light,[1229] and walk in the Light (since God is Light), will be cleansed of all sin by the blood of Jesus Christ.[1230]

[1222] Rom. 4:2: "For if Abraham were justified by works, he hath *whereof* to glory; but not before God."

[1223] 2 Cor. 12:15: "And I will very gladly spend and be spent for you; though the more abundantly I love you, the less I be loved."

[1224] 1 John 1:5: "This then is the message which we have heard of him, and declare unto you, that God is light, and in him is no darkness at all."

[1225] 1 John 4:9: "In this was manifested the love of God toward us, because that God sent his only begotten Son into the world, that we might live through him."

[1226] John 1:9: "*That* was the true Light, which lighteth every man that cometh into the world."

[1227] John 1:7: "The same came for a witness, to bear witness of the Light, that all *men* through him might believe."

[1228] 1 John 1:6: "If we say that we have fellowship with him, and walk in darkness, we lie, and do not the truth."

[1229] John 3:19-21: "And this is the condemnation, that light is come into the world, and men loved darkness rather than light, because their deeds were evil. For

IX.   They are known for their steadfastness and patience in suffering for any part of their testimony. They have suffered banishments, excessive fines, and the seizure of goods and property. They have been beaten and bruised. They have served long imprisonments in crowded and foul dungeons. They have even died for their ministry – four were executed in New England simply for preaching among the people. These things are hard to write about, much less to endure, except by those who have the support of a good and glorious cause. For that cause, they have refused to accept deliverance from these persecutions by any indirect means offered to them.[1231]

X.   Even when it was in their power, they have shown no inclination to take revenge, but forgave their cruel enemies; showing mercy even to those who had displayed none to them.

XI.   They spoke plainly to those in authority – like the ancient prophets, telling them to their faces of their public and private sins. To those enjoying the height of their power, they prophesied their afflictions and downfall. In addition to these personal judgments for individual persecutions, they warned in explicit terms of national judgments, such as the plague and fire of London.[1232] In remarkable ways, these came to pass. In the future, these may be publicly revealed for the glory of God.

---

every one that doeth evil hateth the light, neither cometh to the light, lest his deeds should be reproved. But he that doeth truth cometh to the light, that his deeds may be made manifest, that they are wrought in God."

[1230] 1 John 1:7: "But if we walk in the light, as he is in the light, we have fellowship one with another, and the blood of Jesus Christ his Son cleanseth us from all sin."

[1231] Marmaduke Stephenson, William Robinson, and Mary Dyer were flogged and banished from Massachusetts for being Quakers in 1658. They were warned that they would be executed if they ever came back. Almost immediately, they returned and were arrested for preaching publicly. Both men were hanged on the Boston Commons in 1659. Mary Dyer was sentenced to be hanged with them, but was released at the last minute and again banished. Returning again 1660, she, too, was hung. In 1661, William Leddra followed their example and was also hung.

[1232] In 1664-65, England suffered from a widespread outbreak of the plague. Approximately 70,000 died in London alone and in 1666 fire destroyed more than 80 percent of that city. In his *Journal* (written some years after the event),

This, Reader, is the origin, principles, ministry, and progress of this people, both in its general and particular testimonies. By this account, you can see how and from what root they grew and how they have come to be so numerous a people. What remains is for me to describe for you their care, conduct, and discipline as a Christian and reformed society so that you can judge for yourself if they live up to their principles and their faith. This is important because others have tried to tarnish their character as much by unjust accusations of disorderliness as by the false charges of error. Such slanders have accompanied every true step on the road to reformation. None suffered such contempt more than the primitive Christians themselves, who were the glory of Christianity, the great lights and examples to their own and succeeding ages.

Chapter 4

The Discipline and Practice of This Religious Society

*A*s this people increased daily in both the towns and the country, a holy charge fell on some of the elders among them to provide care and service to the church. Following the example of the primitive saints, the first thing they undertook was charity to provide for the needs of the poor. Collections were early organized and donations liberally made for that and various other services within the church. These funds were entrusted to faithful, God-fearing, well-respected people who had the energy to carry out the work. They made sure that no one would be in need – often adding sizeable amounts of their own without desire for repayment or acknowledgment. Nor was any service held back or allowed to fail for lack of money.

They also ensured that anyone who received such support lived up to God's standards on all occasions – that they lived peaceably and were in all ways good examples. They were careful to maintain careful records. All sufferings and services were written down. Because they could not perform weddings in the world's way, they took particular care that everything was clear between the parties and with all others. It was rare that any problem was brought up publicly that had not already been taken quietly to some well-known and weighty Friends for careful consideration. The support and unity of the society was of great concern to them. But the needs of the

---

George Fox reports that he had a premonition of these events while in Lancaster Prison.

poor, the number of orphans, marriages, sufferings, and other matters multiplied. Instances arose in which a member of one meeting was involved with a member of another meeting, and it became clear that individual meetings needed in some way to better communicate with each other and to work together. It pleased the Lord in wisdom and goodness to reveal a good and orderly way of proceeding to the First Instrument of this Dispensation.[1233] He felt called to visit the meetings throughout England in person and to establish this gospel order among them. By letters and later by visits, he set up the same system in other nations and provinces abroad. I will say more about this when I speak of him below.

The care, conduct, and discipline that I have been speaking of, and which is practiced by this people, are as follows:

In every county where he traveled, this good elder [Fox] urged that some in each Meeting for Worship meet together once each month to discuss what has been happening in and what the needs are of the meeting. While the number of Meetings for Worship varied in different counties, four to six usually joined together at a Monthly Meeting for Business. As he requested, these meetings began to meet and consider the poor, orphans, any who had been disorderly or unfaithful, births, marriages, burials, sufferings, etc.

The Monthly Meetings in each county made up a Quarterly Meeting, where the most devoted and well-known Friends of the county could meet to talk with each other and to offer advise or assistance to each other – especially when a particular piece of business seemed especially difficult or when a Monthly Meeting was unable to settle a matter. These Quarterly Meetings also reviewed reports from each constituent Monthly Meeting and prepared one for the whole county to be sent to the Yearly Meeting.

This is composed of all the Quarterly Meetings and is held in London. Chosen members of the various meetings in England, from other nations, and from the provinces meet yearly to communicate with each other, to advise and be advised, to help each other, and to build up the church. They also ensure that there are sufficient funds to meet the general expenses of the Yearly Meeting – these do not need to be detailed here.

Any member of the church may come to these meetings and all are free, in the fear of God, to speak their minds on any matter, but the

---

[1233] George Fox is "the First Instrument of this Dispensation."

decisions of the Quarterly Meeting are delivered to the Yearly Meeting by persons assigned or chosen for that service by the Quarterly Meetings.

Careful records are kept of all matters that are considered by the Monthly, Quarterly, and Yearly Business Meetings by someone who has volunteered or has been appointed for that service. The Monthly and Quarterly Meetings refer cases to the Yearly Meeting and depend on it to maintain order. Care is taken by a number of persons, chosen by the body as a whole, to make copies of the Yearly Meeting minutes. These are distributed to the Monthly and Quarterly Meetings along with a general Appeal to Holiness, Unity, and Charity.

Meetings for Business are opened and usually concluded by all present solemnly waiting upon God, who is sometimes graciously pleased to provide them with evidence of his love and presence, as in any of their Meetings for Worship.

It should be noted that no one presides over these solemn assemblies for the churches' service, as in the meetings of other people. Christ is their only President and he is pleased to provide life and wisdom to them through any of those present. All are listened to equally – despite differences in education, ability, or personal authority – out of confidence in the divine authority and in the expression of Christ's Power and Spirit through his people. In these meetings, Christ makes good on his blessed promise, that whenever and wherever any meet together in his name, he would be in their midst,[1234] even to the end of the world.[1235] So it is.

[1234] Matt. 18:20: "For where two or three are gathered together in my name, there am I in the midst of them."

[1235] Matt. 28:20: "Teaching them to observe all things whatsoever I have commanded you: and, lo, I am with you always, *even* unto the end of the world. Amen."

The Church Power they Own and Exercise

Now it may be expected that I will delineate what sort of authority this people exercises over those members of their society whose lives are not consistent with their beliefs or who defy the good and upright order which has been established – especially because they have been roundly criticized, both verbally and in writing, on this account.[1236]

The authority that they exercise is that given by Christ through his disciples to his own people until the end of the world. It is to oversee, preach, censure, and, after longsuffering and waiting for the disobedient to change, to disown those who refuse to mend their ways. When this happens, the society publicly repudiates their behavior and way of life and informs everyone that, until they repent, such people are no longer part of their fellowship. This authority is exercised when there is a breach either in relation to ordinary and general practices or when an individual violates those standards by which this people are distinguished from all others who profess to be Christians. Great care is taken to avoid both acts of persecution and of excessive permissiveness which have caused so many splits within Christianity.

What They Reject and Condemn

People cannot be whipped into the temple; those who cannot conform for reasons of faith or conscience should not be punished either physically or financially. Likewise, people cannot claim to be part of that people but left loose and unaccountable to anyone but God and the civil authorities. And nothing has contributed more to this kind of careless and extreme behavior than the abuse of churchly power by those who use force and physical punishment to advance their own desires and interests. From its own grievous sufferings, this people has learned to loathe this practice and are well known for their support of universal liberty of conscience.

In the other hand, they equally disapprove of complete autonomy – a lack of accountability on the part of individuals to the other members of their religious communion that their behavior and life styles are consistent

---

[1236] The establishment of an administrative system consisting of Monthly, Quarterly, and Yearly Meetings was opposed by some Friends. Opposition was particularly strong to Fox's decision to set up separate Women's Business Meetings. Moreover, the shift of power from the north of England to London was a source of friction within the society.

with the values of that community. They distinguish between imposing any restriction on others' faith or worship (which is never done or accepted or submitted to) and requiring members to comply in Christian humility with the body's standards in their day-to-day lives. Such is necessary to maintain the distinct character and order of the society as a serious, religious community. In short, they expect behavior that promotes holiness and charity and that supports members in practicing what they preach. Members are expected to live up to their own principles and are not free to bring shame on their fellowship without condemnation. No one is compelled to associate with them, but those who chose to do so are obligated to behave accordingly. If they do not, they will be disowned. This is their ultimate act of repudiation and is the limit of authority they exercise, or that any Christian community can rightly exercise, upon its own members.

Their Method for Proceedings against Erring and Disorderly Members

This is the disciplinary procedure for those who have lapsed or transgressed. First, the offender is visited by some of them and he or she is confronted with the offense – an act that violates either known, general standards of the wider society or the particular beliefs of their own community. For the good of the offender's soul, the honor of God, and the reputation of the society, these visitors will endeavor by love and tenderness to convince the offender to acknowledge the wrongdoing and repudiate it as publicly as it was committed. For the most part, this is done in writing. If, after repeated attempts and patient waiting for a sign of repentance, the offender is still unwilling to clear the reputation of the society from the stain of his or her evildoing or unfaithfulness, a public statement disowning the offense and the offender is published. That document serves as public testimony to their care for the honor of the Truth that they accept.

If offenders later repudiate their former behavior, offering a sincere acknowledgment of their responsibility and Godly sorrow for their acts, they are received back and looked upon again as members of their communion. God does not turn his back on those who have repented, nor do God's true people.

This then is my report on the origins, principles, and practices of the people of God called Quakers, including descriptions of their faith, worship, discipline, and way of life. I believe that this is a very proper preface to the *Journal* of the first, blessed, and glorious instrument of this

work. It is a testimony to his extraordinary qualifications and services –
remarkable in his own day and worthy to be set out as an example to all
succeeding generations. It has been written for the glory of the Most High
God and as a fitting memorial to that worthy and excellent man, God's
faithful servant and apostle to this generation.

Chapter 5

I have now come to the third topic of my *Preface*, that is, God's chosen
instrument and earthly originator. It is natural for some to say, "We
can see the work and the resulting people, but who was the man, the
instrument, that was sent to this generation to begin this work and this
people?" With God's help, I will describe who and what he was, not only
from the reports of others, but from my own intimate knowledge of him.
For this long and dear friendship, my soul has frequently blessed God and,
by the time this *Preface* is read, a serious Reader will understand that I had
good reason to do so.

George Fox, the Primary Instrument by Whom God Gathered this People

The blessed instrument for and to this day of God was George Fox.

He was born in Leicestershire in about 1624, the child of honest and
capable parents, who tried to bring up all their children in the religious ways
and worship of the nation. But from a young age, George seemed to have a
different frame of mind than the rest of his family, being more religious,
inward, still, solid, and observant beyond his years. The answers he gave,
and the questions he would ask – especially about divine things – on
occasion astonished those who heard him.[1237]

His mother was a very accomplished woman – more so than most in
that area. She took notice of his remarkable abilities – the gravity, wisdom,

---

[1237] Penn seems to be drawing a parallel to the story of Jesus at 12 years old
astonishing the elders in the temple: Luke 2:41-43, 46-47 ("Now his parents
went to Jerusalem every year at the Feast of the Passover. And when he was
twelve years old, they went up to Jerusalem after the custom of the feast. And
when they had fulfilled the days, as they returned, the child Jesus tarried behind
in Jerusalem; and Joseph and his mother knew not *of it*. ... And it came to pass,
that after three days they found him in the temple, sitting in the midst of the
doctors, both hearing them, and asking them questions. And all that heard him
were astonished at his understanding and answers").

and piety that very early shined forth through him – how even when he was very young, he refused to participate in childish and wasteful games or useless social events. She was very tender and indulgent of this behavior, so that he met little difficulty from her. He was trained in country work and took great delight in working with sheep – the simplicity and solitude of this work being well suited to his mind – and became very skillful with them. This early shepherding foreshadowed his later ministry and service.

I will try not to repeat what he has written in his *Journal* – his account being far better than I could achieve – but will add some details to it. When he was in his early twenties, he left his friends and visited with the most thoughtful and religious people in that area – who night and day waited for the consolation of Israel as Zacharias,[1238] Anna,[1239] and Simeon[1240] did in the old times. He sought them out in the neighboring counties and stayed with them until he was called by God to a more advanced ministry.

At that time, he taught, and was an example of, silence, trying to turn them from acts of worship that they chose for themselves and toward the Light of Christ within. He encouraged them to wait patiently, to feel the power of the Light in their hearts, so that their knowledge and worship of God could be rooted in the power of the endless life to be found in obedience to the inward Light. In the Word was Life and that Life was the Light of all people.[1241] Life was in the Word and Light was in all – and, if the Light is obeyed, Life is in them as well. The children of the Light live by the Life of the Word and the Word makes them children of God.[1242] This is the regeneration and new birth without which no one comes into the

---

[1238] Zacharias was a priest in the temple in Jerusalem and father of John the Baptist (see Luke 1).

[1239] Luke 2:36: "And there was one Anna, a prophetess, the daughter of Phanuel, of the tribe of Aser: she was of a great age, and had lived with an husband seven years from her virginity."

[1240] Luke 2:25: "And, behold, there was a man in Jerusalem, whose name *was* Simeon; and the same man *was* just and devout, waiting for the consolation of Israel: and the Holy Ghost was upon him."

[1241] John 1:1&4: "In the beginning was the Word, and the Word was with God, and the Word was God ... In him was life; and the life was the light of men."

[1242] Rom. 8:14: "For as many as are led by the Spirit of God, they are the sons of God."

kingdom of God.[1243] Everyone who comes to that kingdom is greater than John the Baptist,[1244] that is, greater than John's ministry which was not gospel ministry, but merely the capstone of the earlier legal dispensation. George Fox spent his time in this ministry for several years and several Meetings were gathered in that part of the country.

In 1652, he withdrew to the top of a very high mountain in the hinterlands of Yorkshire.[1245] As he waited on the Lord there, he had a vision of a great work of God on the earth and that he was to go forth in public ministry to begin it. He saw people, as thick as the dust in a sunbeam, who would in time be brought home to the Lord, so that there would be one Shepherd and one sheepfold for the whole earth.[1246] His eye was directed northward to a great people that would receive him and his message. On that mountain, God directed him to sound the great Day of the Lord[1247] as if there was a great audience present.

From there he went north, as the Lord had shown him. As he came to each place (if not before he had even arrived) a particular service and task

---

[1243] John 3:3: "Jesus answered and said unto him, Verily, verily, I say unto thee, Except a man be born again, he cannot see the kingdom of God."

[1244] Luke 7:28: "For I say unto you, Among those that are born of women there is not a greater prophet than John the Baptist: but he that is least in the kingdom of God is greater than he."

[1245] Pendle Hill.

[1246] John 10:16: "And other sheep I have, which are not of this fold: them also I must bring, and they shall hear my voice; and there shall be one fold, *and* one shepherd."

[1247] It seems likely that Penn is depicting Fox as engaged in an event of biblical proportions on Pendle Hill, but it is not clear exactly what he is alluding to. Penn's use of 'high mountain' evokes Isa. 40:9 ("O Zion, that bringest good tidings, get thee up into the high mountain; O Jerusalem, that bringest good tidings, lift up thy voice with strength; lift it up, be not afraid; say unto the cities of Judah, Behold your God!"), but there are also strong echoes of Joel 2:1-2 ("Blow ye the trumpet in Zion, and sound an alarm in my holy mountain: let all the inhabitants of the land tremble: for the day of the LORD cometh, for it is nigh at hand; A day of darkness and of gloominess, a day of clouds and of thick darkness, as the morning spread upon the mountains: a great people and a strong; there hath not been ever the like, neither shall be any more after it, even to the years of many generations") in the text.

was revealed to him – the Lord truly was his Leader.[1248] His travels were not in vain; in most places, God endorsed his work with the convincement of a variety of people, from the lowest sinners to the most serious religious leaders. Among the first and most well-known of them, were Richard Farnsworth, James Naylor, William Dewsberry, Thomas Aldam, Francis Howgill, Edward Burroughs, John Camm, John Audland, Richard Hubberthorn, T. Taylor, T. Holmes, Alexander Parker, William Simpson, William Caton, John Stubbs, Robert Widders, Thomas Lowe, Josiah Coale, John Burnyeat, Robert Lodge, and Thomas Salthouse – all now dead – and many more, equally worthy of mention, as well as many still living from that great, first wave of convincements. After gaining knowledge of God's purifying judgment within themselves, and spending some time in silence, waiting to feel and receive power from on high[1249] to speak God's name (which no one else can rightly do otherwise, even though they use the same words), they felt God's promptings. Frequently, they were led forth, especially to public places – markets, fairs, and the sides of the highways – to preach, inform, criticize, and urge others to repent and turn their hearts as well as their words to God. They directed all to the Light of Christ within them and by it to truly see and examine and consider their lives; to shun evil and to do the good and pleasing will of God.

They suffered great hardships for this work – for their love and goodwill – often being put into the stocks, stoned, beaten, whipped, and imprisoned even though they were honest, hard-working people, well-respected by their neighbors. They left husbands, wives, and children, house and home, to carry forth a living call to repentance. The priests generally opposed them, and wrote against them, and fabricated false and scandalous stories to slander them, provoking the civil authorities to suppress them, especially in the north of England. Yet God filled them with living power, opening the door for them, and there was a mighty convincement throughout that part of the country.[1250]

[1248] Isa. 55:4: "Behold, I have given him *for* a witness to the people, a leader and commander to the people."

[1249] Luke 24:49: "And, behold, I send the promise of my Father upon you: but tarry ye in the city of Jerusalem, until ye be endued with power from on high."

[1250] Rev. 3:8: "I know thy works: behold, I have set before thee an open door, and no man can shut it: for thou hast a little strength, and hast kept my word, and hast not denied my name."

In those early days, Judges Bradshaw[1251] and Fell[1252] presided in the courts of that area and Colonel West[1253] was the Clerk of Assize. Though the priests in that area worked hard in opposition, hoping, Herod-like, to use civil power to cut them off and root them out of the county, these men treated them with kindness and gave them protection. Judge Fell especially had little regard for the accusations of ignorant and evil-minded people and was not only a check on their rage in the course of legal proceedings, but looked after these people in other ways as well. His wife was among the first to receive the Truth and, being a wise and just man, her choice influenced his Spirit. In her and others in his family, he saw all the popular vilifications against the way of Truth refuted. He protected them whenever he could, even opening the doors of his home to his wife's friends. In their tenderness, humility, love, and zeal for the Truth and the people of the Lord, both the judge and his wife will be remembered as an honor and a blessing to all who have that name.

In the early years, before the Truth had spread throughout southern England, their house[1254] was a safe-harbor for this people. Other notable and substantial persons in those northern counties also opened their homes and their hearts to the many that God had called to declare salvation to the people in that area. Meetings of the Lord's messengers were frequently held in those homes. There, they reported to one another their services and activities, comforted, and instructed each other in their blessed ministry.

His Many Excellent Qualifications

But I have touched on all this before. Let me return to George Fox and his personal qualities – natural, moral, and divine – both in his interactions with other people and in the Church of God.

I.   He was a man that God endowed with a clear and wonderful spiritual depth – a discerner of others' Spirits and very much a master of his own Spirit. And, though his manner of expression might have sounded

---

[1251] Judge John Bradshaw (1602-1659) presided at the trial of King Charles I in 1648-49 and was a President of the Council of State from 1649-51.

[1252] Thomas Fell (c. 1598-1658) of Swarthmoor Hall was a religious non-conformist and the husband of Margaret Fell (1614-1702) who was later to marry George Fox.

[1253] Colonel William West refused to issue a warrant for Fox's arrest.

[1254] Swarthmoor Hall.

uncouth and unpolished to more refined listeners, the content of his speech was nevertheless very profound. It deserved to be considered more than once and the more often it was, the weightier and more instructive it was. Although sometimes his words poured forth abruptly or ungrammatically, it was obvious that they were often closer to Truth than many finely composed speeches. Indeed his words demonstrated beyond all doubt that he was sent directly by God.

As a man, he was an original, being no one's copy. Training and education made no contribution to the content or the presentation of his ministry – human wit and wisdom had nothing to do with the many great, excellent, and necessary Truths that he was sent to preach. There can be no doubt that his ministry and writings are not the products of human teachings or learned by studying other human works. They were not theory or speculation, but sensible and practical Truths aimed at pointing people to conversion and regeneration – to setting up the kingdom of God in their hearts. This was his work. I myself have many times been overcome by the power of his preaching, crying out with my Lord and Master, "I thank you, Father, Lord of heaven and earth, because you have hidden these things from the wise and learned, and revealed them to little children."[1255] Many times has my soul bowed in humble thankfulness to the Lord for not choosing any of the wise and learned of this world to be the leading messenger of God's Blessed Truth to our age. God chose one who was not born to wealth or power, or elegant speech, or highly educated, so that there would be no suspicion that his message and work grew out of human wisdom or personal interests. As a result, that message was clearer to, and worked more forcefully on, the consciences of those who sincerely sought the way of Truth.

With an inner eye, opened in me by God, I can clearly see the marks of God's finger and hand in this testimony: in the clearness of the principle, in its serious, powerful, and effective example, in its simplicity, zeal, steadiness, humility, solemnity, precision, charity, and all-inclusive care. All this shined through in his life and this people's lives and in the testimony God gave him to deliver. This confirmed to me that his work was the Lord's, and it engaged my soul in a deep love, fear, reverence, and

---

[1255] Matt. 11:25: "At that time Jesus answered and said, I thank thee, O Father, Lord of heaven and earth, because thou hast hid these things from the wise and prudent, and hast revealed them unto babes."

thankfulness for God's love and mercy. In that state, I am now and, with God's help, hope to remain to the end of my days.

II.   In his testimony or ministry, he worked hard to reveal Truth to everyone's understanding and to ground them in the principle (and Principal), Christ Jesus, the Light of the World. By bringing them to that something of God that is within themselves, they were better able to know and understand God and themselves.

III.   He had an extraordinary gift for revealing the meaning of the Scriptures. He could go straight to the essence of things and plainly lay out their purpose, unity, and fulfillment, providing great comfort and instruction.

IV.   The mysteries of the first and second Adam, of the fall and restoration, of the Law and Gospel, of shadows and substance, of the servant's and child's state, and the fulfillment of the scriptures in Christ, and by Christ the True Light within all, through obedience and faith, were the heart and soul of his testimonies. In this, all could see that he was God's – preaching what Christ, who never errs or fails, had given him directly.

V.   But above all, he excelled in prayer. The inwardness and weight of his Spirit, the reverence and solemnity of his language and behavior – the fewness and fullness of his words – have often filled even strangers with reverence and brought others consolation. I must say that the most awe-filled, spiritually alive, and worshipful body I have ever felt or seen was his in prayer. Truly, his life was prayer and he lived nearer to the Lord than other people – those who best know God best understand that God is to be approached with reverence and fear.

VI.   He lived an innocent life – not a busybody nor a self-seeker, neither irritable nor critical. He was very instructive, without being condescending. He was so meek, contented, modest, easygoing, steady, and tender that it was a pleasure just to be in his company. He exercised no authority, except over evil – and that in all things and everywhere – without love, compassion, and patience. He was a most merciful man, always ready to forgive, never giving or taking offense at anything. Thousands can testify that in truth he had an excellent spirit and reputation and, because of it, other excellent spirits felt genuine and lasting love for him.

VII.   He worked tirelessly. When he was young, before many great and deep sufferings and travels had sapped his energy, he labored much in the word – preaching doctrine and discipline in England, Scotland, and

Ireland. He turned many to God, strengthened those who were convinced of the Truth, and established good order for church business among them. Near the end of his travels, between the years 1671 and 1677, he visited the meetings in the American colonies, the Netherlands, and in Germany (as described in his *Journal*) – convincing and consoling many in those places. After that time, he lived mostly in and around the city of London. Besides his frequent and valuable service and ministry, he wrote often, both to those within and those who were outside the fellowship. Above all, he exercised great care for the affairs of the church.

VIII.   He was often where the church records are kept and occasional letters from the Meetings of God's People throughout the world were received. He had these letters read to him and shared them with the weekly meetings held there.[1256] He was sure to stir up the meeting to address the needs of those writing, especially in cases of sufferings.[1257] He showed great sympathy and compassion on those occasions, carefully looking into each case, and strenuously working for speedy and suitable relief. The Meetings and any suffering members of them knew they would not be forgotten or help delayed if he was there.

IX.   In his services for God and God's people, he knew neither fatigue nor fear – as free from fright as from anger. His behavior at Derby, Litchfield, Appleby, before Oliver Cromwell, at Launceston, Scarborough, Worcester, and Westminster Hall,[1258] and in many other places, gave abundant evidence of his character to friends and foes alike.

[1256] Early on, a group of 'weighty Friends' met in London on Monday mornings in what was called the Second Morning Meeting to attend to the ongoing business of Friends. This committee was later formalized as the Meeting for Sufferings and is today the executive body of Britain Yearly Meeting.

[1257] 'Sufferings' refers to the deaths, fines, imprisonment, beatings, etc. that resulted from persecution.

[1258] Fox was imprisoned in Derby, Launceston, Scarborough, and Worcester. He was twice on trial in Westminster Hall. He felt called by God to walk barefoot through Lichfield in 1651, crying out, "Woe to the bloody city of Lichfield!" He also met several times with Oliver Cromwell during Cromwell's tenure as Lord Protector of England.

His Troubles and Sufferings, Both Within and Without the Society

In the primitive church, some rose up against the blessed Apostles of our Lord Jesus Christ – even among those they had personally led to the hope of the gospel – and became their greatest enemies. In the same way, this man of God had his share of suffering from some who had been convinced by him, but through prejudice or misunderstanding turned against him and accused him of attempting to dominate them against their consciences. He worked tirelessly, in person and in writing, to win willing and enthusiastic agreement with good and wholesome things – in particular with respect to the orderly conduct of the affairs of the church and in their outward behavior. Some were jealous of the love and esteem this meek man received and deserved in the hearts of the people. Others believed the groundless accusations that he unilaterally imposed his judgment and required blind obedience.

They favored complete autonomy for each person. Since each has direct access to the Light within, each should be answerable only to that and to no one else. They ignore the fact that the Light is One in all and, although the measure of Light or grace differs in each person, it is ultimately the same in all. In so doing, they attacked the essential spiritual unity into which people, who are all guided by the same principle, will naturally be led. What is evil to one person must be evil to all. What is virtuous, honest, or honorable to one, must be so to all – if they are led in common by the One Universal Principle. Those who are disaffected claim to be led by that principle. It is the root of all true Christian fellowship, the spring from which all people of God drink, that leads them to become spirit-led – and therefore of one heart and one soul.

Some, on weak grounds, misrepresented the purpose of church governance. They claimed that Fox and others were, in the guise of seeking good order, attempting to control the content of worship. On that basis, they were ready to object (as the dissenters from the national church of England rightly had) that they were being forced to conform to a creed and a fixed form of worship. But the good order that was presented dealt only with external behavior and the governance of the outward (one might say civil) aspects of the church – that members should live up to the principles they profess to believe and be generous in care for others and in charity. Some have stumbled and fallen because of such mistakes, unreasonable stubbornness, and even prejudice, but, Blessed be God! most have returned to their first love. They have recognized the work of the enemy, who looks for every opportunity or advantage to hold up or hinder the work of God, to disrupt the peace of God's church, and to chill the love of God's people for the Truth and for one another. There is still hope even for those who have not yet returned.

In all these things, there was no one that the discontented attacked as sharply as this good man. He accepted all their weaknesses and prejudices, refused to answer blow for blow, and forgave them all for their weak and bitter words. He prayed that they understand the harm they were doing and see how slyly the enemy acts to tear apart and divide. He prayed for their return to their first love that forgives all things.

Proof that he was Led by a Divine Power – Not a Human One

Truly, I must say that even though God had visibly clothed him in divine preference and authority – indeed, his very presence expressed a religious majesty – he never abused it. He held his position in the church of God with gentleness, humility, and restraint. At all times, like his blessed master, he was the servant of all – holding and exercising his eldership in the invisible power that had gathered them – with reverence for the true head of the church and with care for its members. It was only by the Spirit and power of Christ that he was the first and chief elder of this age. As such he was doubly worthy of respect and, for that reason, it was given him by the faithful. His authority was inward, not outward. He received it and kept it by the love of God and by the power of an endless life.[1259] I write this from my own knowledge, not based on the reports of others, and what I tell you is true. I have been with him for weeks and months at a time on various occasions – some of a most interesting and dangerous nature – by night and day, by land and sea, at home and abroad. I can say that I never saw him abuse his position nor did he ever fail to accept any service or responsibility that it required.

In all things, he acted as a man, a strong man, a new and heavenly minded man. He understood both divine and natural things, by God Almighty's making. I have been surprised by his questions and answers in natural things. Even though he was never educated in the (useless and hairsplitting) sciences, he drew on a strong foundation of useful and valuable knowledge which he cultivated every where. His behavior was courteous

---

[1259] Heb. 7:16: "Who is made [a priest], not after the law of a carnal commandment, but after the power of an endless life."

and respectful – more than can be taught. He was a very temperate person, eating little and, though a large man, sleeping less.

His End and Triumph

This is how he lived among us and, as he lived, so he died – feeling in his final moments the same eternal power that had called him forth and preserved him. He was so confident of God's love that he triumphed over death – hardly giving it any attention, right up to the end. On his deathbed, he talked with those of us present about sending out an epistle that he had just written to the churches of Christ throughout the world. His mind was on his books, but above all on Friends, especially those in Ireland and America. Twice he told us, "Care for the poor Friends in Ireland and America."

About four or five hours before his departure from this world, some who had come in asked him how he was feeling. He replied, "Never mind that – the Lord's power is over all weakness and death! The seed reigns! Blessed be the Lord!" He was at the meeting near Lombard Street on the first day of the week, and it was two days later, at about 10 PM when he left us, dying just a few doors away in Henry Gouldney's house.

He had reached a ripe old age, living to see his children's children to many generations in the Truth. He suffered only a short final illness and was blessed that his mind remained clear to the end. Like the author of Hebrews, we can truly say, "Even though he is dead, he still speaks to us."[1260] Though he is absent in body, he is present in spirit[1261] – neither time nor place can interrupt the communion of the saints or dissolve the fellowship of the spirits of the just.[1262] His works praise him[1263] because were performed to the praise of the One who made him. His memory is and will be blessed. I will finish this section with a short epitaph:

[1260] Heb. 11:4: "By faith Abel offered unto God a more excellent sacrifice than Cain, by which he obtained witness that he was righteous, God testifying of his gifts: and by it he being dead yet speaketh."

[1261] 1 Cor. 5:3: "For I verily, as absent in body, but present in spirit, have judged already, as though I were present, *concerning* him that hath so done this deed."

[1262] Heb. 12:23: "To the general assembly and church of the firstborn, which are written in heaven, and to God the Judge of all, and to the spirits of just men made perfect."

[1263] Ps. 145:10: "All thy works shall praise thee, O LORD; and thy saints shall bless thee."

Many have lived upright lives in this day, but dear George, you surpass them all.

Chapter 6

Five Distinct Exhortations

Reminding this People of their Primitive Integrity and Simplicity

Now, Friends, you who claim to walk in the path to which God sent this blessed man to guide us, listen carefully to this exhortation – parents as much as children, elders as much as youths. The glory of this day, and the foundation for the hope that has sustained us since we became a distinct people, is that blessed principle of Light and Life of Christ that we possess. We point all people to it as the greatest means to conversion and help in turning them to God. This is what first touched and enlightened us – showing us our inward condition, leading us to consider our final end, directing our eyes to God, and teaching us to number our days so that we might fix our hearts on wisdom.[1264] After that time, we did not depend on the sight of our eyes or the hearing of our ears. Our judgments and actions – of things and people, ourselves and others, even toward God, our maker – were guided by the Light on our inward senses that this blessed principle gave us. Being inwardly enlivened by it, we could easily discern the differences between things – what was right and what was wrong, what was appropriate and what was not –with respect to both religious and civil concerns. It is the ground on which the fellowship of all saints is built and on it, our fellowship stood. In it, we desired to know each other and act toward each other, and all people, in love, faithfulness, reverence and fear.

Feeling the work of this principle in our hearts, we drew near to the Lord. Before we approached the Lord in prayer or opened our mouths in ministry, we waited to be prepared by it. Our comfort, service, and instruction began and ended with it. When we tried to outrun this guide or stopped short of it, we made burdens for ourselves to bear – finding our work rejected instead of accepted. Hearing "Who required this?"[1265] instead

---

[1264] Ps. 90:12: "So teach *us* to number our days, that we may apply *our* hearts unto wisdom."

[1265] Isa. 1:12: "When ye come to appear before me, who hath required this at your hand, to tread my courts?"

of "Well done!"[1266] At that time, we were a faithful and disciplined people –
everything about us declared it!

We were then very concerned to provide care for others, as well as for
ourselves, especially for the newly convinced. Often we were compelled to
carry the word of the Lord to our neighbors, relatives, and acquaintances –
even to strangers. We worried about each other's well-being. We did not
seek out any coldness or misunderstandings, but treated each other as
people who believed in and felt God's presence. Our way of life was
innocent, serious, and sincere. We guarded ourselves against the cares and
friendships of the world. We understood Truth according to its own Spirit,
not our own spirits, our own needs, or our own desires.

When others saw our behavior, they were humbled by it and frequently
joined us. We did not think of ourselves as free to do as we pleased, to go
when or where we choose, or to say whatever we desired. Our freedom was
in devotion to the Spirit of Truth – no pleasure, no profit, no fear or favor
could distract us from this careful, strict, and private state. We did not seek
out the company of others – indeed, we avoided it when we could –
preferring to attend to our own business, rather than unnecessarily
meddling in that of others.

Our words were few and carefully chosen, our expressions calm but
serious, and our way of life open for all to see. It is true that this reserved
and careful sort of life contrasted greatly with the world's idea of liberty,
and this exposed us to criticism by many so-called humorists and by
conceited or self-righteous persons. But such a life protected us from many
of the snares into which others so often fall – lured by the appeals to the
desires of the eyes, to the cravings of the flesh, and to earthly pride that are
so common in the wider world.[1267]

I cannot forget the humility and uncorrupted passion of that day. Oh!
How faithful in meetings – how humble in them! How firm in living
Truth's life and following Truth's principles! How completely united our

---

[1266] Matt. 25:23: "His lord said unto him, Well done, good and faithful servant; thou
hast been faithful over a few things, I will make thee ruler over many things:
enter thou into the joy of thy lord."

[1267] 1 John 2:16: "For all that *is* in the world, the lust of the flesh, and the lust of the
eyes, and the pride of life, is not of the Father, but is of the world."

communion was, as would be expected from a body that acknowledged only one head, Christ Jesus the Lord.[1268]

This was the testimony and example that George Fox was sent to proclaim and to leave with us, and we embraced it as a merciful gift from God. My exhortation is that today, even more than before, we must continue to walk in the path of that testimony with zeal and integrity – for the day draws near.[1269]

Particularly to the Ministry

First, to you beloved and honored brothers and sisters in Christ who offer ministry, feel the life in your ministry! Let Life be your mission, your well-spring and treasury on all occasions. Otherwise, you know very well that there is no way to get to God. Since nothing can spiritually awaken or enliven people but the Life of God, only a ministry in and from that Life can turn any people to God. We have seen the fruit of all other ministries by the few who are turned from the evil of their ways by it. It is not our abilities or our memories, or the repetition of an earlier revelation – it is not anything that we choose or any time that we choose to do it – that will accomplish God's work.

A dry, doctrinal ministry, no matter how sound it is, can only reach the ear. At best, it is a pleasant act of our imaginations. There is another way for ministry to be sound that is the soundest of all – Christ, the power of God. This is the key of David – what it opens, no one can shut, and what it shuts, no one can open.[1270] As oil is to a lamp and the soul is to the body, so that Life is to the best of words. This is what Christ meant when he said, "The words that I have spoken to you are Spirit and Life."[1271] – that is, they are from Life and therefore they make those who receive them alive. The disciples who lived with Jesus were commanded to stay in Jerusalem until

---

[1268] Col. 1:18: "And he is the head of the body, the church: who is the beginning, the firstborn from the dead; that in all *things* he might have the preeminence."

[1269] Eze. 7:12: "The time is come, the day draweth near: let not the buyer rejoice, nor the seller mourn: for wrath *is* upon all the multitude thereof."

[1270] Rev. 3:7: "And to the angel of the church in Philadelphia write; These things saith he that is holy, he that is true, he that hath the key of David, he that openeth, and no man shutteth; and shutteth, and no man openeth."

[1271] John 6:63: "It is the spirit that quickeneth; the flesh profiteth nothing: the words that I speak unto you, *they* are spirit, and *they* are life."

they received it.[1272] Even more so, we must wait to receive before we minister if we are going to turn the people from darkness to Light and from Satan's power to God.[1273]

I fervently bow my knee to the God and Father of our Lord Jesus Christ, praying that you will always do likewise – that you will always wait reverently for the Word of Life to come to you and be revealed to you and that you will attend to it in your ministry and service. Only in that way will you serve God in his Spirit. It doesn't matter whether you receive only a little or in abundance – much is not too much and the least bit is enough if it comes from God's Spirit. But, if it does not, even the smallest amount is too much and will produce no benefit.

It is the Spirit of the Lord, either acting directly or through the ministry of the Lord's servants, that teaches and benefits God's people. To be sure, to the extent that we take that Spirit along with us in our service will we be useful – to that degree and no more. It is the Lord who does all things in us and for our salvation – even more, it is the Lord that must work through us for the conversion of others. Sometimes, it has been difficult for us to speak when the Lord required it – but never consider it a burden to remain silent when the Lord requires that.

It is one of the more frightening sayings in the book of God that if anyone adds to its words of prophesy, God will inflict the plagues written about in that book on that person.[1274] To withhold the counsel of God is just as terrible: If anyone takes words away from the book of prophecy, God will take their share out of the book of life.[1275] Beyond doubt, this is a terrible warning to those who use the name of the Lord. They must be sure

---

[1272] Acts 1:4: "And, being assembled together with *them*, commanded them that they should not depart from Jerusalem, but wait for the promise of the Father, which, *saith he*, ye have heard of me."

[1273] Acts 26:18: "To open their eyes, *and* to turn *them* from darkness to light, and *from* the power of Satan unto God, that they may receive forgiveness of sins, and inheritance among them which are sanctified by faith that is in me."

[1274] Rev. 22:18: "For I testify unto every man that heareth the words of the prophecy of this book, If any man shall add unto these things, God shall add unto him the plagues that are written in this book."

[1275] Rev. 22:19: "And if any man shall take away from the words of the book of this prophecy, God shall take away his part out of the book of life, and out of the holy city, and *from* the things which are written in this book."

that it is the Lord who is speaking through them and that they are not among those who add to the words of testimony that God has given them to say, nor those who hold back or change those words. Both of these things are offensive to God.

Therefore, Brothers and Sisters, let us be careful neither to run ahead of our Guide nor to fall behind it. Those who make haste may lose their way, and those who lag behind may lose their Guide entirely. Even those who have received the Word of the Lord need to wait for wisdom so that they know how to properly share the Word. Plainly, it is possible, out of impatience, for someone who has received the Word to misunderstand its importance or, with his or her own interpretation, create an unsound and dangerous mixture of Truth and imaginings. This can hardly result in a right-minded and living people of God.

Above all else, this is my most serious advice to public ministers. I know very well how much it can influence the present and future state and the preservation of the Church of Jesus Christ that was gathered up and built by a living and powerful ministry. The ministry must continue to be rooted in the revelations, workings, and nurturance of the same Life and Power.

Wherever it is observed that anyone ministers more from their own ability and training than from the Life and Power of the Spirit, even though they are enlightened and doctrinally sound, let them be counseled and cautioned for their own good. Otherwise, little by little, they will come to depend on themselves, forsaking Christ, the living fountain, and dig cisterns for themselves that cannot hold the living water.[1276] Bit by bit, they will draw others away from waiting for the gift of God in themselves, to feel it instead in others, to turn again from God to mere humans for spiritual strength and refreshment. This makes a shipwreck of the faith that was delivered to the saints and of a good conscience toward God.[1277] These are preserved only by the divine gift of life that first awakened and blessed the conscience and imparted faith.

[1276] Jer. 2:13: "For my people have committed two evils; they have forsaken me, the fountain of living waters, *and* hewed them out cisterns, broken cisterns, that can hold no water."

[1277] 1 Tim. 1:19: "Holding faith, and a good conscience; which some having put away concerning faith have made shipwreck."

Nor is it enough that we once knew this divine gift and through it preached to the spirits in prison[1278] or served as God's instrument in convincing others to follow the way of the Lord, if we do not remain humble and recognize that we depend on God for everything. There must be Life in what we say – the repetition of old advices and revelations, the memories of past joys, will not bring a soul to God, or bread to the hungry, or water to the thirsty. We must wait for it, each time.

Oh! That we may depend on no other fountain or treasury! That no one would ever presume that they could act on their own for God – even if they have previously acted under God's direction. We cannot substitute our own wisdom for the wisdom we get by waiting. No matter how blessed we have been in the past, we cannot take less care, or more liberty, in speaking than we did before. Whatever the expectations we may feel from others, if we do not feel the power of God opening us and enlarging us, we must not fill up the time with words of our own.

I hope we will always remember who it was who said, "By yourselves, you can do nothing."[1279] All of our abilities come from God.[1280] We are not to speak our own words, or give any thought to our defense, when we are attacked for our testimony.[1281] Surely then, we are not to use our own words or plan out ministry offered in the name of the Lord to the souls of the people. Then, above all other times and all other occasions, let the words, "It is not you who speak, but the Holy Spirit,"[1282] be fulfilled in us.

True ministry of the Spirit must be born in and remain in agreement with the Spirit. Just as no one can enter the kingdom of God who is not born of the Spirit,[1283] no ministry can turn a soul to God unless it comes from the Spirit. For this, as I said before, the disciples waited before going

---

[1278] 1 Pet. 3:19: "By which also he went and preached unto the spirits in prison."

[1279] John 15:5: "I am the vine, ye *are* the branches: He that abideth in me, and I in him, the same bringeth forth much fruit: for without me ye can do nothing."

[1280] 2 Cor. 3:5: "Not that we are sufficient of ourselves to think any thing as of ourselves; but our sufficiency *is* of God."

[1281] Matt. 10:19: "But when they deliver you up, take no thought how or what ye shall speak: for it shall be given you in that same hour what ye shall speak."

[1282] Matt. 10:20: "For it is not ye that speak, but the Spirit of your Father which speaketh in you."

[1283] John 3:5: "Jesus answered, Verily, verily, I say unto thee, Except a man be born of water and *of* the Spirit, he cannot enter into the kingdom of God."

forth and in this, our spiritual ancestors – the messengers of God in our day – waited, watched, and reached out to us. Having begun in the Spirit, no one should hope to become perfect in the flesh.[1284] What is flesh to spirit? No more than chaff to wheat. If we remain in the Spirit, we will find unity in the Spirit. This is the foundation on which we build. By drinking from the Spirit, we are made one people for God and are sustained in the unity of the faith and the bond of peace.[1285] Envy, bitterness, and strife have no place in our hearts.[1286] We will watch always for good and not for evil in one another. Each will be overjoyed at, and not resent, another's increase in the riches of grace with which God replenishes all faithful servants.

Brothers and Sisters, the oracles of God have been revealed to you. You have many opportunities and are greatly respected by the people among whom you labor. I beseech you not to think it is sufficient to simply declare the Word of Life in their assemblies, no matter how comforting and instructive that is to you or to them. Follow Fox's example when he was among us. Look into the condition of the meetings that you visit. Who within them is sick or troubled? Who is tempted? Are any unfaithful or obstinate? Try to speak to these things in the wisdom and power of God – this will be a glorious crown on your ministry. This will prepare the way for you to be received into the hearts of the people as servants of God and give your advice authority. The afflicted will be comforted by you; the tempted will be strengthened; the sick will be refreshed; the unfaithful will condemn themselves and be restored; and the obstinate will be softened and prepared for reconciliation. Your care for individuals in need will demonstrate how your general testimony is applied and erase any doubts that they might have about it.

Although good and wise people, even elders, may live in such places – people who are worthy of respect and important among us generally – sometimes, they are undervalued by the people they live with. Other times, circumstances will make them unable to exercise their authority. But you, who travel as God's messengers, if they accept you in general, can they rebuff in particular? How can they accept the principle and ignore the

---

[1284] Gal. 3:3: "Are ye so foolish? having begun in the Spirit, are ye now made perfect by the flesh?"

[1285] Ephesians 4:3: "Endeavouring to keep the unity of the Spirit in the bond of peace."

[1286] James 3:14: "But if ye have bitter envying and strife in your hearts, glory not, and lie not against the truth."

application of it? In that way, you can prove yourselves to be God's workers indeed, carrying out the business before you to the praise of the One who called you from darkness to Light – turning others from Satan's power to God and the kingdom of God, which is within. Oh! If only there were more such faithful laborers in the vineyard of the Lord![1287] There has never been a time when they were needed more!

I cannot help but cry out and call to you who have for so long been proclaiming the Truth, who know the convincing power of the Truth, and who lead serious lives in the world, but who are content to know the Truth only for yourselves. You go to meetings and regularly practice charity in the church. You live honestly and humbly. You have no desire for recognition or glory. You feel no concern to spread Truth across the face of the earth, but are simply glad to see others succeed in that service. Arise in the name and power of the Lord Jesus! Behold, the fields are ripe and ready for the harvest[1288] in this and other nations, but there are only a few laborers to work in them.[1289] Your friends, neighbors, and relatives want to know the Lord and his Truth and to walk in the Truth. Do you owe them nothing? Look within yourselves, I implore you! Lose no time; the Lord will soon be here.

I do not judge you, but there is one who will judge all and that judgment will be final. You have greatly increased your outward riches – increase your inward treasures as much, and do good with both while there is still time to do good. Once, in God's name, your enemies would have taken whatever you had; but in the face of your enemies, God has given you much in this world. Let it be your servant and not your master – your diversion, not your business! Make the Lord first in your heart. Think about how you live and whether or not God still has more for you to do. If you find that you owe more, then wait to be prepared and receive the word of

---

1287 Matt. 20:1: "For the kingdom of heaven is like unto a man *that is* an householder, which went out early in the morning to hire labourers into his vineyard."

1288 John 4:35: "Say not ye, There are yet four months, and *then* cometh harvest? behold, I say unto you, Lift up your eyes, and look on the fields; for they are white already to harvest."

1289 Luke 10:2: "Therefore said he unto them, The harvest truly *is* great, but the labourers *are* few: pray ye therefore the Lord of the harvest, that he would send forth labourers into his harvest."

command. When you have put your hand to the plow,[1290] do not grow weary of doing what is right, because, if you do not faint, you will surely reap the fruit of your heavenly labors in God's everlasting kingdom.[1291]

To the Young Convinced

You younger convinced ones, be diligent and faithful in waiting for God's blessed appearance and revelations to you. Do not look outwardly, but within yourselves. Do not be misled by someone else's bad example or feel a need to imitate others. Let your inward sense and feeling of God's power guide you. Do not crush the tender new growth of that sense in your soul or, in your desire and love, outrun the holy and gentle work of it. Remember that it is a still voice[1292] that speaks to us in this day and that it is not to be heard in the noises and busyness of the mind, but is heard distinctly in private. Jesus loved and sought out solitude, often going into the mountains, gardens, or the seaside to avoid the swarming crowds, to show his disciples the importance of time alone, and to get away from the clamoring of the world. Imagination and freedom are your potential enemies, but the plain, practical, living, holy Truth that has convinced you will protect you. Let it guide you; use it to test all your thoughts, ideas, and affections and to determine if they come from God, or from the enemy, or from yourselves. In this way, you will have a true test, a true discernment, and a true judgment of what you should do and what you should leave undone. If you are diligent and faithful in this, you will grow in understanding and Christ, the eternal Wisdom, will fill your treasury. When you are converted, as well as convinced, then take your place publicly and be ready for every good word and work that the Lord will call you to. Then your life itself will be praise to God who has chosen you to share with the saints in the Light of an unshakable kingdom, in an incorruptible and eternal inheritance.[1293]

[1290] Luke 9:62: "And Jesus said unto him, No man, having put his hand to the plough, and looking back, is fit for the kingdom of God."

[1291] Gal. 6:9: "And let us not be weary in well doing: for in due season we shall reap, if we faint not."

[1292] 1 Kings 19:12: "And after the earthquake a fire; *but* the LORD *was* not in the fire: and after the fire a still small voice."

[1293] 1 Pet. 1:4: "To an inheritance incorruptible, and undefiled, and that fadeth not away, reserved in heaven for you."

To the Children of Friends

As for you who are the children of God's people, there is a great concern on my spirit for your good. Often, I am on my knees before the God of your parents on your behalf – asking that you might join in that same divine life and power, that holy nation and peculiar people[1294] – eager to do good works[1295] when your predecessors have all been laid in the dust. Young men and women! It is not enough to be the children of the people of the Lord! You must also be born again to inherit the kingdom of God.[1296] Those are merely your physical parents and through them you are children of the first Adam, but you must be spiritually regenerated to become children of the last Adam.[1297]

Look carefully, you children of the children of God! Consider your position and where you are in relation to this divine family and birth! Have you obeyed the Light and walked in the Spirit – the imperishable seed of the Word and the kingdom of God – by which you must be born again?[1298] God does not show favoritism.[1299] The parent cannot save or answer for the child, or the child for the parent – the one who sins shall die, but for

---

[1294] 1 Pet. 2:9: "But ye *are* a chosen generation, a royal priesthood, an holy nation, a peculiar people; that ye should shew forth the praises of him who hath called you out of darkness into his marvellous light."

[1295] Titus 2:14: "Who gave himself for us, that he might redeem us from all iniquity, and purify unto himself a peculiar people, zealous of good works."

[1296] John 3:3: "Jesus answered and said unto him, Verily, verily, I say unto thee, Except a man be born again, he cannot see the kingdom of God."

[1297] 1 Cor. 15:45-47: "And so it is written, The first man Adam was made a living soul; the last Adam *was made* a quickening spirit. Howbeit that *was* not first which is spiritual, but that which is natural; and afterward that which is spiritual. The first man *is* of the earth, earthy: the second man *is* the Lord from heaven."

[1298] 1 Pet. 1:23: "Being born again, not of corruptible seed, but of incorruptible, by the word of God, which liveth and abideth for ever."

[1299] Rom. 2:11: "For there is no respect of persons with God."

the righteousness you do, through Jesus Christ, you will live.[1300] The willing and obedient will eat the best from the land.[1301]

Do not be deceived; God is not to be mocked – whatever any nation or any people sows, that is what they will reap at the hand of a just God.[1302] In the end, if you have not chosen the way of the Lord, your many and great advantages over the children of other people will be added to the scales against you. You have had more than mere doctrine; you have had lesson upon lesson, rule upon rule;[1303] you have felt the guiding principle within yourselves of which others are ignorant. Unlike your parents, you know that you can be as good as you please, without fear of disapproval or beatings, or of being thrown out of your parents' houses and lives for the sake of God and religion. You have seen and heard how God wondrously protected them and guided them through a sea of troubles, granting them countless earthly as well as spiritual blessings in the sight of their enemies. If after this, you turn your back, you would not only be most ungrateful children to God and to them, but you must expect that God will call the children of others, and take the crown out of your hands, and you will receive a dreadful judgment at the hand of the Lord. Oh! That this will never happen to any of you! Lord forbid it, my soul prays!

Therefore, young men and women, look to the rock of your parents. Choose their God. There is no other God, no other Light, no other grace, no other Spirit to convince you, to enliven you, or to comfort you. There is no other to sustain, guide, and lead you to God's everlasting kingdom. Be possessors as well as professors of the Truth! Embrace it, not only because of what you were taught, but by your own judgment and conviction – from a sense in your souls and through the working of the eternal spirit and power of God in your hearts. By this, you may come to be the children of

---

[1300] Eze. 18:20: "The soul that sinneth, it shall die. The son shall not bear the iniquity of the father, neither shall the father bear the iniquity of the son: the righteousness of the righteous shall be upon him, and the wickedness of the wicked shall be upon him."

[1301] Isa. 1:19: "If ye be willing and obedient, ye shall eat the good of the land."

[1302] Gal. 6:7: "Be not deceived; God is not mocked: for whatsoever a man soweth, that shall he also reap."

[1303] Isa. 28:13: "But the word of the LORD was unto them precept upon precept, precept upon precept; line upon line, line upon line; here a little, *and* there a little; that they might go, and fall backward, and be broken, and snared, and taken."

Abraham by faith and by a circumcision not made with hands.[1304] You are heirs of the promise[1305] made to your parents, of an imperishable crown. As I said before, you can be a generation devoted to God and continuing the proclamation of the blessed Truth in the Life and Power of God.

Religion that is merely the observance of forms and ceremonies is despised by God and by good people – all the more so when the forms and ceremonies are newly invented and practiced with extraordinary zealotry and rigidity. Therefore, I say, continue to worship in the same manner, without the salt and sugar that is added to make worship more palatable for other people. Forms and ceremonies do not return God's love or our parents' care. They are not consistent with the Truth in ourselves – nor in others who do not obey the Truth, but who can see and hear enough to know if those who claim to obey have succeeded. Where the divine power is not felt in the soul, and waited for, and lived in, flaws and deficiencies will quickly become obvious, revealing the unfaithful and exposing their lack of spiritual understanding.

Therefore, dear children, I beg you to shut your eyes to the temptations and enticements of this dreary and short-lived world. Do not allow your affections to be captivated by the desires and vanities that your parents turned their backs on for Truth's sake. As you are able, believe in the Truth, take it into your hearts and become children of God. May it never be said of you, as the evangelist said of the Jews of his time, "Christ, the true Light, came to his own, but his own people did not accept him. But to all who received him, he gave the power to become children of God; they were children, not by natural descent or by a human decision or of the will of their parents, but of God."[1306] This passage is especially appropriate to this topic. You uniquely and exactly correspond to those Jews, in that you bear the name of God's people, being the children of God's people. By his Light within you, God may be said to come to his own and, if you do not obey it,

---

[1304] Ephesians 2:11: "Wherefore remember, that ye *being* in time past Gentiles in the flesh, who are called Uncircumcision by that which is called the Circumcision in the flesh made by hands."

[1305] Gal. 3:29: "And if ye *be* Christ's, then are ye Abraham's seed, and heirs according to the promise."

[1306] John 1:11-13: "He came unto his own, and his own received him not. But as many as received him, to them gave he power to become the sons of God, *even* to them that believe on his name. Which were born, not of blood, nor of the will of the flesh, nor of the will of man, but of God."

but turn away from it and follow the desires of your own minds, you will be among "his own who do not receive him." I pray to God that this will never be your case or your judgment, but that you will be aware of the many, great obligations you have to the Lord for God's love and to your parents for their care. With all your heart and all your soul and all your strength,[1307] turn to the Lord, to this gift and Spirit in you – listen for God's voice within you and obey it, so that based on the Truth and evidence of your own experience you may join in the testimony of your parents. Then, your children's children will bless you and thank the Lord for you as those who gave them a faithful example and a record of the Truth of God. Those of your parents who are still alive will go to their graves with joy, seeing Truth prosper in you and knowing that not only their nature, but their spirits will live on in you when they are gone.

To those who are Still Strangers to this People and their Ways

I will conclude this *Preface* with a few words to those reading this who are not of our society, especially to those who live in England.

Friends, as fellow descendents of Adam and Eve, we are brothers and sisters in the flesh. My prayers have often and earnestly been offered to God on your behalf, that you might come to know the one who made you as your redeemer and reconciler. God sent his son to be the Light and Life of the world. By the power and Spirit of Jesus Christ, the image of God you have lost through sin can be restored. Oh! If only you, who are called Christians, would take him into your hearts! It is there that you need him. He stands knocking at its door,[1308] hoping that you would let him in, but you do not open it for him. You have filled your heart with other guests, so that now, as long ago, only a manger is available for him.[1309] But, you are full of declarations of faith – as were the Jews when he came among them – they did not recognize him, but rejected him and treated him evilly. If you

---

[1307] Mark 12:30: "And thou shalt love the Lord thy God with all thy heart, and with all thy soul, and with all thy mind, and with all thy strength: this *is* the first commandment."

[1308] Rev. 3:20: "Behold, I stand at the door, and knock: if any man hear my voice, and open the door, I will come in to him, and will sup with him, and he with me."

[1309] Luke 2:7: "And she brought forth her firstborn son, and wrapped him in swaddling clothes, and laid him in a manger; because there was no room for them in the inn."

do not come to know by direct experience what you claim to believe, all your careful religious practices will do you no good on the day of God's final judgment.

I beseech you! Consider for yourselves your eternal condition. Judge for yourselves what you call Christianity – the foundation, ground, and rock on which it is built – is there more to it than mere words and a traditional belief in the gospel? Have you known the baptism of fire and the Holy Spirit and the fan of Christ that blows away the chaff of bodily desires and hungers?[1310] Do you feel the divine leaven that transforms the lump of a person, sanctifying the body, soul, and spirit?[1311] If this is not the basis of your faith, you are truly miserable.

You might answer that although you are sinners, and daily commit more sins, and are not sanctified in the way that I talk about it, you are saved by belief in Christ because his righteousness has been imputed to you – that he has accepted the curse for you and you are whole in Christ.

My Friends, do not deceive yourselves in something as important as your immortal souls. If you have true faith in Christ, your faith will cleanse you and sanctify you. For the saints, faith was their victory – by faith, they overcame sin within and the sinful without. If you are in Christ, you follow the way of the Spirit, not of the flesh,[1312] and its fruits are obvious. If you are in Christ, you are a new creature, re-made and re-fashioned according to God's will and design. The old things are gone and, behold, all things have become new[1313] – new love, new desires, new will, new affections, new behavior. It is no longer you who live – disobedient, worldly, and greedy –

[1310] Luke 3:16-17: "John answered, saying unto *them* all, I indeed baptize you with water; but one mightier than I cometh, the latchet of whose shoes I am not worthy to unloose: he shall baptize you with the Holy Ghost and with fire: Whose fan *is* in his hand, and he will thoroughly purge his floor, and will gather the wheat into his garner; but the chaff he will burn with fire unquenchable."

[1311] 1 Cor. 5:6-8: "Know ye not that a little leaven leaveneth the whole lump? Purge out therefore the old leaven, that ye may be a new lump, as ye are unleavened. For even Christ our passover is sacrificed for us: Therefore let us keep the feast, not with old leaven, neither with the leaven of malice and wickedness; but with the unleavened *bread* of sincerity and truth."

[1312] Rom. 8:1: "*There is* therefore now no condemnation to them which are in Christ Jesus, who walk not after the flesh, but after the Spirit."

[1313] 2 Cor. 5:17: "Therefore if any man *be* in Christ, *he is* a new creature: old things are passed away; behold, all things are become new."

but Christ living within you.[1314] For you, living is Christ and dying is eternal gain[1315] because you know that your corruptible body will be replaced by an incorruptible one, your mortality by immortality.[1316] If you are in Christ, you have a glorious and eternal home in the heavens that will never become old or fall into ruin.[1317] As surely as heat comes from fire and light from the sun, all of this comes from being in Christ.

Therefore, be careful what you rely on. Do you presume to be in Christ while still having a fallen nature? What fellowship does Light have with darkness or Christ with Belial?[1318] Listen to what the beloved disciple tells you, "If we claim to have fellowship with God but walk in the darkness, we lie and do not live the truth."[1319] That is, if we go our own way, prisoners of our bodily desires, and have not turned our lives to God, we walk in darkness and can have no fellowship with God. Christ clothes with his righteousness those who receive his grace into their hearts, who rid themselves of their own desires, and who daily take up their cross and follow him. Christ's righteousness makes them inwardly holy – with holy minds, holy wills, and holy behavior. Even though we have received it as a gift from God, it remains Christ's – it is not ours by birth, but by adoption and faith. Still, even though it is not ours by nature, we must embrace it if we are to get any good from it – if we do not, Christ's righteousness will gain us nothing. This is the way in which Christ was the righteousness, sanctification, justification, and redemption of the primitive Christians. If

---

[1314] Gal. 2:20: "I am crucified with Christ: nevertheless I live; yet not I, but Christ liveth in me: and the life which I now live in the flesh I live by the faith of the Son of God, who loved me, and gave himself for me."

[1315] Phil. 1:21: "For to me to live *is* Christ, and to die *is* gain."

[1316] 1 Cor. 15:53: "For this corruptible must put on incorruption, and this mortal *must* put on immortality."

[1317] 2 Cor. 5:1: "For we know that if our earthly house of *this* tabernacle were dissolved, we have a building of God, an house not made with hands, eternal in the heavens."

[1318] 2 Cor. 6:14-15: "Be ye not unequally yoked together with unbelievers: for what fellowship hath righteousness with unrighteousness? and what communion hath light with darkness? And what concord hath Christ with Belial? or what part hath he that believeth with an infidel?"

[1319] 1 John 1:6: "If we say that we have fellowship with him, and walk in darkness, we lie, and do not the truth."

you ever hope to know the heart, core, and true comfort of the Christian religion, you must come to know and possess it.

Now, my Friends, from what you have read, you may see that God has given one poor people among you redemptive knowledge and revelations. They have been protected and increased in number, despite the fierce opposition they have faced. Do not take these revelations lightly, we know it was and still is a day of small things[1320] and of no significance to many. Numerous cruel and wicked names have been given to their work, but it was of God – it came from and leads back to God. Although we know this, we cannot make anyone else believe it unless they follow the same path to knowledge that we have walked.

What does the world do when it talks of God? They pray for power, but reject the Principle in which that power exists. If you want to know God – and to worship and serve God as you should – you must come to the path that God has provided. Some seek it in books, some seek it in scholars, but what they seek is within themselves, but not of themselves, and there, they overlook it. The voice is too still,[1321] the seed is too small,[1322] and the Light shines in darkness.[1323] They look everywhere else and therefore cannot share in its riches.[1324] But the woman who lost her silver found it at home after she lit a candle and swept the house.[1325] Do the same

---

[1320] Penn seems to be making an allusion to Zech. 4:10 ("For who hath despised the day of small things? for they shall rejoice, and shall see the plummet in the hand of Zerubbabel *with* those seven; they *are* the eyes of the LORD, which run to and fro through the whole earth"). The 'small things' in this passage are the meager start that had been made at rebuilding the temple in Jerusalem.

[1321] 1 Kings 19:12: "And after the earthquake a fire; *but* the LORD *was* not in the fire: and after the fire a still small voice."

[1322] Mark 4:31: "*It is* like a grain of mustard seed, which, when it is sown in the earth, is less than all the seeds that be in the earth."

[1323] John 1:5: "And the light shineth in darkness; and the darkness comprehended it not."

[1324] Isa. 53:12: "Therefore will I divide him *a portion* with the great, and he shall divide the spoil with the strong; because he hath poured out his soul unto death: and he was numbered with the transgressors; and he bare the sin of many, and made intercession for the transgressors."

[1325] Luke 15:8: "Either what woman having ten pieces of silver, if she lose one piece, doth not light a candle, and sweep the house, and seek diligently till she find *it*?"

and you will know what Pilate wanted to discover: Truth[1326] – Truth in your inmost being and of the highest value in the sight of God.

The Light of Christ within, who is the Light of the World (and therefore a Light to you, revealing the truth of your spiritual condition) leads all that obey it out of darkness and into God's marvelous Light. The Light grows within the obedient – it is spread for the righteous,[1327] it is like the dawning sun that shines brighter and brighter until it has fully risen.[1328]

Therefore, Friends, turn in, turn in, I beseech you! Where the poison is, there is the antidote. You need Christ within, there you must seek him, and by God's blessing, there you will find him. "Seek and you shall find."[1329] – I can testify to the truth of that statement. But, you must seek with your whole heart, as if you were seeking your life, indeed your eternal life. Diligently, humbly, patiently – seek as if you can find no pleasure, comfort, or satisfaction in anything else until you find the One your souls want, and desire to know, and to love above all else. Oh! It is hard work, hard spiritual work! Let the ordinary, irreverent world think and say what it will about you. And by this path, and it alone, you must walk to eternal foundations of the city of God.

What does this blessed Light do for you? First, it displays all your sins to you. It reveals the spirit of this world with all its baits and lures. It shows you how mankind fell from grace and what a lowly state it is now in. Second, it stirs up grief and sorrow, in those who believe in it, for this fearful state. You will see distinctly how you have pierced him[1330] – what blows and wounds you have given him by your disobedience – and how you have made him suffer for your sins. You will weep and mourn for it and your sorrow will be a godly sorrow. Third, it will make you vigilant, so

---

[1326] John 19:9: "And [Pilate] went again into the judgment hall, and saith unto Jesus, Whence art thou? But Jesus gave him no answer."

[1327] Ps. 97:11: "Light is sown for the righteous, and gladness for the upright in heart."

[1328] Prov. 4:18: "But the path of the just *is* as the shining light, that shineth more and more unto the perfect day."

[1329] Matt. 7:7: "Ask, and it shall be given you; seek, and ye shall find; knock, and it shall be opened unto you."

[1330] Rev. 1:7: "Behold, he cometh with clouds; and every eye shall see him, and they *also* which pierced him: and all kindreds of the earth shall wail because of him. Even so, Amen."

that you will not sin again and so the enemy cannot sneak up on you again. Then your thoughts, as well as your words and deeds, will be judged – this is the way to holiness, the way in which God's redeemed walk. Here, you will come to love God above all else and your neighbors as yourselves.[1331] Nothing will hurt or harm or frighten on this Holy Mountain.[1332] Now, you have in truth become Christ's, for you are his in your nature and your spirit. You have given up being your own. And when you are Christ's, then Christ is yours, and not before. You will come into communion with the Father and the Son. You will be wholly cleansed by the blood of Jesus Christ that speaks a better word than the blood of Abel.[1333] The blood of that immaculate lamb will cleanse all sin from the consciences of those who, through living faith, have come to be sprinkled with it. They are free of the acts that lead to death and brought to serve the living God.[1334]

In conclusion, behold the testimony and doctrine of the people called Quakers! Behold their practice and discipline! And behold George Fox, the blessed man, and the other blessed ones who were sent by God to do this excellent work and service! All of this is better described in the *Journal* of that man. I heartily recommend serious study of that book to all my readers. And I ask the blessings of Almighty God to go with it, so that many who are still strangers to that holy dispensation may be turned to God and so that the church in general could be instructed by it.

For the many mercies and repeated blessings to his people, all glory, honor, thanksgiving, and fame are God's in this day of great love. May it be offered with love and reverence through the Lamb of God, in whom he is well pleased – our Light and Life, who sits with God on the throne, world without end. Amen.

[1331] Mark 12:30-31: "And thou shalt love the Lord thy God with all thy heart, and with all thy soul, and with all thy mind, and with all thy strength: this *is* the first commandment. And the second *is* like, *namely* this, Thou shalt love thy neighbour as thyself. There is none other commandment greater than these."

[1332] Isa. 65:25: "The wolf and the lamb shall feed together, and the lion shall eat straw like the bullock: and dust *shall be* the serpent's meat. They shall not hurt nor destroy in all my holy mountain, saith the Lord."

[1333] Heb. 12:24: "And to Jesus the mediator of the new covenant, and to the blood of sprinkling, that speaketh better things than *that of* Abel."

[1334] Heb. 9:14: "How much more shall the blood of Christ, who through the eternal Spirit offered himself without spot to God, purge your conscience from dead works to serve the living God?"

So says one whom God has mercifully visited and who was not disobedient to the heavenly vision and call – to whom the way of Truth is more lovely and precious than ever and who knows the beauty and benefit of it above all worldly treasure and who has chosen it as his highest joy. Therefore, he recommends it to your love and choice because he is with greatest sincerity and affection

Your soul's friend,

William Penn

Printed in the United States
19076LVS00004BB/37-81